THE SEVEN DEADLY SINS

nakaba suzuki presents

20

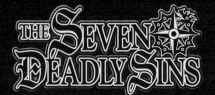

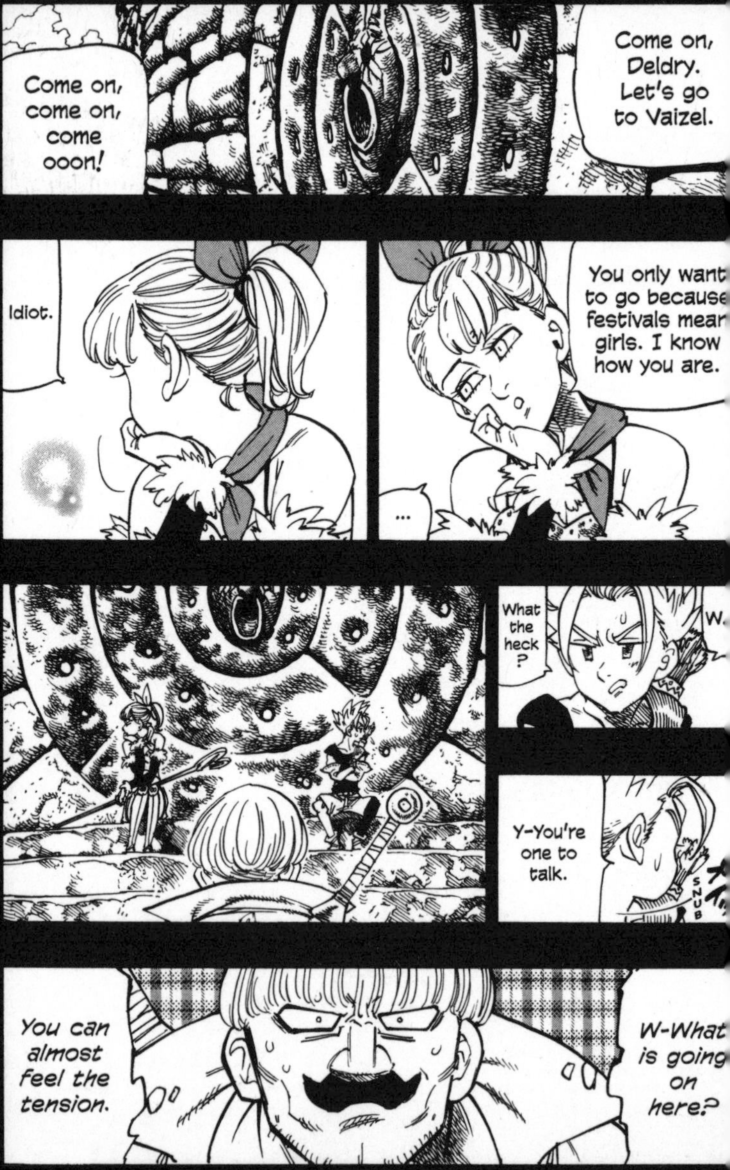
Come on, Deldry. Let's go to Vaizel.
Come on, come on, come ooon!
You only want to go because festivals mean girls. I know how you are.
...
Idiot.
What the heck?
W...
Y-You're one to talk.
SNUB
W-What is going on here?
You can almost feel the tension.

C O N T E N T S

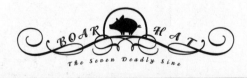

BOAR HAT

The Seven Deadly Sins

Chapter 154 - The Demon Smiles

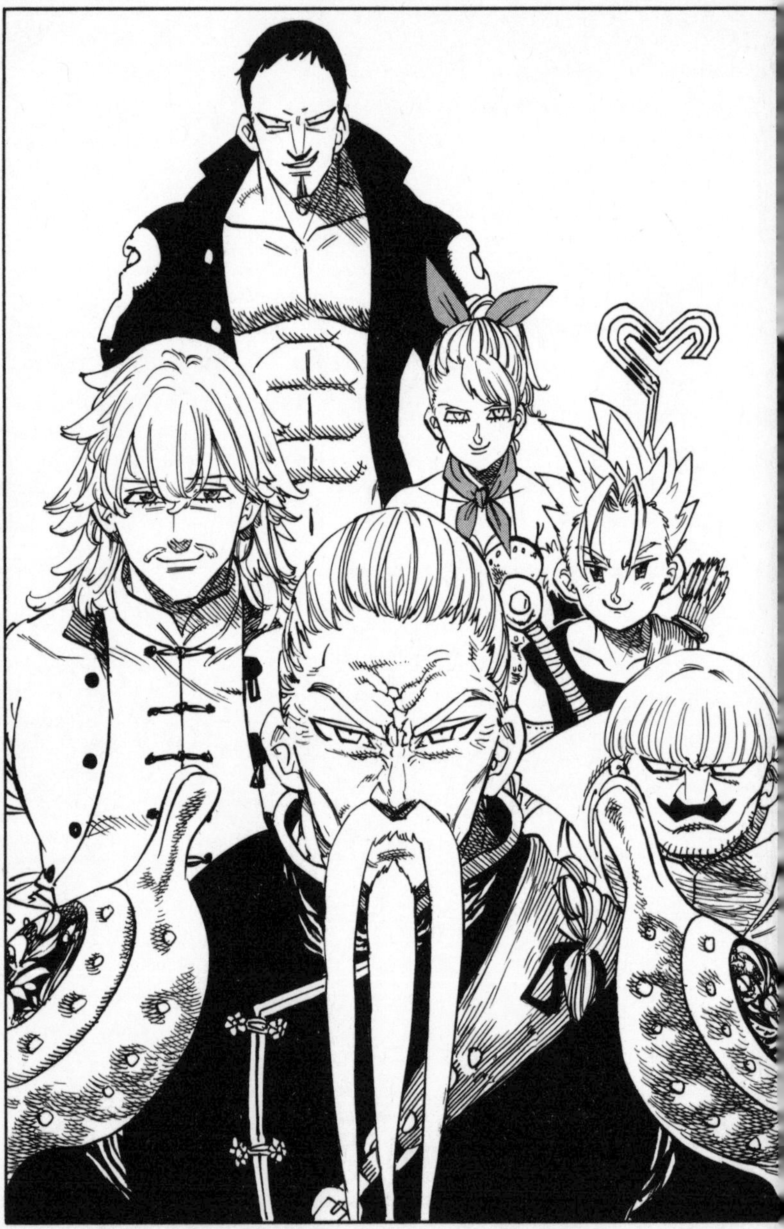

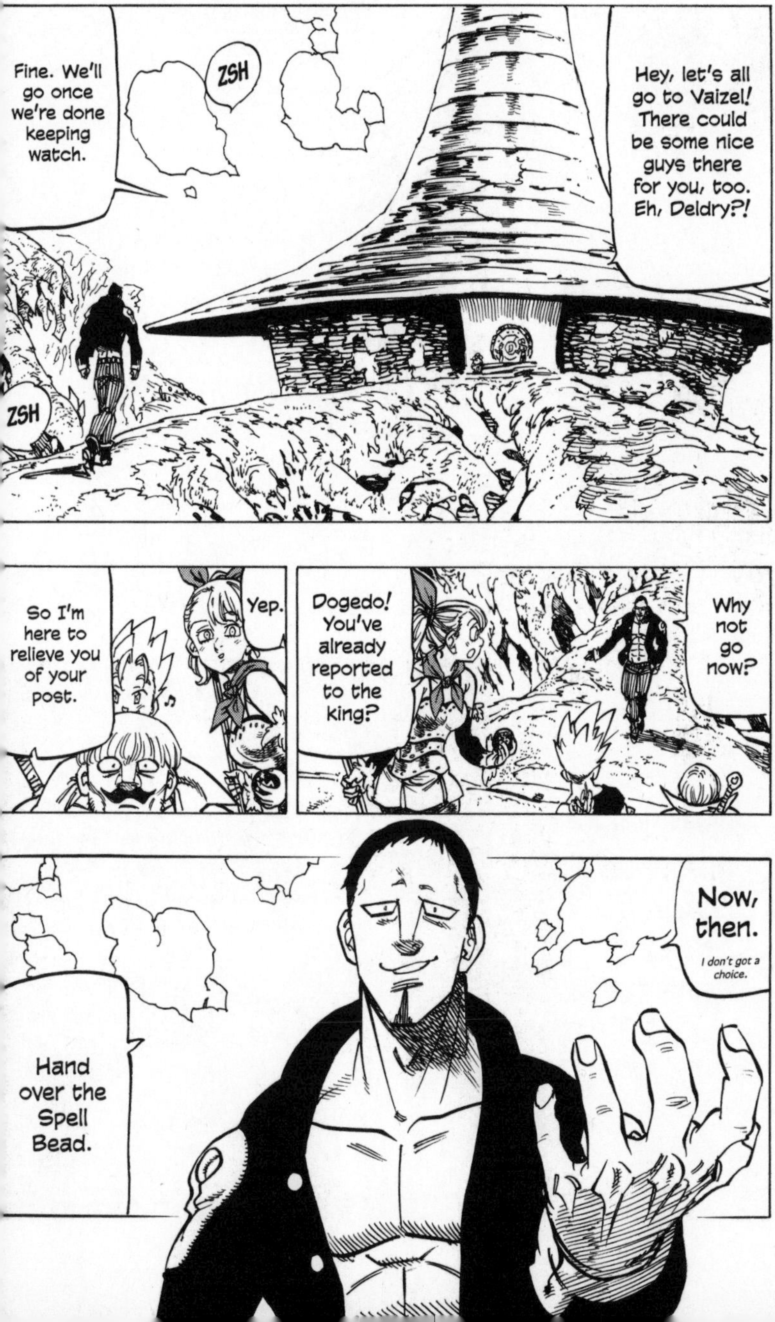
Hey, let's all go to Vaizel! There could be some nice guys there for you, too. Eh, Deldry?!
ZSH
Fine. We'll go once we're done keeping watch.
ZSH
Why not go now?
Dogedo! You've already reported to the king?
Yep.
So I'm here to relieve you of your post.
Now, then.
I don't got a choice.
Hand over the Spell Bead.

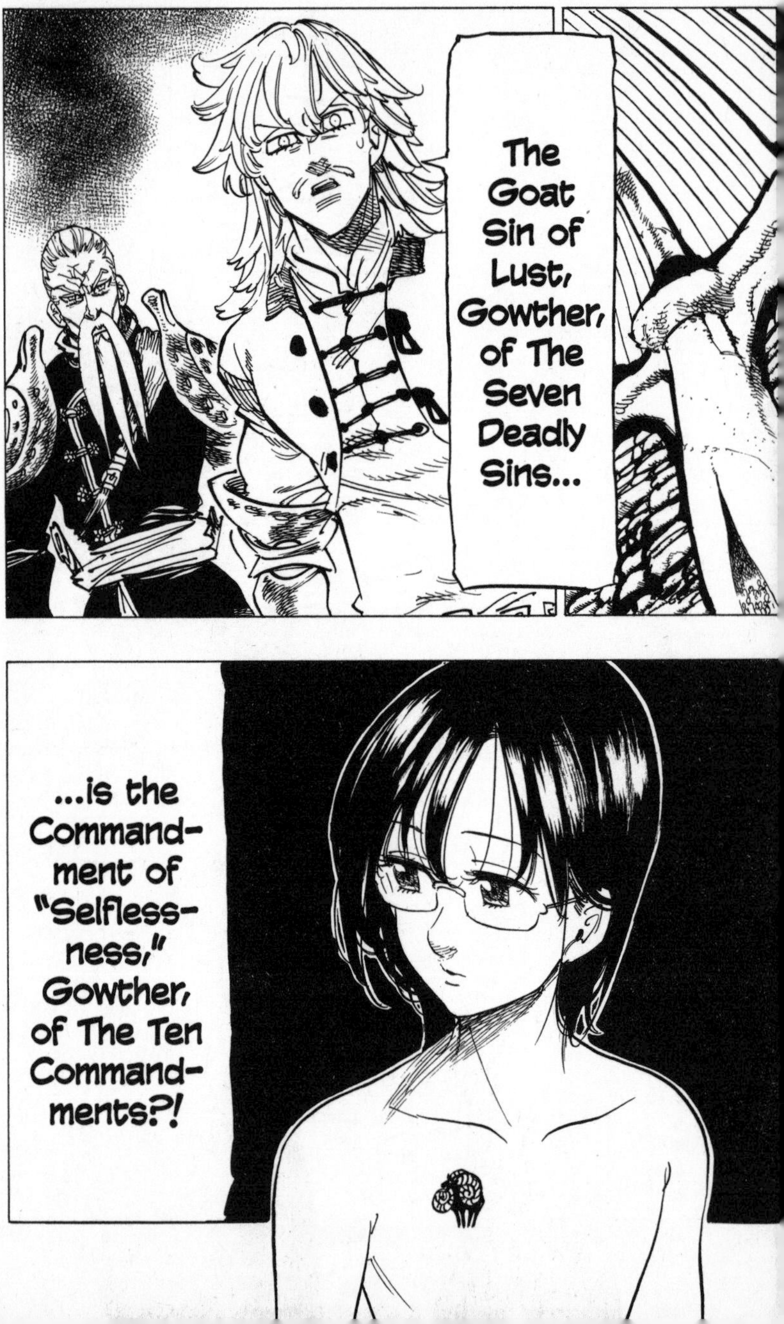
The Goat Sin of Lust, Gowther, of The Seven Deadly Sins...
...is the Commandment of "Selflessness," Gowther, of The Ten Commandments?!

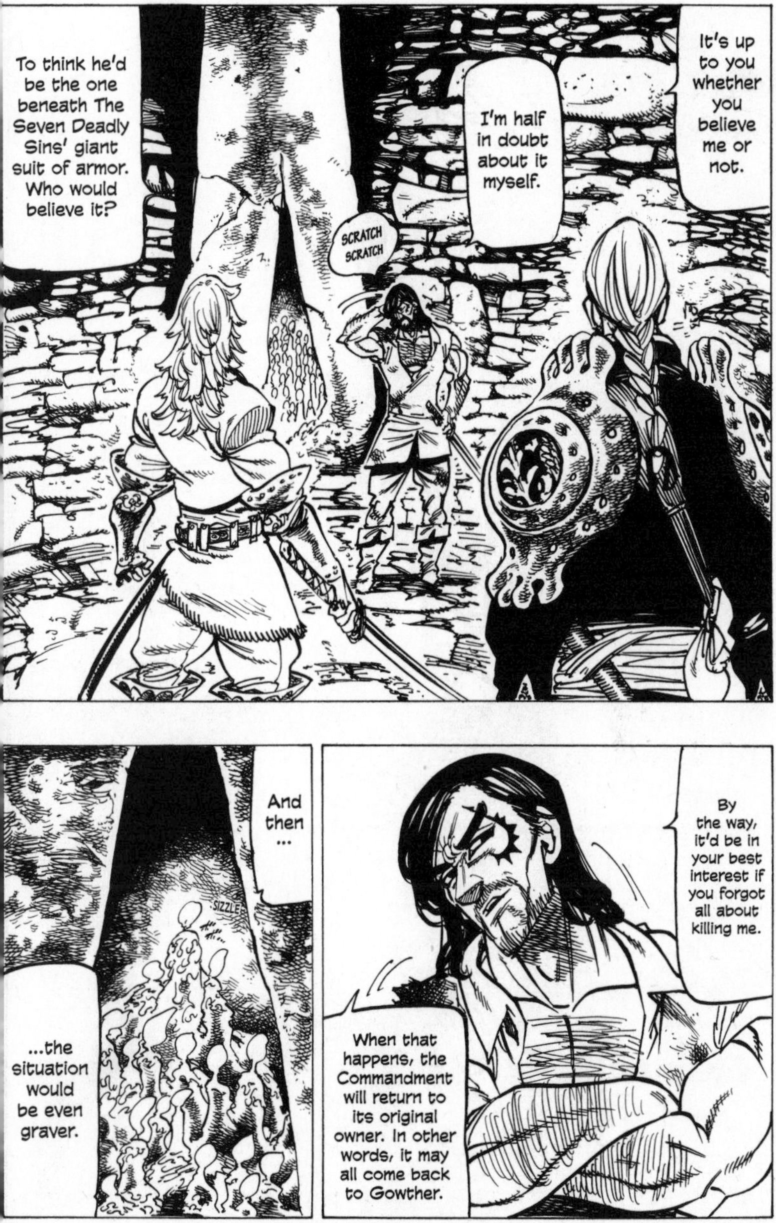
It's up to you whether you believe me or not.
I'm half in doubt about it myself.
SCRATCH SCRATCH
To think he'd be the one beneath The Seven Deadly Sins' giant suit of armor. Who would believe it?
By the way, it'd be in your best interest if you forgot all about killing me.
When that happens, the Commandment will return to its original owner. In other words, it may all come back to Gowther.
And then...
SIZZLE
...the situation would be even graver.

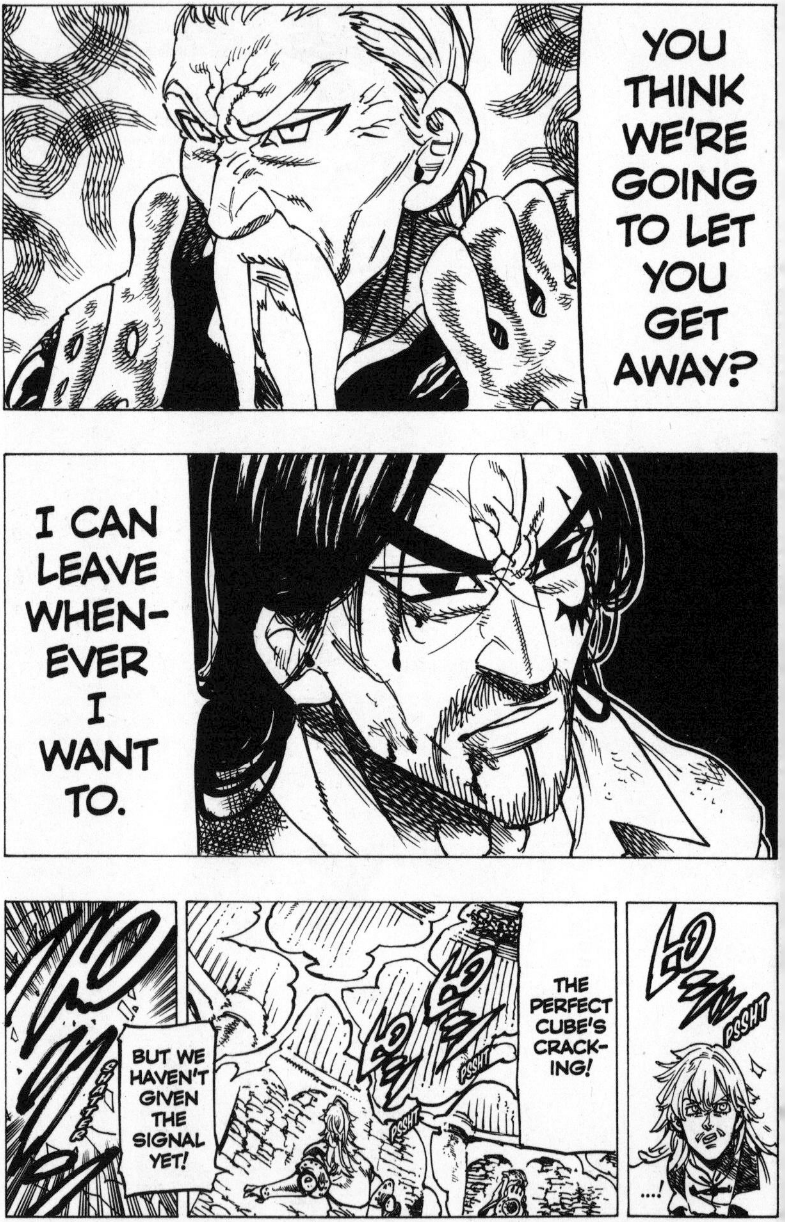
YOU THINK WE'RE GOING TO LET YOU GET AWAY?
I CAN LEAVE WHEN-EVER I WANT TO.
PSSHT
....!
THE PERFECT CUBE'S CRACK-ING!
PSSHT
PSSHT
BUT WE HAVEN'T GIVEN THE SIGNAL YET!

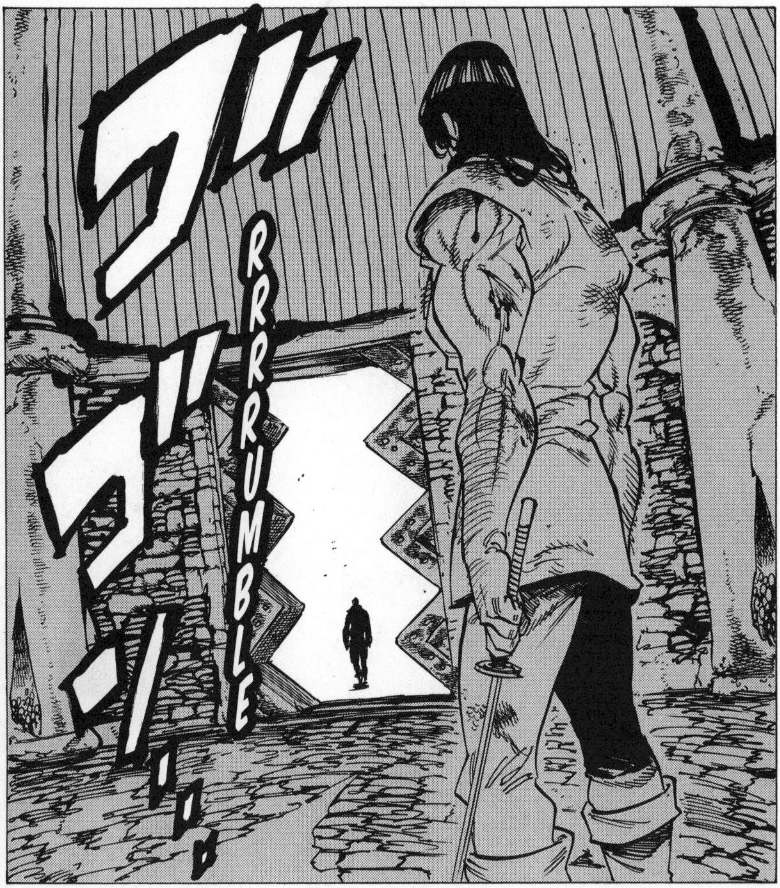
RRRRUMBLE

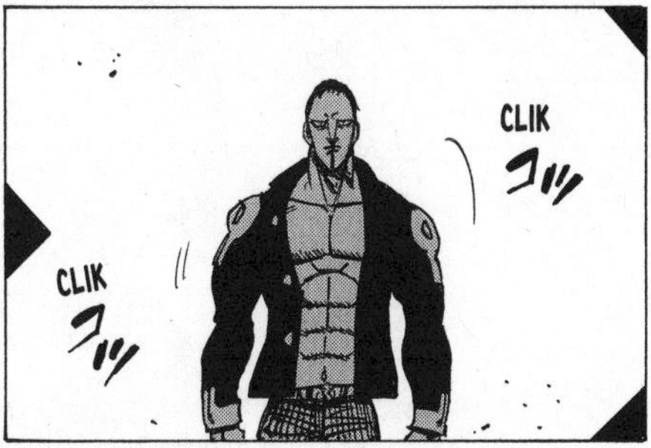
CLIK
コッ
CLIK
コッ

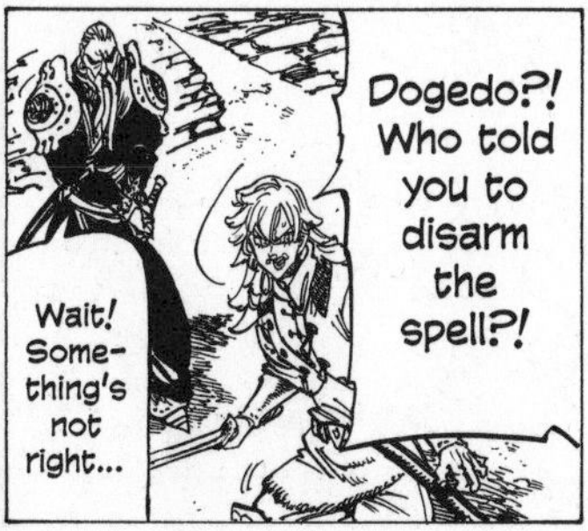
Dogedo?! Who told you to disarm the spell?!
Wait! Something's not right...

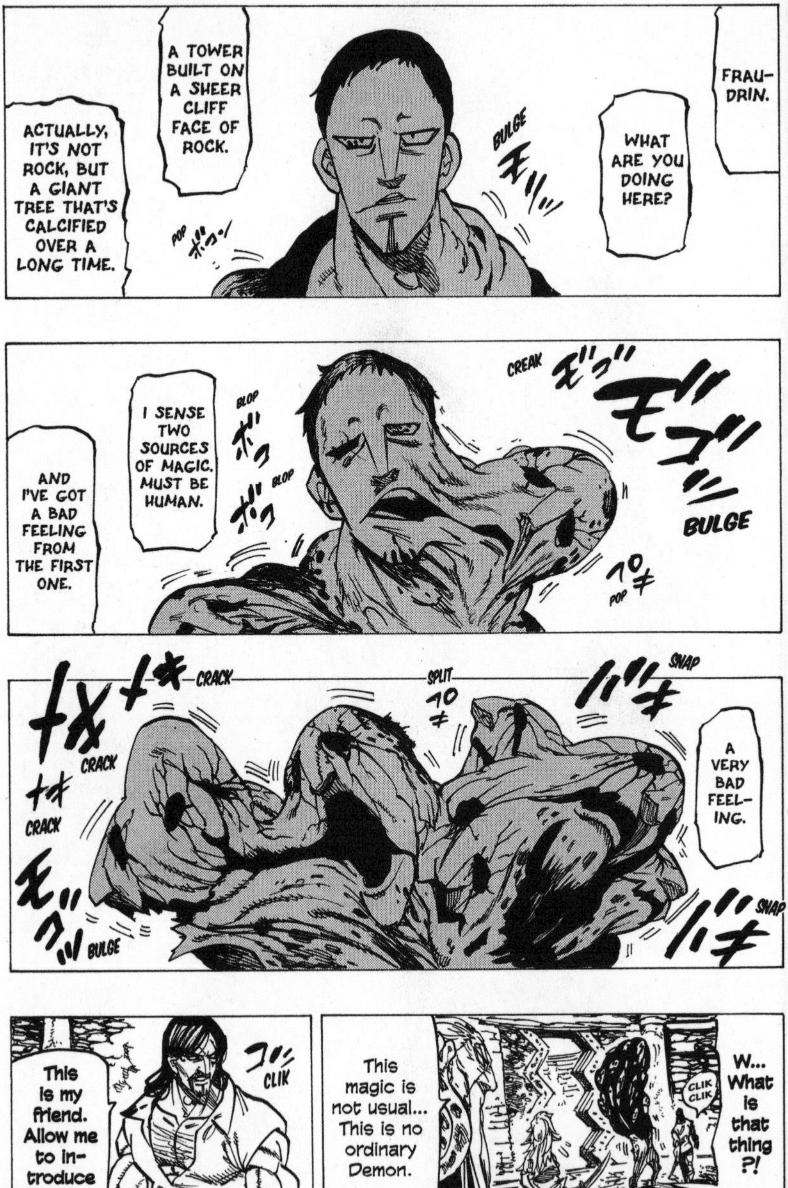
FRAU-DRIN.
WHAT ARE YOU DOING HERE?
BULGE
A TOWER BUILT ON A SHEER CLIFF FACE OF ROCK.
POP
ACTUALLY, IT'S NOT ROCK, BUT A GIANT TREE THAT'S CALCIFIED OVER A LONG TIME.
CREAK
BULGE
POP
BLOP
BLOP
I SENSE TWO SOURCES OF MAGIC. MUST BE HUMAN.
AND I'VE GOT A BAD FEELING FROM THE FIRST ONE.
SNAP
A VERY BAD FEEL-ING.
SPLIT
CRACK
SNAP
CRACK
CRACK
BULGE
W... What is that thing?!
CLIK CLIK
This magic is not usual... This is no ordinary Demon.
CLIK
This is my friend. Allow me to in-troduce you.

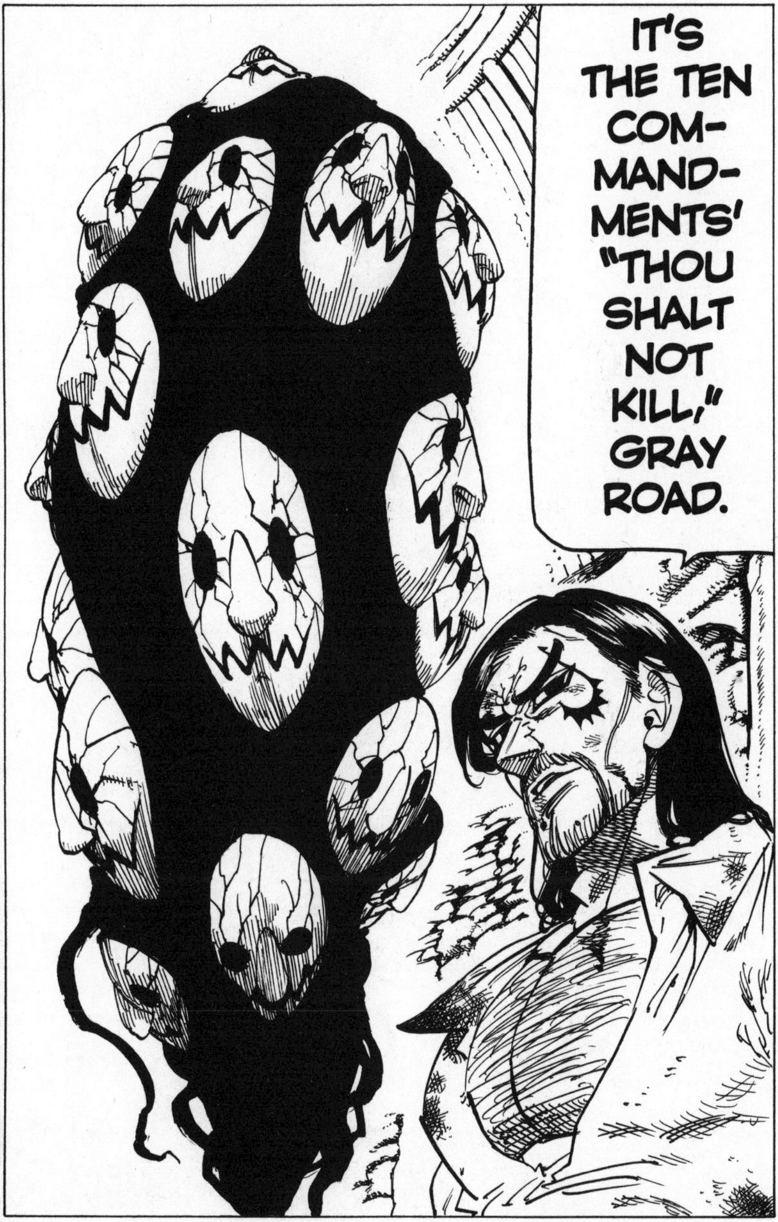
IT'S THE TEN COMMANDMENTS' "THOU SHALT NOT KILL," GRAY ROAD.

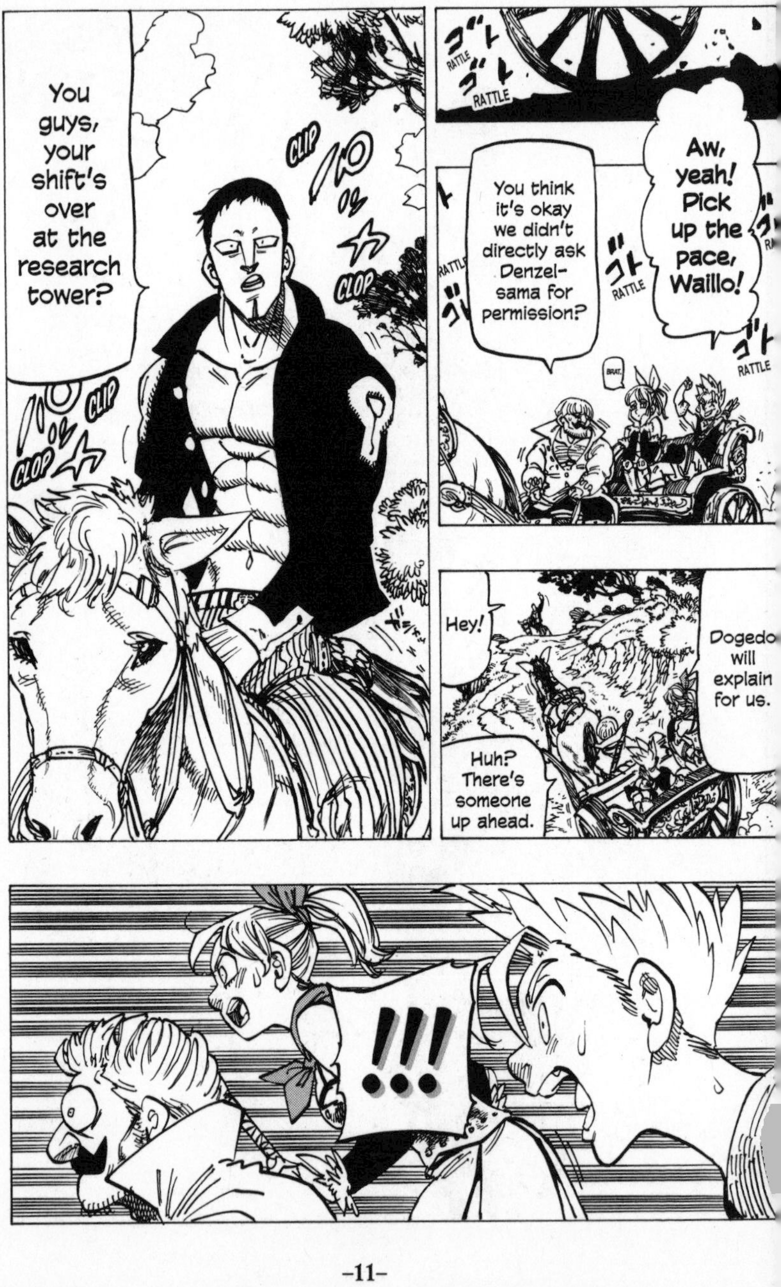
RATTLE
RATTLE
Aw, yeah! Pick up the pace, Waillo!
RATTLE
RATTLE
RATTLE
You think it's okay we didn't directly ask Denzel-sama for permission?
BRAT.
Dogedo will explain for us.
Hey!
Huh? There's someone up ahead.
CLIP
CLOP
You guys, your shift's over at the research tower?
CLIP
CLOP
!!!

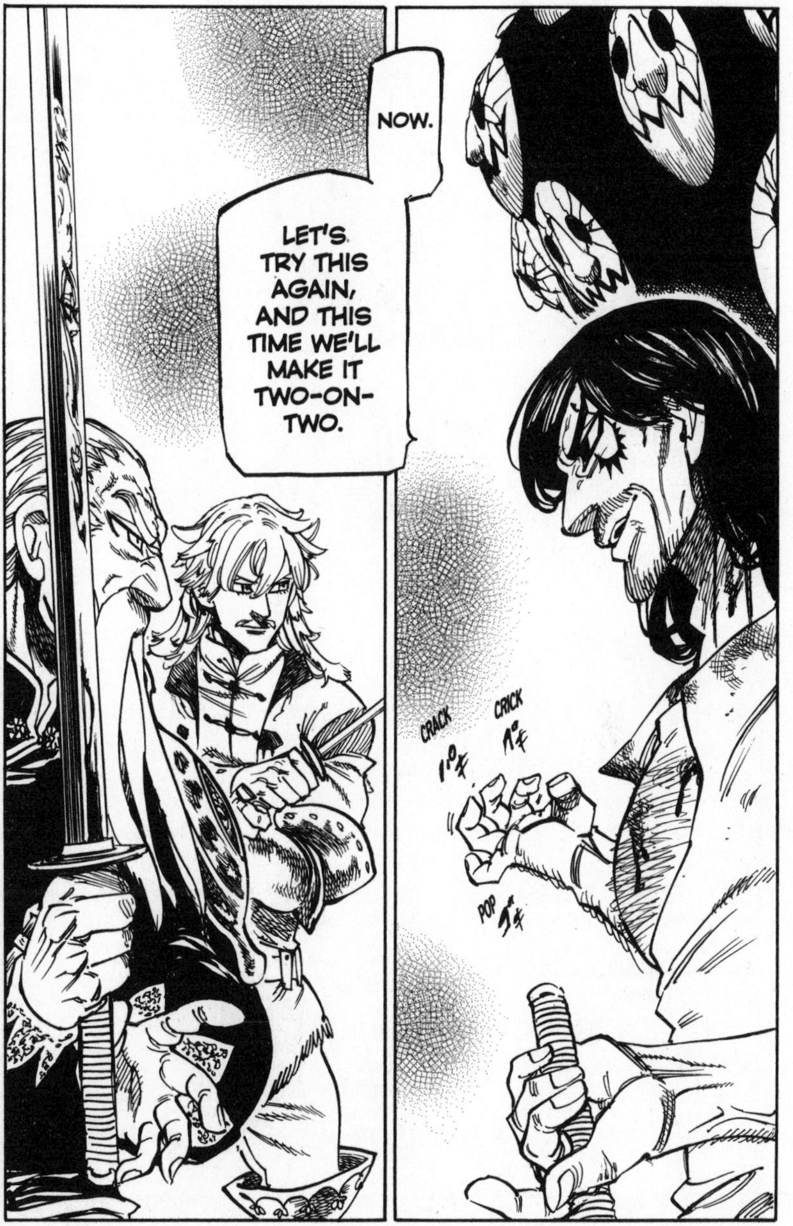
NOW.
LET'S TRY THIS AGAIN, AND THIS TIME WE'LL MAKE IT TWO-ON-TWO.
CRICK
CRACK
POP

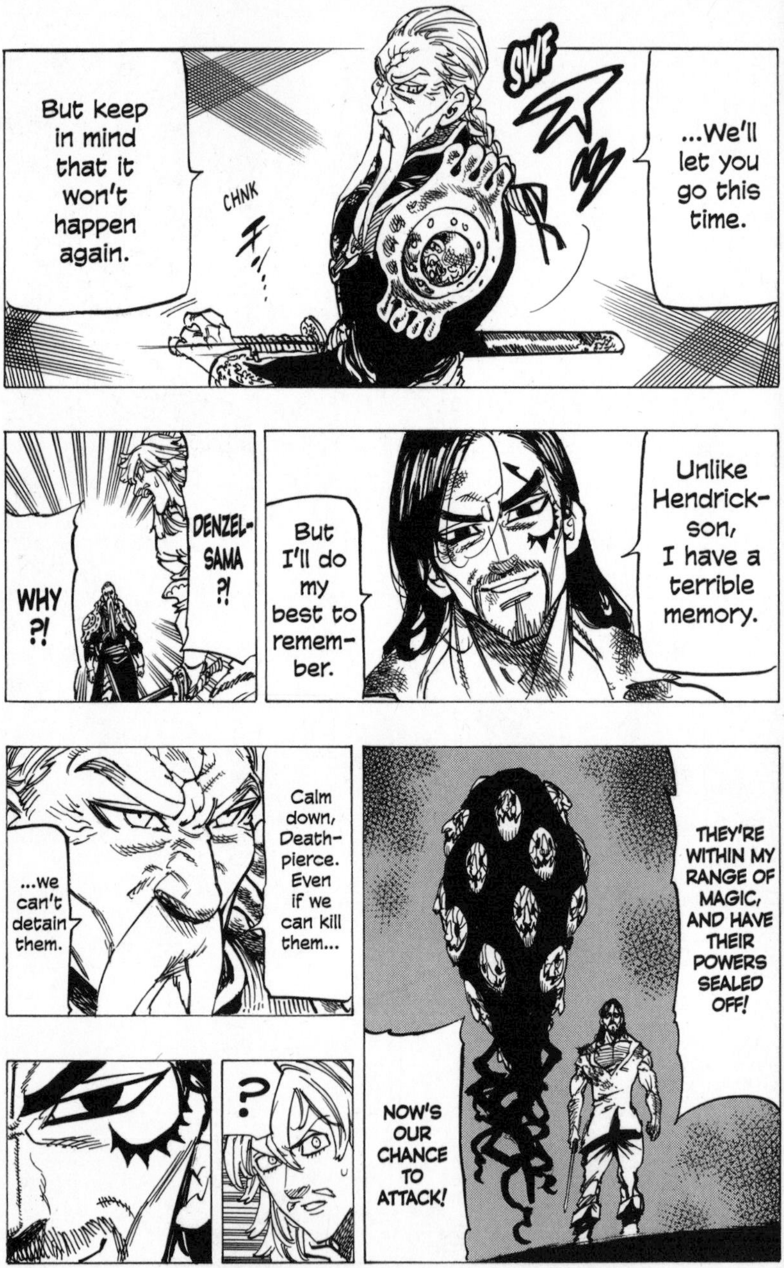
SWF
...We'll let you go this time.
CHNK
But keep in mind that it won't happen again.
Unlike Hendrickson, I have a terrible memory.
But I'll do my best to remember.
DENZEL-SAMA ?!
WHY ?!
THEY'RE WITHIN MY RANGE OF MAGIC, AND HAVE THEIR POWERS SEALED OFF!
NOW'S OUR CHANCE TO ATTACK!
Calm down, Deathpierce. Even if we can kill them...
...we can't detain them.
?

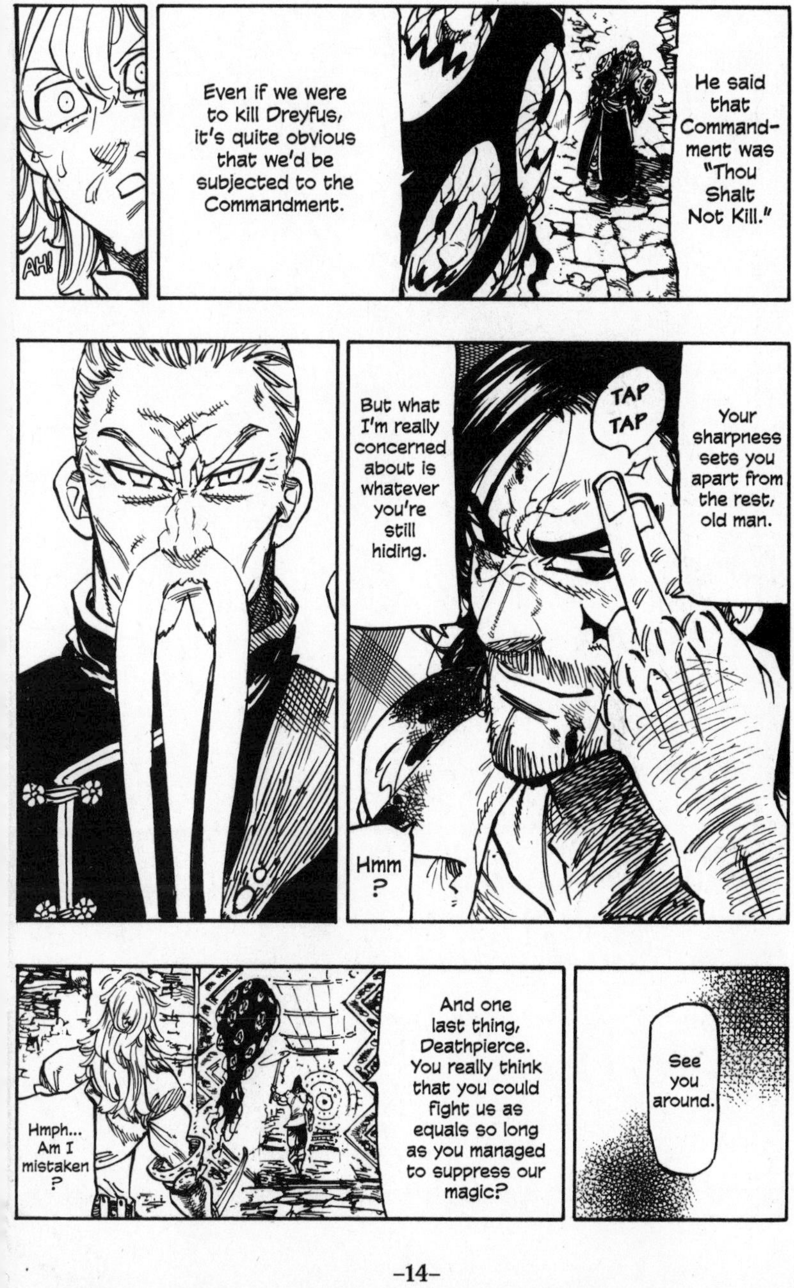
He said that Commandment was "Thou Shalt Not Kill."
Even if we were to kill Dreyfus, it's quite obvious that we'd be subjected to the Commandment.
AH!
Your sharpness sets you apart from the rest, old man.
TAP TAP
But what I'm really concerned about is whatever you're still hiding.
Hmm?
See you around.
And one last thing, Deathpierce. You really think that you could fight us as equals so long as you managed to suppress our magic?
Hmph... Am I mistaken?

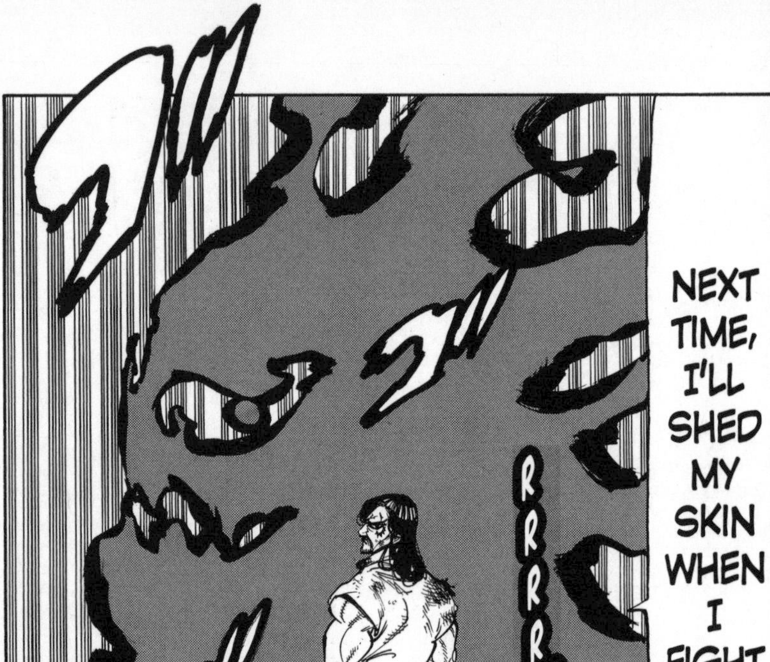
NEXT TIME, I'LL SHED MY SKIN WHEN I FIGHT YOU.
RRRRRUMBLE

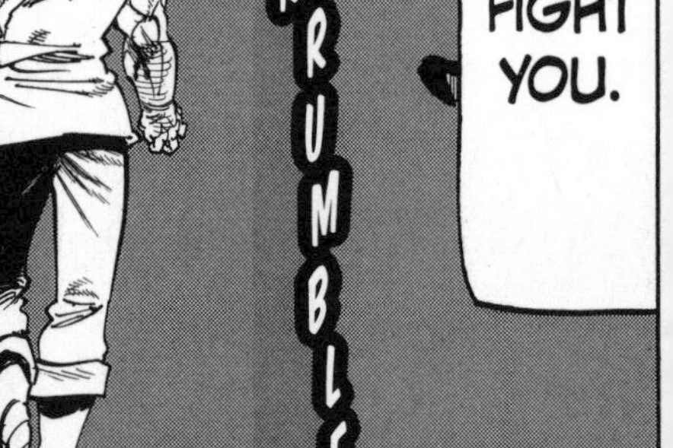
...!!
THADUMP

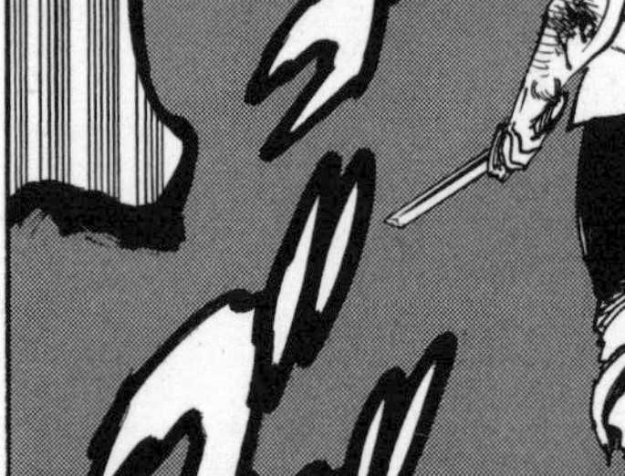
SSHF

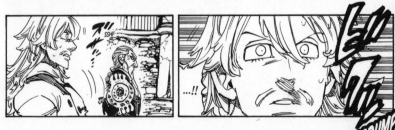

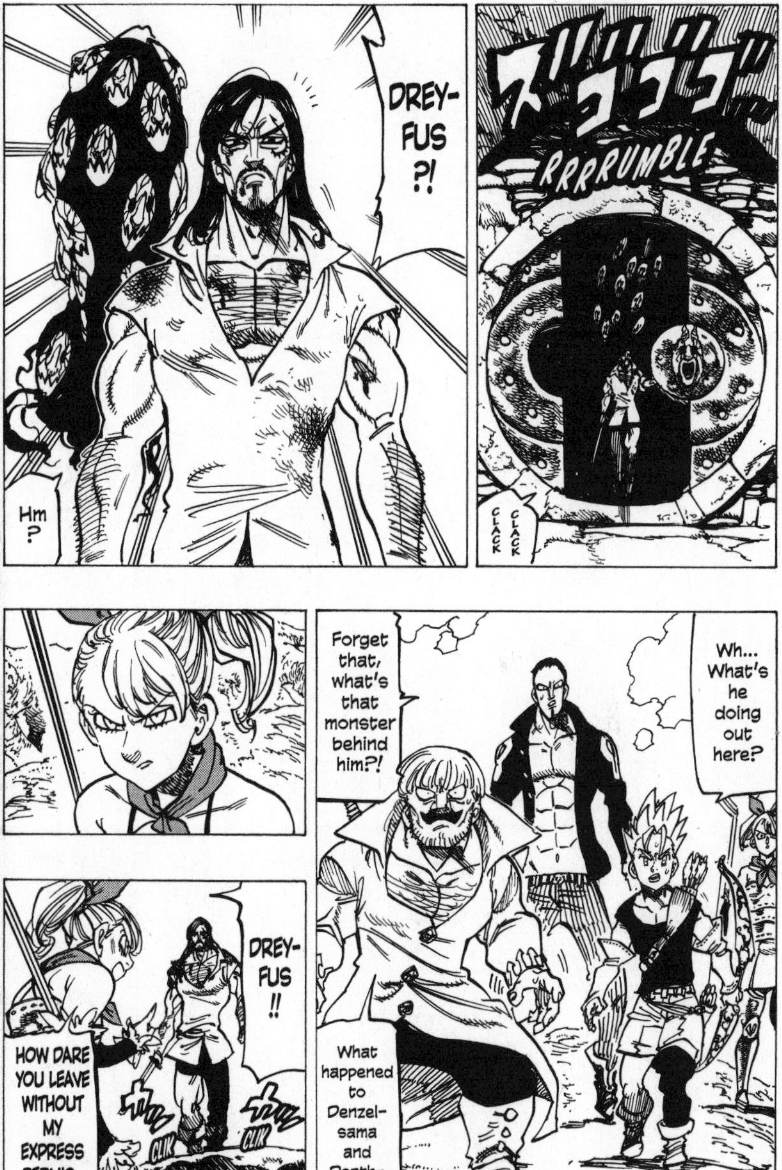
RRRRUMBLE
CLACK CLACK
DREY-FUS ?!
Hm ?
Wh... What's he doing out here?
Forget that, what's that monster behind him?!
What happened to Denzel-sama and Death-pierce?!
DREY-FUS !!
HOW DARE YOU LEAVE WITHOUT MY EXPRESS PERMIS-SION—
CLIK
CLIK

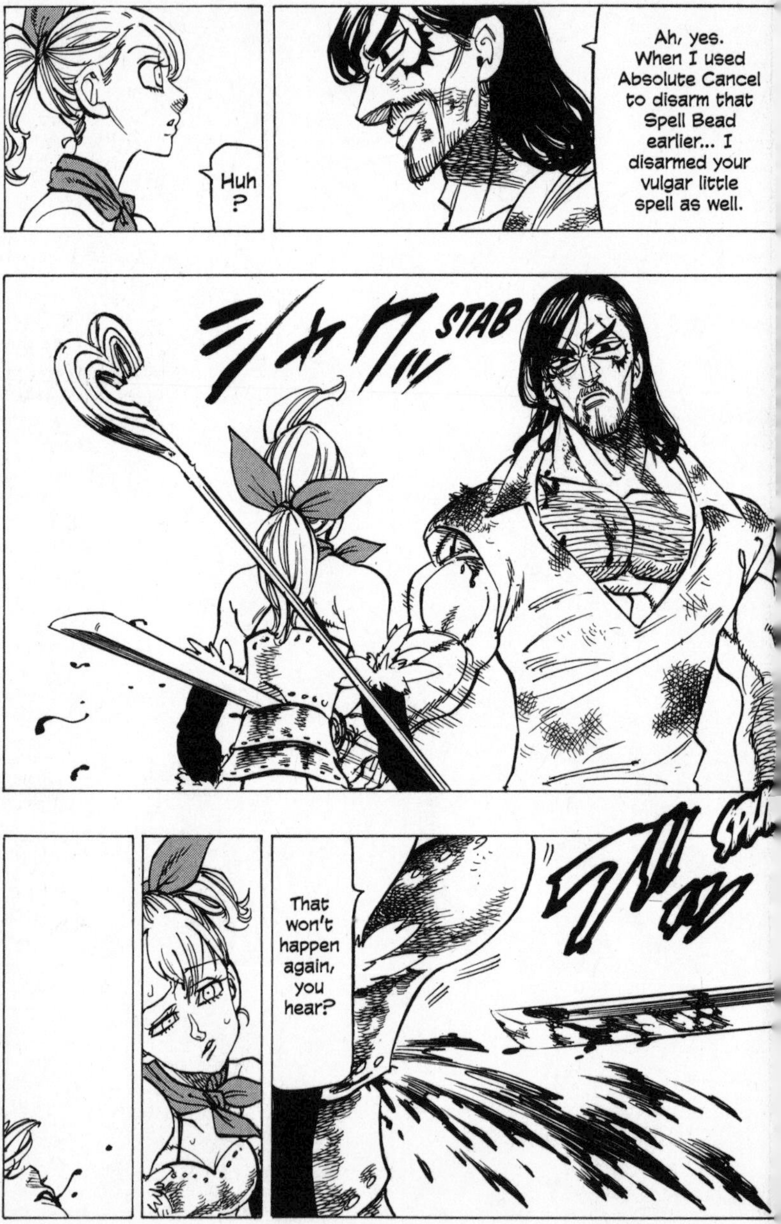
Ah, yes. When I used Absolute Cancel to disarm that Spell Bead earlier... I disarmed your vulgar little spell as well.
Huh?
STAB
That won't happen again, you hear?

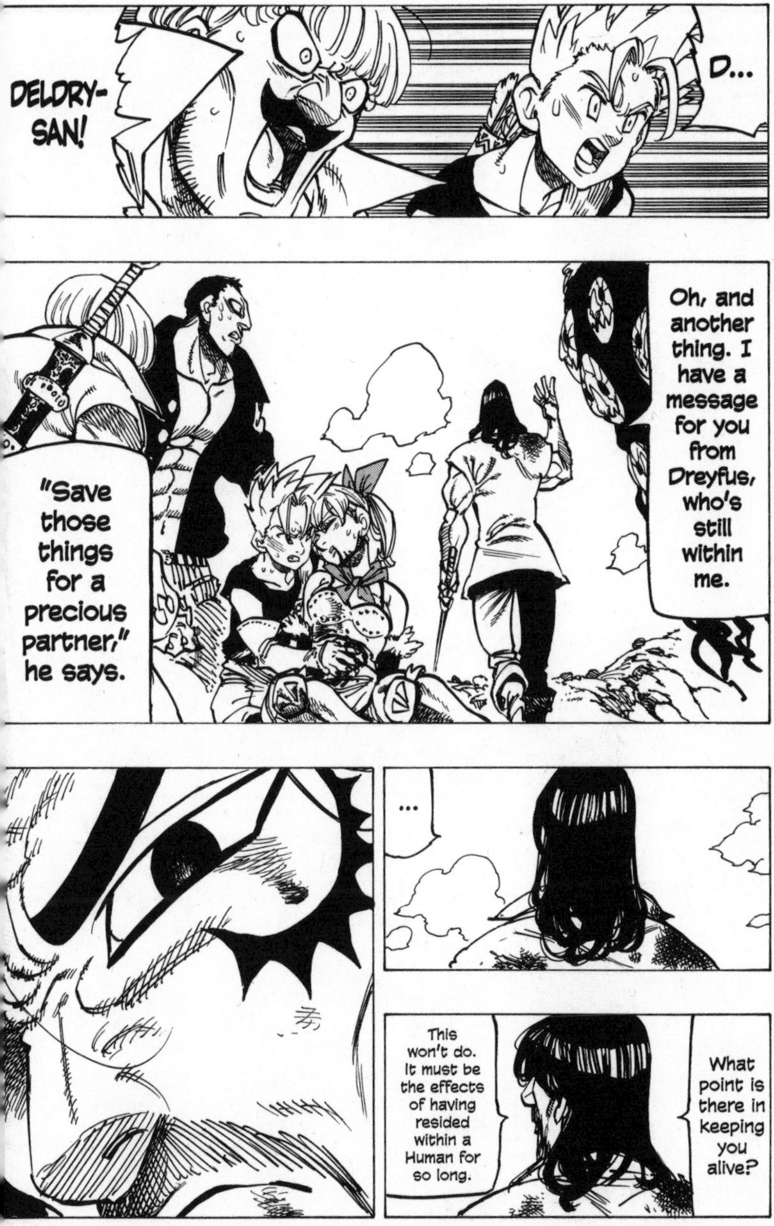
D...
DELDRY-SAN!
Oh, and another thing. I have a message for you from Dreyfus, who's still within me.
"Save those things for a precious partner," he says.
...
What point is there in keeping you alive?
This won't do. It must be the effects of having resided within a Human for so long.

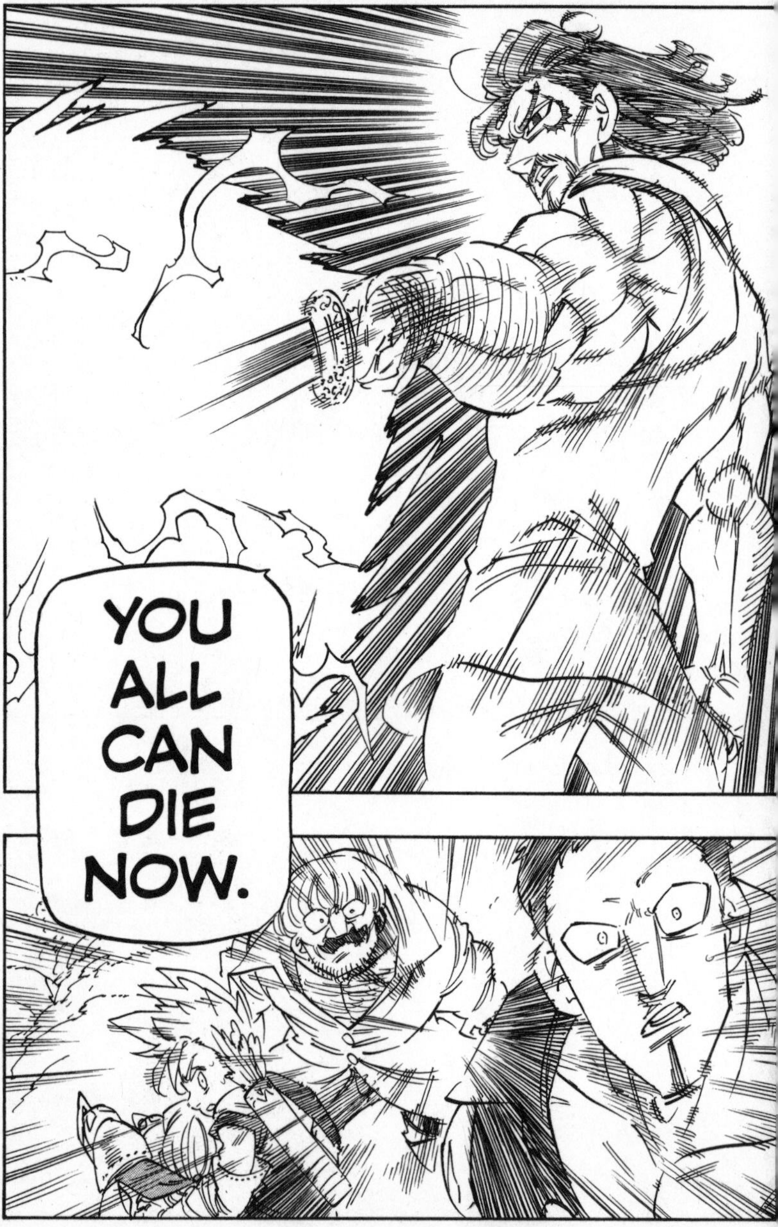
YOU ALL CAN DIE NOW.

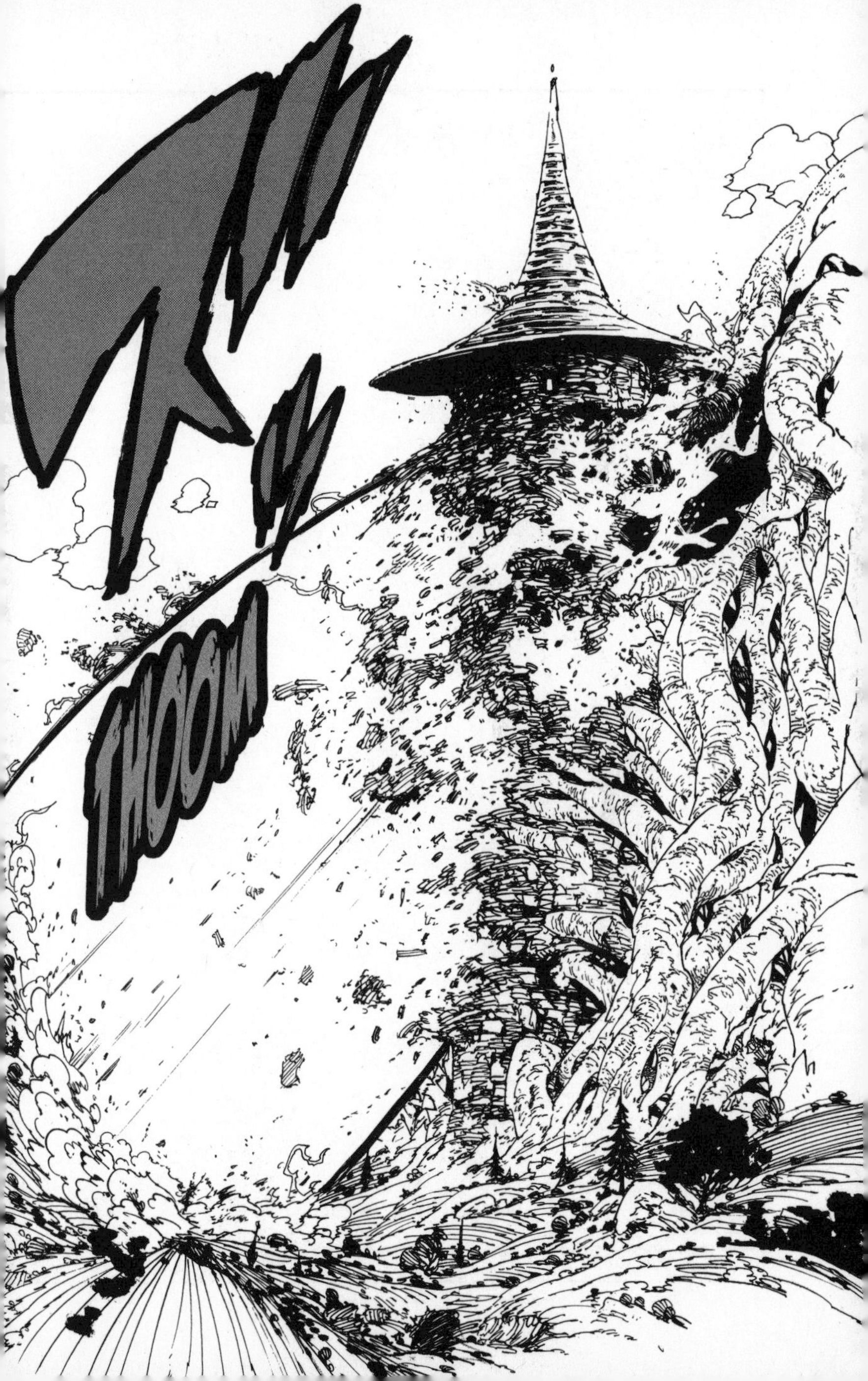
ズッ
THOOM

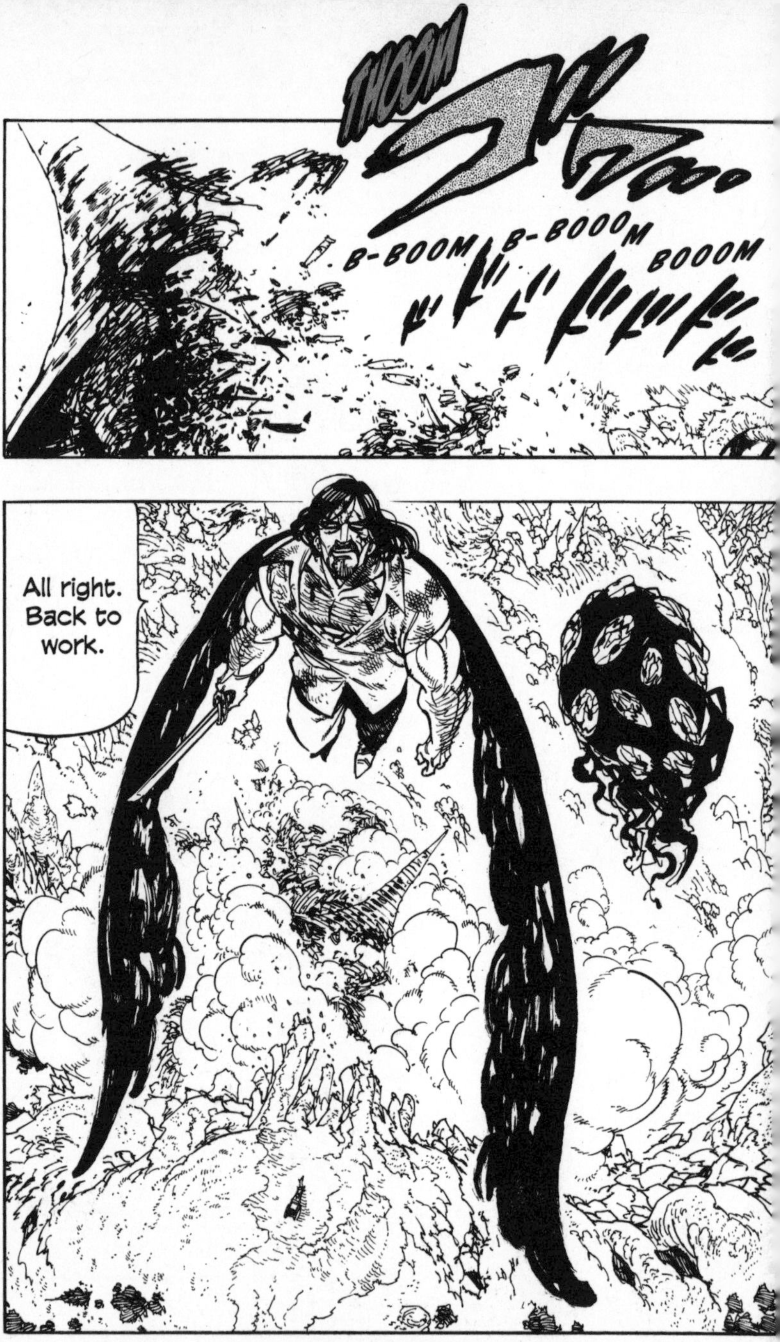
THOOM
B-BOOM
B-BOOOM
BOOOM
All right. Back to work.

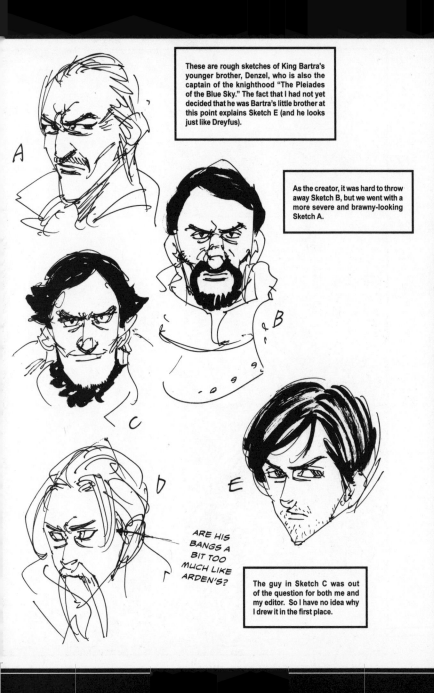

These are rough sketches of King Bartra's younger brother, Denzel, who is also the captain of the knighthood "The Pleiades of the Blue Sky." The fact that I had not yet decided that he was Bartra's little brother at this point explains Sketch E (and he looks just like Dreyfus).

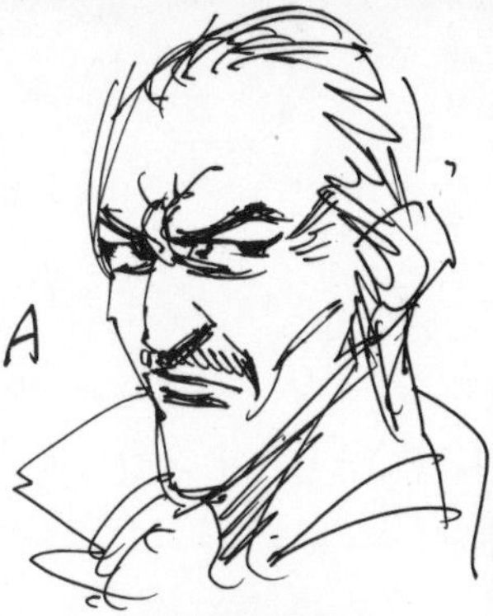
A

As the creator, it was hard to throw away Sketch B, but we went with a more severe and brawny-looking Sketch A.

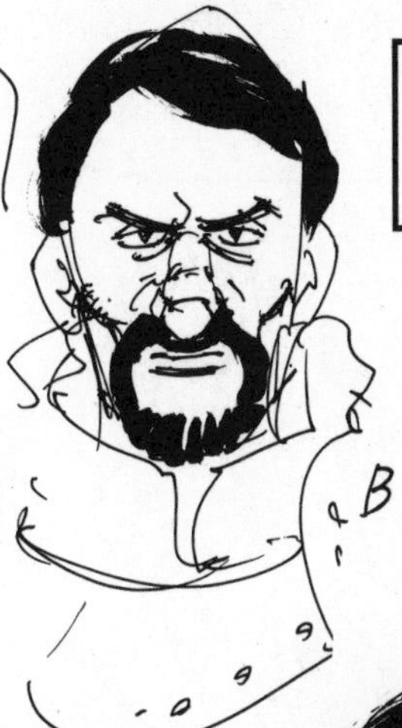
B

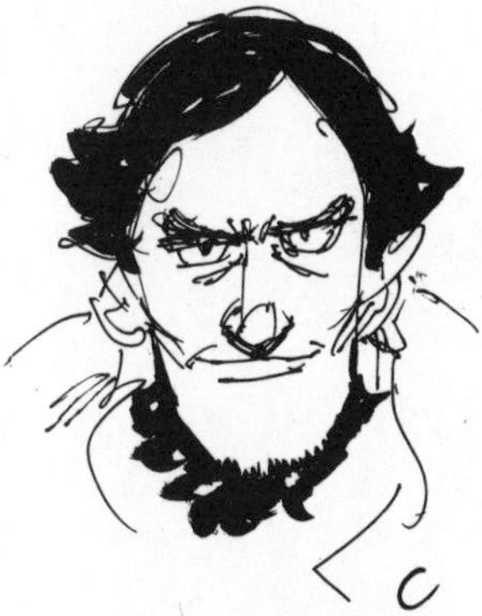
C

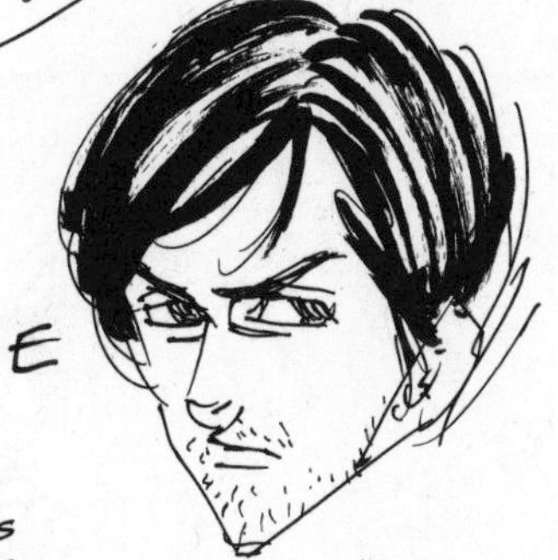
E

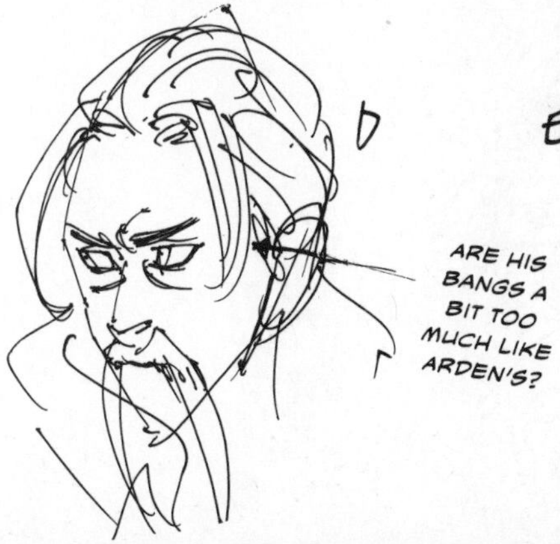
D
ARE HIS BANGS A BIT TOO MUCH LIKE ARDEN'S?

The guy in Sketch C was out of the question for both me and my editor. So I have no idea why I drew it in the first place.

Chapter 155 - Death-Trap Maze

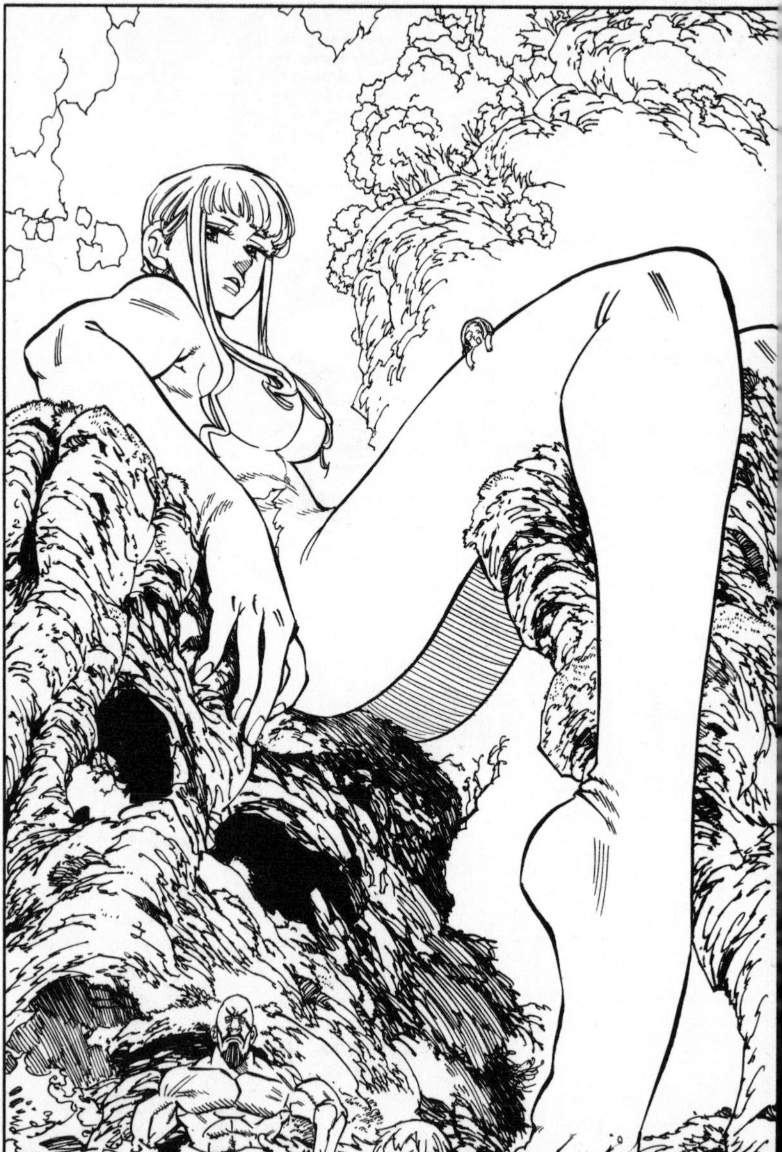

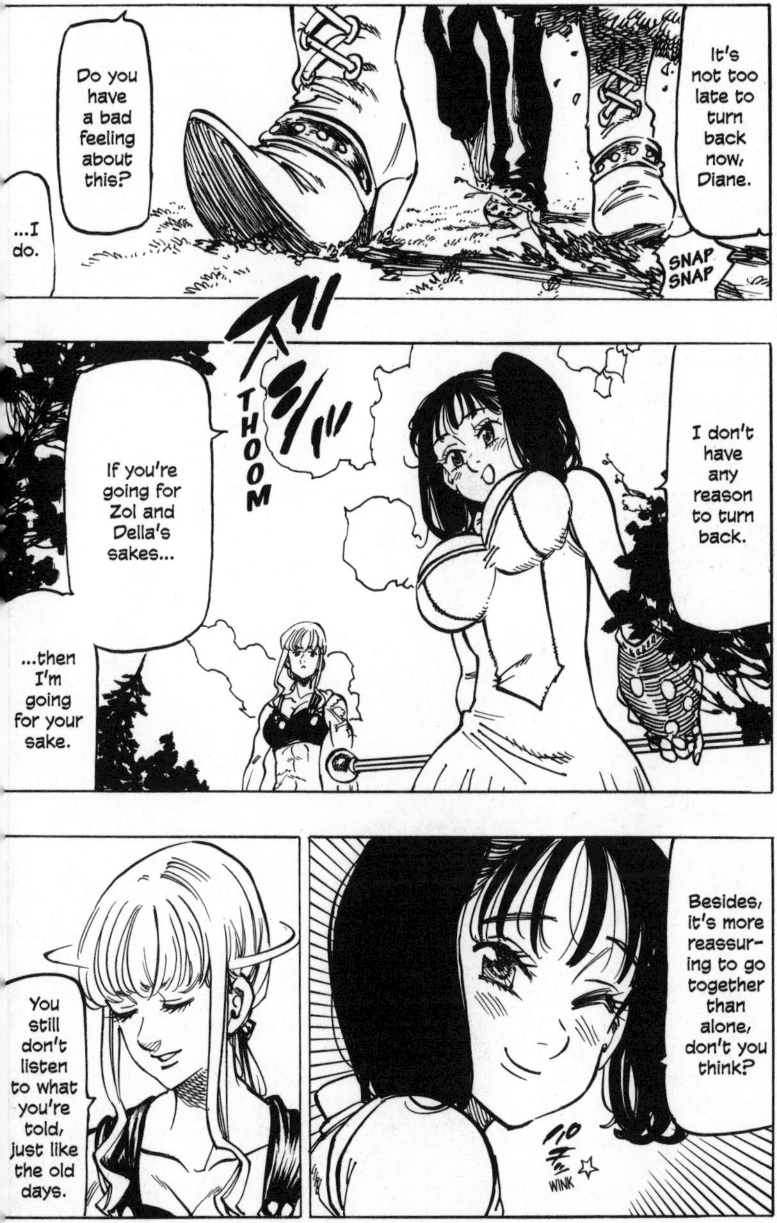
It's not too late to turn back now, Diane.
SNAP SNAP
Do you have a bad feeling about this?
...I do.
THOOM
I don't have any reason to turn back.
If you're going for Zol and Della's sakes...
...then I'm going for your sake.
Besides, it's more reassuring to go together than alone, don't you think?
WINK
You still don't listen to what you're told, just like the old days.

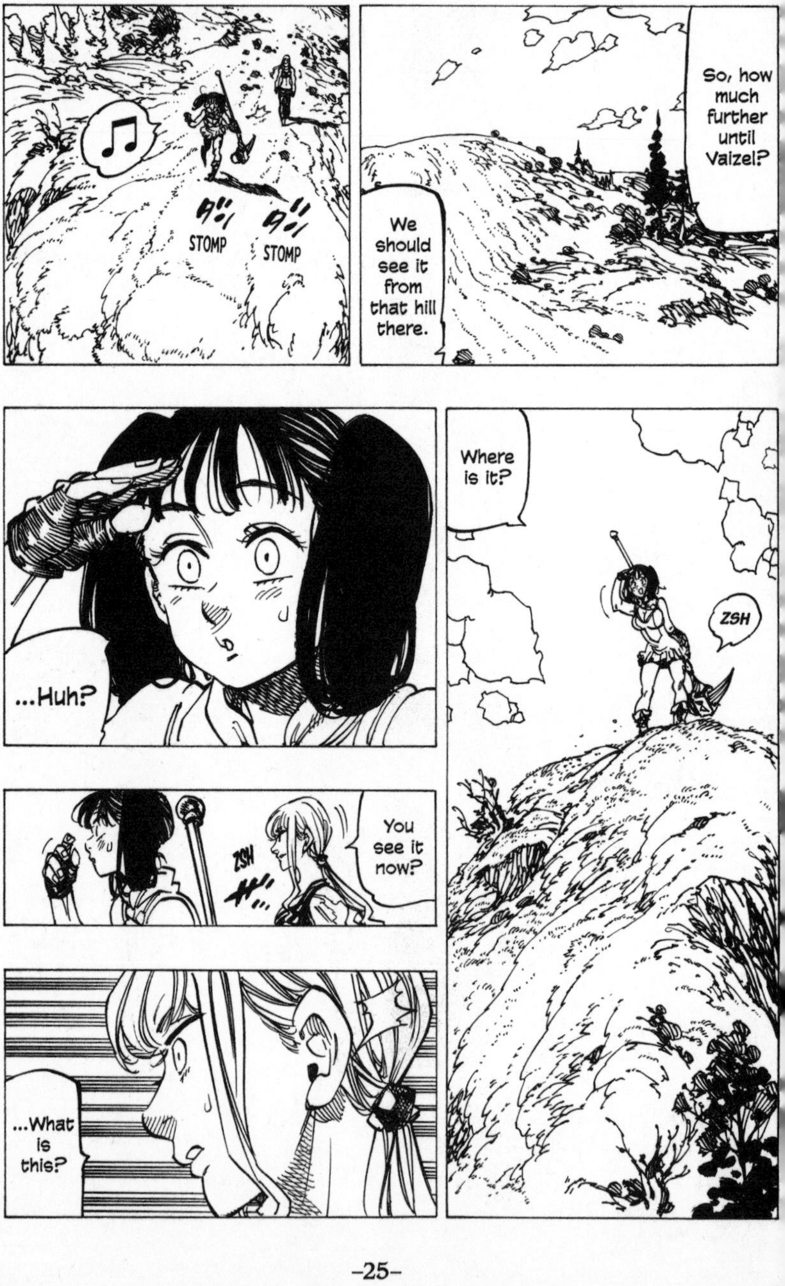
So, how much further until Vaizel?
We should see it from that hill there.
♫
STOMP
STOMP
Where is it?
ZSH
...Huh?
You see it now?
ZSH
...What is this?

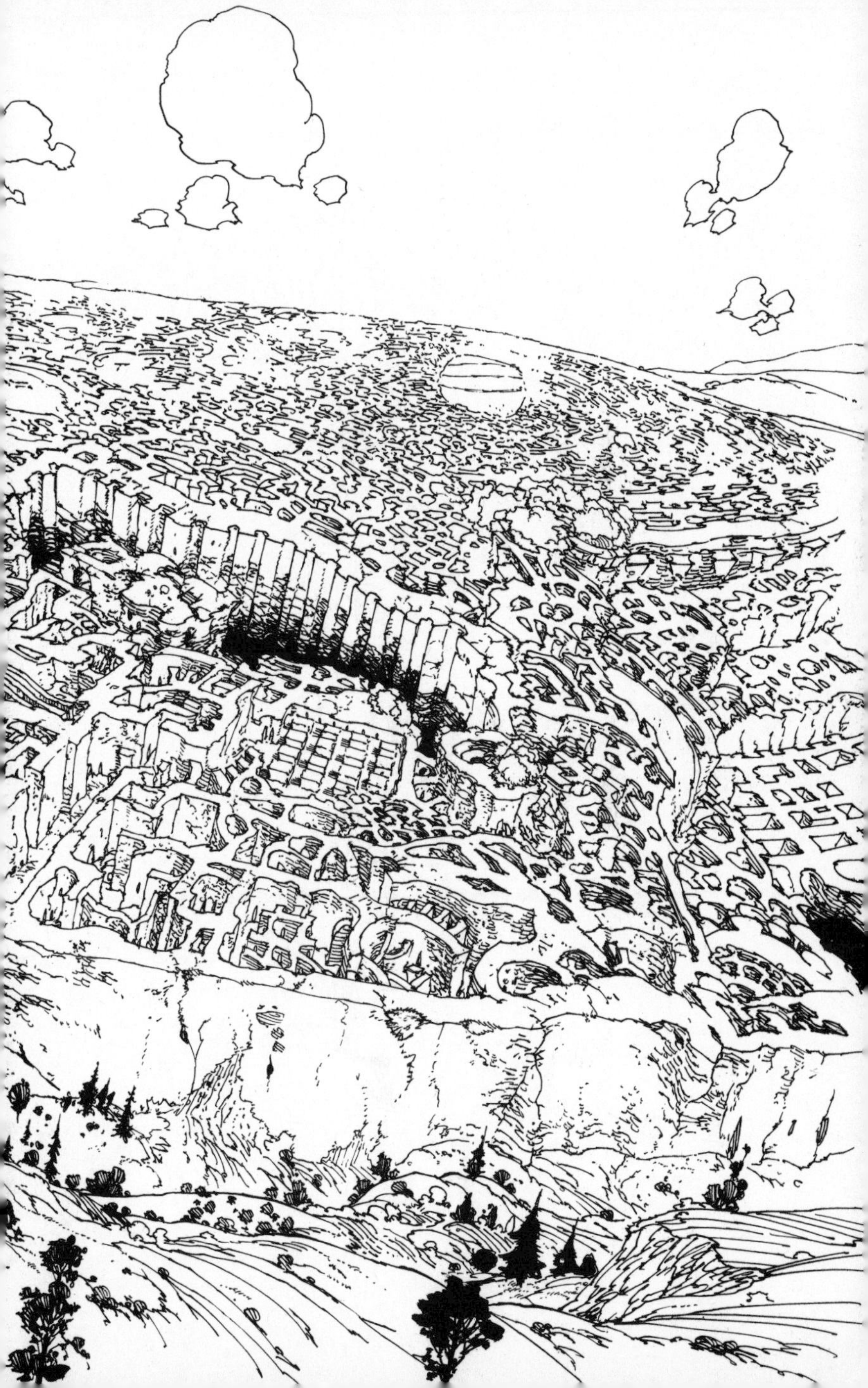

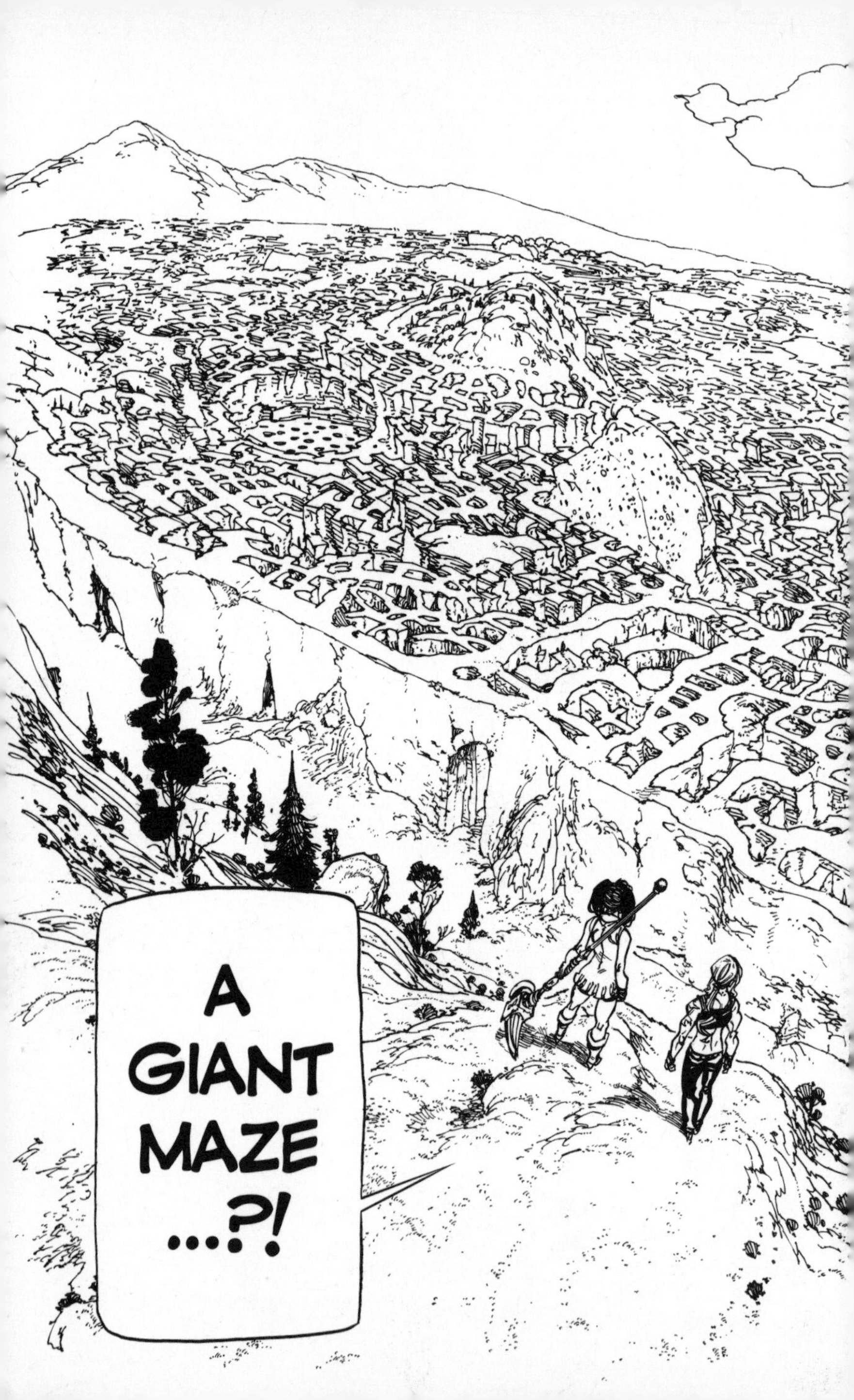
A GIANT MAZE ...?!

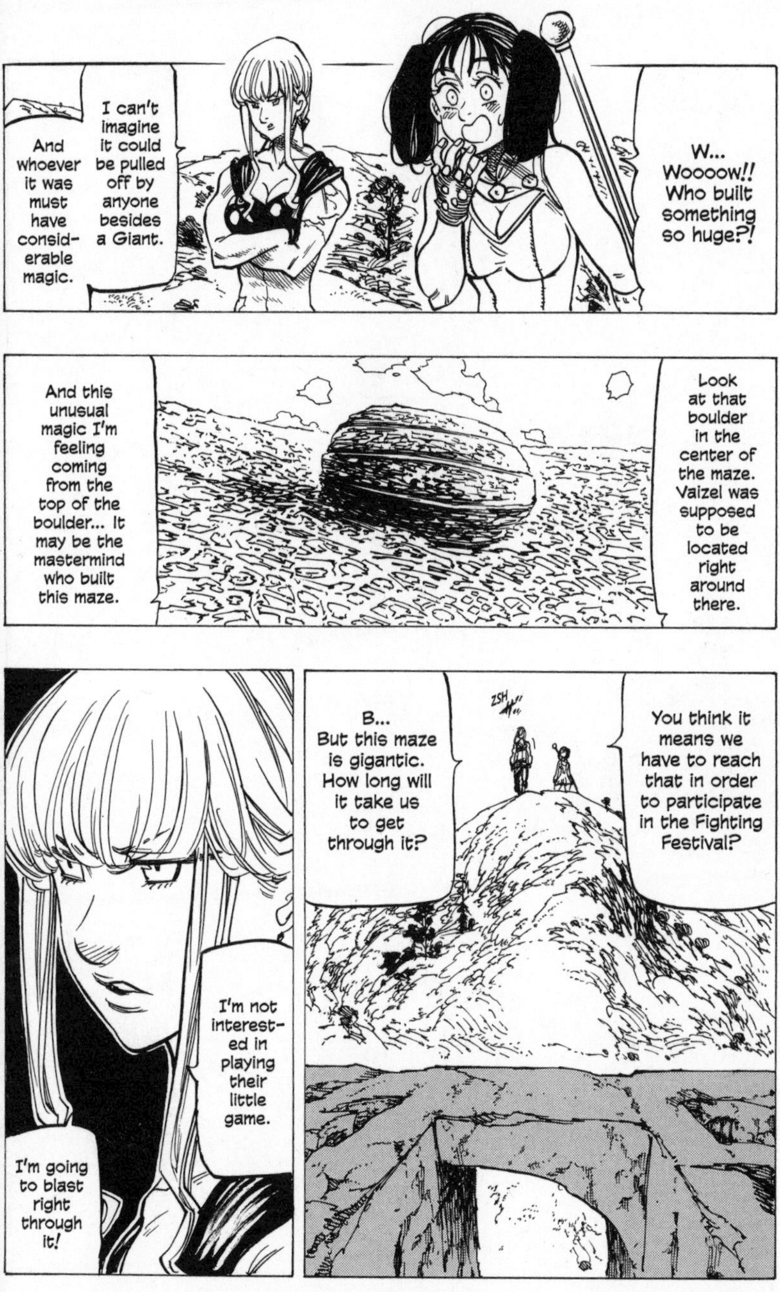
W... Wooooow!! Who built something so huge?!
I can't imagine it could be pulled off by anyone besides a Giant.
And whoever it was must have consid-erable magic.
Look at that boulder in the center of the maze. Vaizel was supposed to be located right around there.
And this unusual magic I'm feeling coming from the top of the boulder... It may be the mastermind who built this maze.
You think it means we have to reach that in order to participate in the Fighting Festival?
ZSH
B... But this maze is gigantic. How long will it take us to get through it?
I'm not interest-ed in playing their little game.
I'm going to blast right through it!

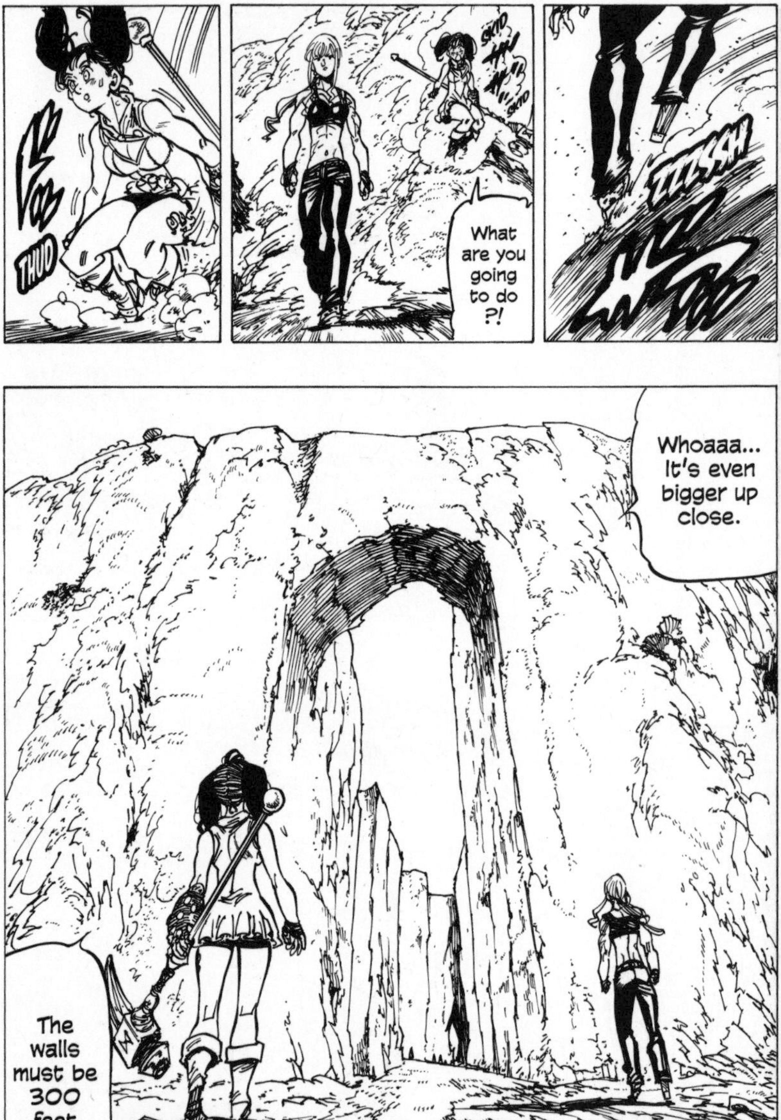
ZZZSSH
SKID
SKID
What are you going to do ?!
THUD
Whoaaa... It's even bigger up close.
The walls must be 300 feet high!

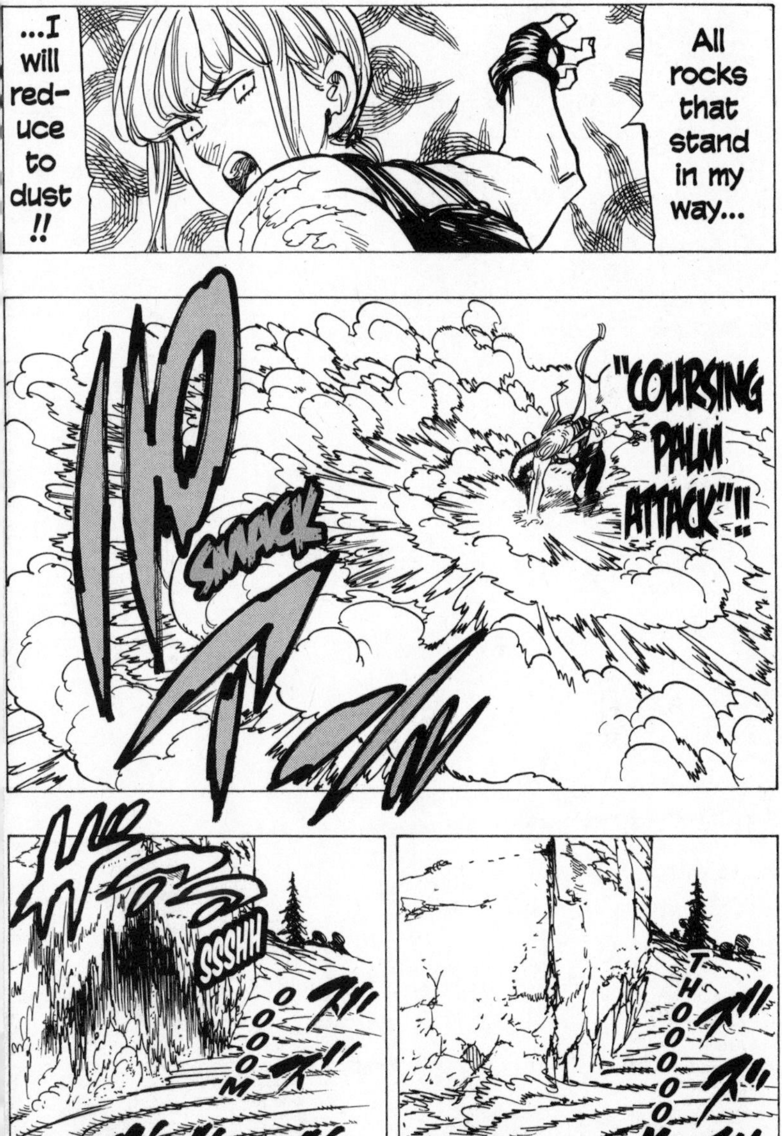
All rocks that stand in my way...
...I will red-uce to dust!!
"COURSING PALM ATTACK"!!
SMACK
THOOOOOOM
SSSHH
OOOOM

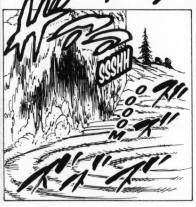

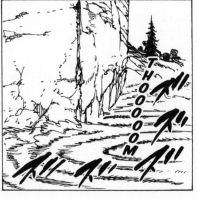

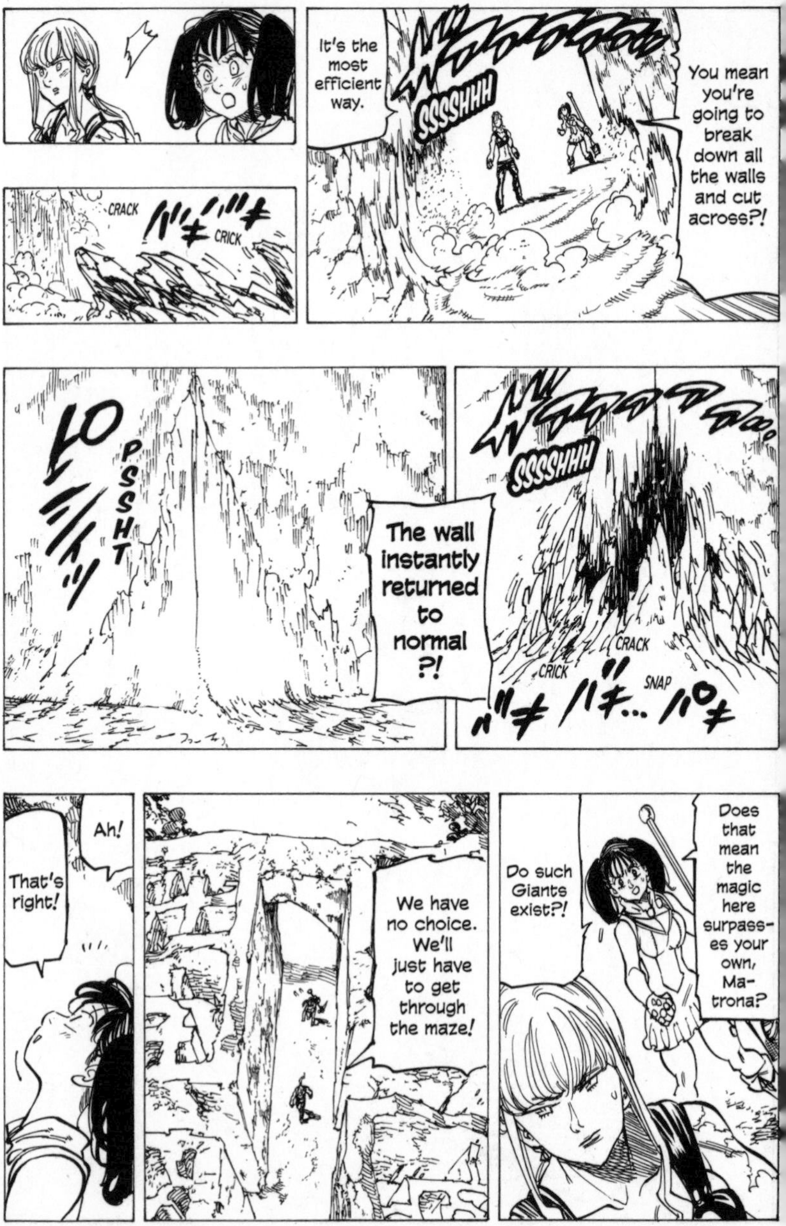
You mean you're going to break down all the walls and cut across?!
It's the most efficient way.
SSSSHHH
CRACK
CRICK
SSSSHHH
CRACK
CRICK
SNAP
The wall instantly returned to normal?!
PSSHT
Does that mean the magic here surpasses your own, Matrona?
Do such Giants exist?!
We have no choice. We'll just have to get through the maze!
Ah!
That's right!

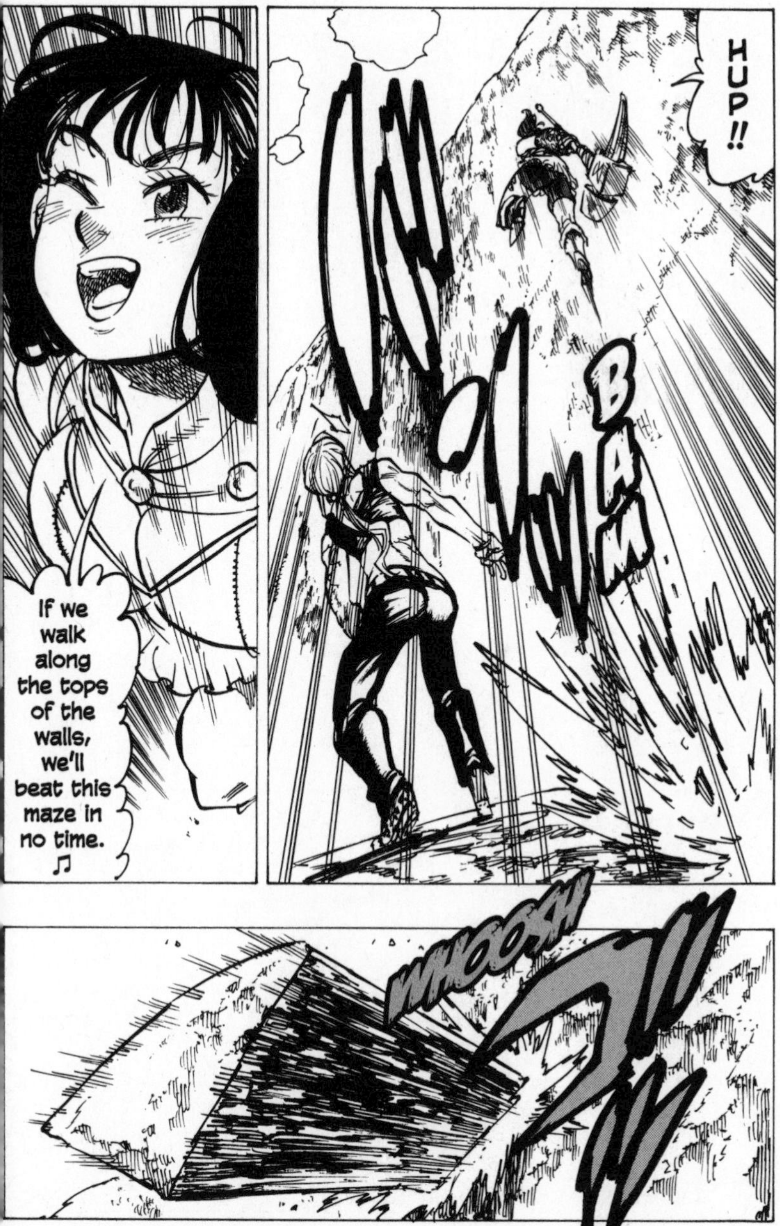
HUP!!
BAM
If we walk along the tops of the walls, we'll beat this maze in no time. ♫
WHOOSH

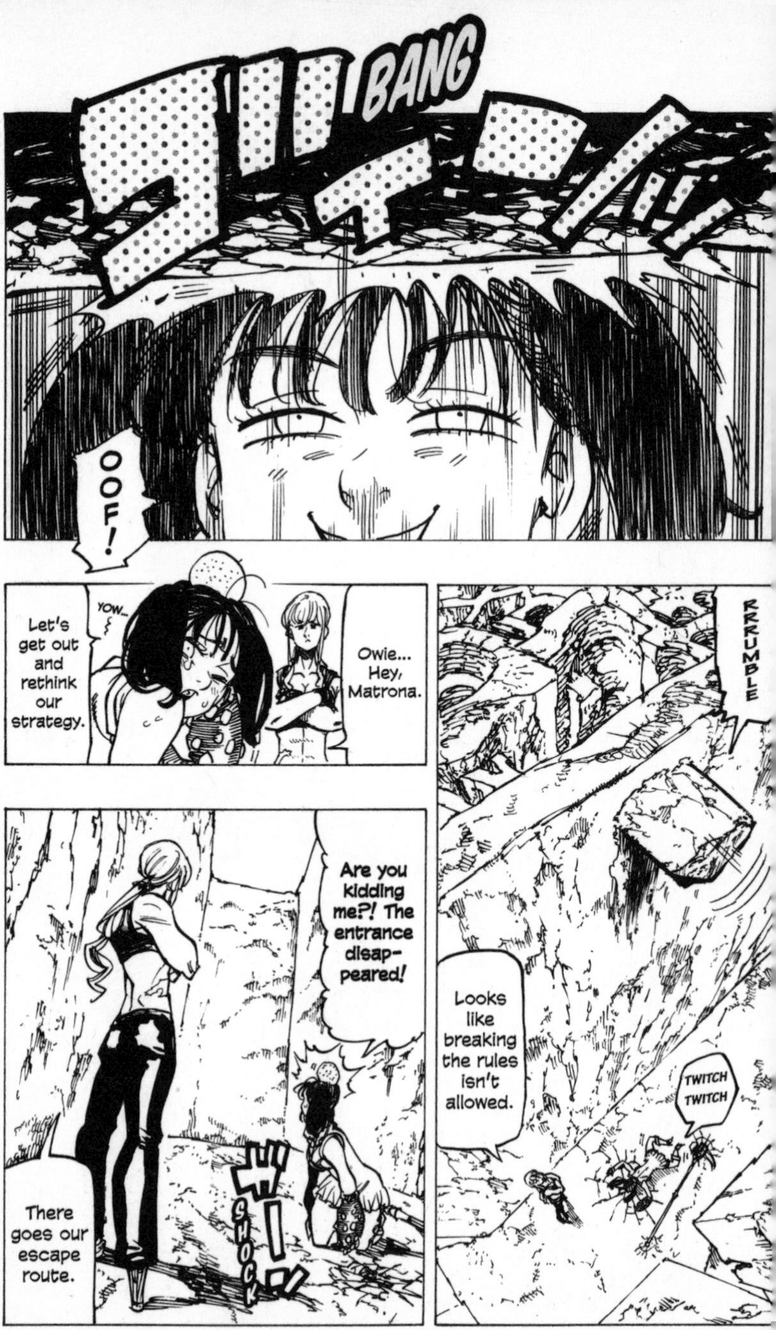
BANG
OOF!
RRRUMBLE
Looks like breaking the rules isn't allowed.
TWITCH TWITCH
Owie... Hey, Matrona.
YOW...
Let's get out and rethink our strategy.
Are you kidding me?! The entrance disappeared!
SHOCK
There goes our escape route.

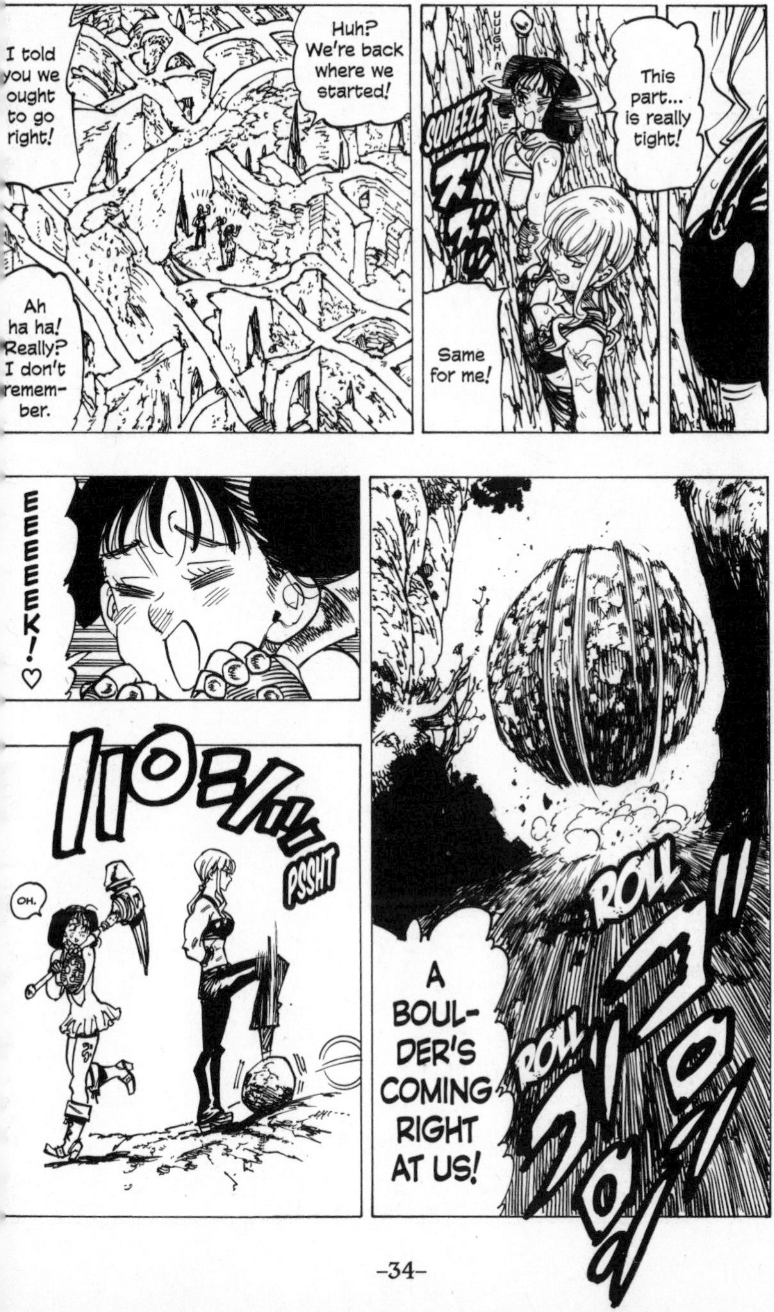
UUUGH!N
SQUEEZE
This part... is really tight!
Same for me!
Huh? We're back where we started!
I told you we ought to go right!
Ah ha ha! Really? I don't remember.
A BOULDER'S COMING RIGHT AT US!
ROLL
ROLL
EEEEEEK!♡
PSSHT
OH.

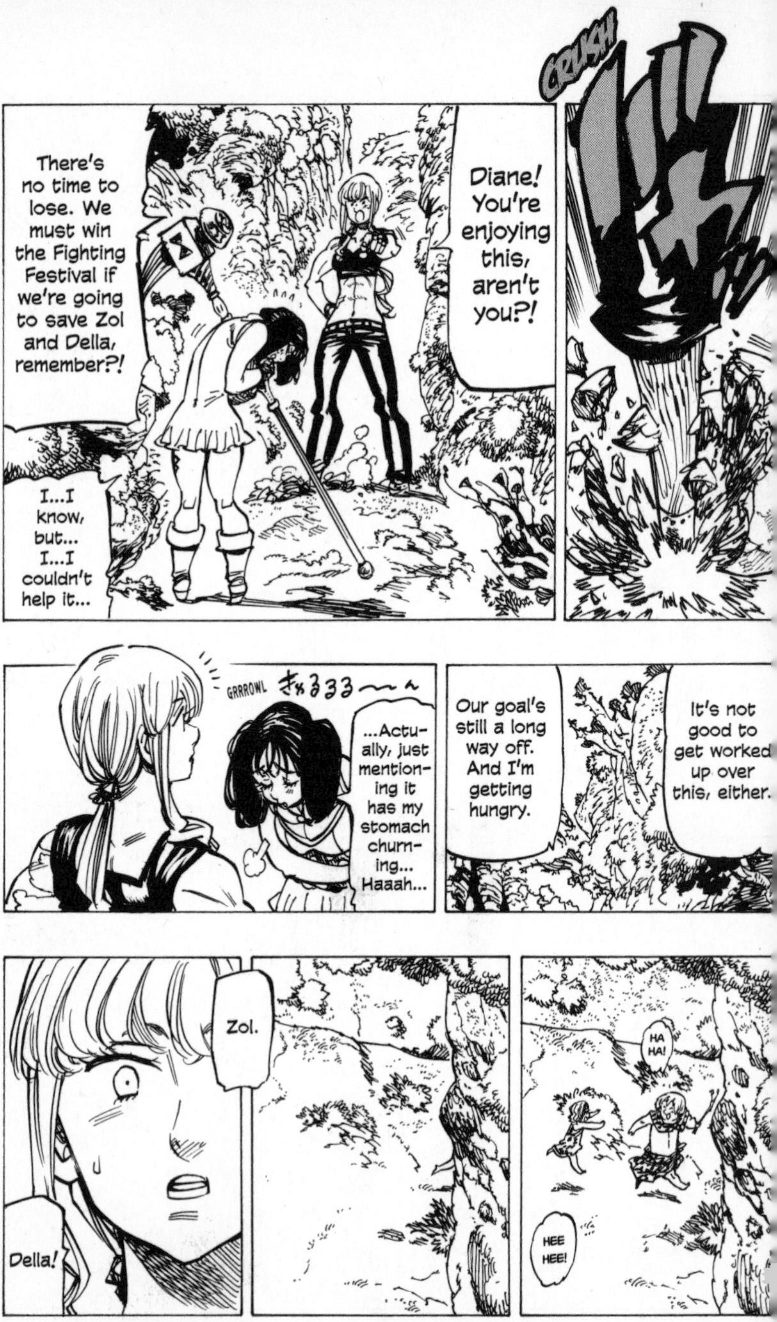
CRUSH
Diane! You're enjoying this, aren't you?!
There's no time to lose. We must win the Fighting Festival if we're going to save Zol and Della, remember?!
I...I know, but... I...I couldn't help it...
It's not good to get worked up over this, either.
Our goal's still a long way off. And I'm getting hungry.
GRRROWL
...Actually, just mentioning it has my stomach churning... Haaah...
HA HA!
HEE HEE!
Zol.
Della!

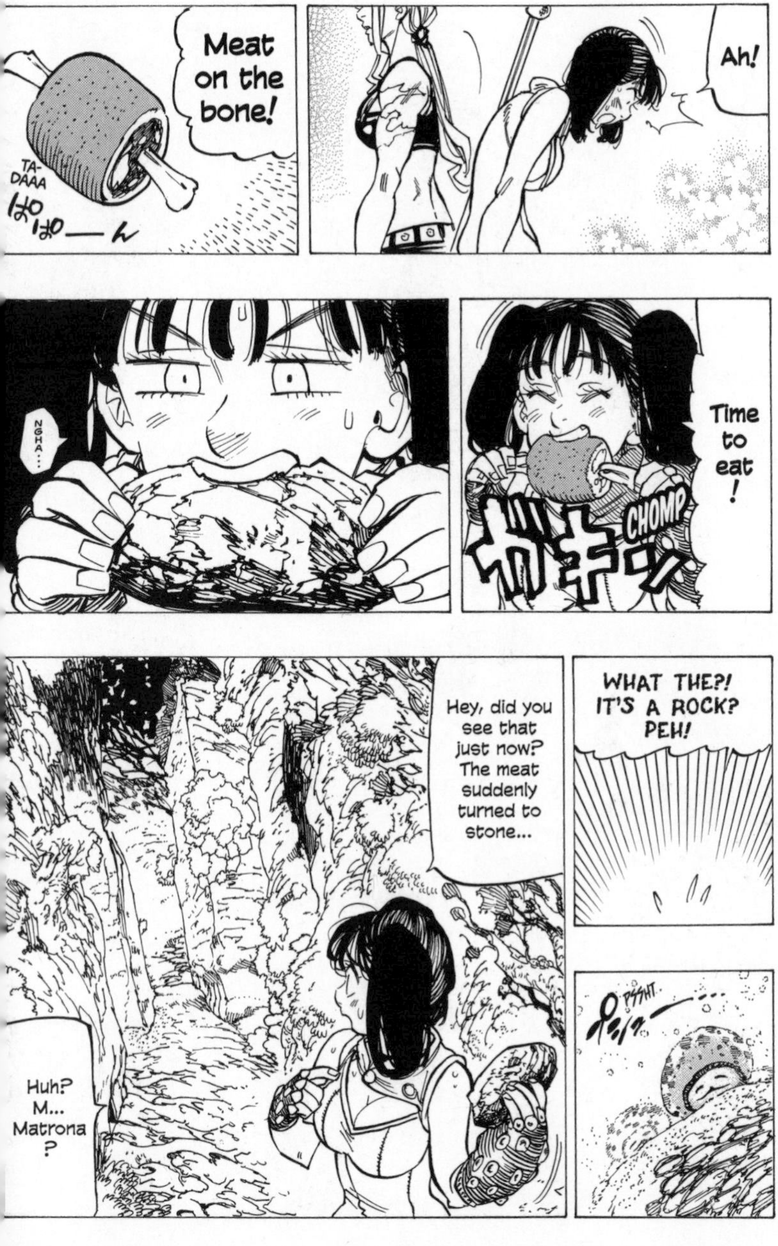
Ah!
Meat on the bone!
TA-DAAA
Time to eat!
CHOMP
ガキッ
NGHA...
WHAT THE?! IT'S A ROCK? PEH!
PSSHT
Hey, did you see that just now? The meat suddenly turned to stone...
Huh? M... Matrona?

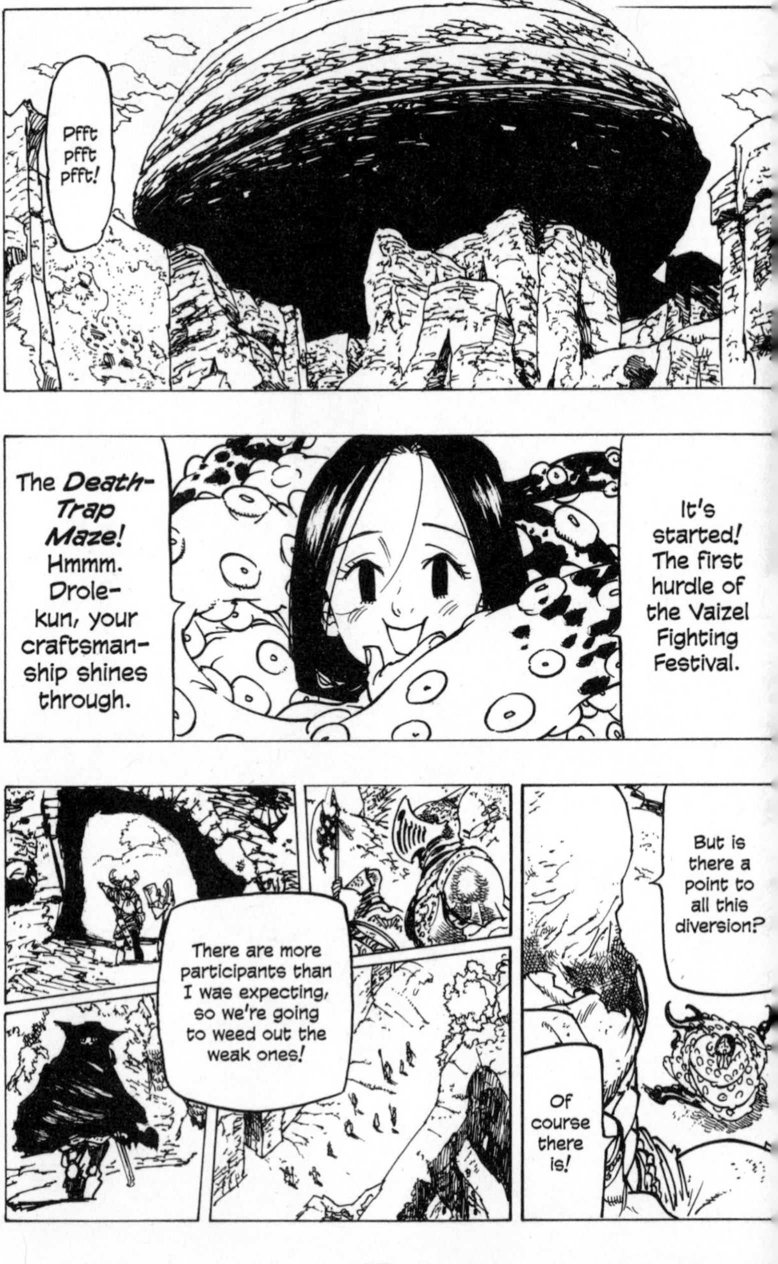
Pfft pfft pfft!
It's started! The first hurdle of the Vaizel Fighting Festival.
The *Death-Trap Maze!* Hmmm. Drole-kun, your craftsmanship shines through.
But is there a point to all this diversion?
Of course there is!
There are more participants than I was expecting, so we're going to weed out the weak ones!

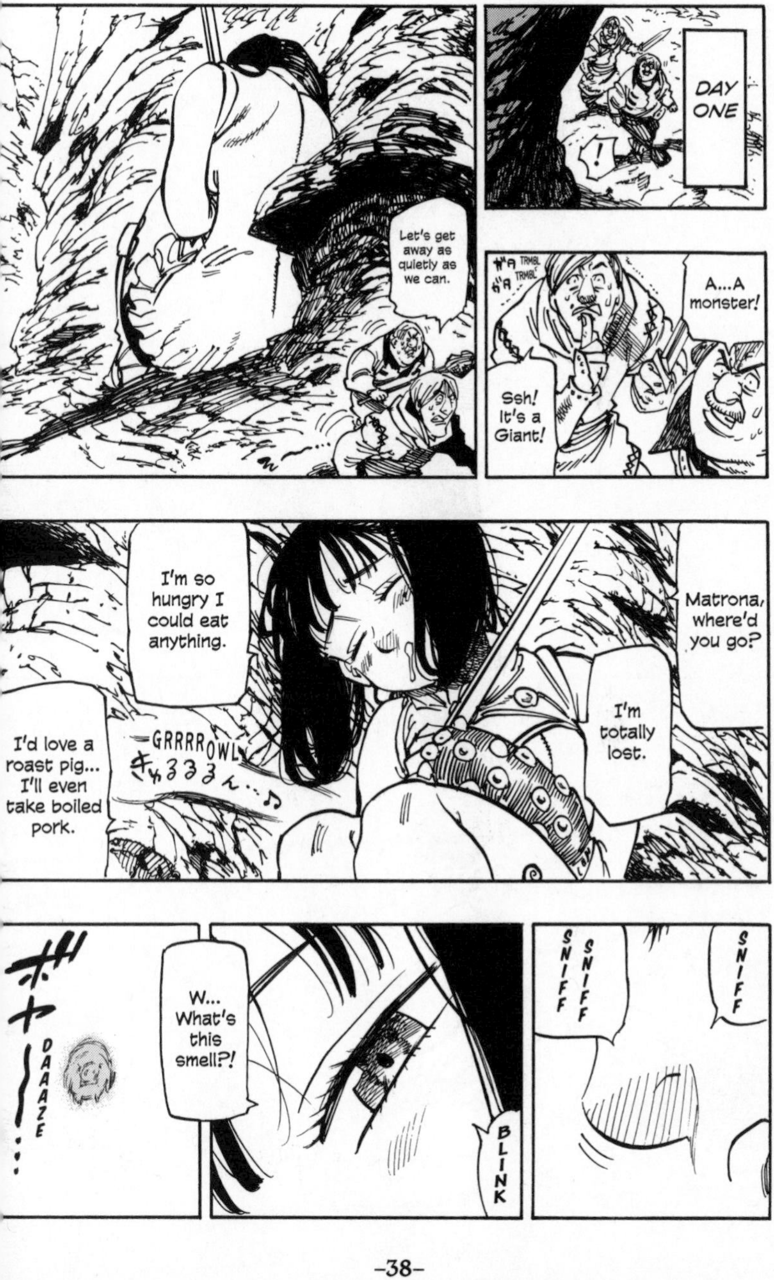
DAY ONE
!
A...A monster!
TRMBL TRMBL
Ssh! It's a Giant!
Let's get away as quietly as we can.
Matrona, where'd you go?
I'm totally lost.
I'm so hungry I could eat anything.
I'd love a roast pig... I'll even take boiled pork.
GRRRROWL
SNIFF
SNIFF SNIFF
W... What's this smell?!
BLINK
DAAAZE

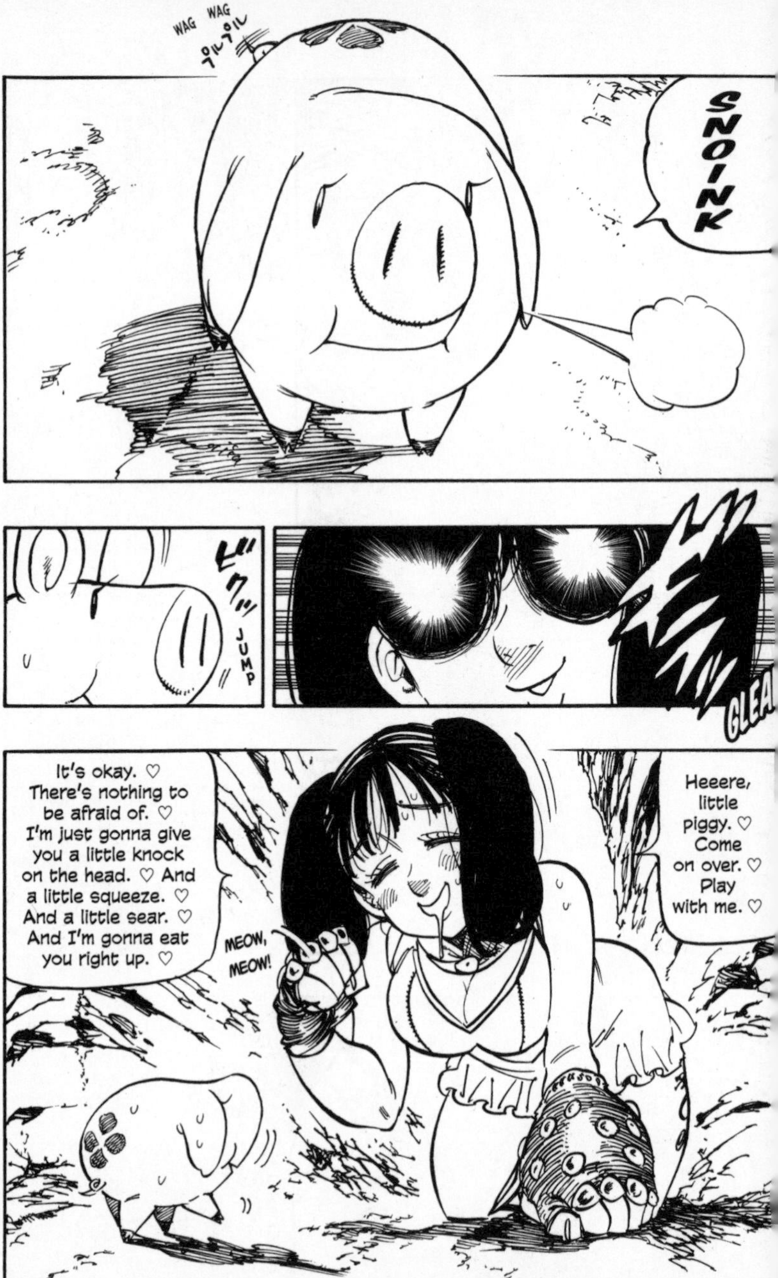
WAG WAG
SNOINK
GLEA
JUMP
Heeere, little piggy. ♡ Come on over. ♡ Play with me. ♡
It's okay. ♡ There's nothing to be afraid of. ♡ I'm just gonna give you a little knock on the head. ♡ And a little squeeze. ♡ And a little sear. ♡ And I'm gonna eat you right up. ♡
MEOW, MEOW!

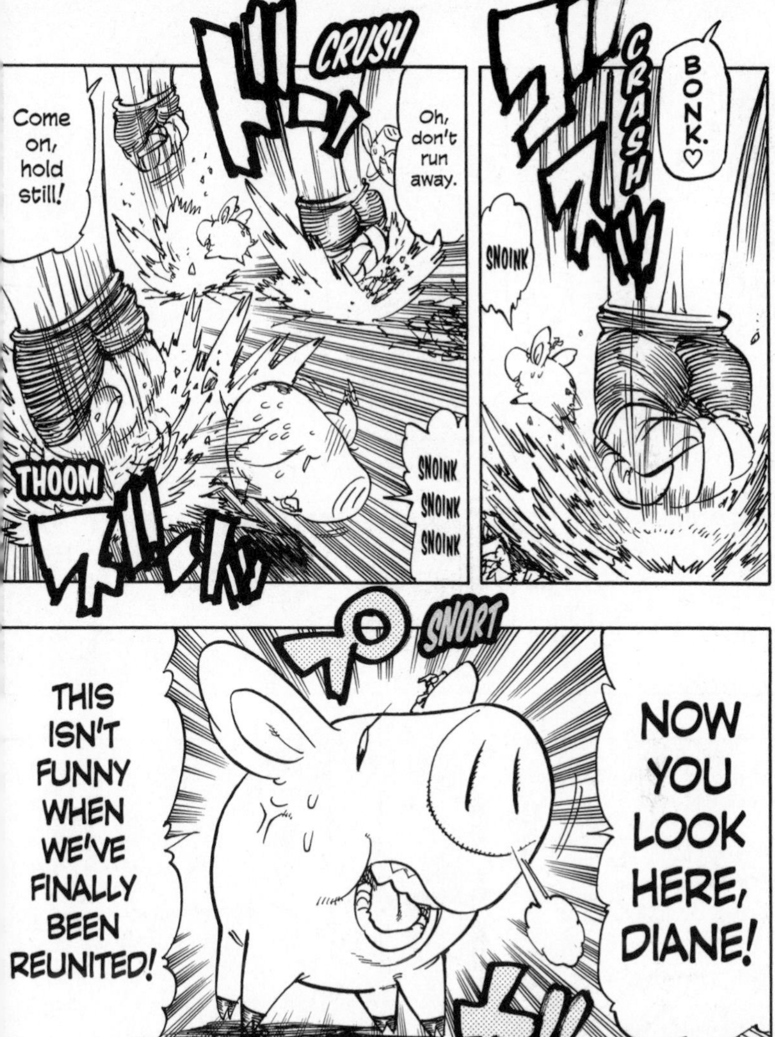
BONK.♡
CRASH
SNOINK
CRUSH
Oh, don't run away.
Come on, hold still!
SNOINK SNOINK SNOINK
THOOM
SNORT
NOW YOU LOOK HERE, DIANE!
THIS ISN'T FUNNY WHEN WE'VE FINALLY BEEN REUNITED!
A...
A talking pig!!

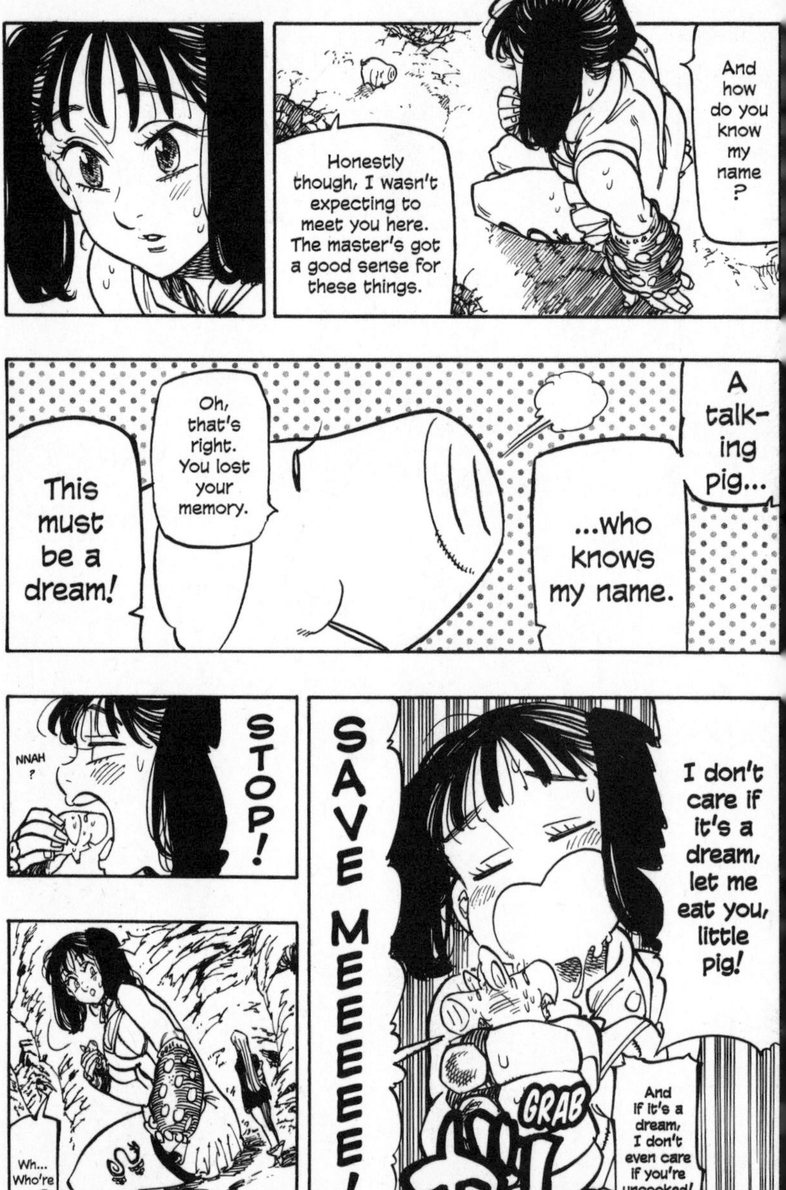
And how do you know my name?
Honestly though, I wasn't expecting to meet you here. The master's got a good sense for these things.
A talking-ing pig...
...who knows my name.
Oh, that's right. You lost your memory.
This must be a dream!
I don't care if it's a dream, let me eat you, little pig!
GRAB
And if it's a dream, I don't even care if you're uncooked!
SAVE MEEEEEE!
STOP!
NNAH?
Wh... Who're you?

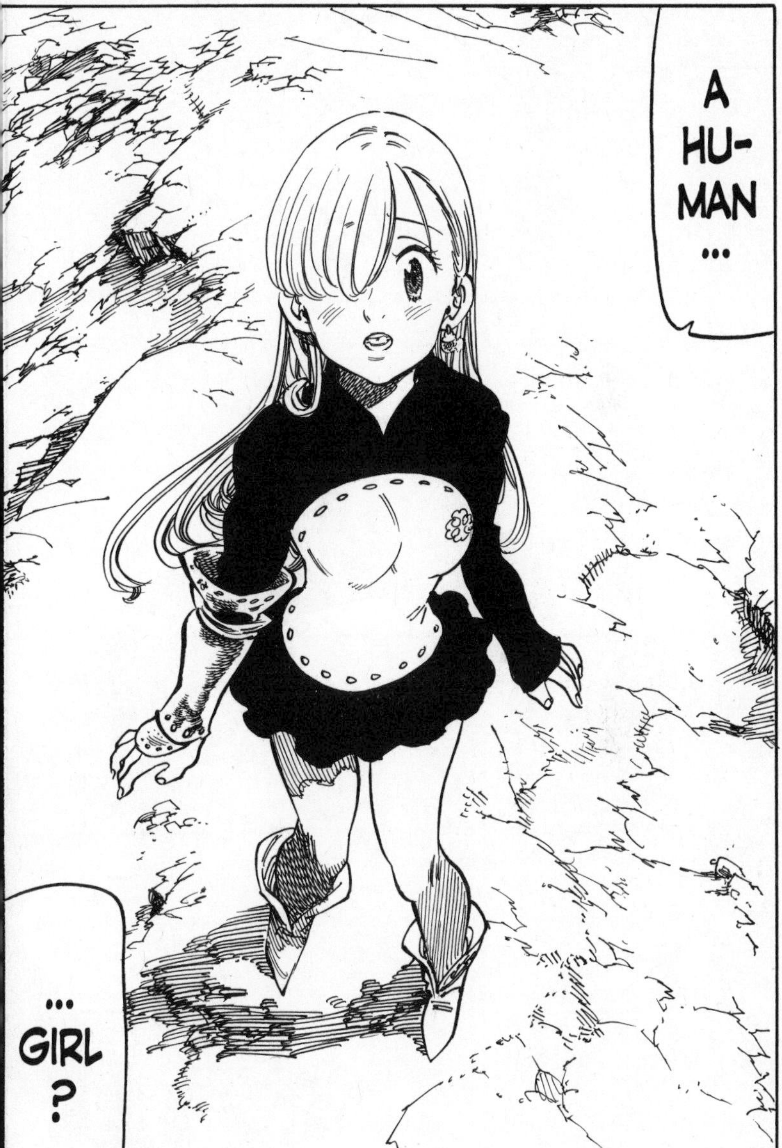
A HU-MAN ...
... GIRL ?

Chapter 156 - The Maze Exploration Contest

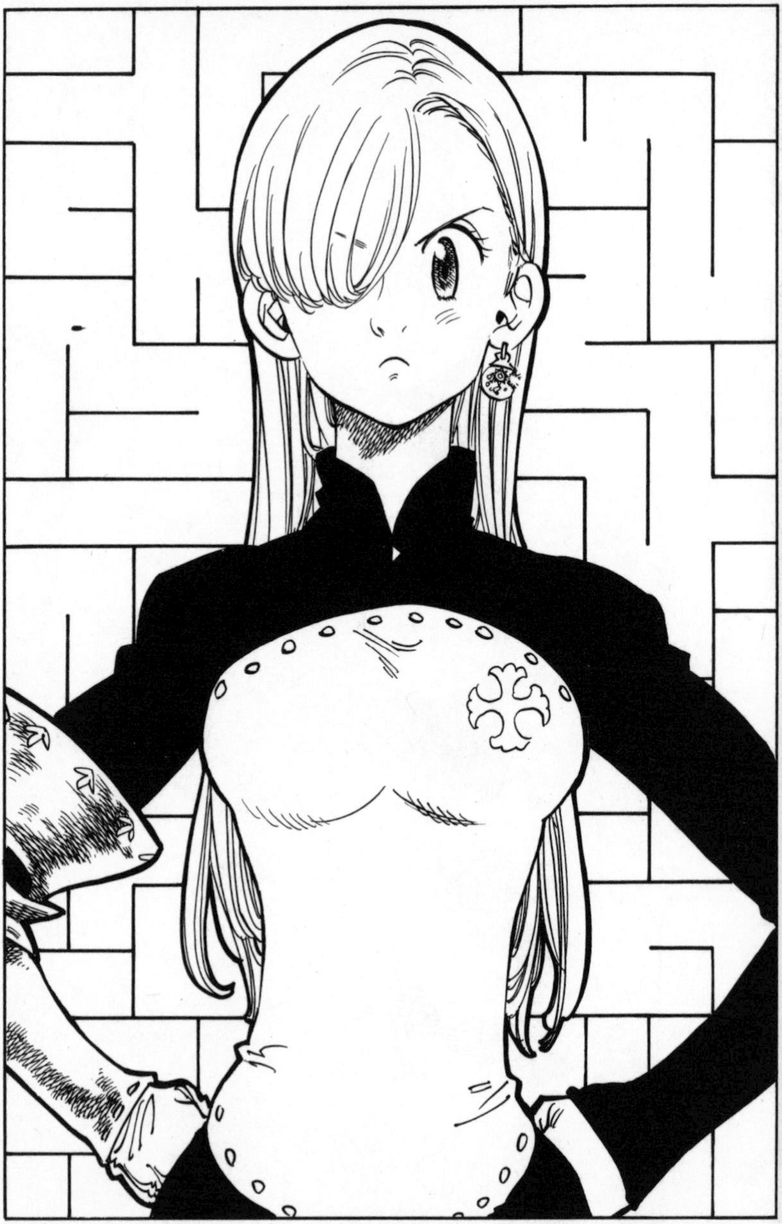

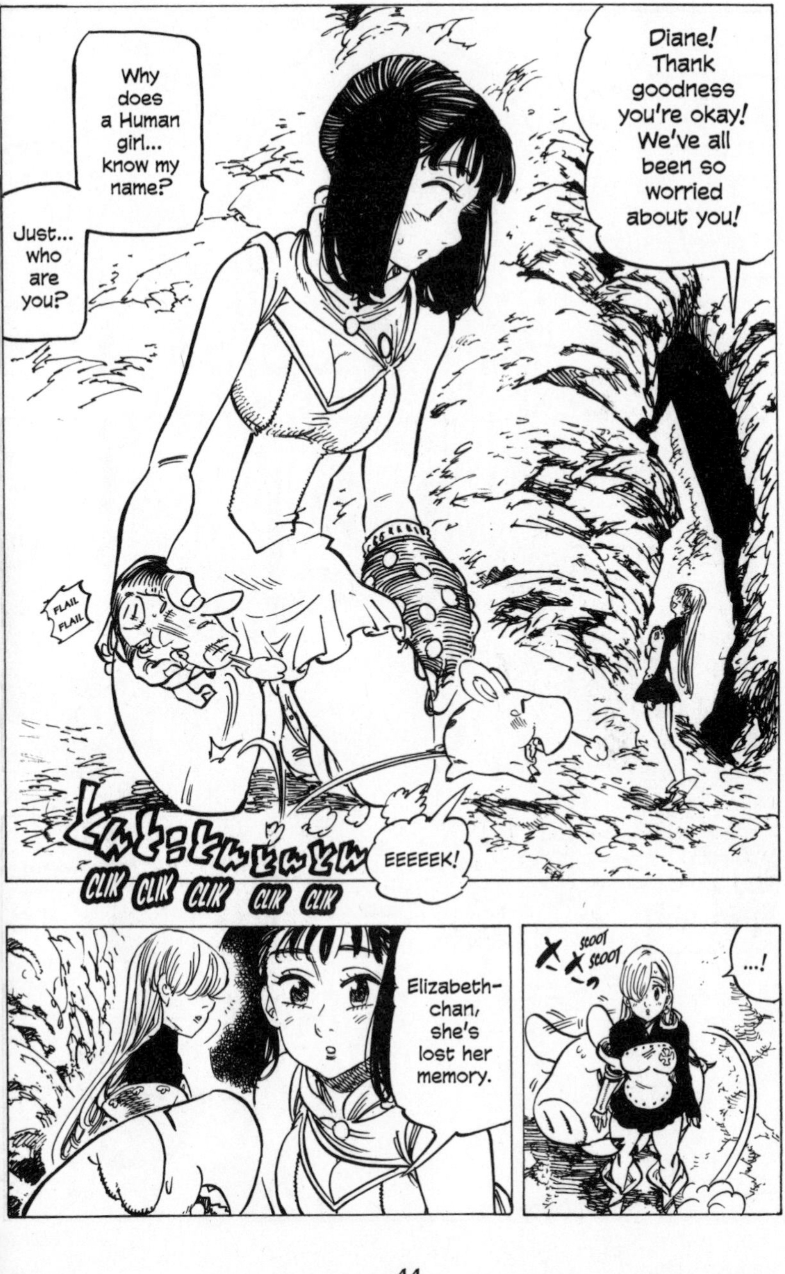
Diane! Thank goodness you're okay! We've all been so worried about you!
Why does a Human girl... know my name?
Just... who are you?
FLAIL FLAIL
EEEEEK!
CLIK CLIK CLIK CLIK CLIK
...!
SCOOT SCOOT
Elizabeth-chan, she's lost her memory.

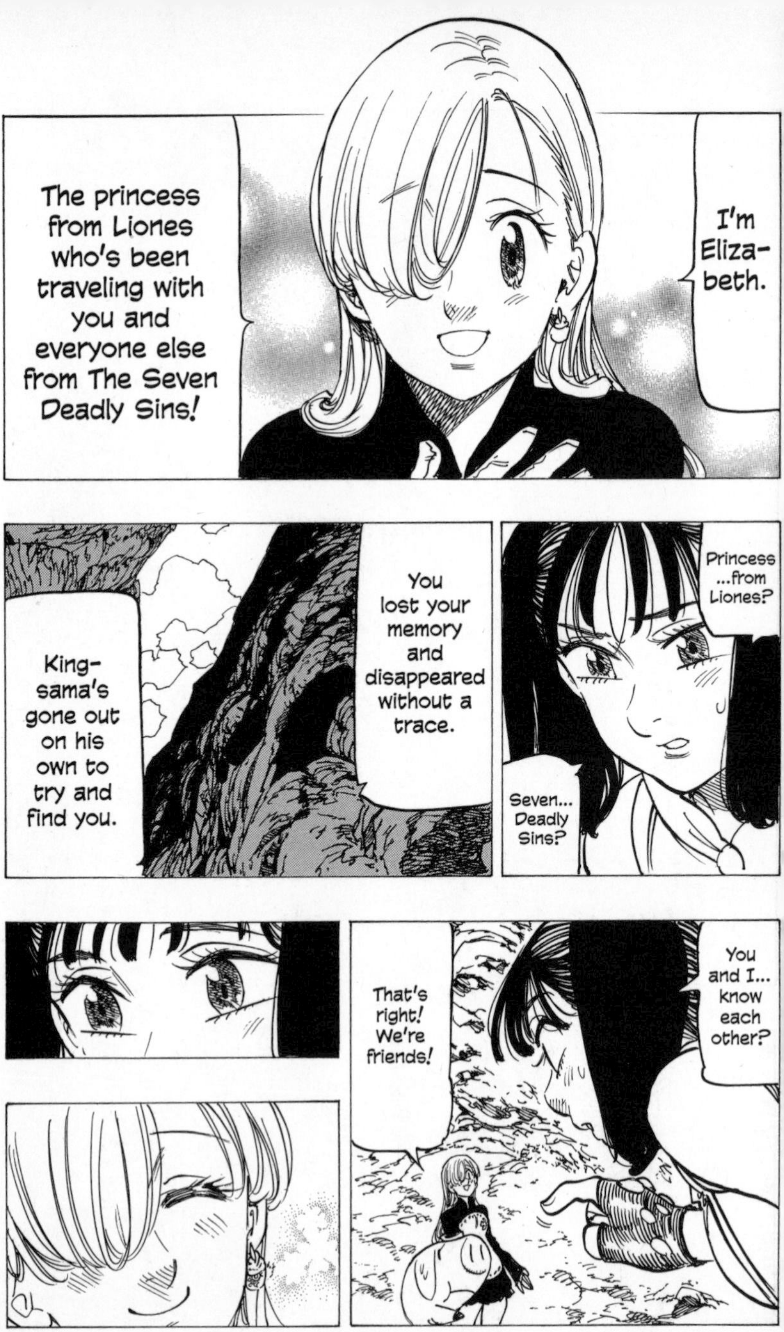
I'm Eliza-beth.
The princess from Liones who's been traveling with you and everyone else from The Seven Deadly Sins!
Princess ...from Liones?
Seven... Deadly Sins?
You lost your memory and disappeared without a trace.
King-sama's gone out on his own to try and find you.
You and I... know each other?
That's right! We're friends!

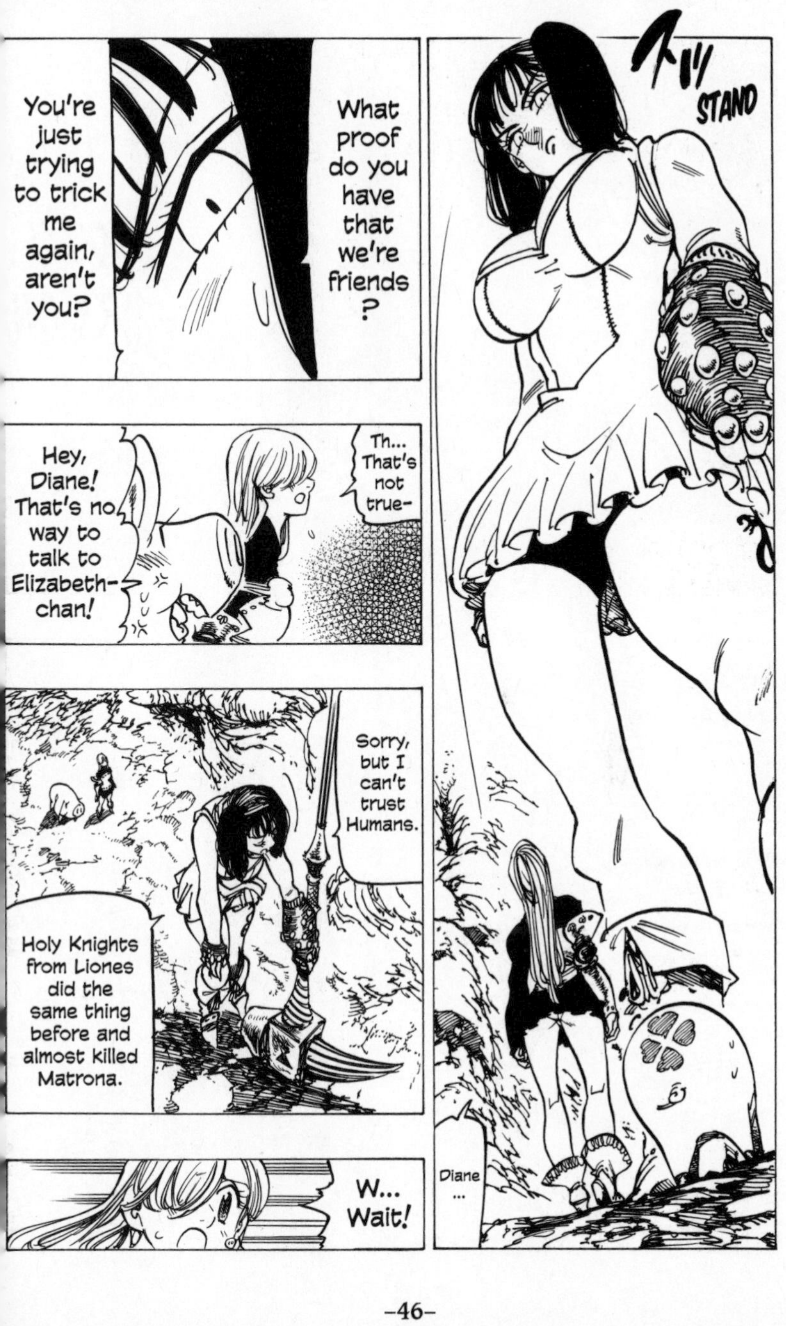
STAND
Diane...
What proof do you have that we're friends?
You're just trying to trick me again, aren't you?
Th... That's not true-
Hey, Diane! That's no way to talk to Elizabeth-chan!
Sorry, but I can't trust Humans.
Holy Knights from Liones did the same thing before and almost killed Matrona.
W... Wait!

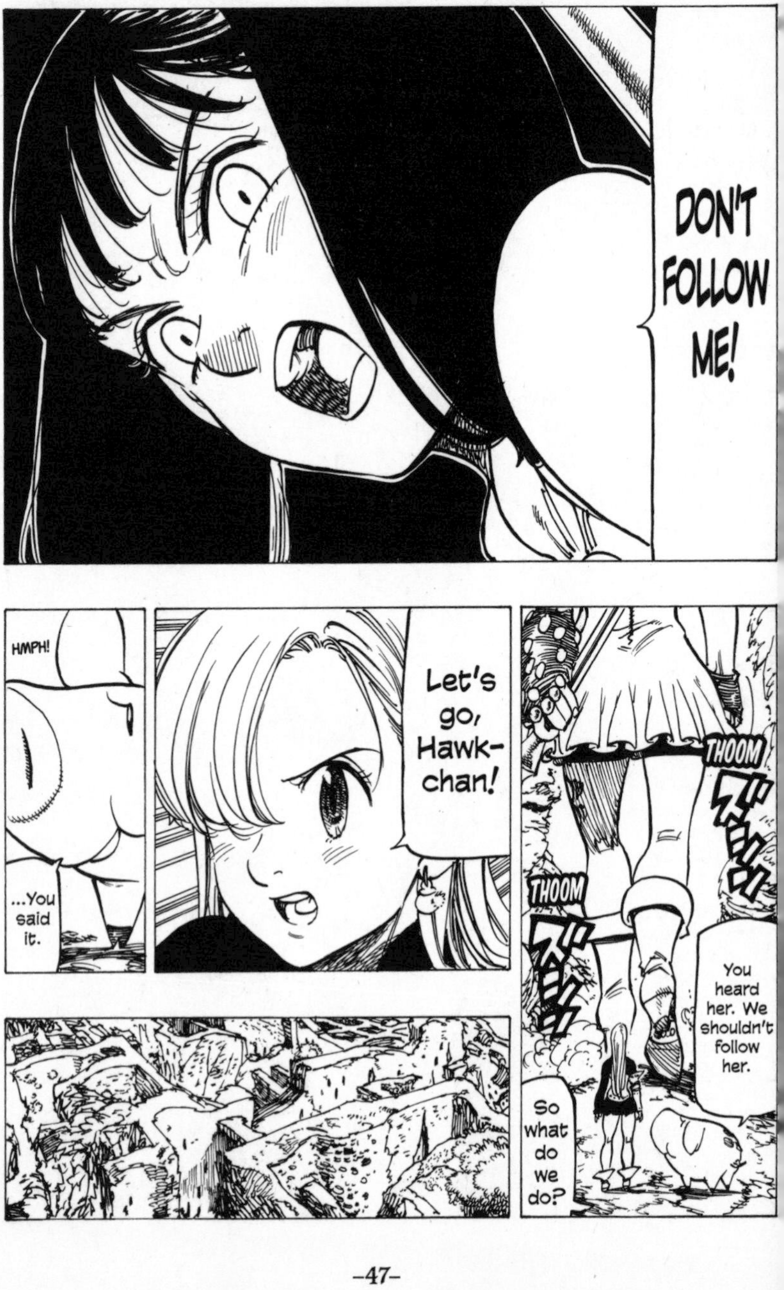
DON'T FOLLOW ME!
THOOM
THOOM
You heard her. We shouldn't follow her.
So what do we do?
Let's go, Hawk-chan!
HMPH!
...You said it.

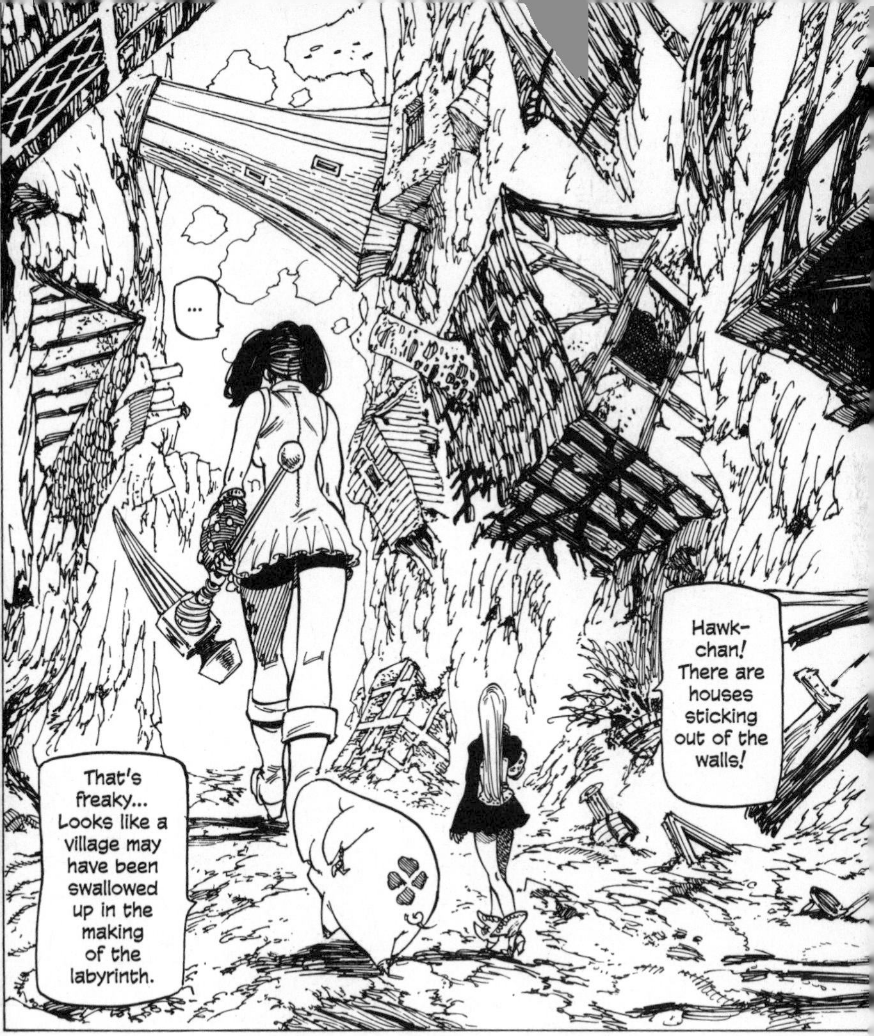
...
Hawk-chan! There are houses sticking out of the walls!
That's freaky... Looks like a village may have been swallowed up in the making of the labyrinth.
This is terrible... Where are all the people?
Why are you following after me?
Hmph! We just so happen to be walking in the same direction to get where we want to go!
SNORK
SNORK

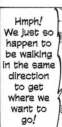

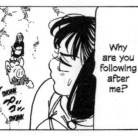

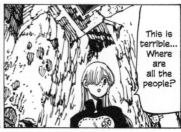

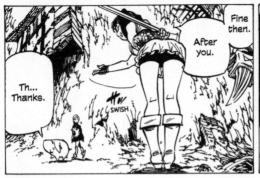

Fine then.

After you.

Th... Thanks.

SWISH

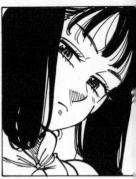

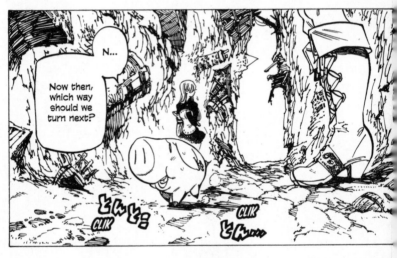

N...

Now then, which way should we turn next?

CLIK

CLIK

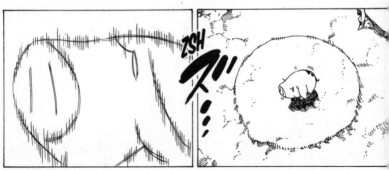

ZSH

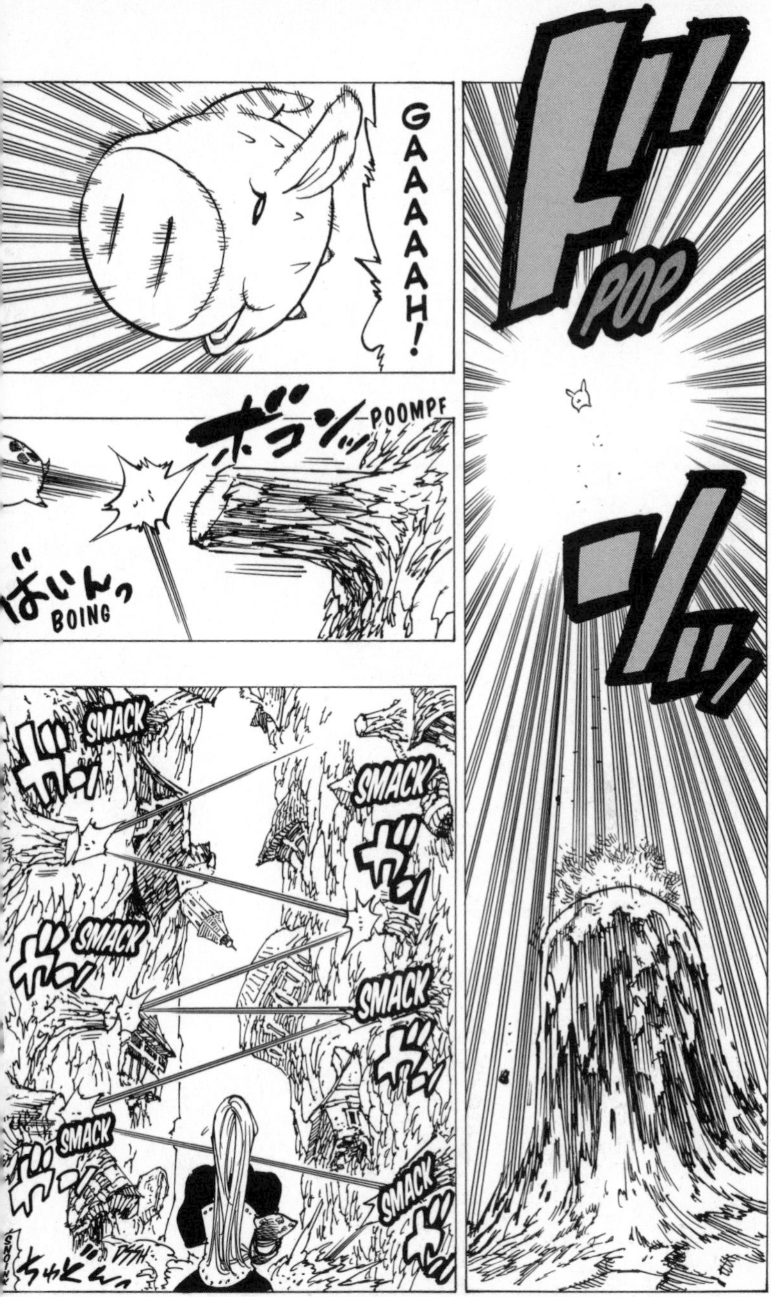
POP
GAAAAAAH!
ボコンッ
POOMPF
ばいんっ
BOING
SMACK
SMACK
SMACK
SMACK
SMACK
SMACK

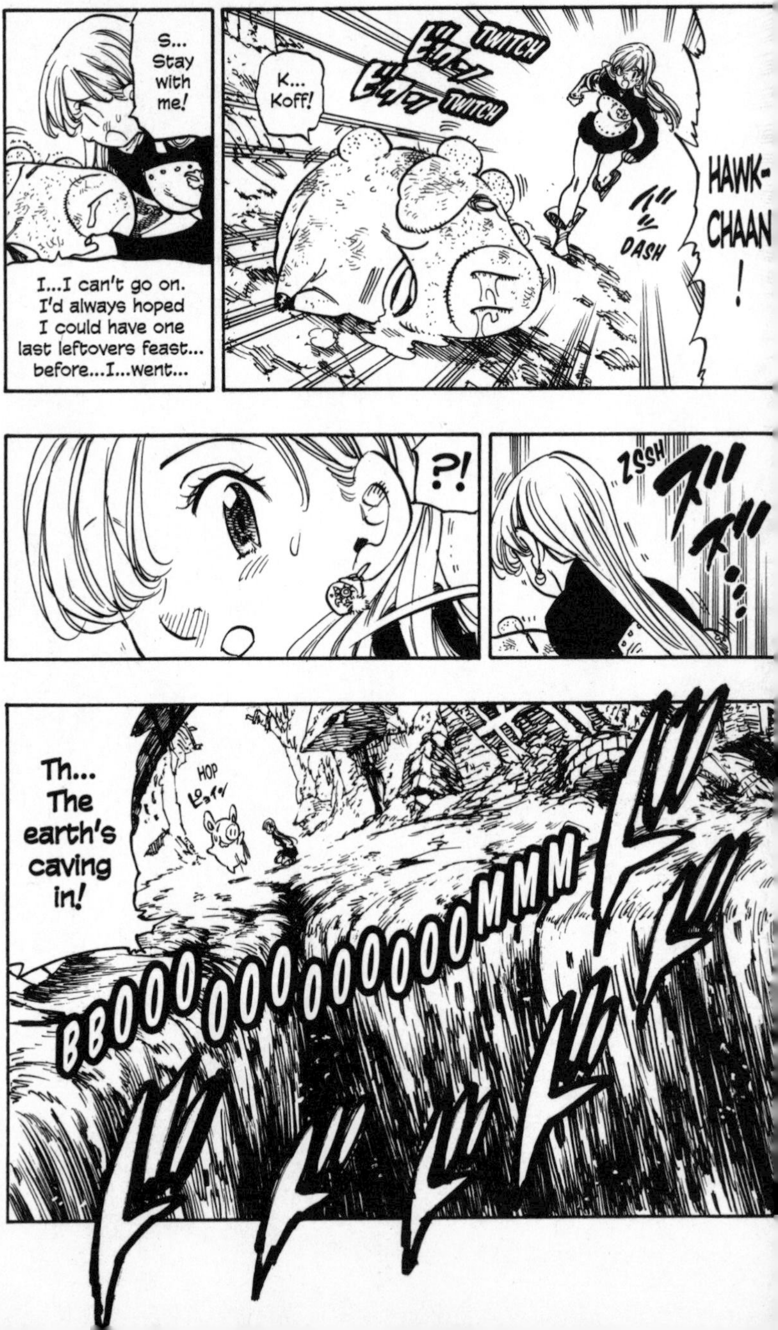
HAWK-CHAAN!
DASH
TWITCH
TWITCH
K... Koff!
S... Stay with me!
I...I can't go on. I'd always hoped I could have one last leftovers feast... before...I...went...
ZSSH
?!
Th... The earth's caving in!
HOP
BBOOOOOOOOOOOOMMM

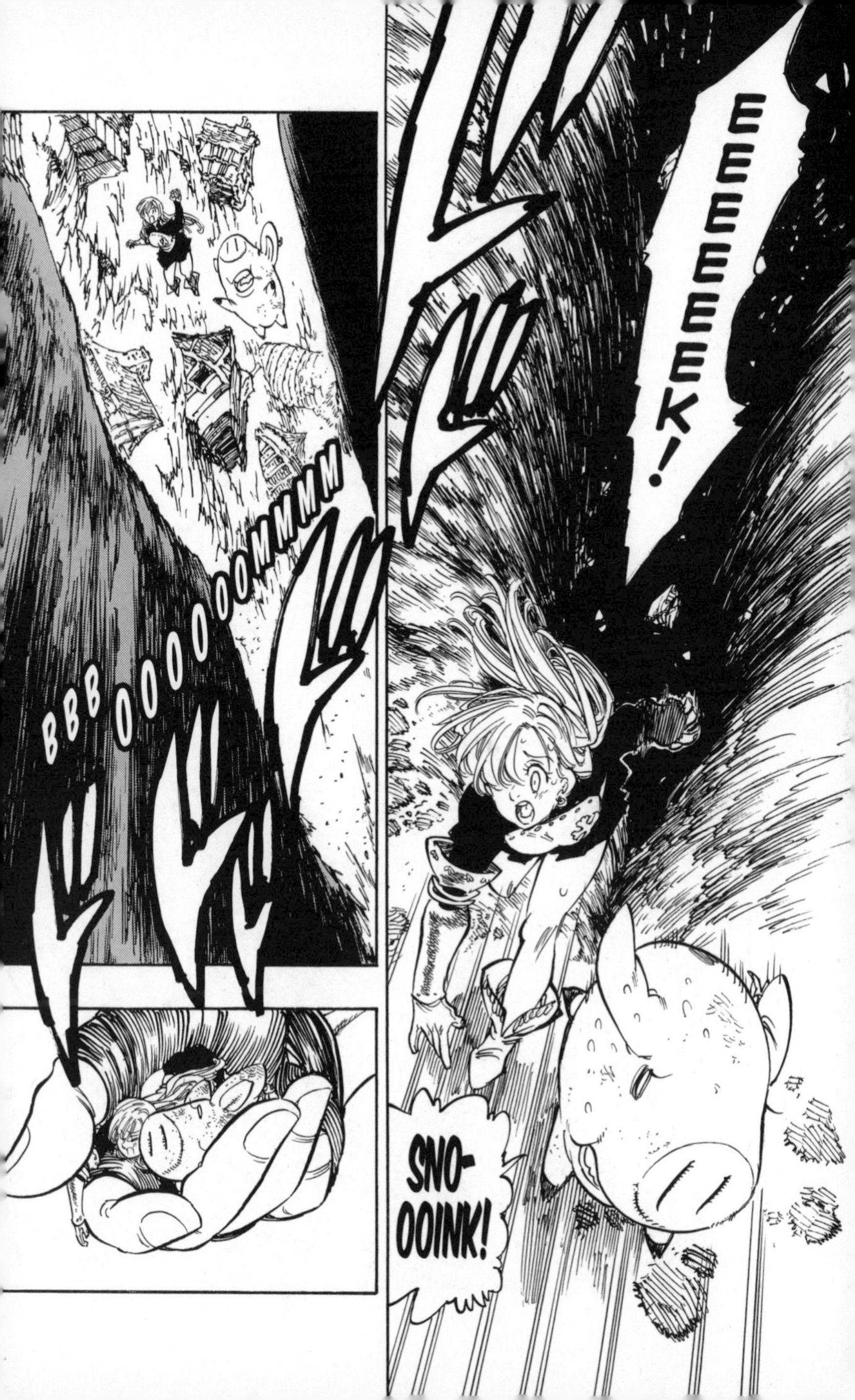
EEEEEEEK!
SNO-OOINK!
BBBOOOOOMMMM

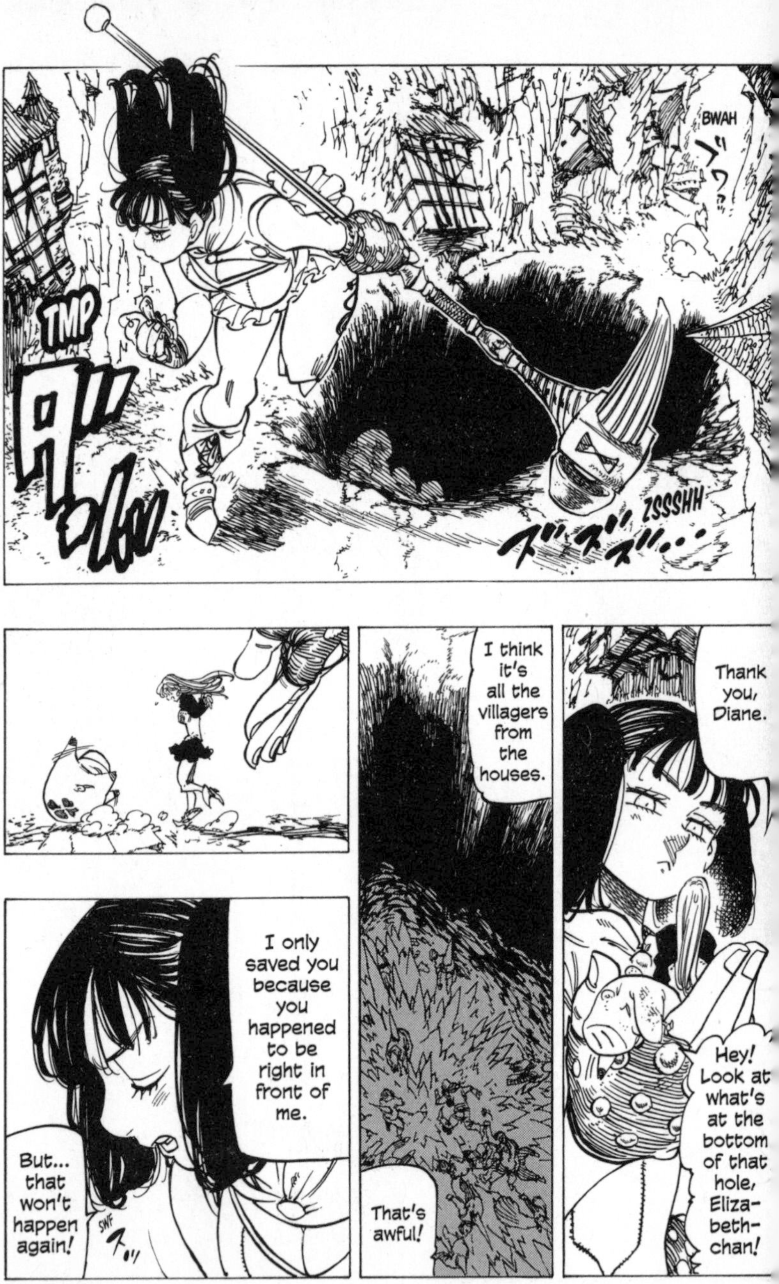
BWAH
ZSSSHH
TMP
Thank you, Diane.
Hey! Look at what's at the bottom of that hole, Eliza-beth-chan!
I think it's all the villagers from the houses.
That's awful!
I only saved you because you happened to be right in front of me.
But... that won't happen again!
SWF

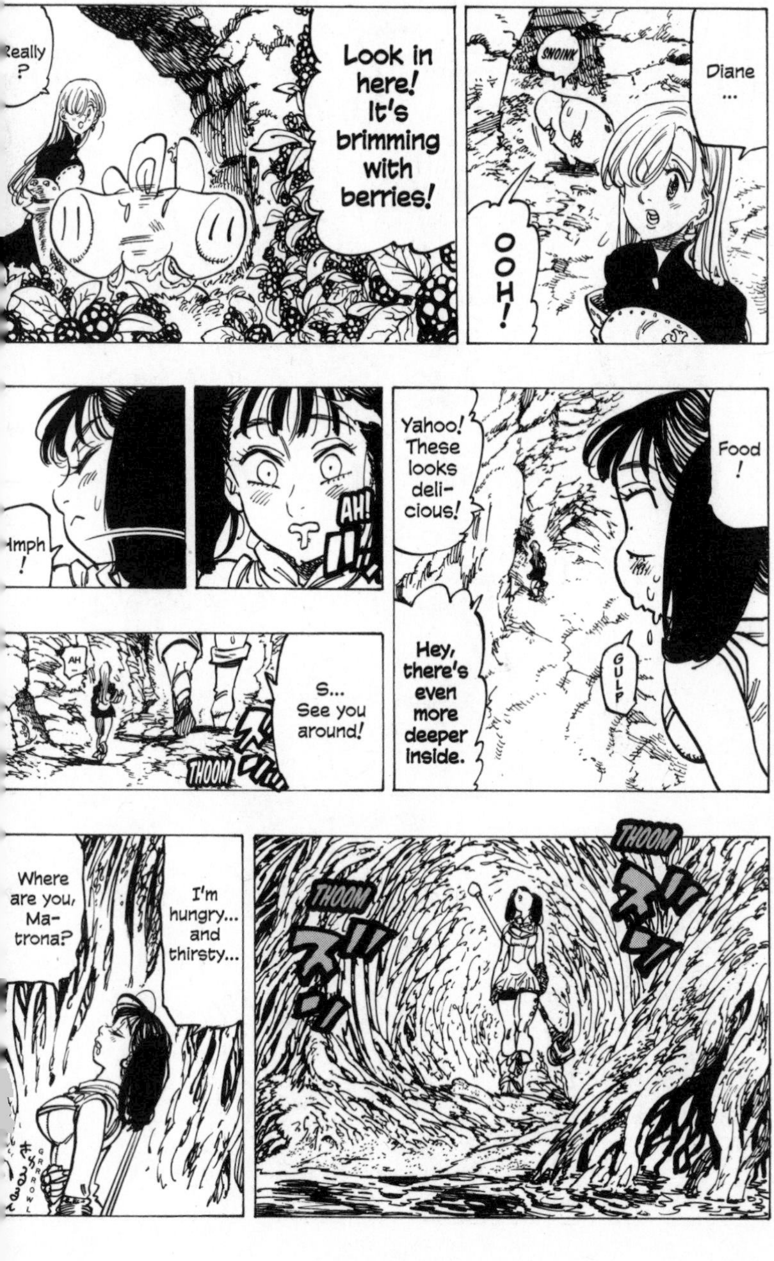
Diane ...
SNOINK
OOH!
Look in here! It's brimming with berries!
Really ?
Food!
GULP
Yahoo! These looks deli-cious!
Hey, there's even more deeper inside.
AH!
Hmph!
S... See you around!
AH ...
THOOM
THOOM
THOOM
I'm hungry... and thirsty...
Where are you, Ma-trona?
GRROWL

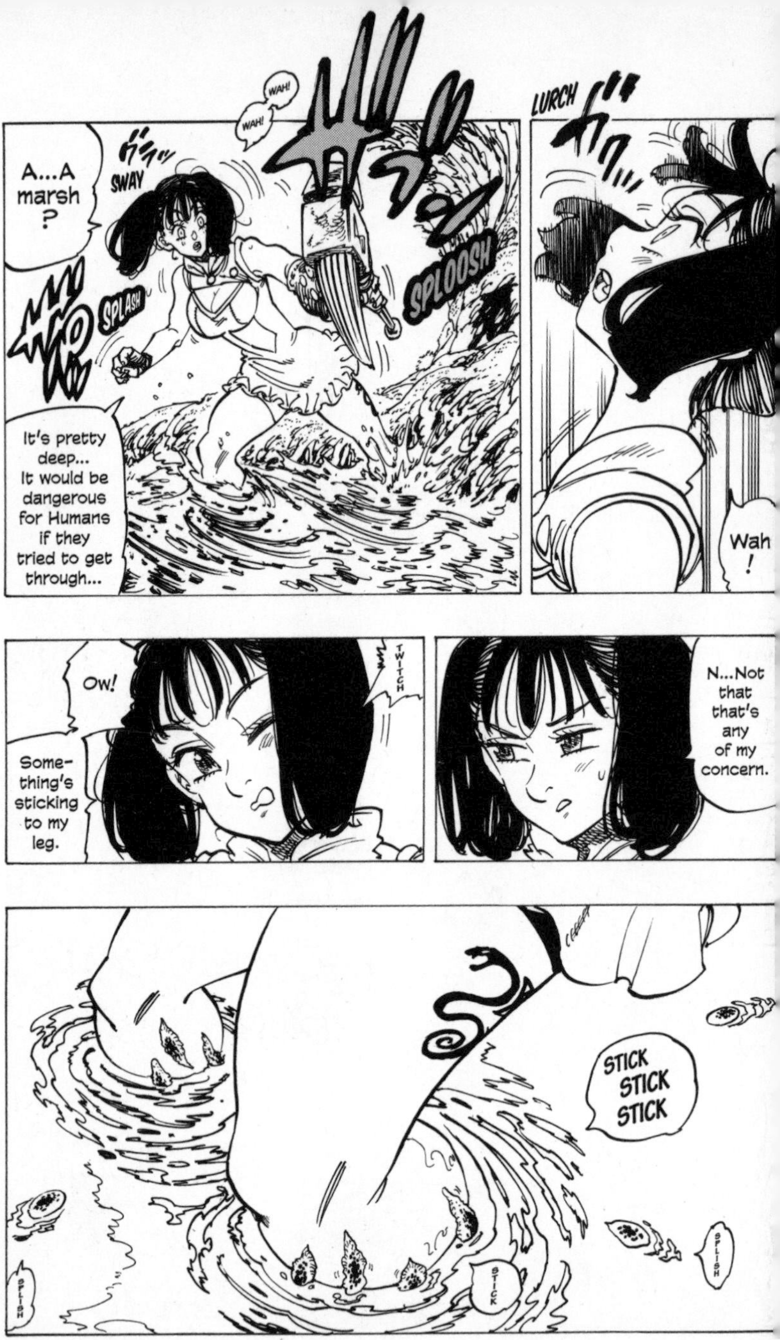
LURCH
Wah!
WAH!
WAH!
A...A marsh?
SWAY
SPLOOSH
SPLASH
It's pretty deep... It would be dangerous for Humans if they tried to get through...
N...Not that that's any of my concern.
TWITCH
Ow!
Something's sticking to my leg.
STICK STICK STICK
SPLISH
STICK
SPLISH

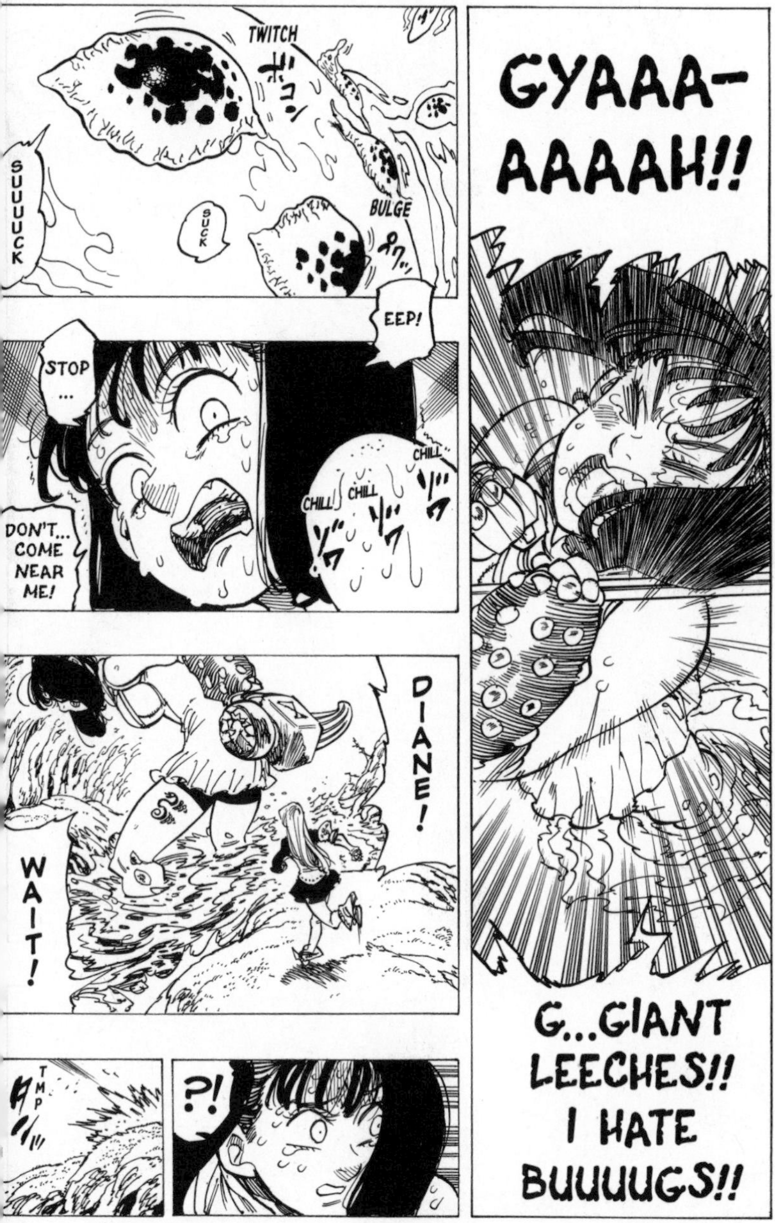
GYAAA-AAAAH!!
G...GIANT LEECHES!! I HATE BUUUUGS!!
TWITCH
BULGE
SUCK
SUUUUUCK
EEP!
STOP ...
DON'T... COME NEAR ME!
CHILL
CHILL
CHILL
DIANE!
WAIT!
?!
TMP

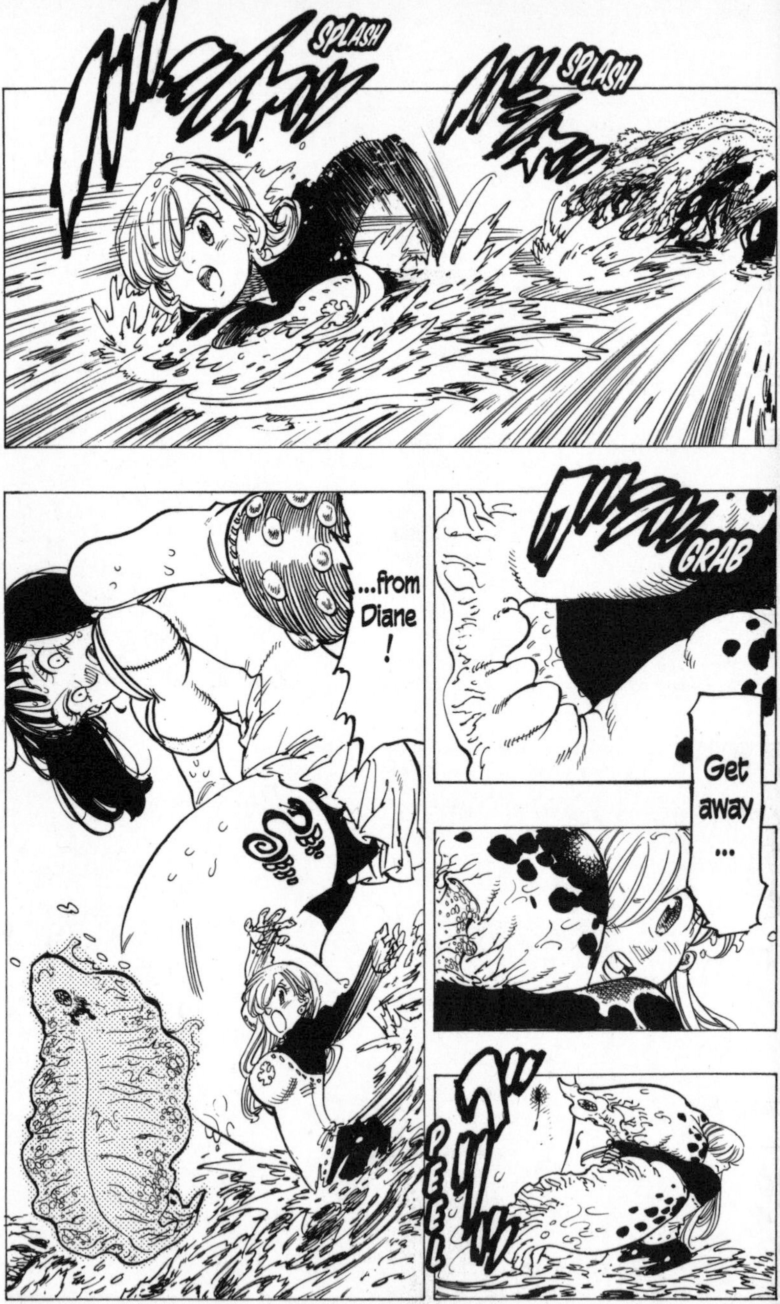
SPLASH
SPLASH
GRAB
Get away ...
PEEL
...from Diane!

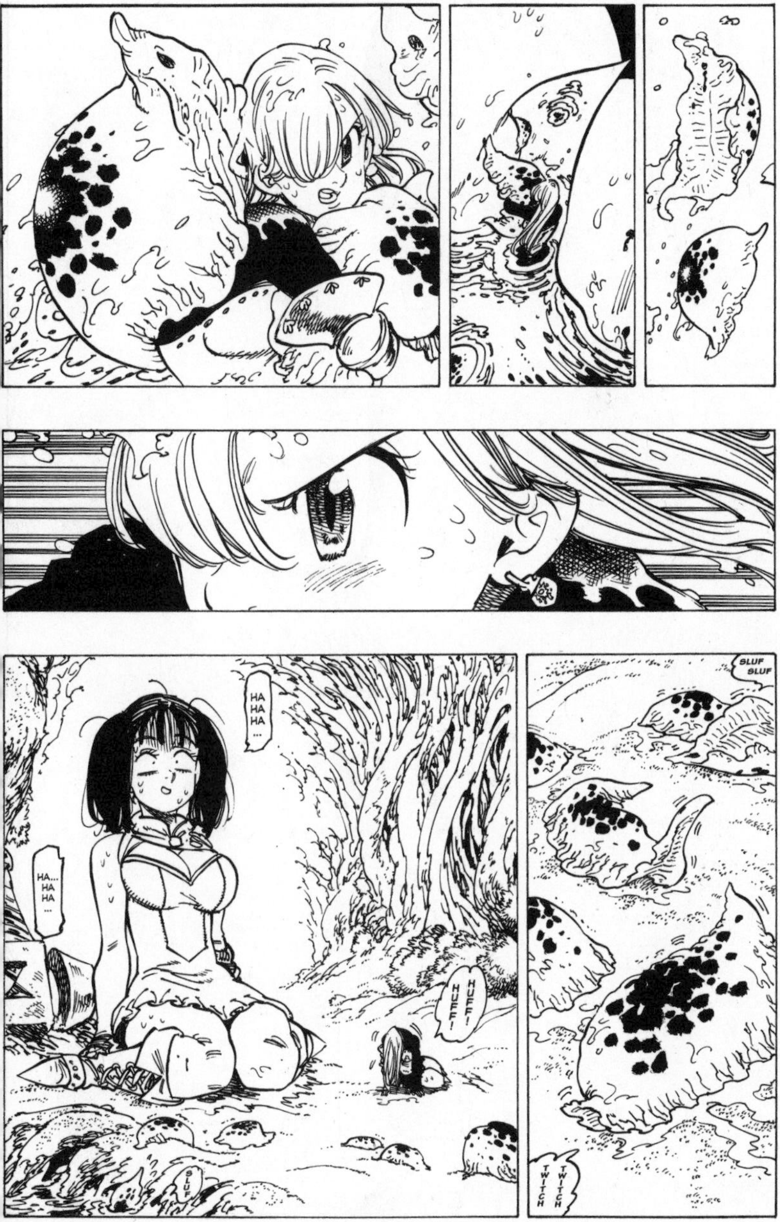
SLUF SLUF
TWITCH TWITCH
HA HA HA ...
HA... HA HA ...
HUFF! HUFF!
SLUF

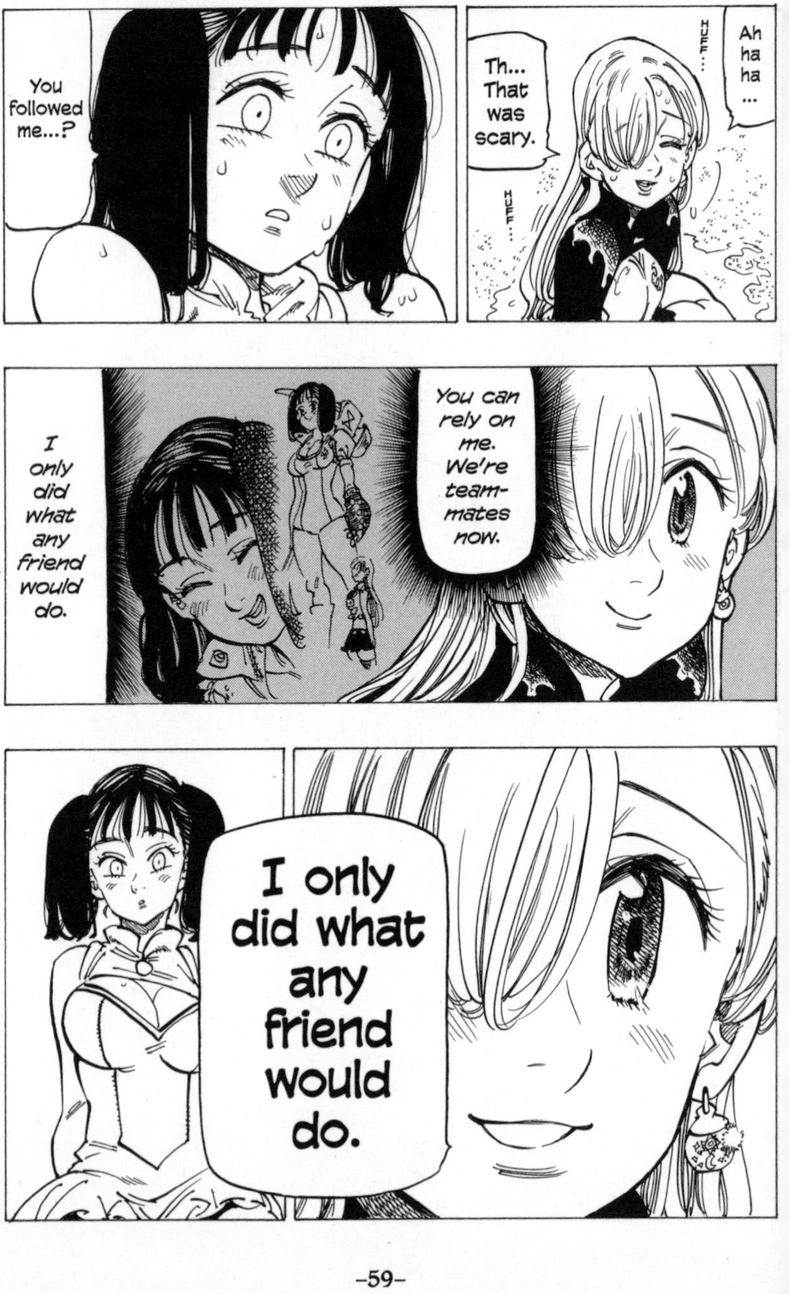
Ah ha ha ...
HUFF...
Th... That was scary.
HUFF...
You followed me...?
You can rely on me. We're team-mates now.
I only did what any friend would do.
I only did what any friend would do.

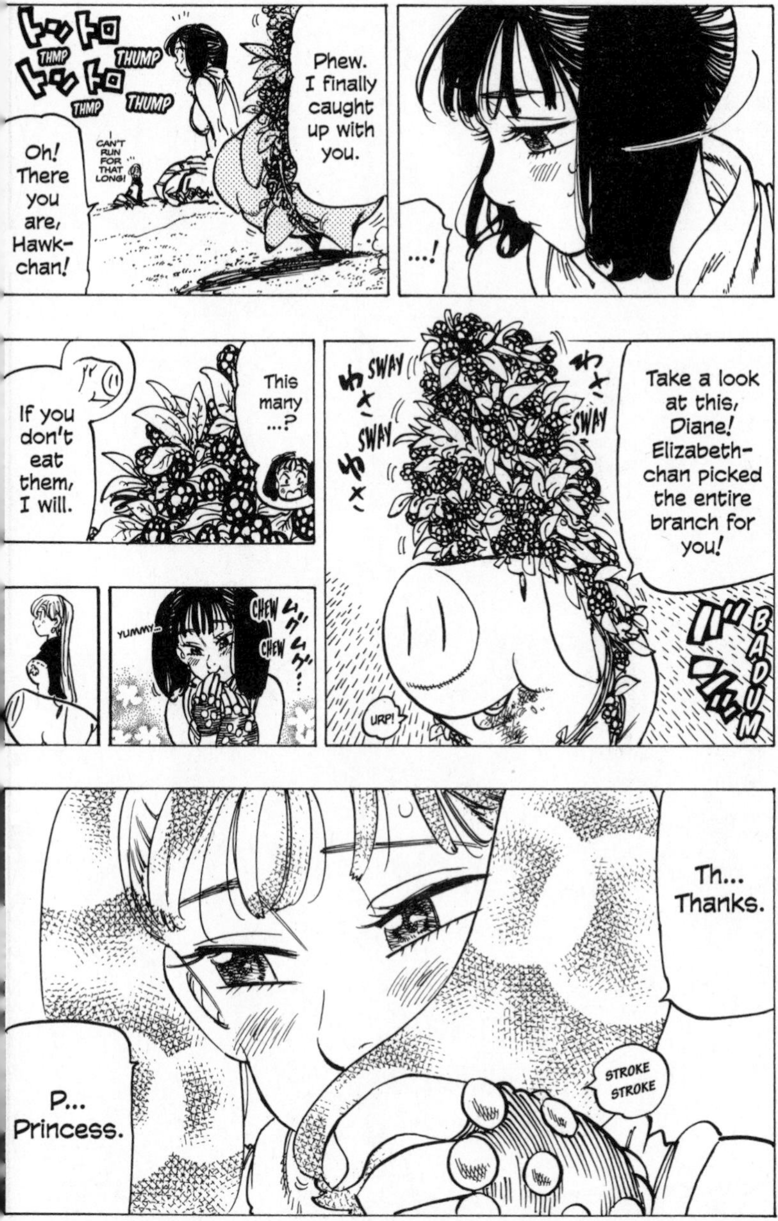
...!
Phew. I finally caught up with you.
THUMP
THUMP
THMP
THUMP
Oh! There you are, Hawk-chan!
I CAN'T RUN FOR THAT LONG!
Take a look at this, Diane! Elizabeth-chan picked the entire branch for you!
SWAY
SWAY
SWAY
BADUM
URP!
This many ...?
If you don't eat them, I will.
CHEW
CHEW
YUMMY...
Th... Thanks.
STROKE STROKE
P... Princess.

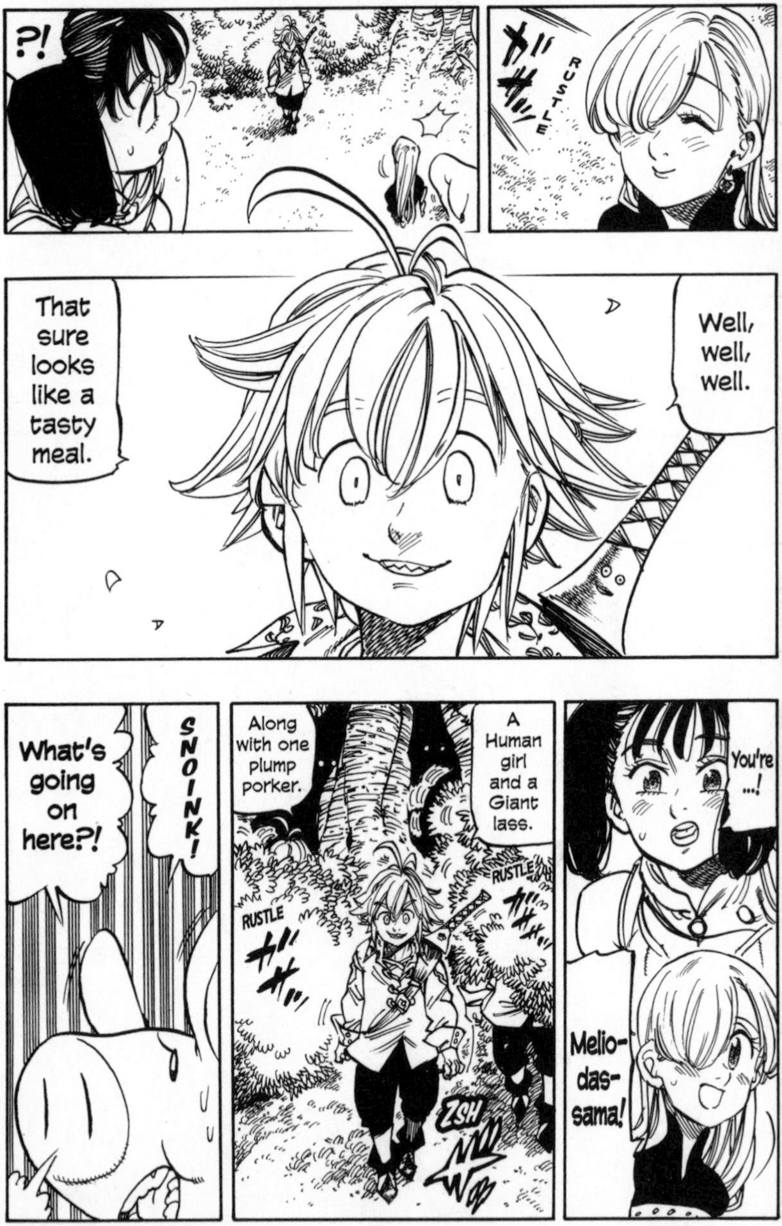
RUSTLE
?!
Well, well, well.
That sure looks like a tasty meal.
You're ...!
Melio-das-sama!
A Human girl and a Giant lass.
Along with one plump porker.
RUSTLE
RUSTLE
ZSH
SNOINK!
What's going on here?!

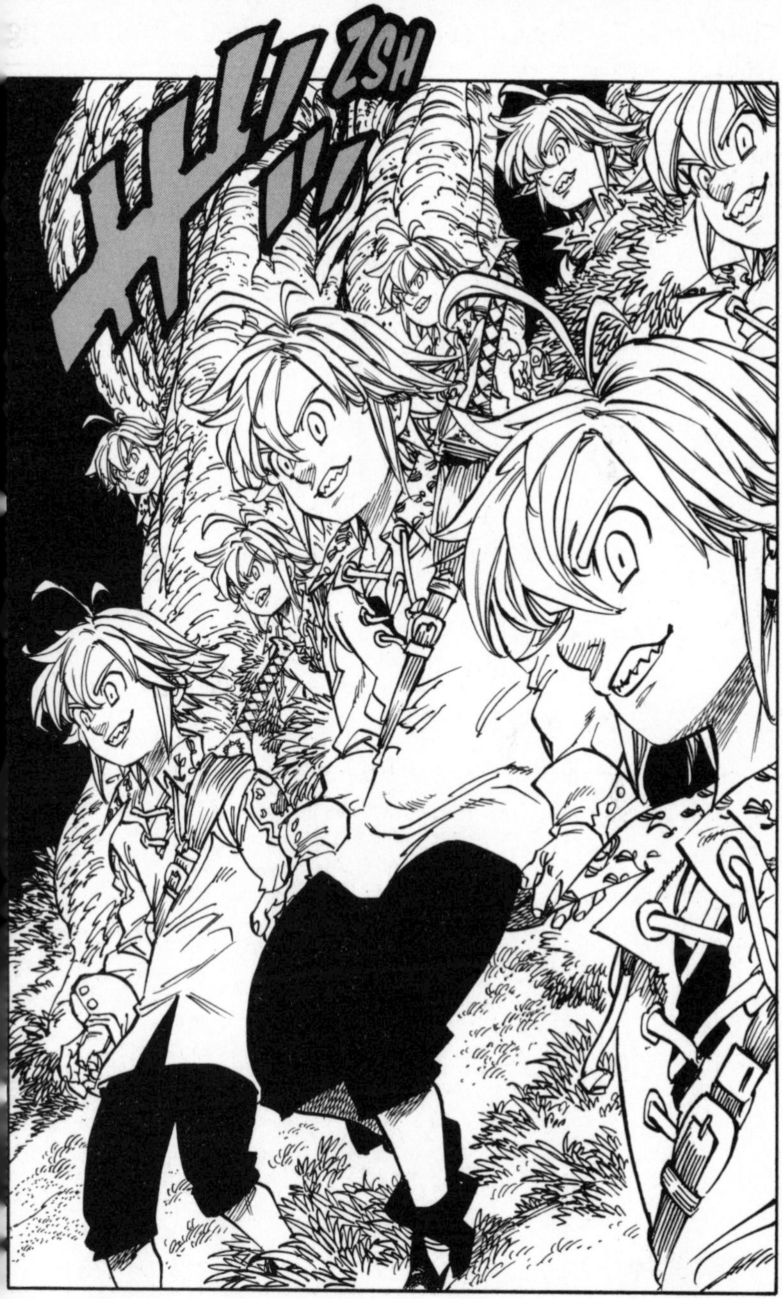
ZSH

Chapter 157 - The Contenders That Dance a Frenzied Jig

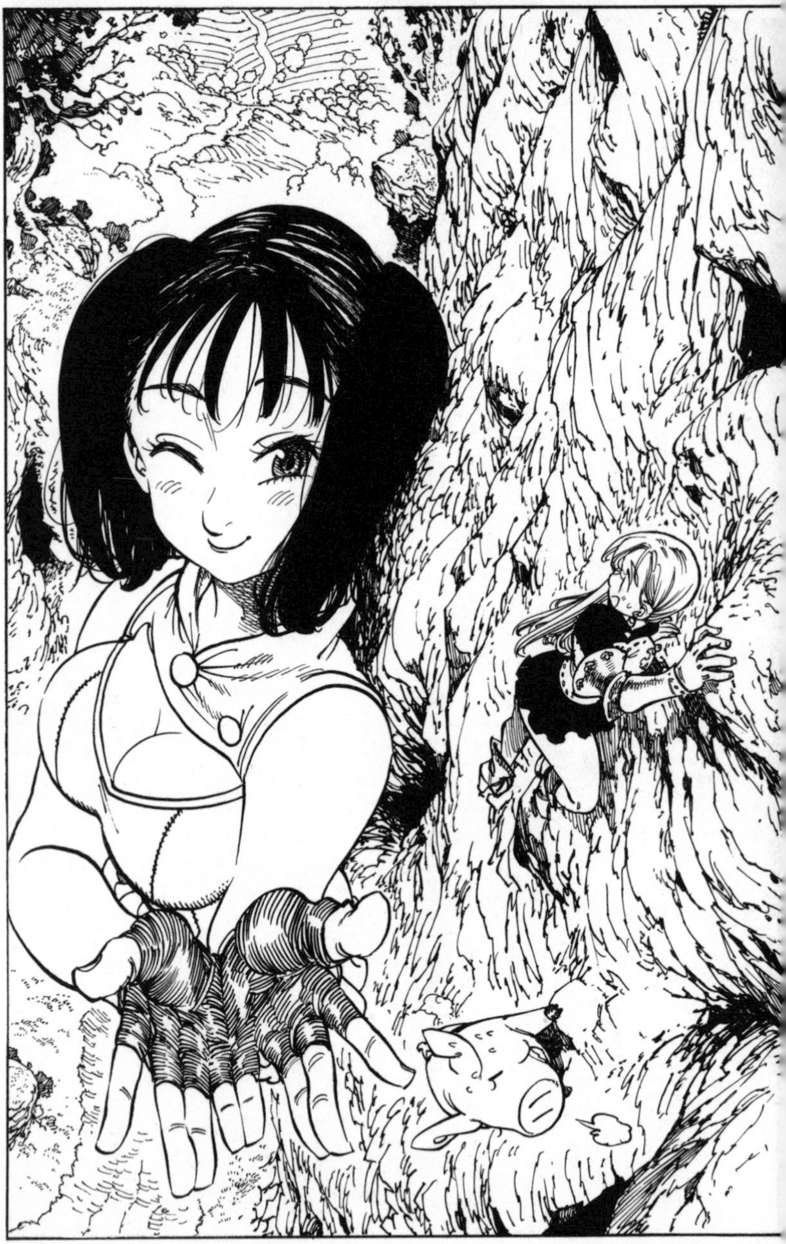

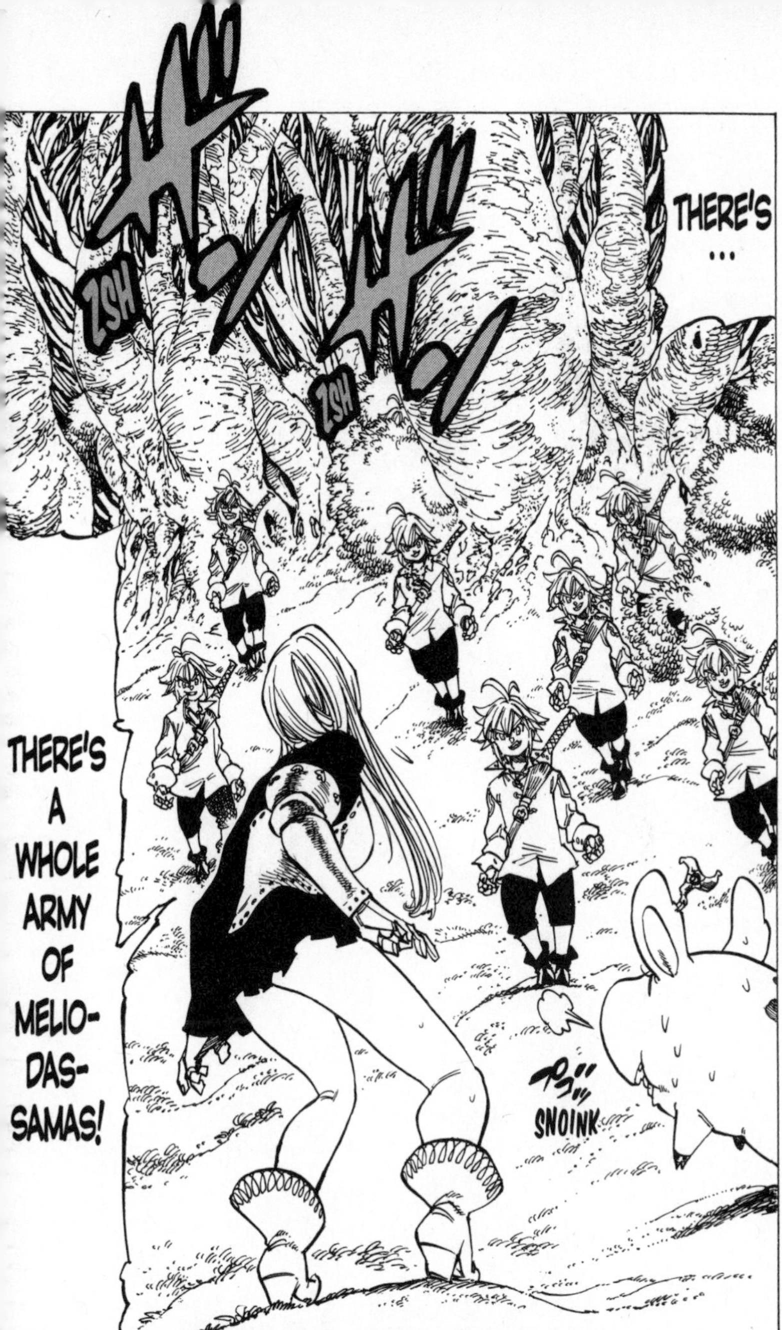
ZSH
ZSH
THERE'S ...
THERE'S A WHOLE ARMY OF MELIO-DAS-SAMAS!
SNOINK

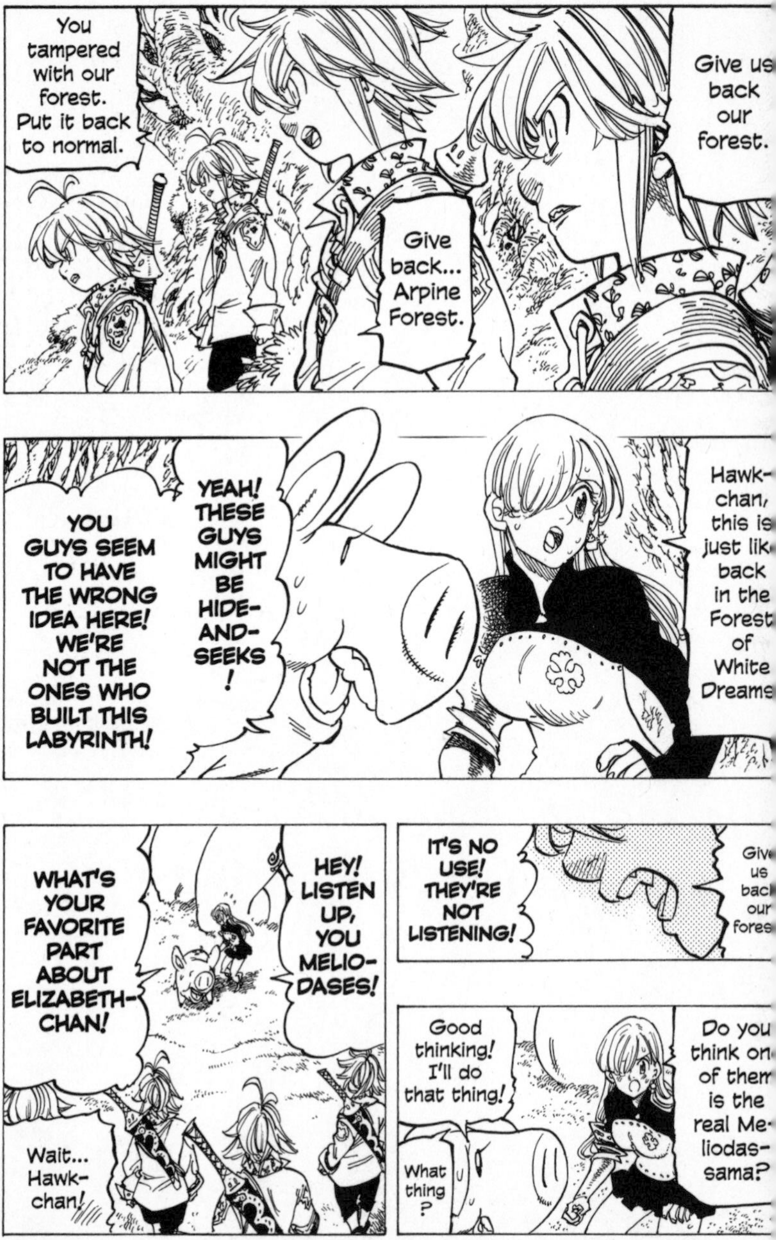

Give us back our forest.
Give back... Arpine Forest.
You tampered with our forest. Put it back to normal.
Hawk-chan, this is just lik back in the Forest of White Dreams
YEAH! THESE GUYS MIGHT BE HIDE-AND-SEEKS!
YOU GUYS SEEM TO HAVE THE WRONG IDEA HERE! WE'RE NOT THE ONES WHO BUILT THIS LABYRINTH!
Give us back our fores
IT'S NO USE! THEY'RE NOT LISTENING!
Do you think one of them is the real Meliodas-sama?
Good thinking! I'll do that thing!
What thing?
HEY! LISTEN UP, YOU MELIODASES!
WHAT'S YOUR FAVORITE PART ABOUT ELIZABETH-CHAN!
Wait... Hawk-chan!

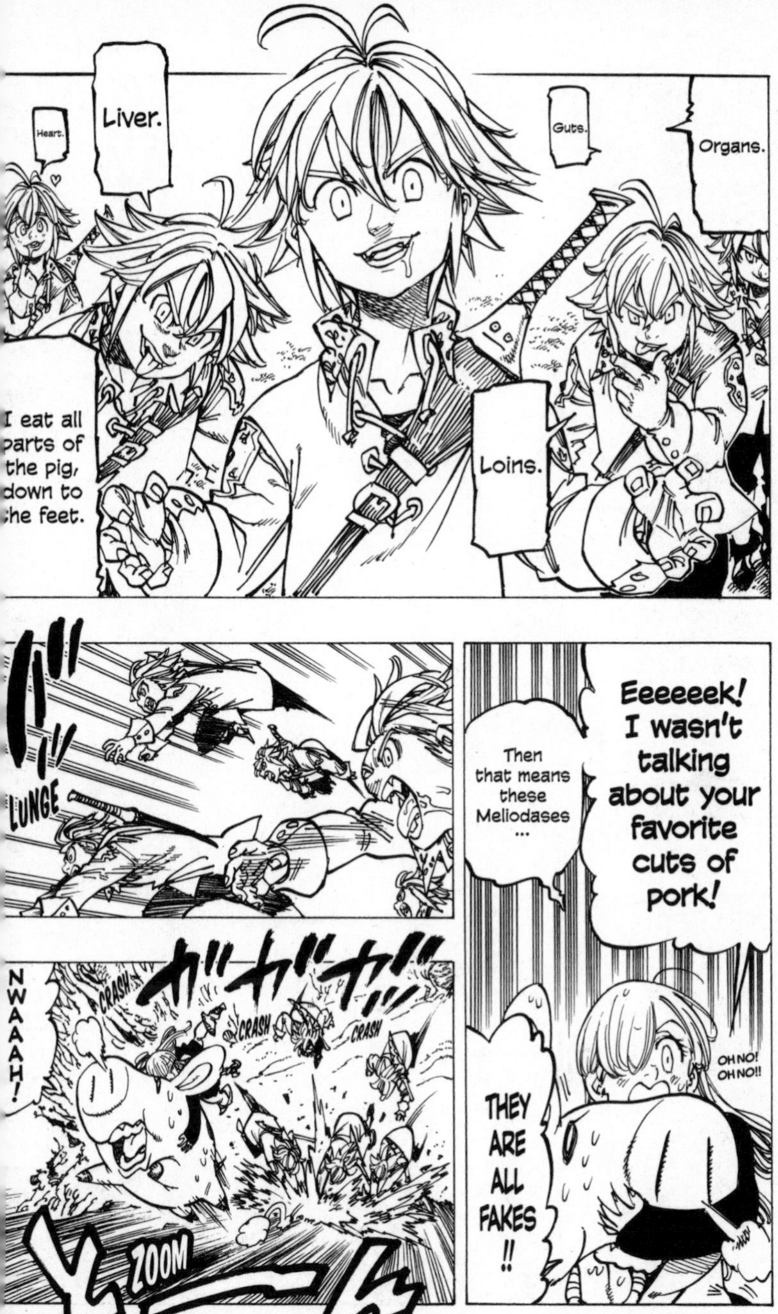
Organs.
Guts.
Loins.
Liver.
Heart.
I eat all parts of the pig, down to the feet.
Eeeeeek! I wasn't talking about your favorite cuts of pork!
Then that means these Meliodases ...
OH NO! OH NO!!
THEY ARE ALL FAKES!!
LUNGE
NWAAAAH!
CRASH
CRASH
CRASH
ZOOM

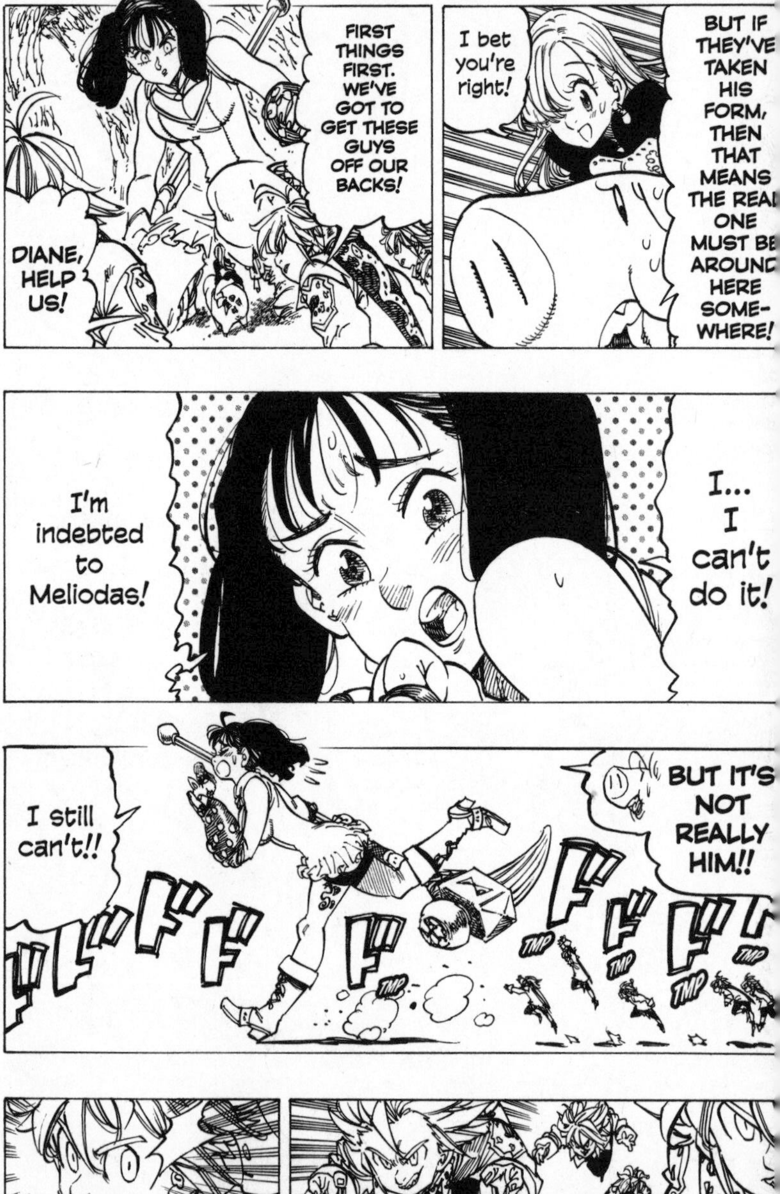
BUT IF THEY'VE TAKEN HIS FORM, THEN THAT MEANS THE REAL ONE MUST BE AROUND HERE SOMEWHERE!
I bet you're right!
FIRST THINGS FIRST. WE'VE GOT TO GET THESE GUYS OFF OUR BACKS!
DIANE, HELP US!
I... I can't do it!
I'm indebted to Meliodas!
BUT IT'S NOT REALLY HIM!!
I still can't!!
TMP
TMP
TMP
TMP
TMP

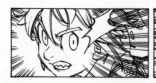

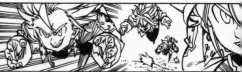

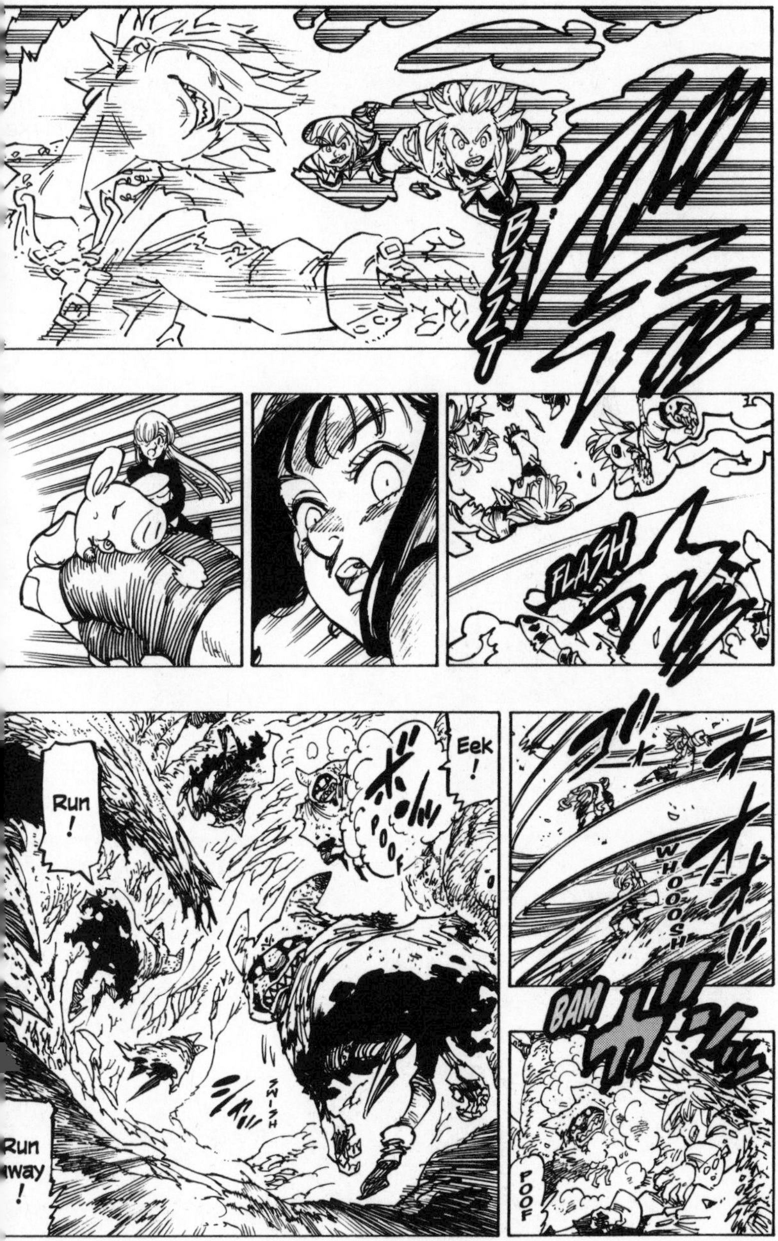
BZZZT
FLASH
WHOOOOSH
BAM
POOF
Eek!
POOF
Run!
SWISH
Run away!

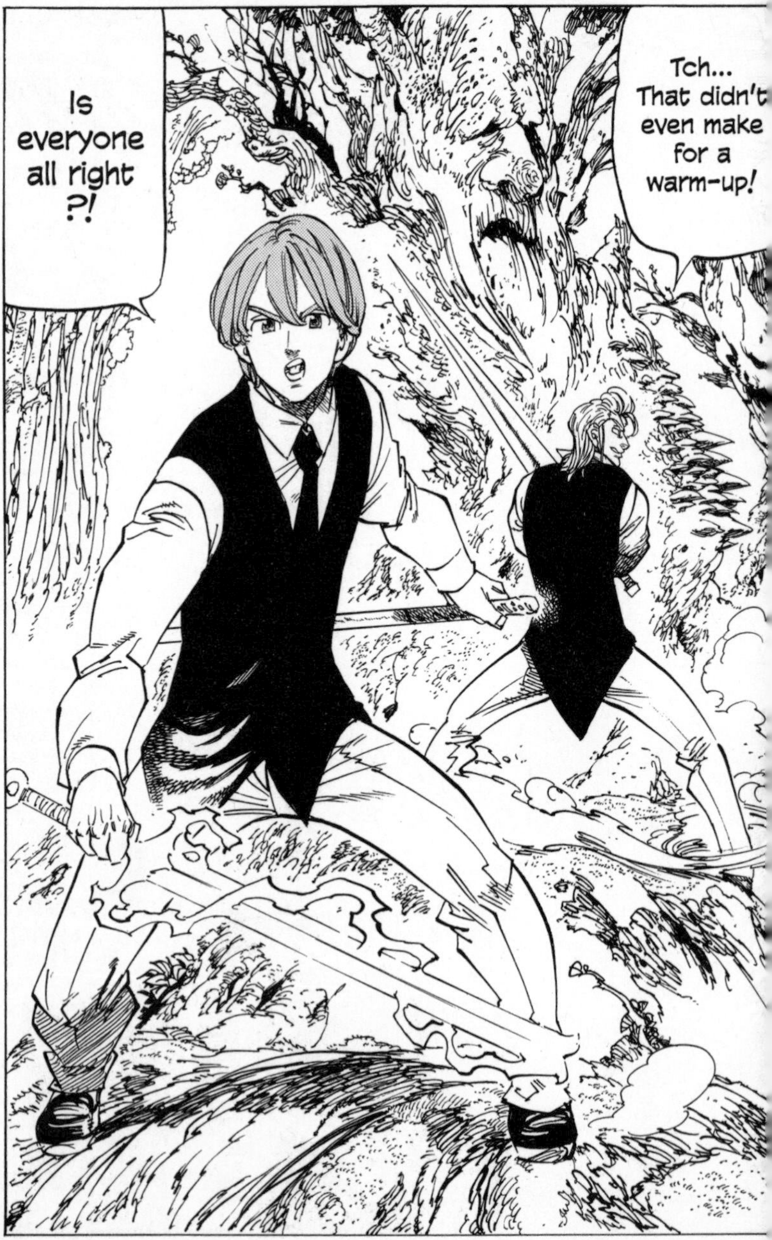
Tch... That didn't even make for a warm-up!
Is everyone all right ?!

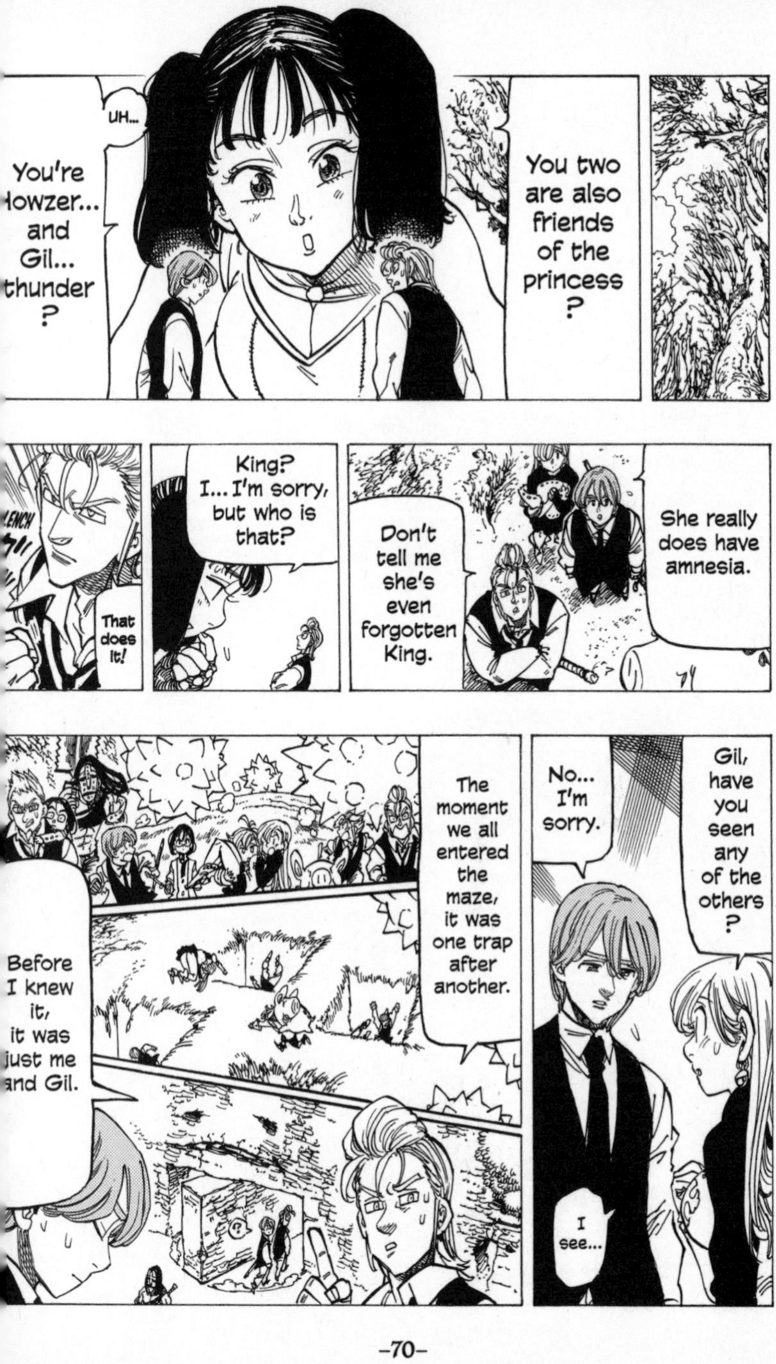
You two are also friends of the princess?
UH...
You're owzer... and Gil... thunder?
She really does have amnesia.
Don't tell me she's even forgotten King.
King? I... I'm sorry, but who is that?
That does it!
Gil, have you seen any of the others?
No... I'm sorry.
I see...
The moment we all entered the maze, it was one trap after another.
Before I knew it, it was just me and Gil.

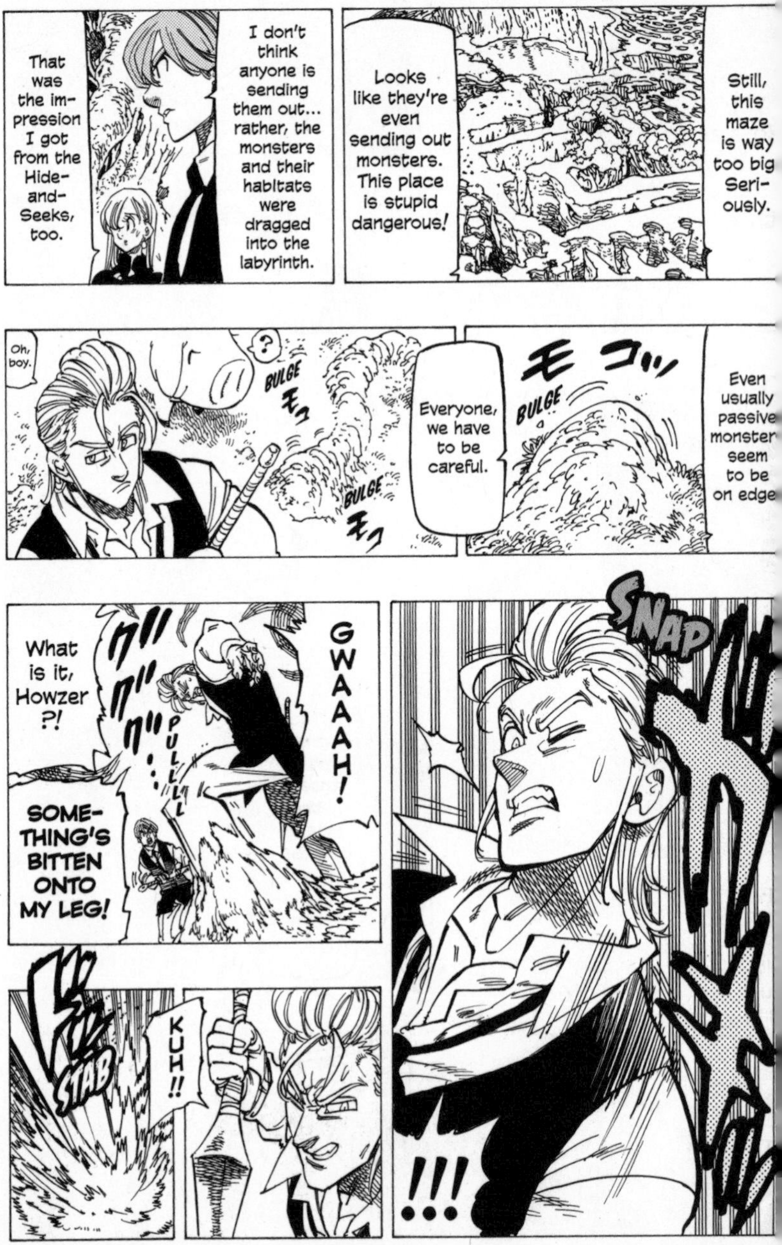
Still, this maze is way too big Seri-ously.
Looks like they're even sending out monsters. This place is stupid dangerous!
I don't think anyone is sending them out... rather, the monsters and their habitats were dragged into the labyrinth.
That was the impression I got from the Hide-and-Seeks, too.
Even usually passive monster seem to be on edge
BULGE
Everyone, we have to be careful.
BULGE
?
BULGE
Oh, boy.
SNAP
!!!
GWAAAH!
What is it, Howzer?!
PULLLL
SOMETHING'S BITTEN ONTO MY LEG!
KUH!!
STAB

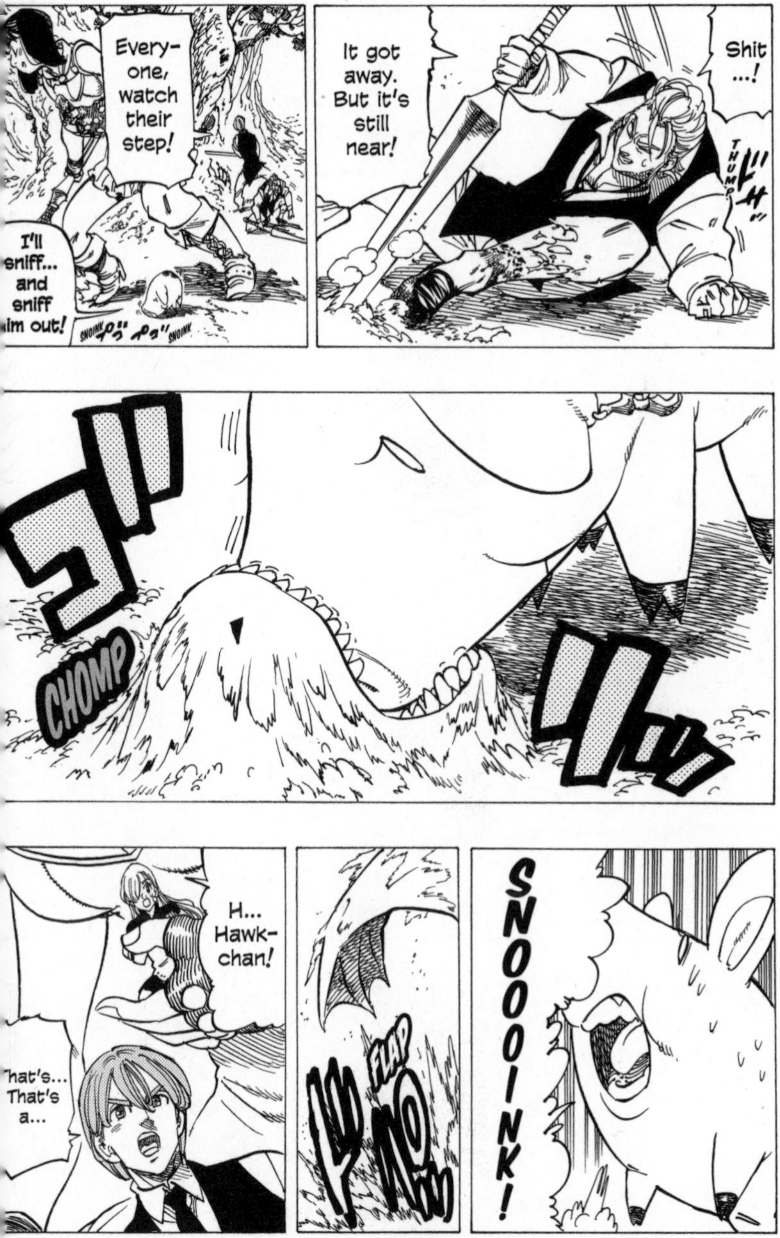
Shit ...!
THUMP
It got away. But it's still near!
Every-one, watch their step!
I'll sniff... and sniff im out!
SNOINK
SNOINK
CHOMP
SNOOOOINK!
FLAP
H... Hawk-chan!
That's... That's a...

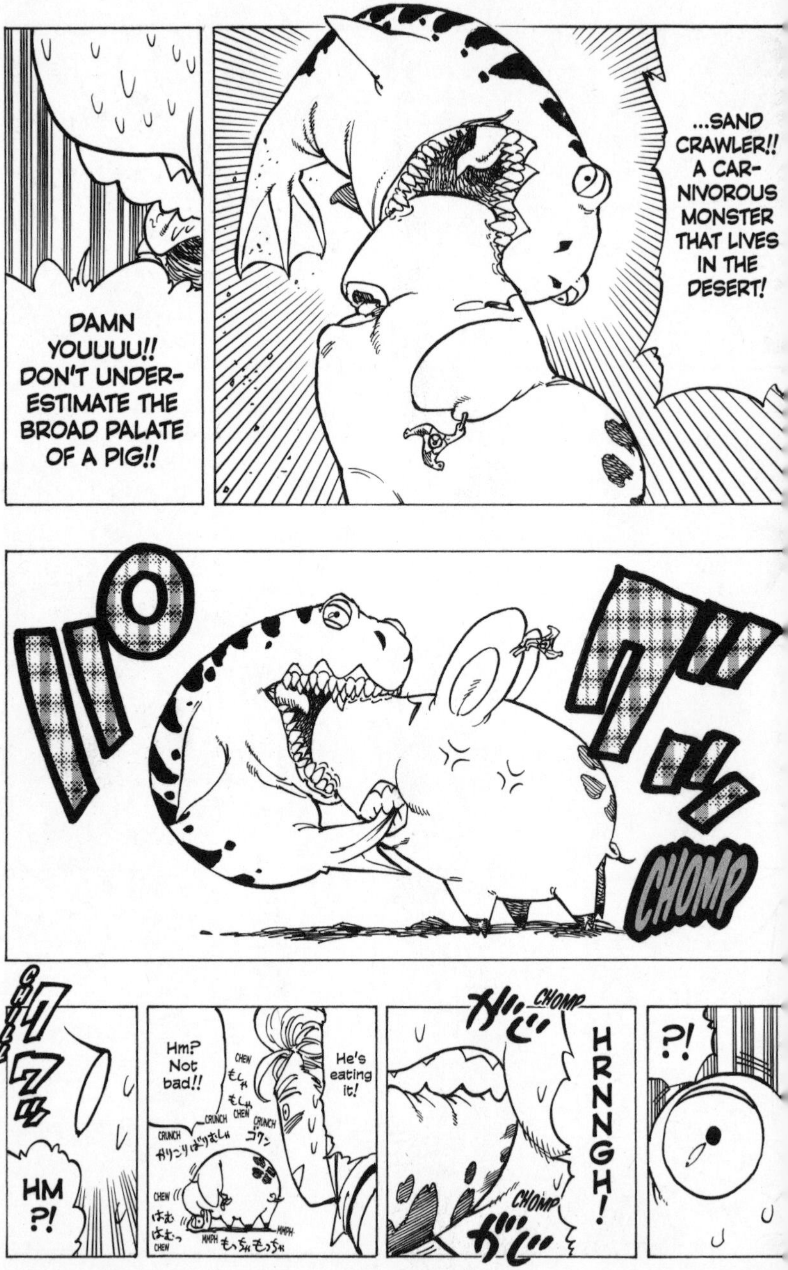
...SAND CRAWLER!! A CARNIVOROUS MONSTER THAT LIVES IN THE DESERT!
DAMN YOUUUU!! DON'T UNDERESTIMATE THE BROAD PALATE OF A PIG!!
パクッ
CHOMP
?!
CHOMP
HRNNGH!
CHOMP
He's eating it!
Hm? Not bad!!
CHEW
CRUNCH
CHEW
CRUNCH
MMPH
HM ?!
CHILL

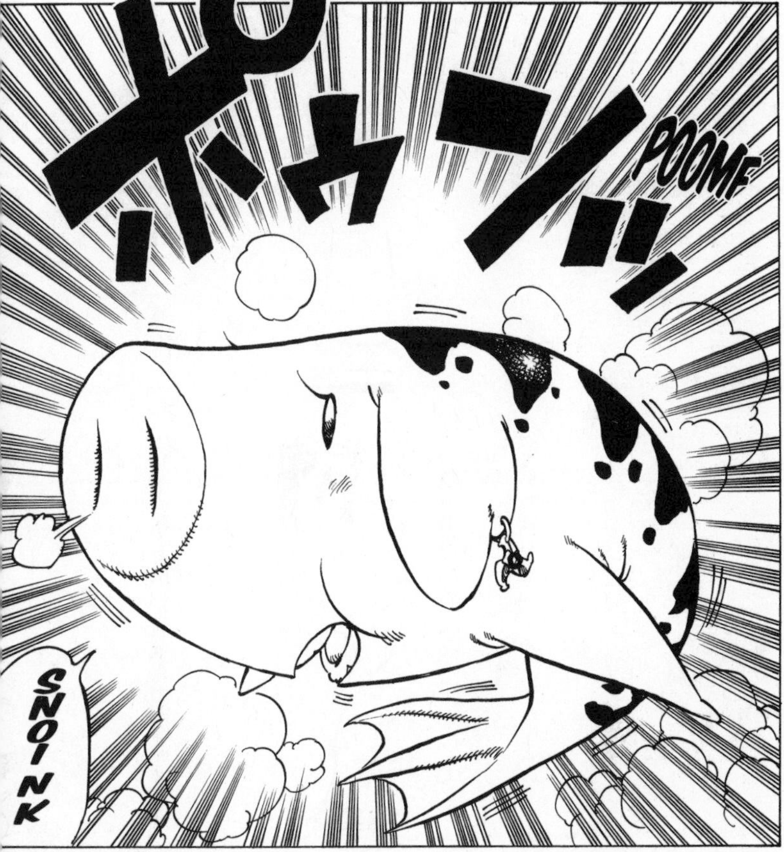
POOMF
SNOINK

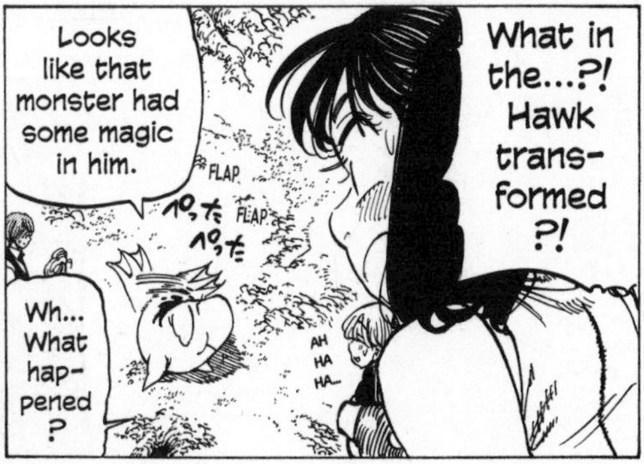
What in the...?! Hawk transformed?!
Looks like that monster had some magic in him.
FLAP
FLAP
Wh... What happened?
AH HA HA...

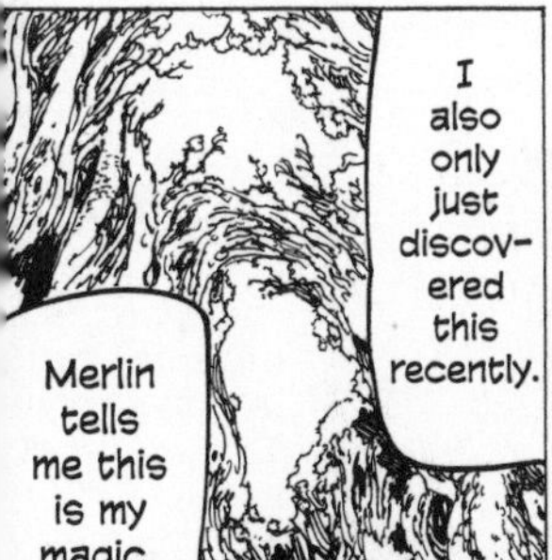
I also only just discovered this recently.
Merlin tells me this is my magic.

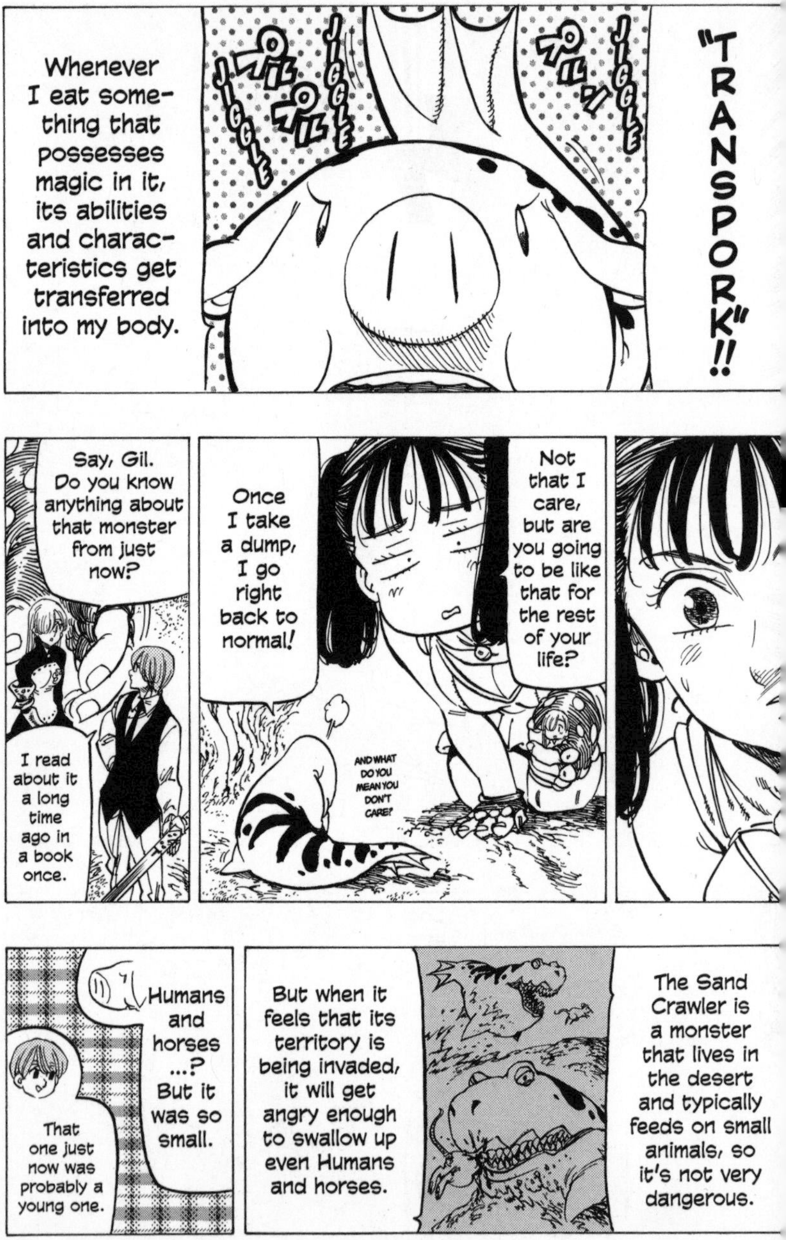
"TRANSPORK"!!
JIGGLE
JIGGLE
JIGGLE
JIGGLE
Whenever I eat something that possesses magic in it, its abilities and characteristics get transferred into my body.
Not that I care, but are you going to be like that for the rest of your life?
Once I take a dump, I go right back to normal!
AND WHAT DO YOU MEAN YOU DON'T CARE?
Say, Gil. Do you know anything about that monster from just now?
I read about it a long time ago in a book once.
The Sand Crawler is a monster that lives in the desert and typically feeds on small animals, so it's not very dangerous.
But when it feels that its territory is being invaded, it will get angry enough to swallow up even Humans and horses.
Humans and horses ...? But it was so small.
That one just now was probably a young one.

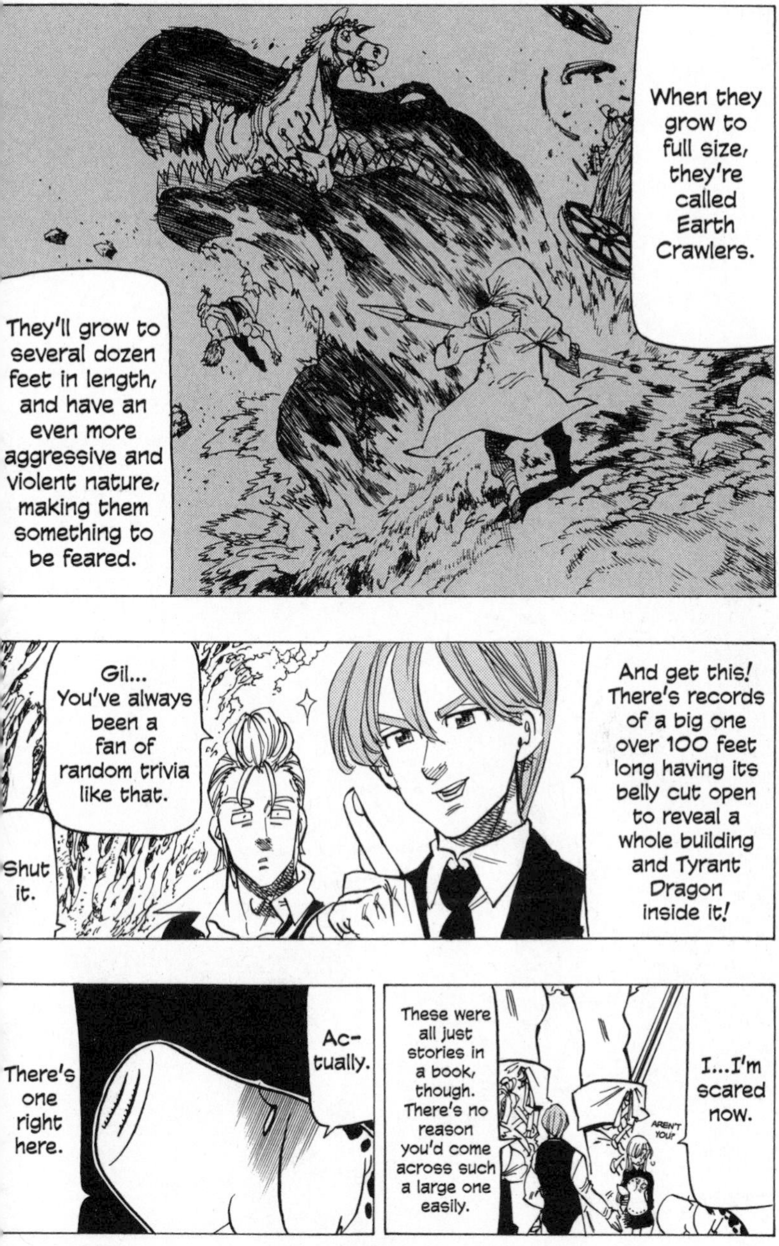
When they grow to full size, they're called Earth Crawlers.
They'll grow to several dozen feet in length, and have an even more aggressive and violent nature, making them something to be feared.
And get this! There's records of a big one over 100 feet long having its belly cut open to reveal a whole building and Tyrant Dragon inside it!
Gil... You've always been a fan of random trivia like that.
Shut it.
I...I'm scared now.
AREN'T YOU?
These were all just stories in a book, though. There's no reason you'd come across such a large one easily.
Ac-tually.
There's one right here.

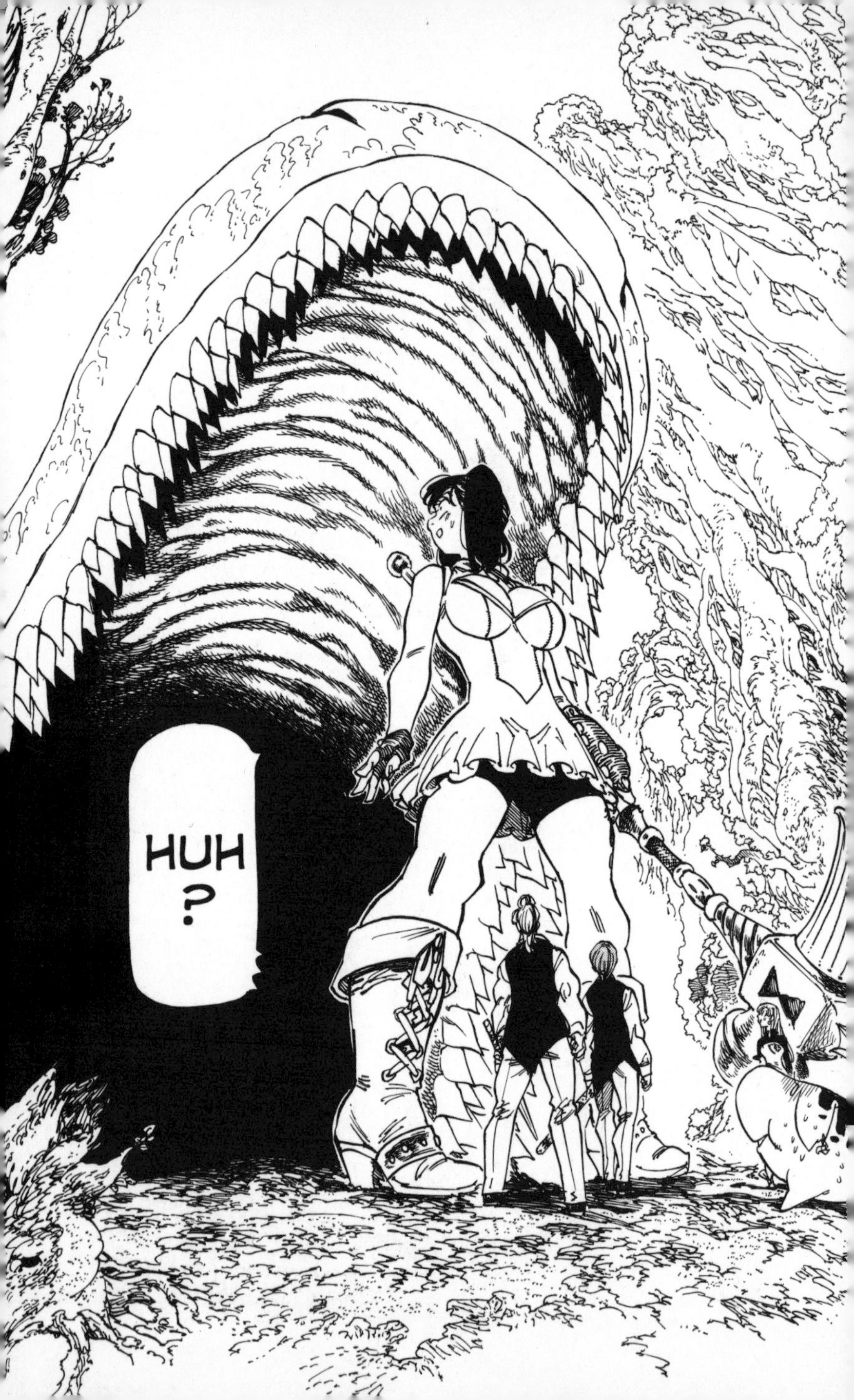
HUH?

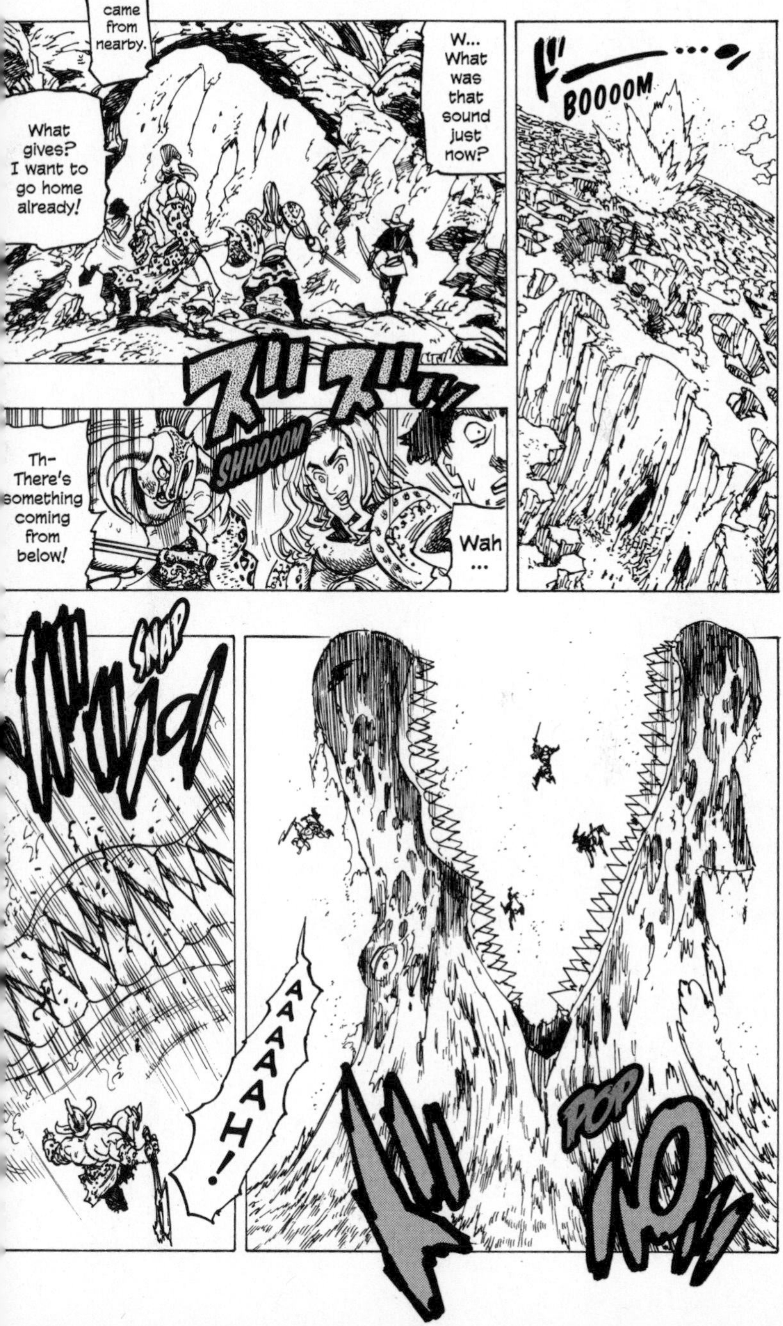
BOOOOM
W... What was that sound just now?
It came from nearby.
What gives? I want to go home already!
SHHOOOM
Wah ...
Th- There's something coming from below!
AAAAAH!
POP
SNAP

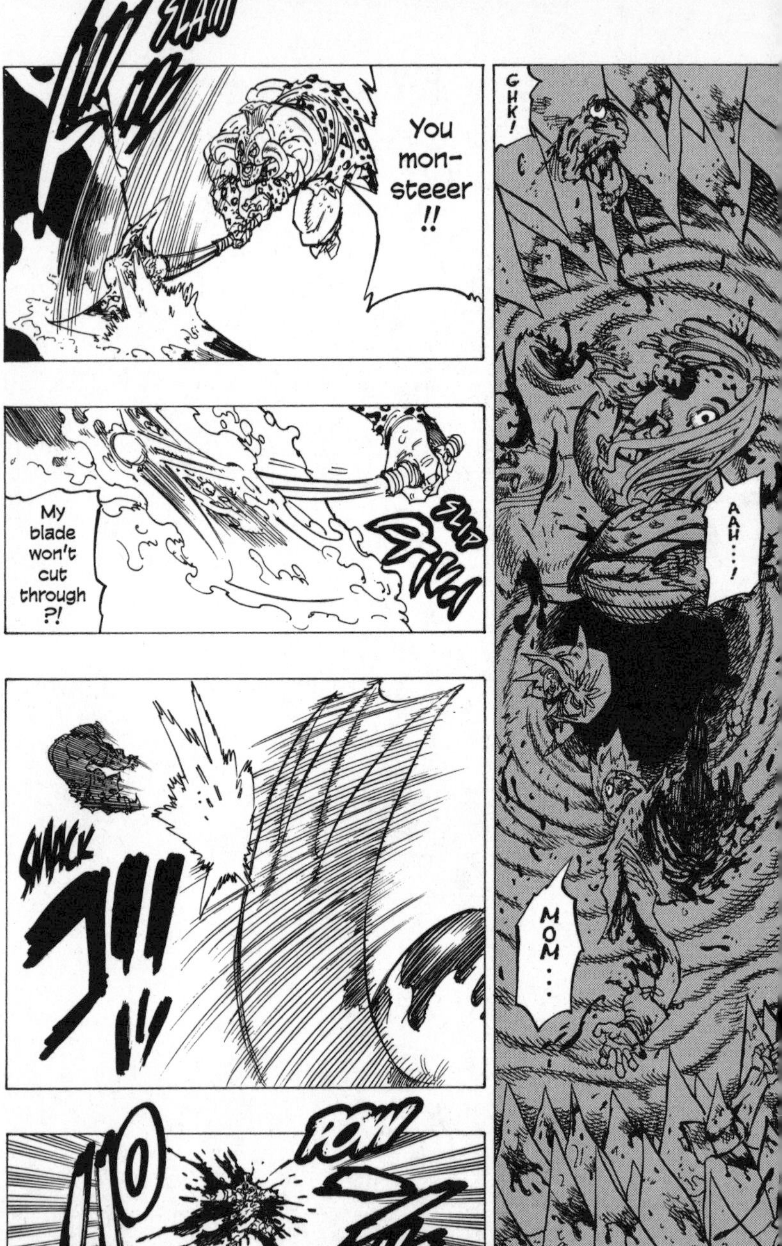
GHK!
AAH...!
MOM...
SLAM
You mon-steeer!!
SLAP
My blade won't cut through?!
SMACK
POW

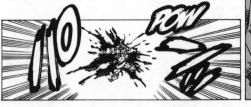

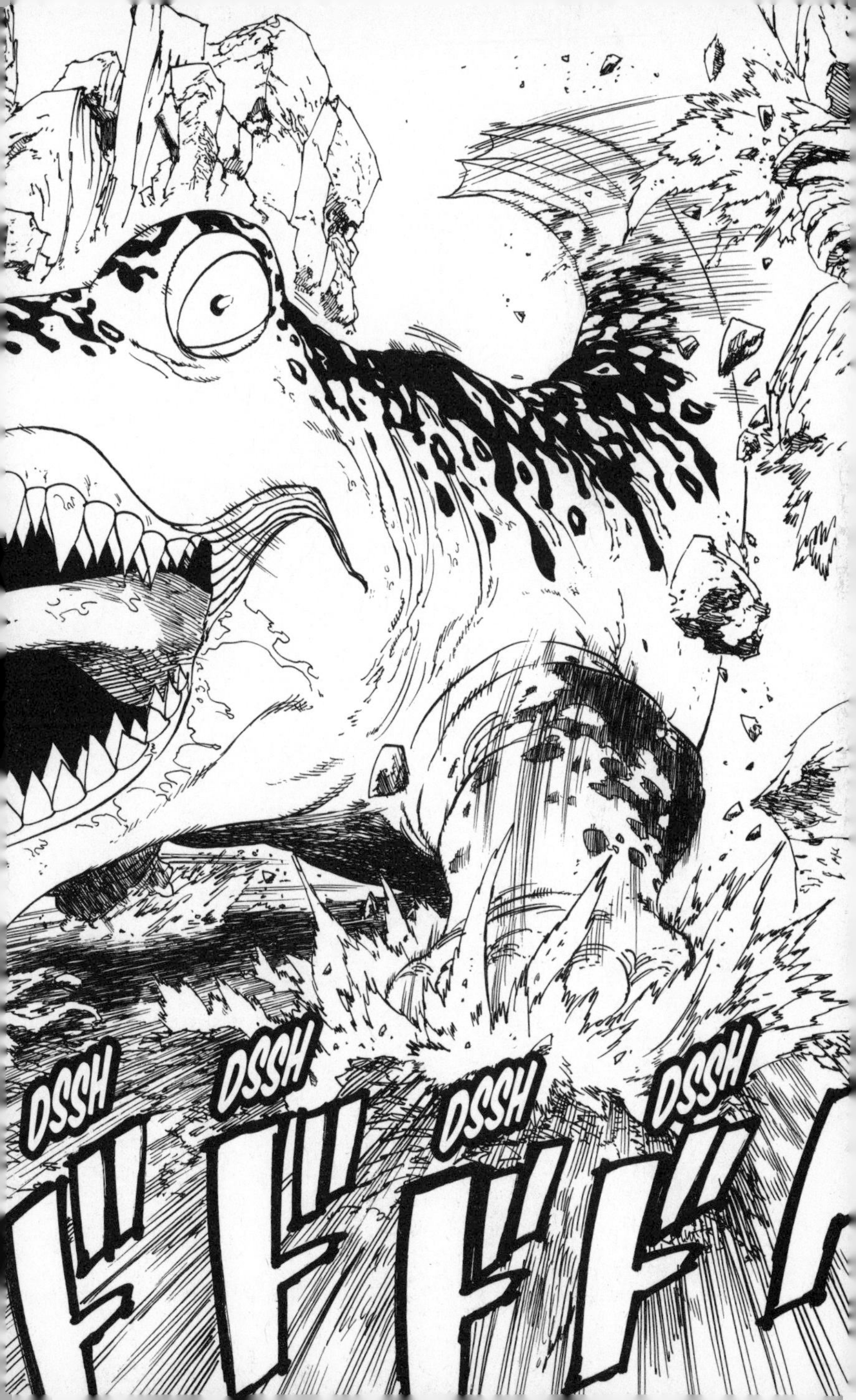
DSSH
DSSH
DSSH
DSSH

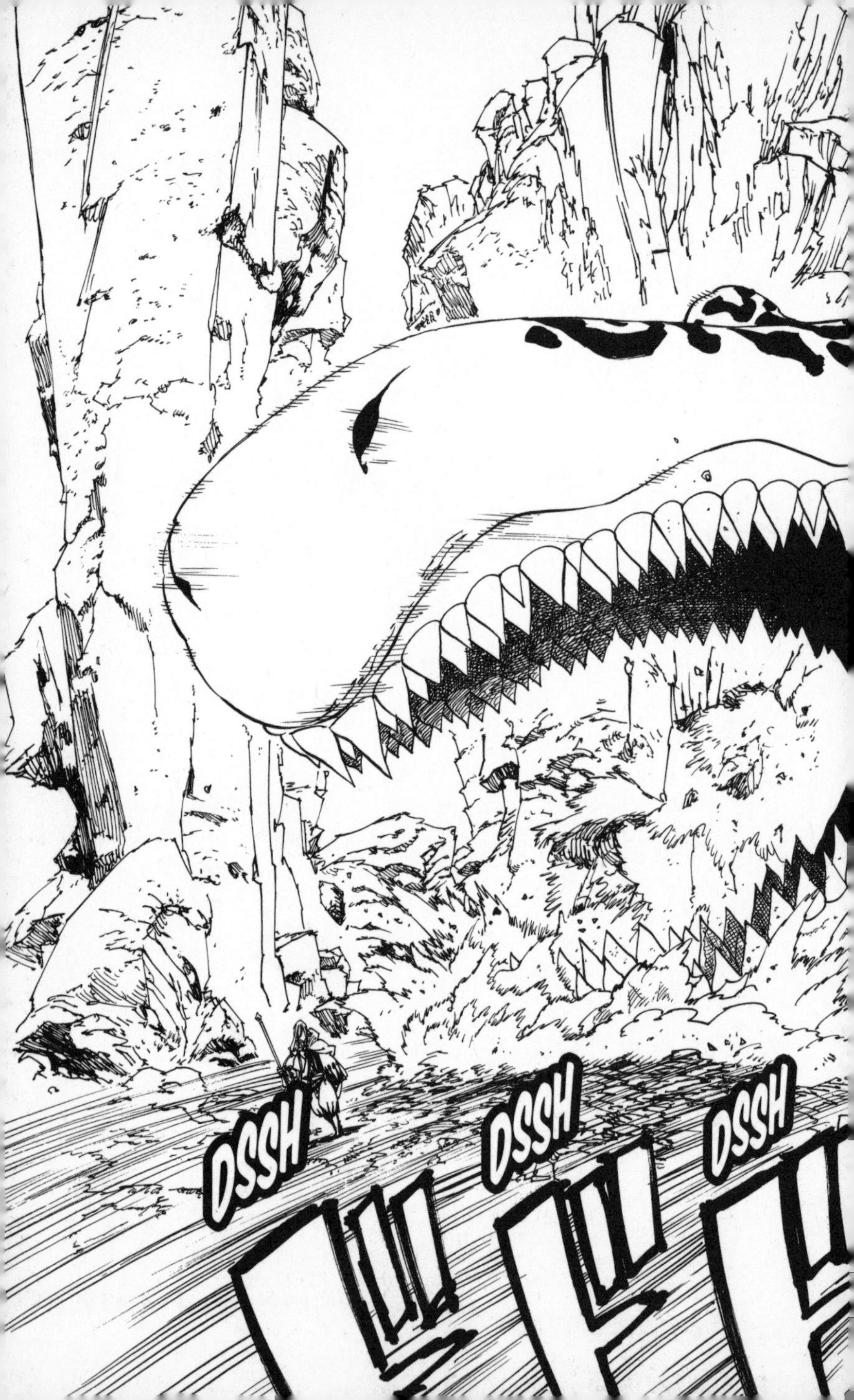
DSSH
DSSH
DSSH

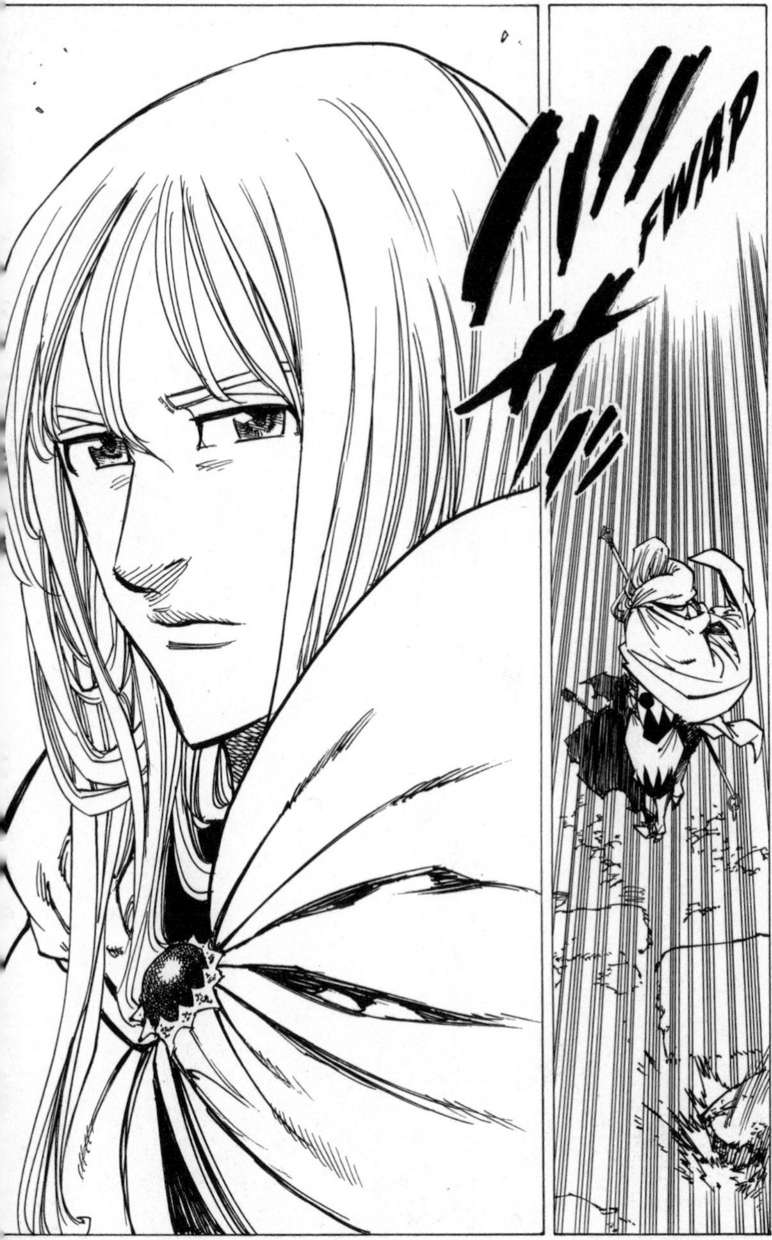
FWAP

Chapter 158 - The Brave Reveler

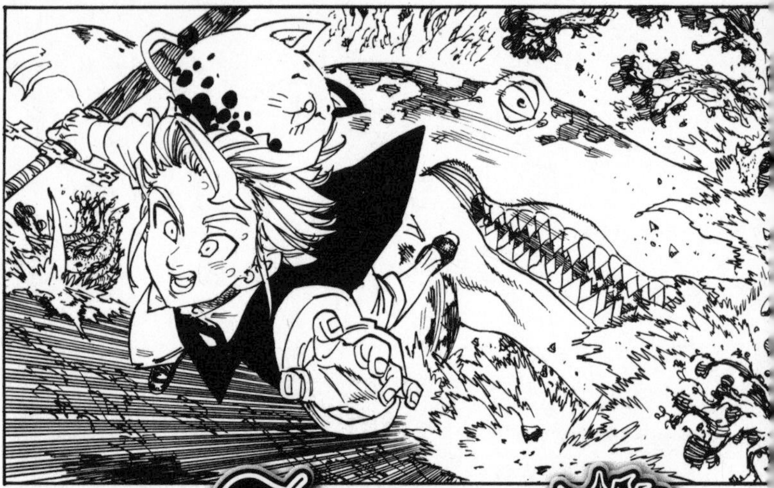

THE SEVEN DEADLY SINS

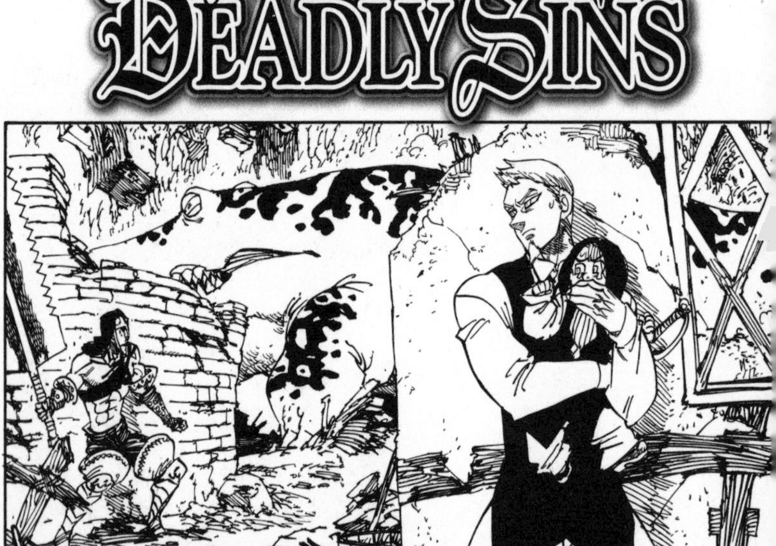

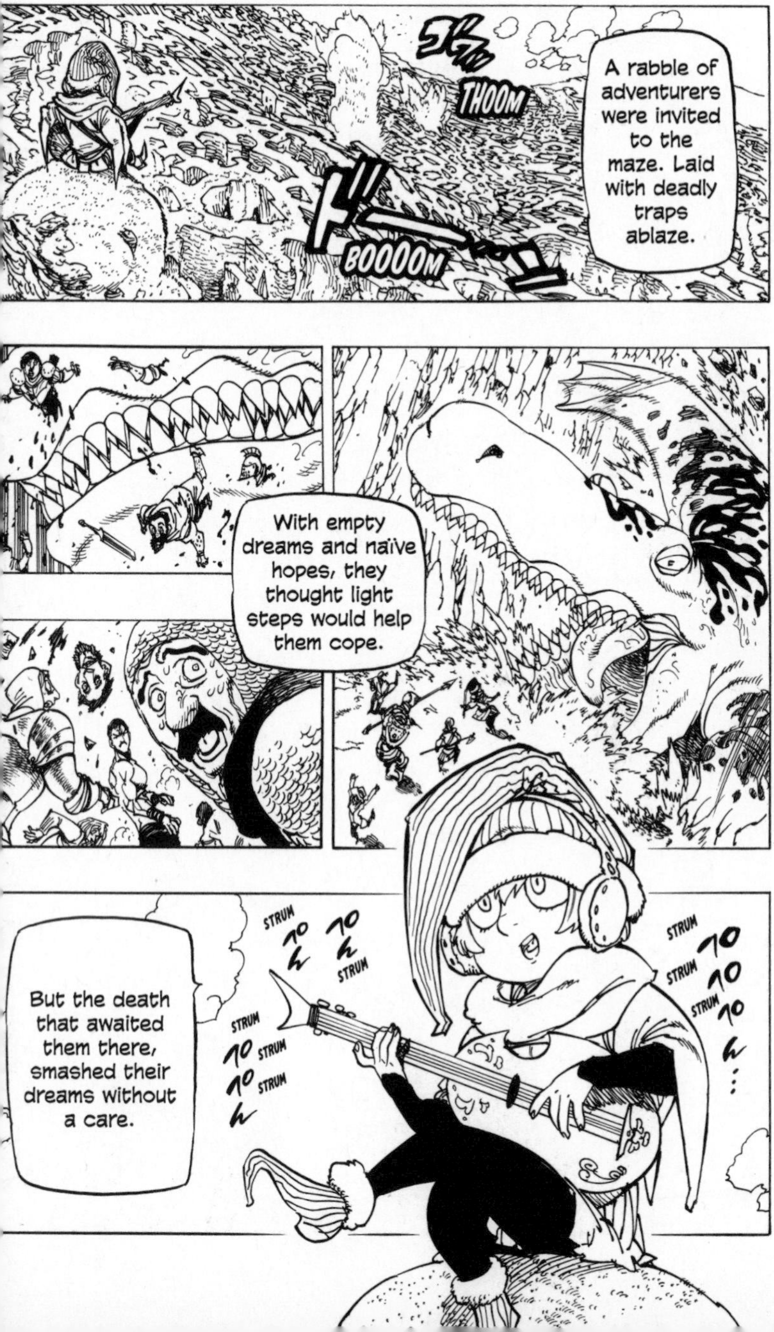
A rabble of adventurers were invited to the maze. Laid with deadly traps ablaze.
THOOM
BOOOOM
With empty dreams and naïve hopes, they thought light steps would help them cope.
STRUM
STRUM
STRUM
STRUM
STRUM
But the death that awaited them there, smashed their dreams without a care.
STRUM
STRUM
STRUM

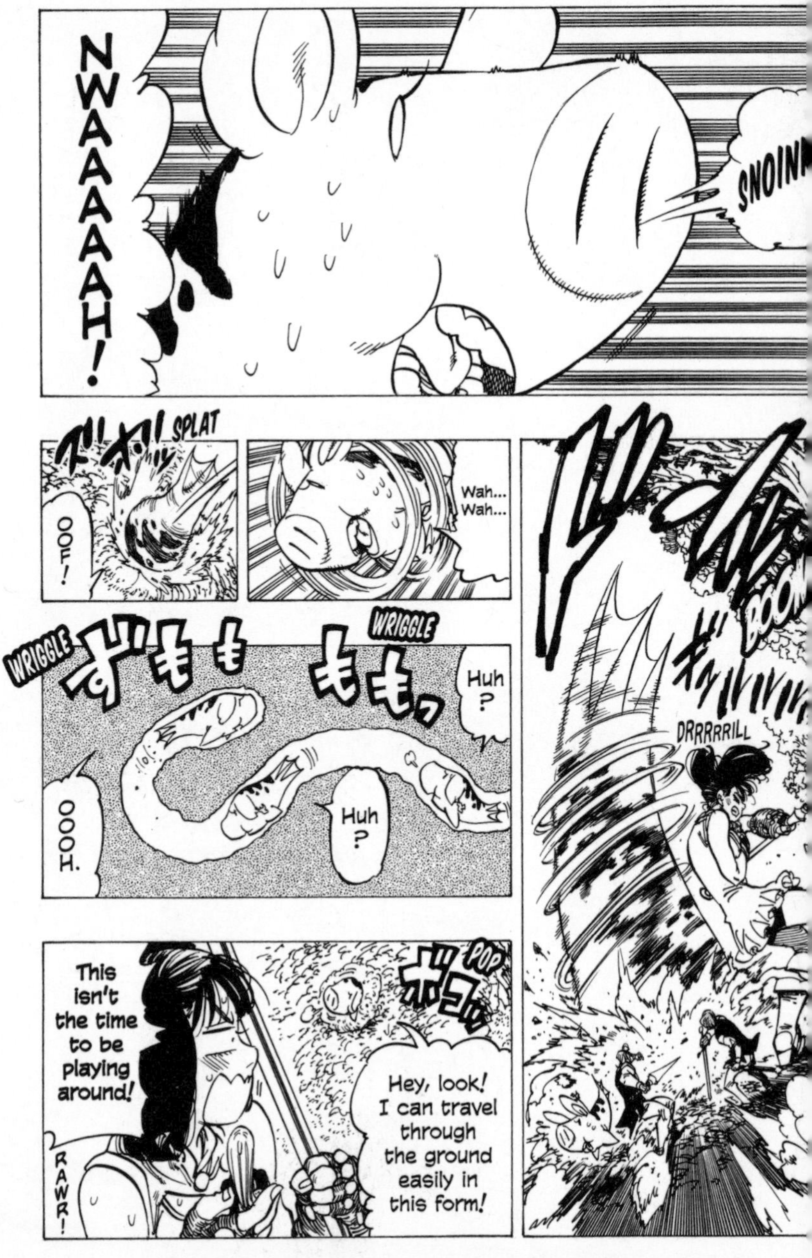
SNOINK
NWAAAAAAH!
BOOM
DRRRRRILL
SPLAT
OOF!
Wah... Wah...
WRIGGLE
WRIGGLE
Huh?
Huh?
OOOH.
POP
Hey, look! I can travel through the ground easily in this form!
This isn't the time to be playing around!
RAWR!

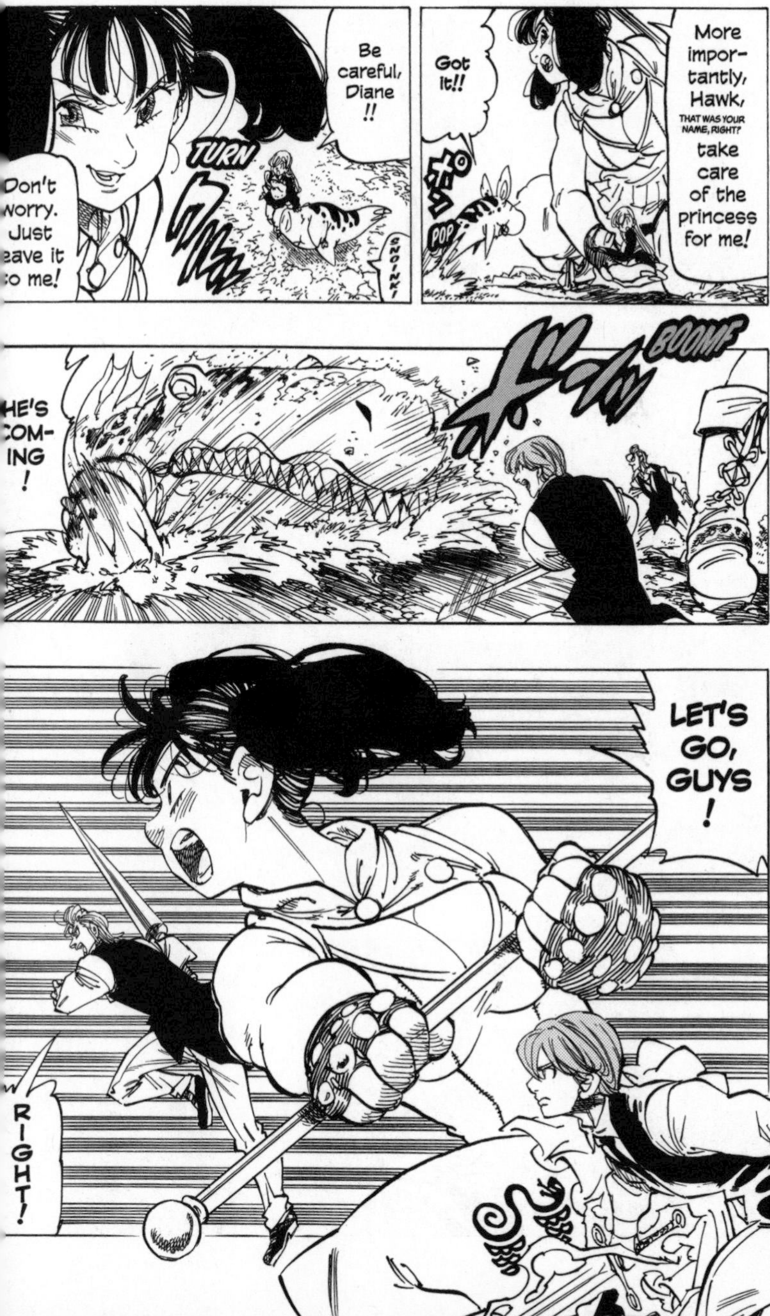
More importantly, Hawk,
THAT WAS YOUR NAME, RIGHT?
take care of the princess for me!
Got it!!
POP
Be careful, Diane!!
TURN
SNOINK!
Don't worry. Just eave it o me!
BOOMF
HE'S COMING!
LET'S GO, GUYS!
RIGHT!

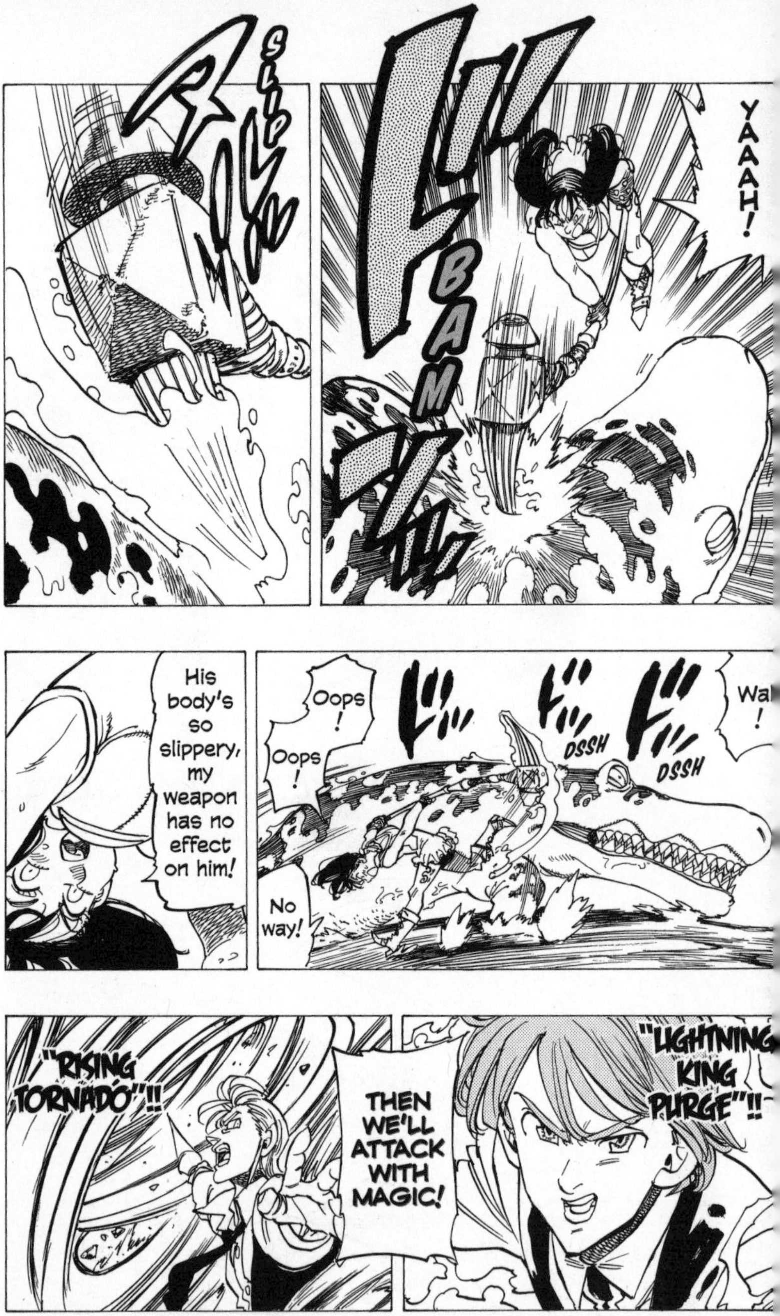
YAAAH!
BAM
SLIP
Wa!
DSSH
DSSH
Oops!
Oops!
No way!
His body's so slippery, my weapon has no effect on him!
"LIGHTNING KING PURGE"!!
THEN WE'LL ATTACK WITH MAGIC!
"RISING TORNADO"!!

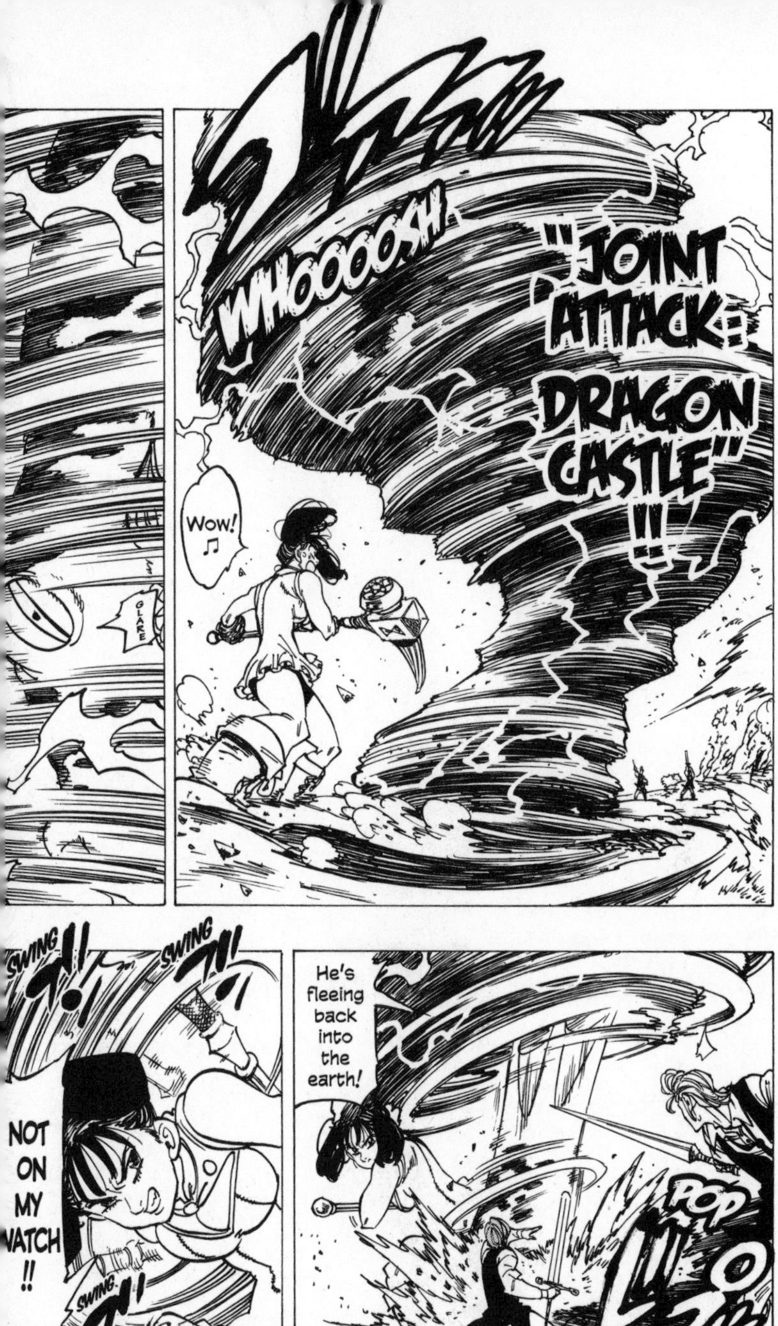
WHOOOOSH
"JOINT ATTACK: DRAGON CASTLE"!!
Wow! ♫
GLARE
He's fleeing back into the earth!
POP
SWING
SWING
NOT ON MY WATCH!!
SWING

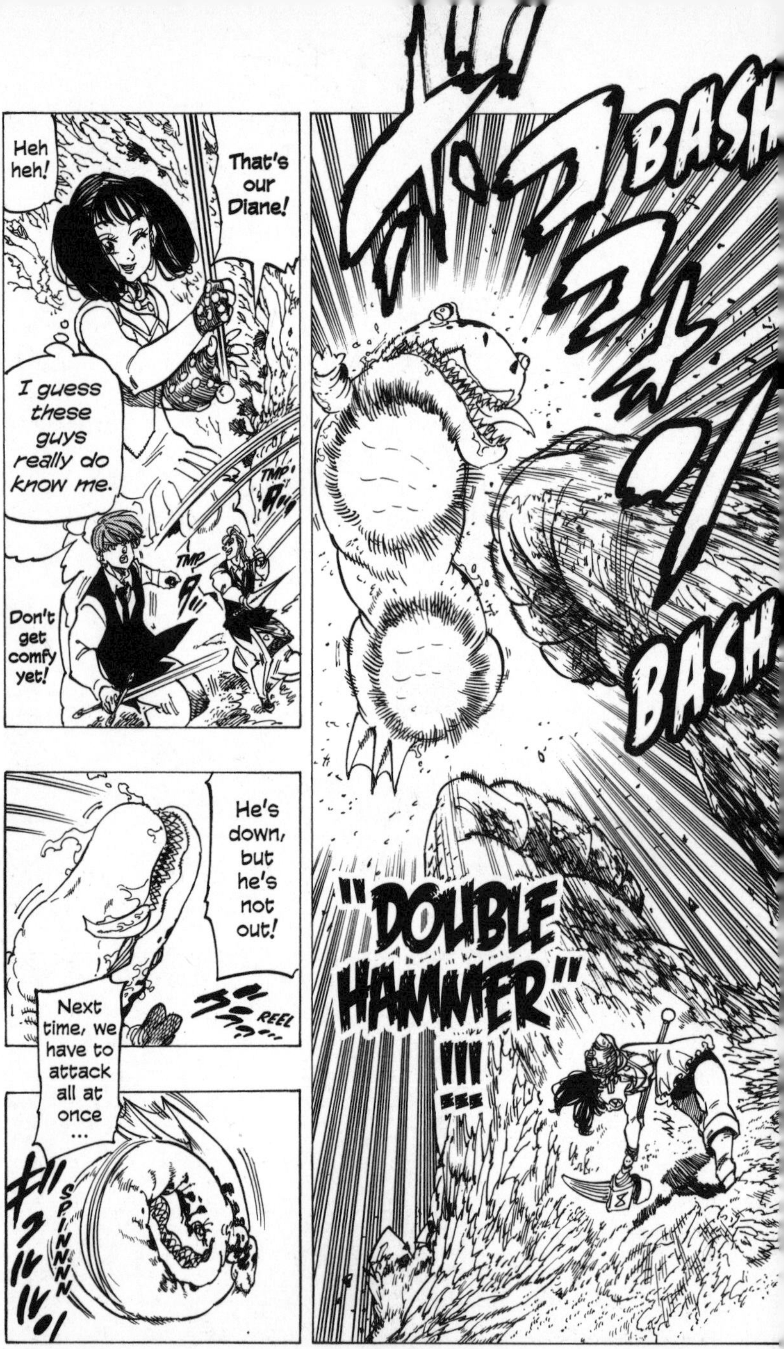

BASH
BASH
"DOUBLE HAMMER"!!!
That's our Diane!
Heh heh!
I guess these guys really do know me.
TMP
TMP
Don't get comfy yet!
He's down, but he's not out!
REEL
Next time, we have to attack all at once...
SPINNNN

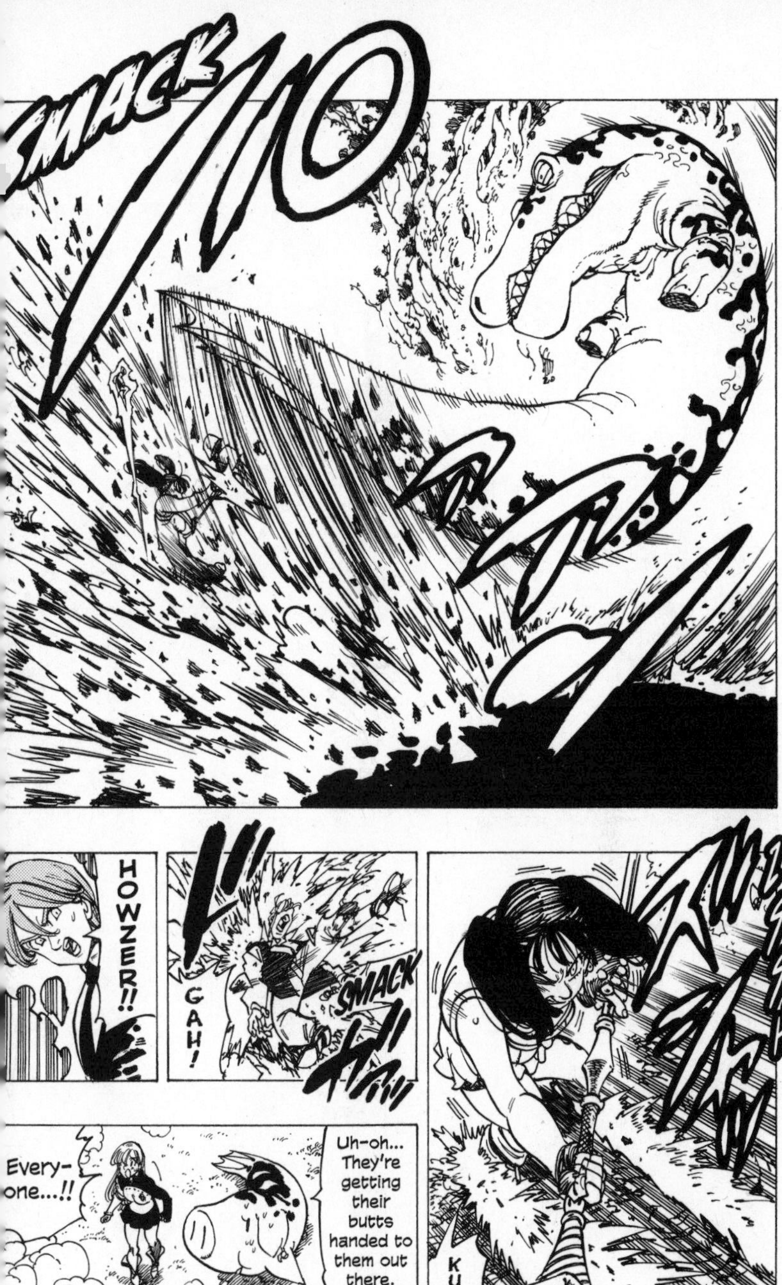
SMACK
KUH!
GAH!
SMACK
HOWZER!!
Uh-oh... They're getting their butts handed to them out there.
Every-one...!!

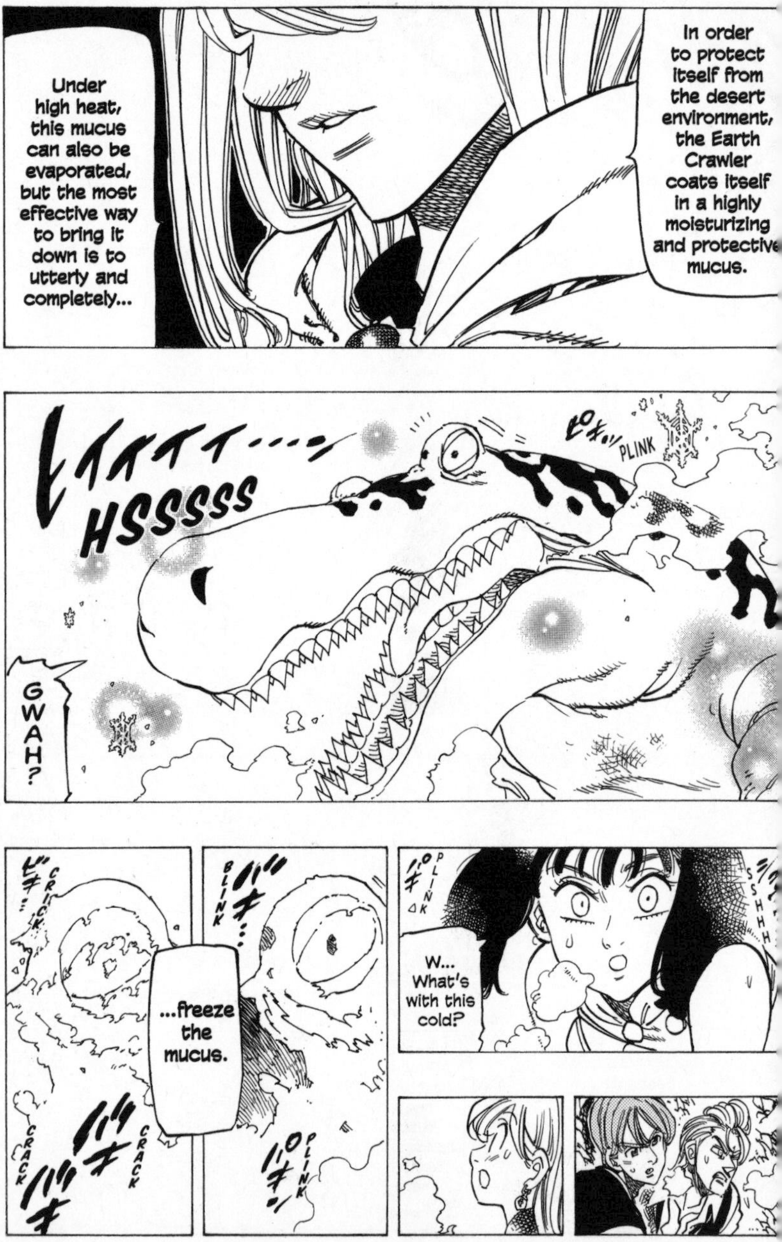
In order to protect itself from the desert environment, the Earth Crawler coats itself in a highly moisturizing and protective mucus.
Under high heat, this mucus can also be evaporated, but the most effective way to bring it down is to utterly and completely...
PLINK
HSSSSS
GWAH?
PLINK
SSHHH
W... What's with this cold?
BLINK
...freeze the mucus.
PLINK
CRICK
CRACK
CRACK

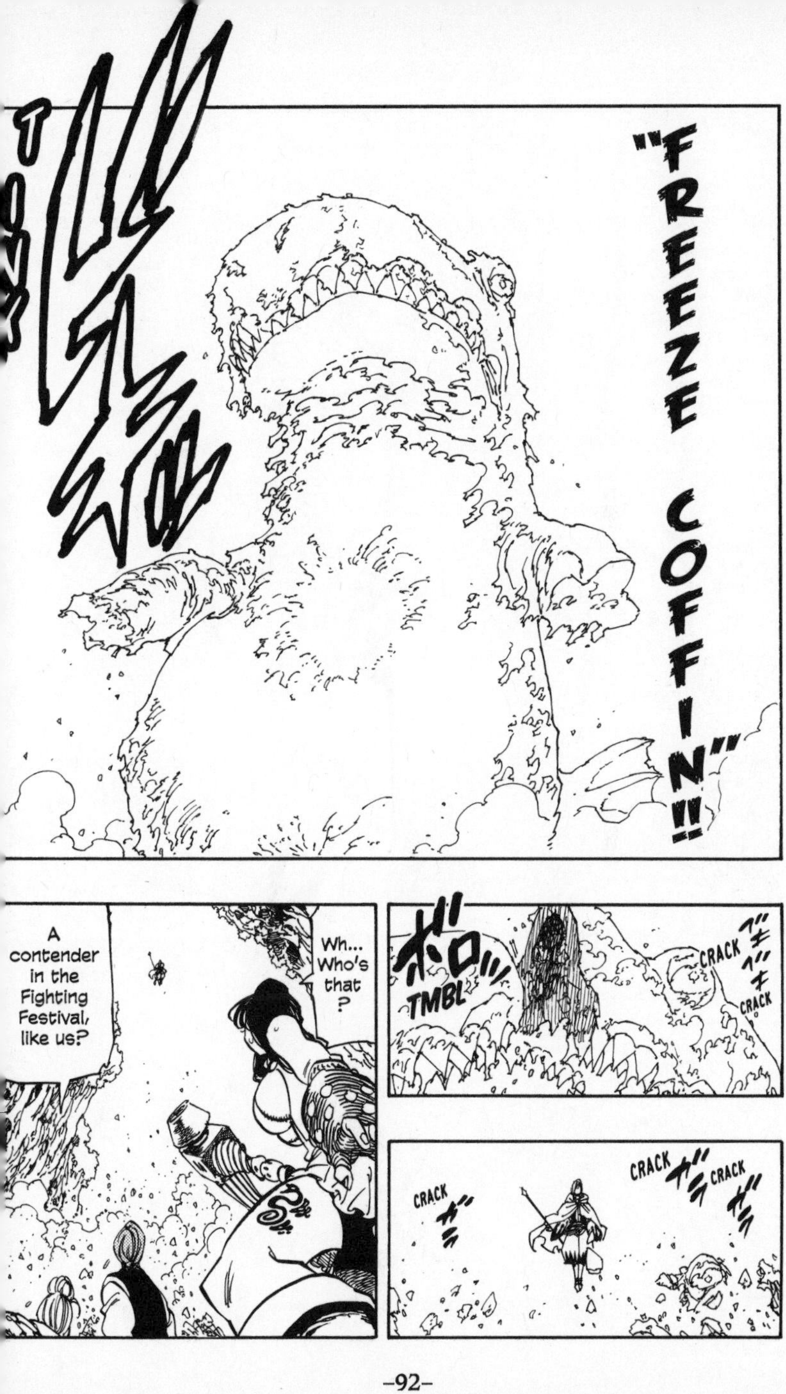
"FREEZE COFFIN"!!
TMBL
CRACK
CRACK
CRACK
CRACK
CRACK
Wh... Who's that?
A contender in the Fighting Festival, like us?

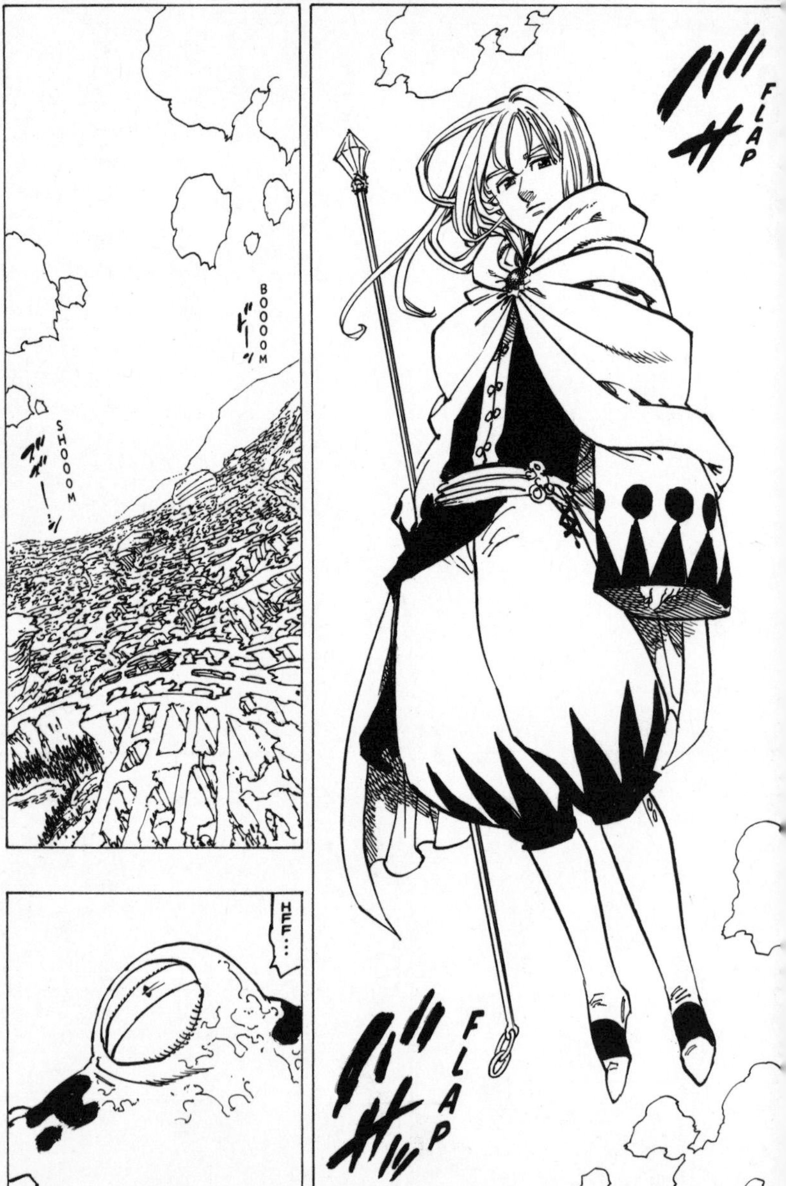
FLAP
FLAP
BOOOOM
SHOOOOM
HFF...
HFF

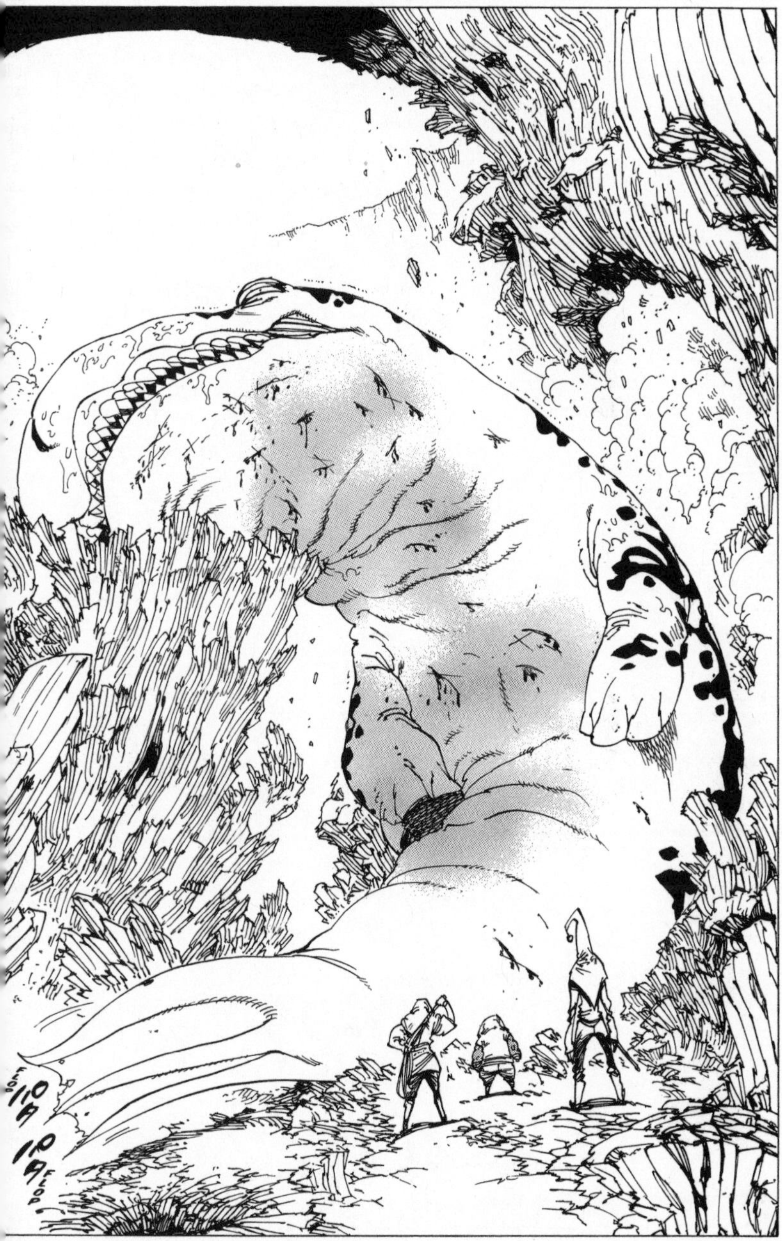
FLOP
FLOP

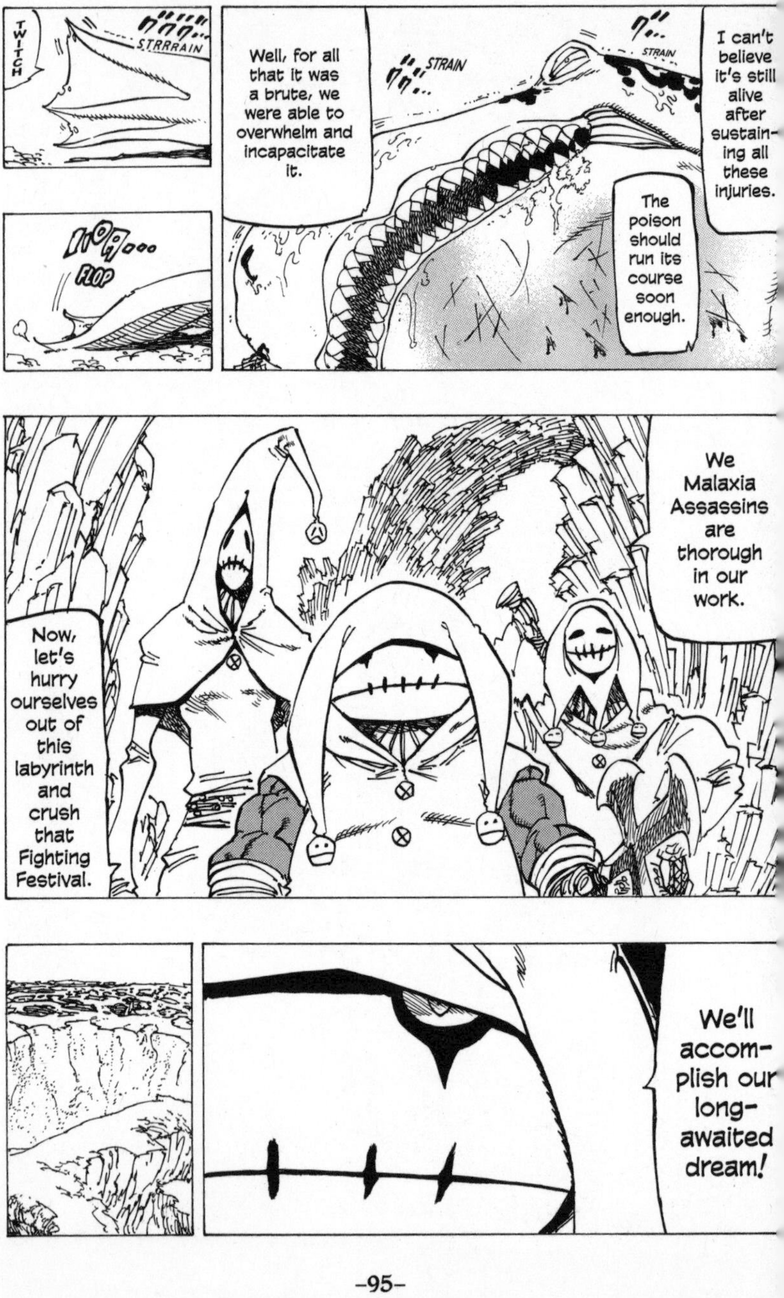
STRAIN
I can't believe it's still alive after sustaining all these injuries.
STRAIN
Well, for all that it was a brute, we were able to overwhelm and incapacitate it.
The poison should run its course soon enough.
STRRRAIN
TWITCH
FLOP
We Malaxia Assassins are thorough in our work.
Now, let's hurry ourselves out of this labyrinth and crush that Fighting Festival.
We'll accomplish our long-awaited dream!

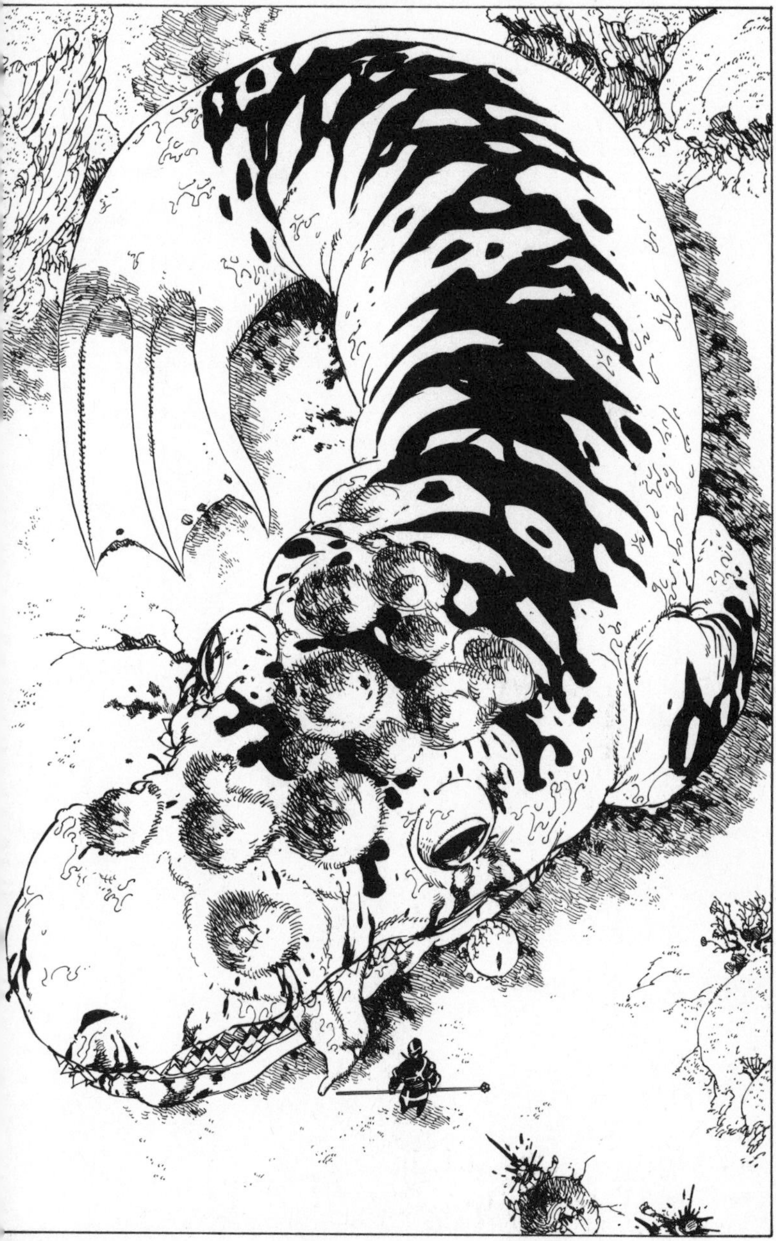

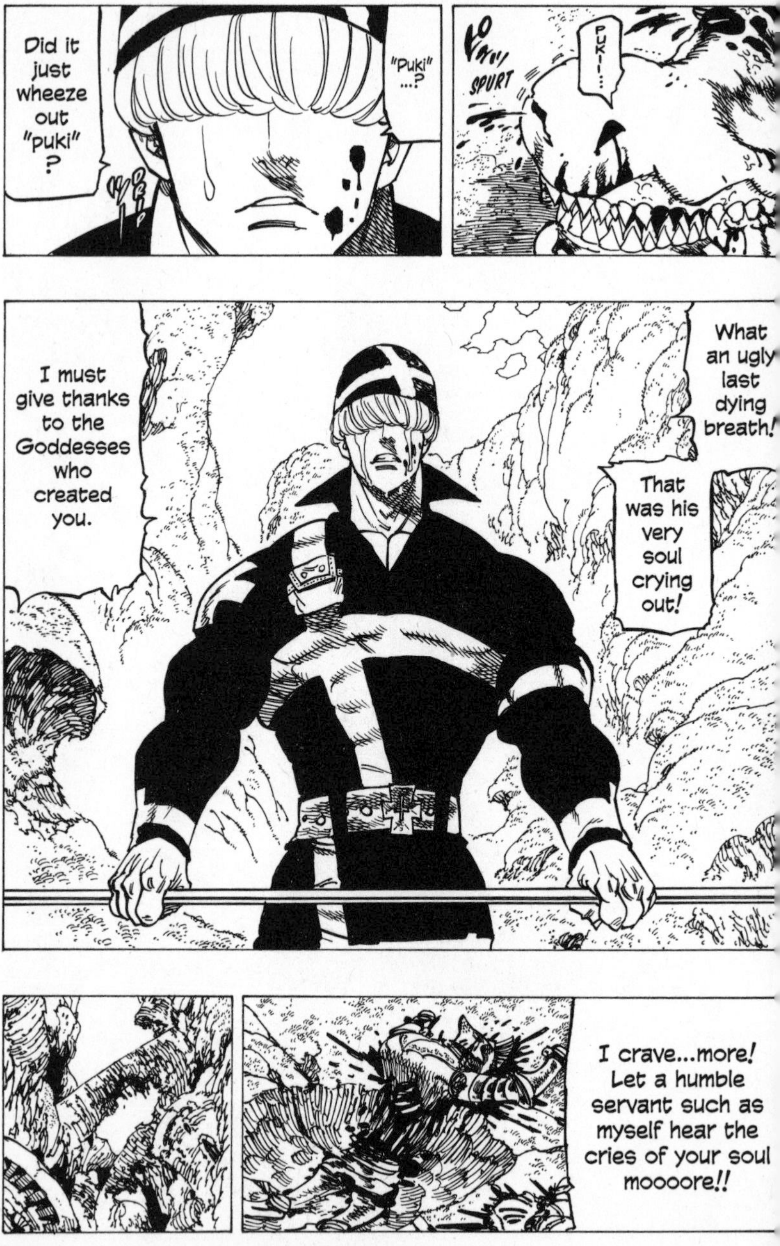
PUKI...
SPURT
"Puki"...?
Did it just wheeze out "puki"?
DRIP
What an ugly last dying breath!
That was his very soul crying out!
I must give thanks to the Goddesses who created you.
I crave...more! Let a humble servant such as myself hear the cries of your soul moooore!!

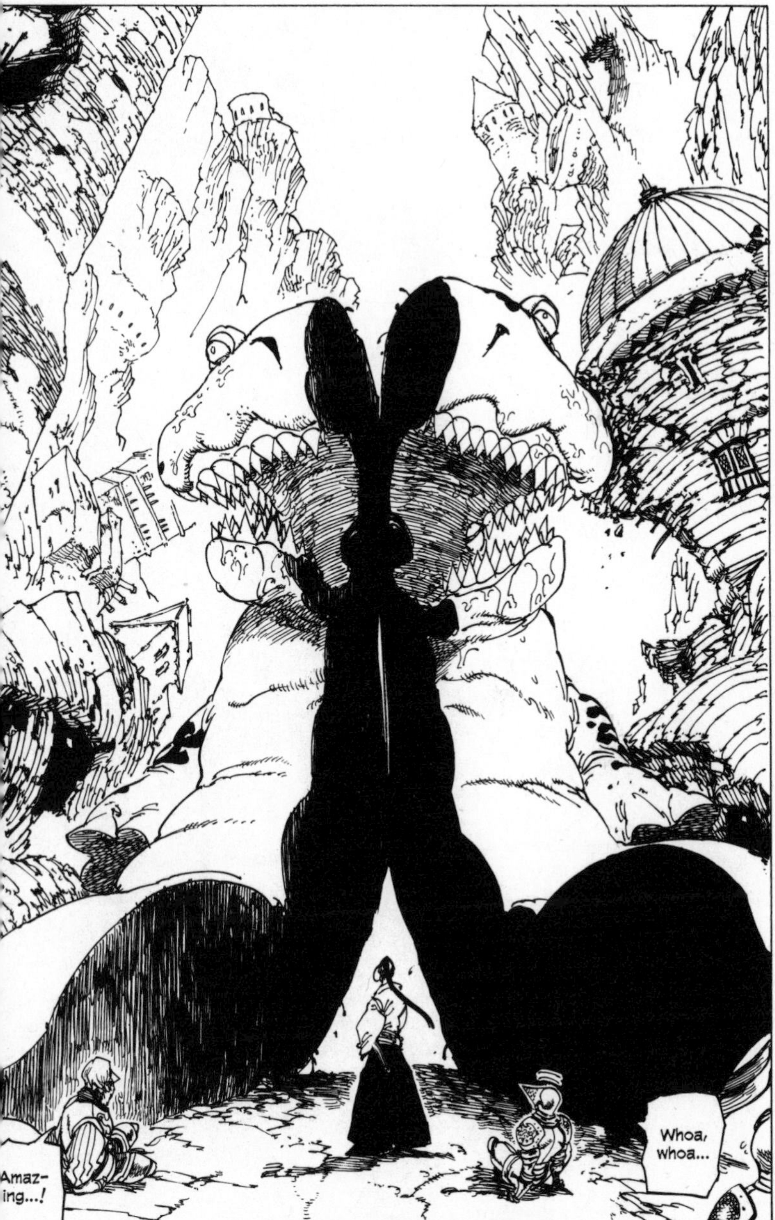
Whoa, whoa...
Amaz-ing...!

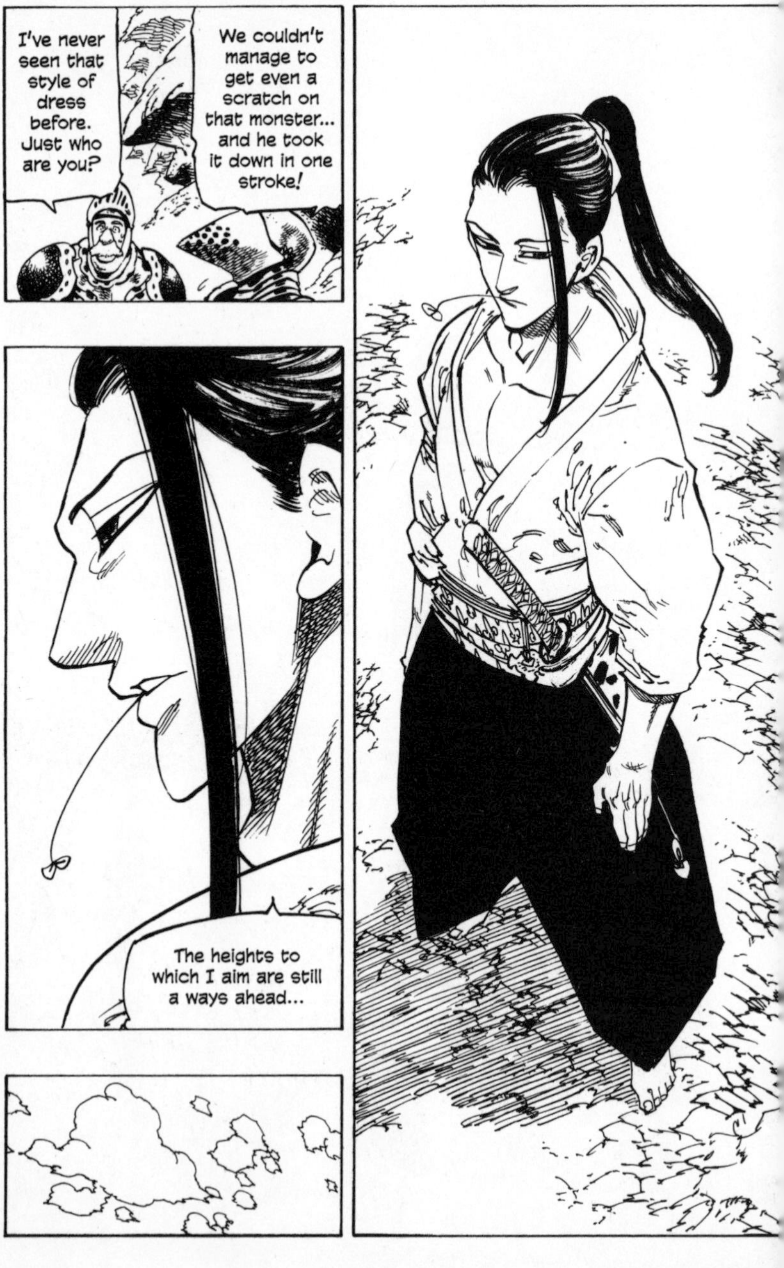
We couldn't manage to get even a scratch on that monster... and he took it down in one stroke!
I've never seen that style of dress before. Just who are you?
The heights to which I aim are still a ways ahead...

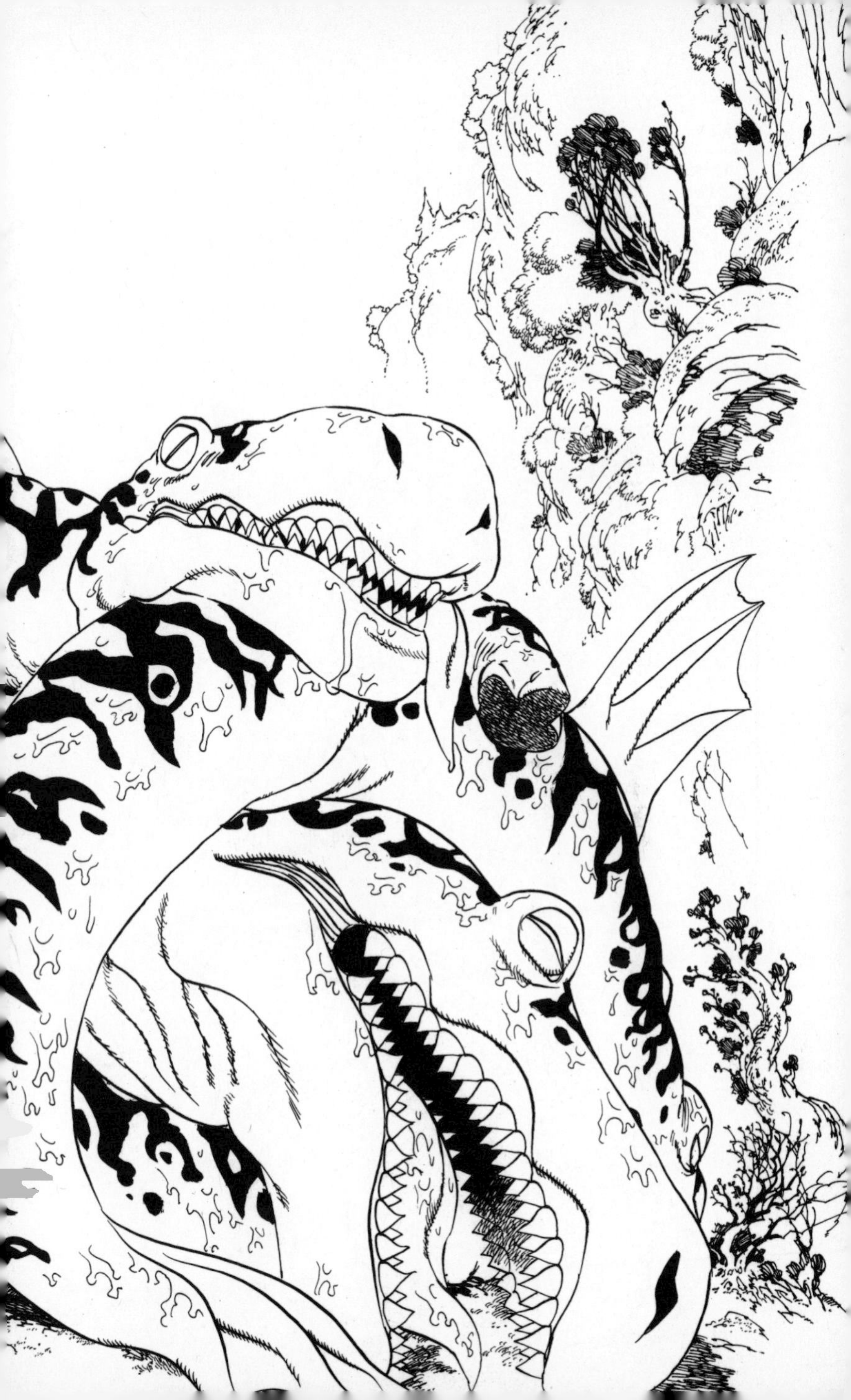

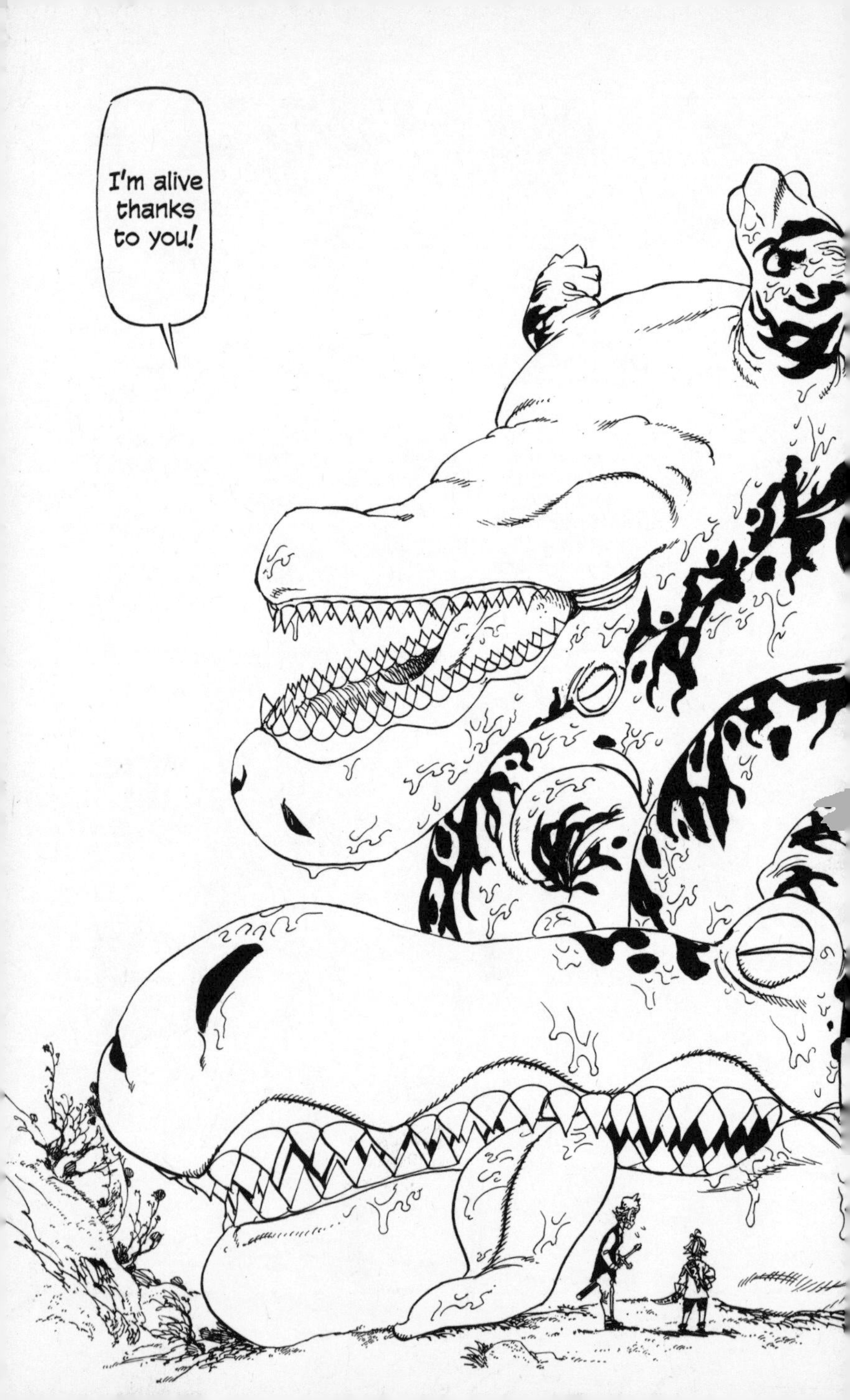
I'm alive thanks to you!

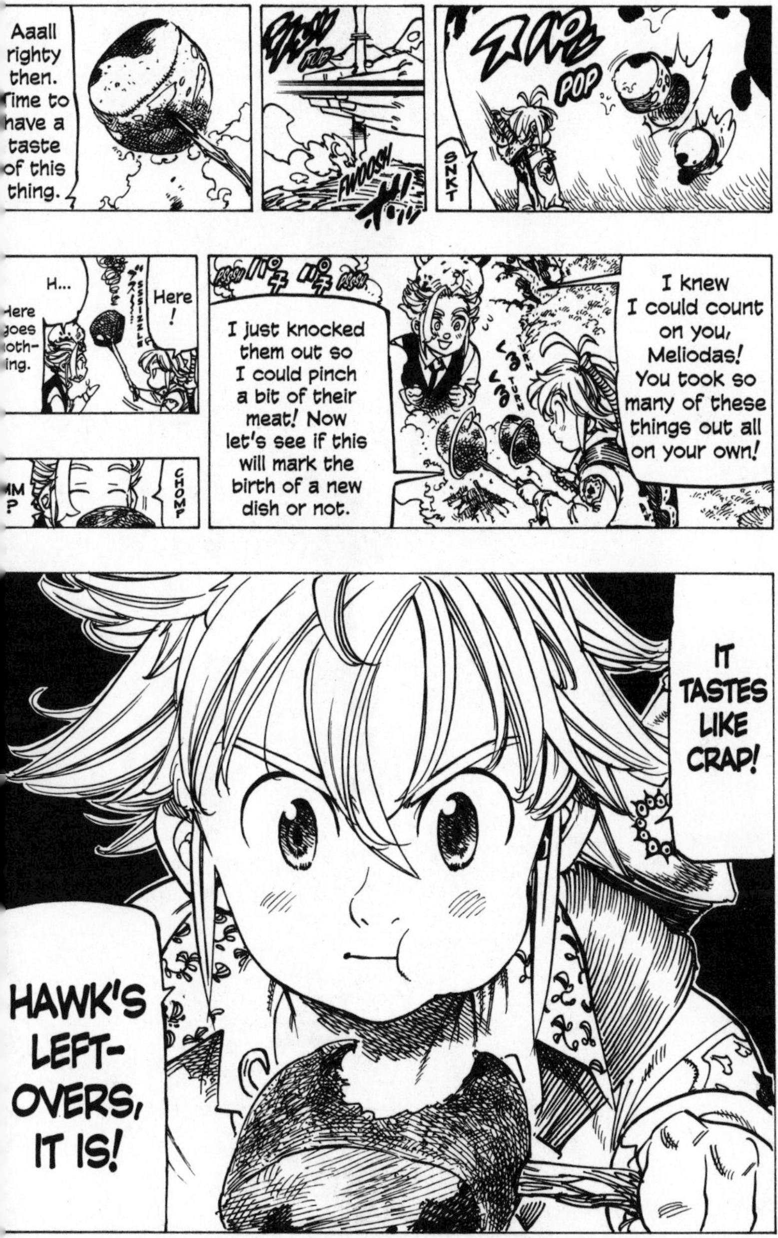
SNKT
POP
FUB
FWOOSH
Aaall righty then. Time to have a taste of this thing.
PSSH
I knew I could count on you, Meliodas! You took so many of these things out all on your own!
TURN TURN
I just knocked them out so I could pinch a bit of their meat! Now let's see if this will mark the birth of a new dish or not.
Here!
SSSIZZLE
H...
CHOMP
IT TASTES LIKE CRAP!
HAWK'S LEFT-OVERS, IT IS!

Chapter 159 - No Words Necessary

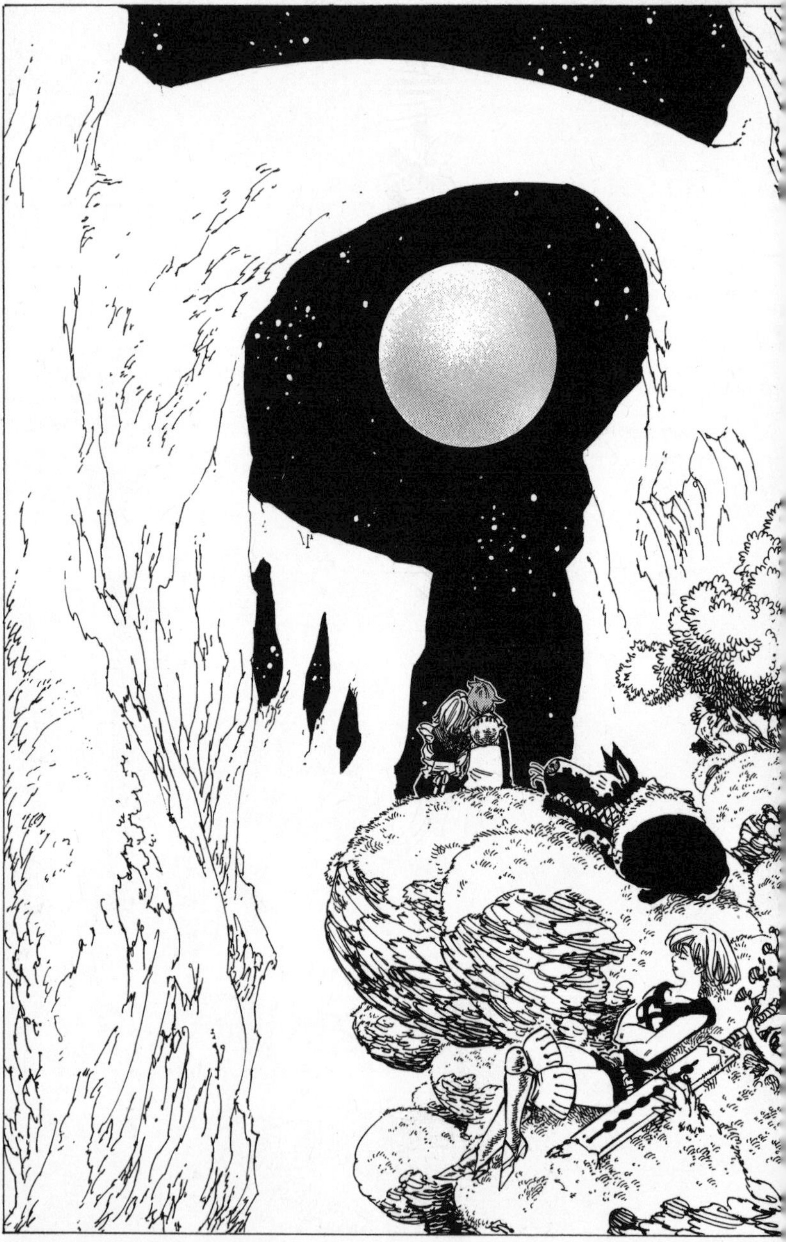

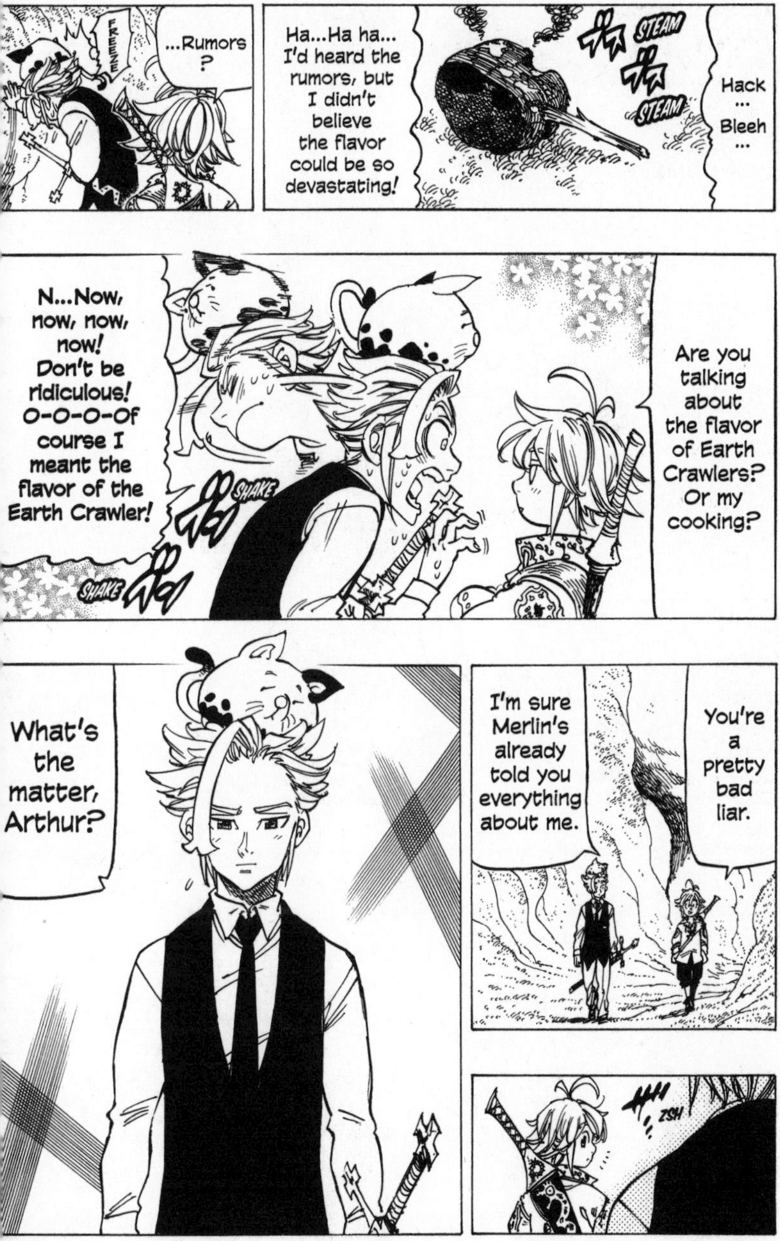
Hack ... Bleeh ...
STEAM
STEAM
Ha...Ha ha... I'd heard the rumors, but I didn't believe the flavor could be so devastating!
FREEZE
...Rumors ?
Are you talking about the flavor of Earth Crawlers? Or my cooking?
N...Now, now, now, now! Don't be ridiculous! O-O-O-Of course I meant the flavor of the Earth Crawler!
SHAKE
SHAKE
You're a pretty bad liar.
I'm sure Merlin's already told you everything about me.
ZSH
What's the matter, Arthur?

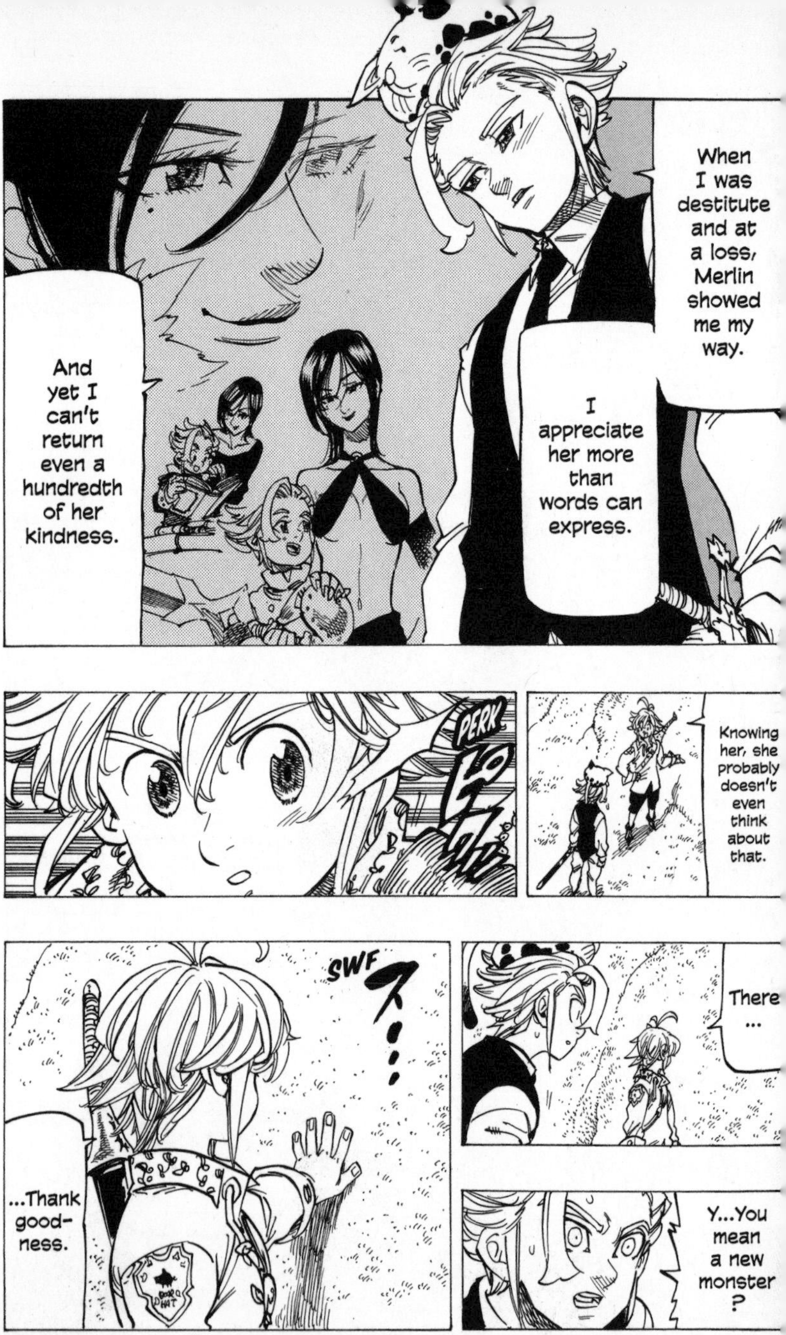
When I was destitute and at a loss, Merlin showed me my way.
I appreciate her more than words can express.
And yet I can't return even a hundredth of her kindness.
Knowing her, she probably doesn't even think about that.
PERK
There...
Y...You mean a new monster?
SWF
...Thank goodness.

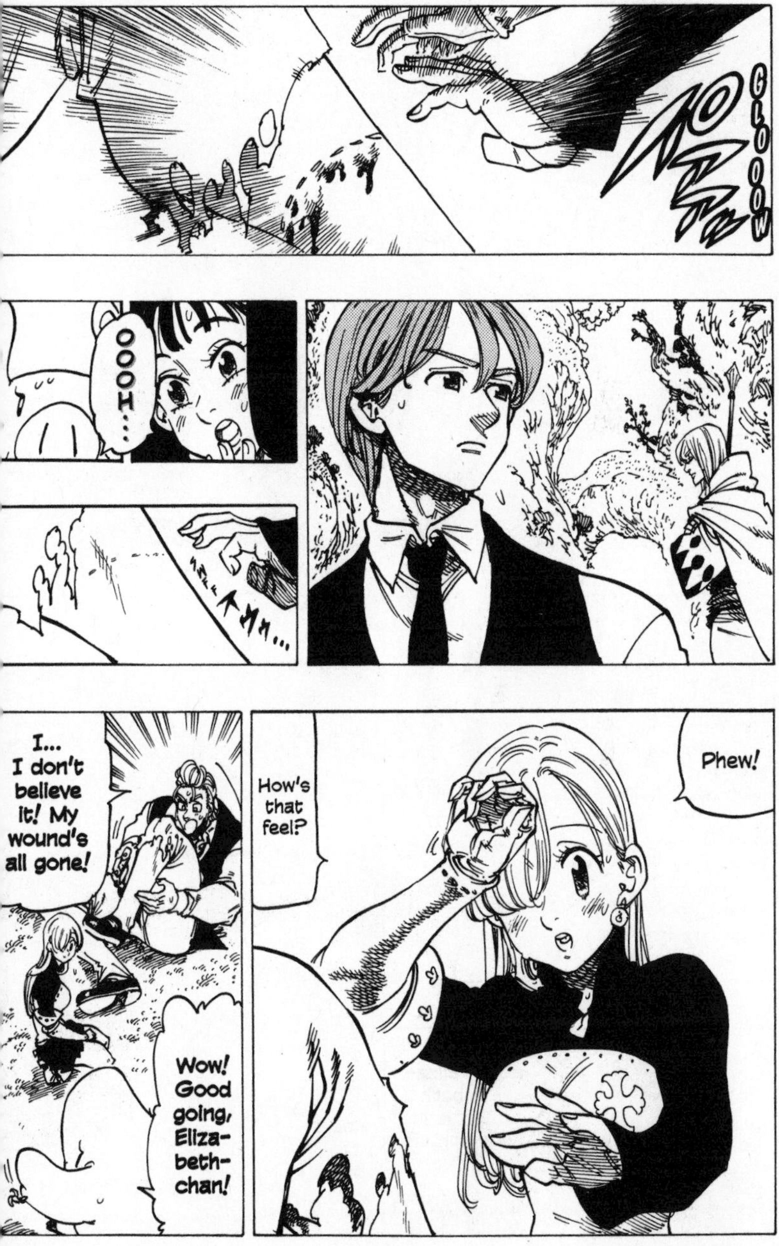
GLOOOW
OOOH...
SNFF
Phew!
How's that feel?
I... I don't believe it! My wound's all gone!
Wow! Good going, Eliza-beth-chan!

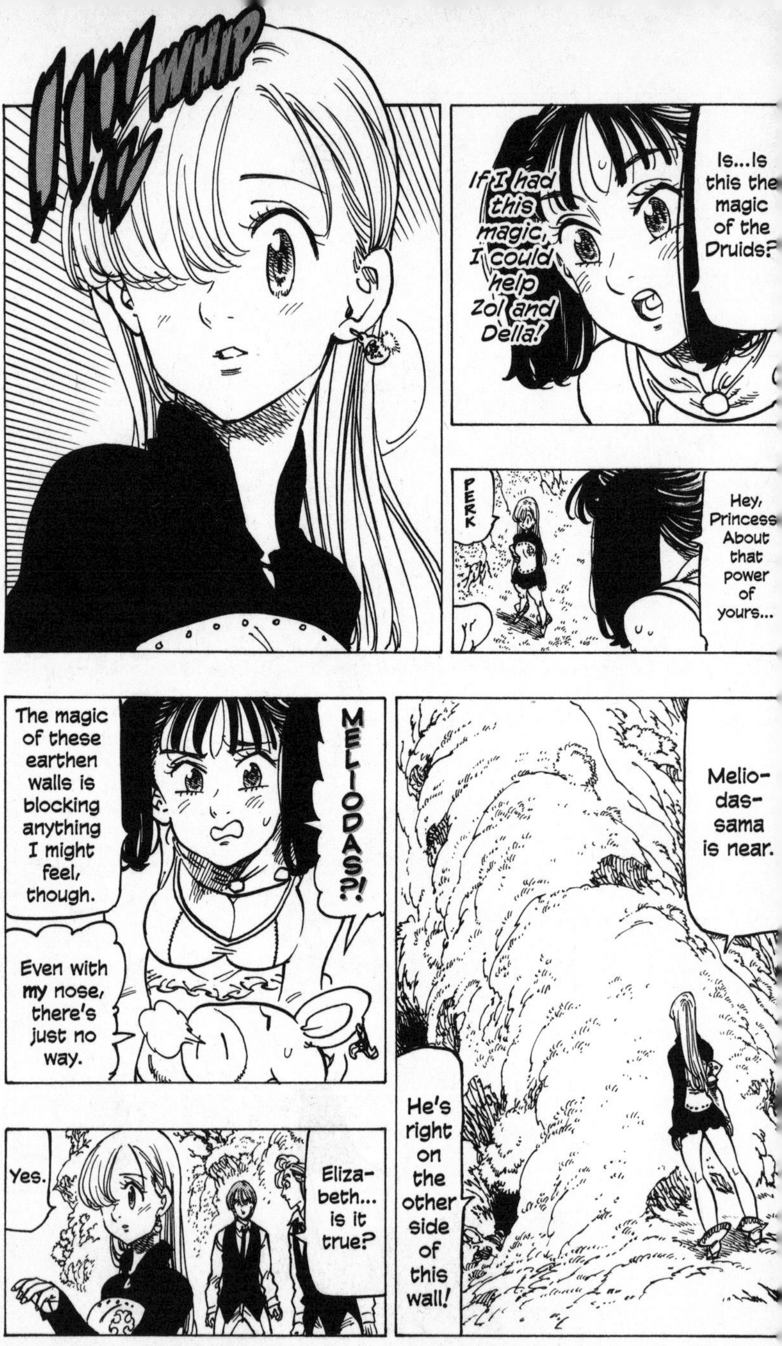

Is...Is this the magic of the Druids?
If I had this magic, I could help Zol and Della!
Hey, Princess About that power of yours...
PERK
WHIP
Melio-das-sama is near.
He's right on the other side of this wall!
MELIODAS?!
The magic of these earthen walls is blocking anything I might feel, though.
Even with my nose, there's just no way.
Eliza-beth... is it true?
Yes.

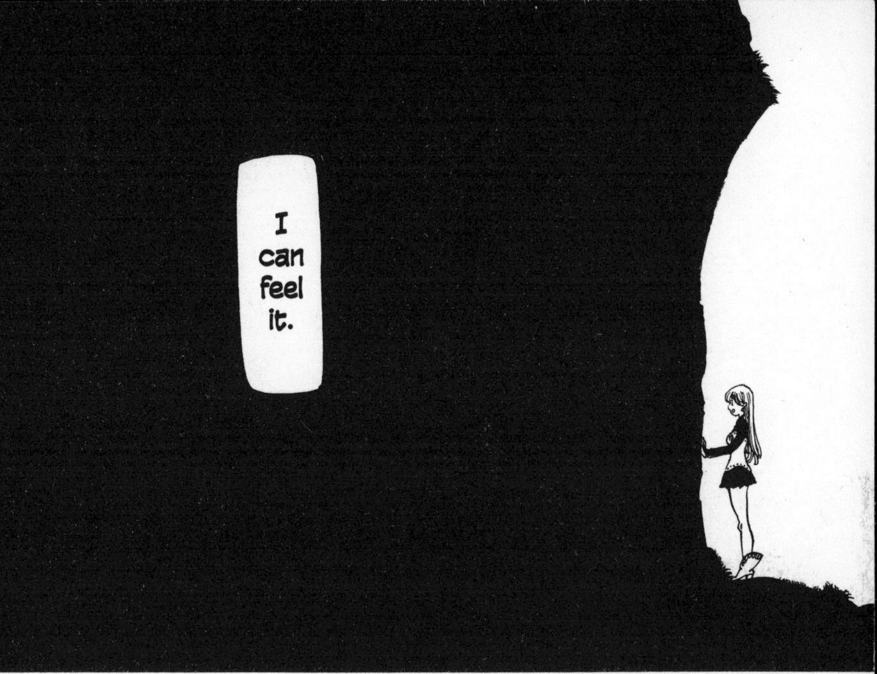
I can feel it.
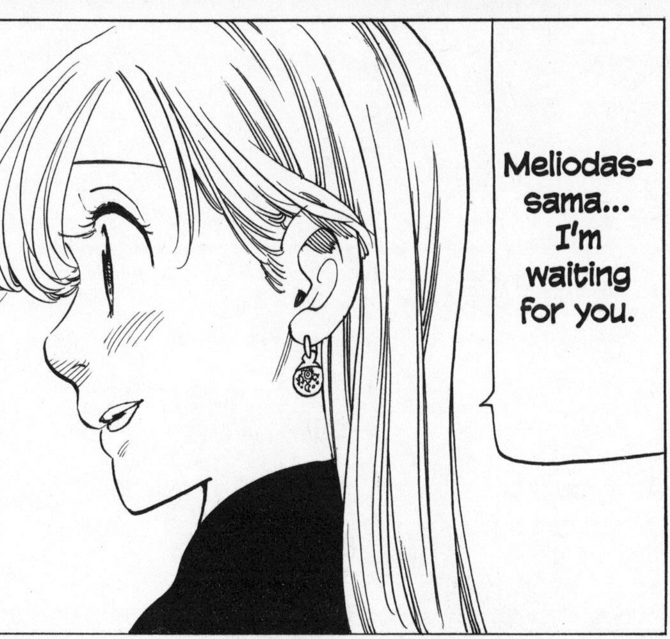
Meliodas-sama... I'm waiting for you.

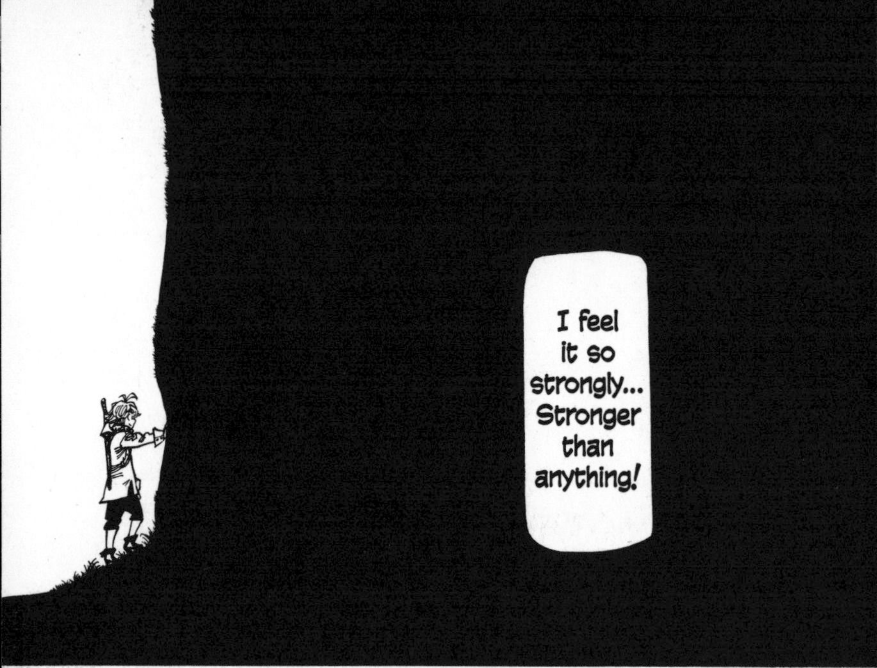
I feel it so strongly... Stronger than anything!
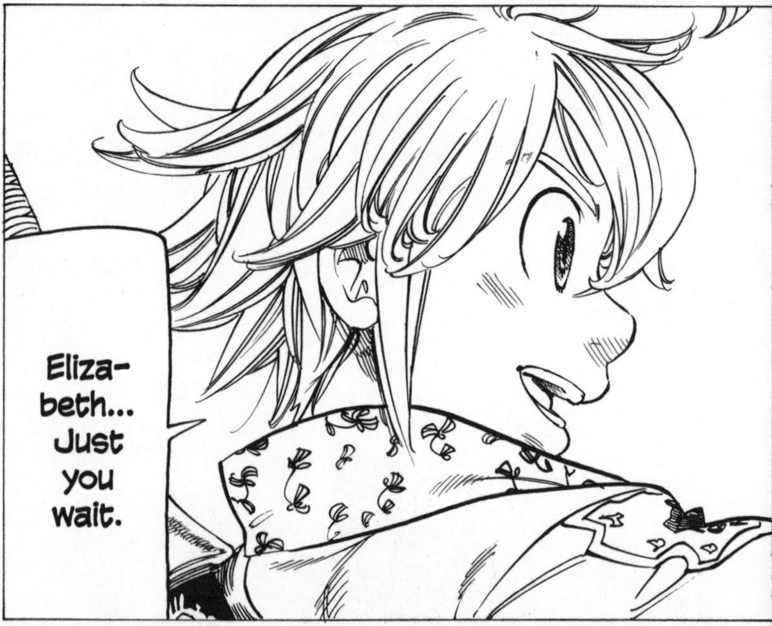
Eliza-beth... Just you wait.

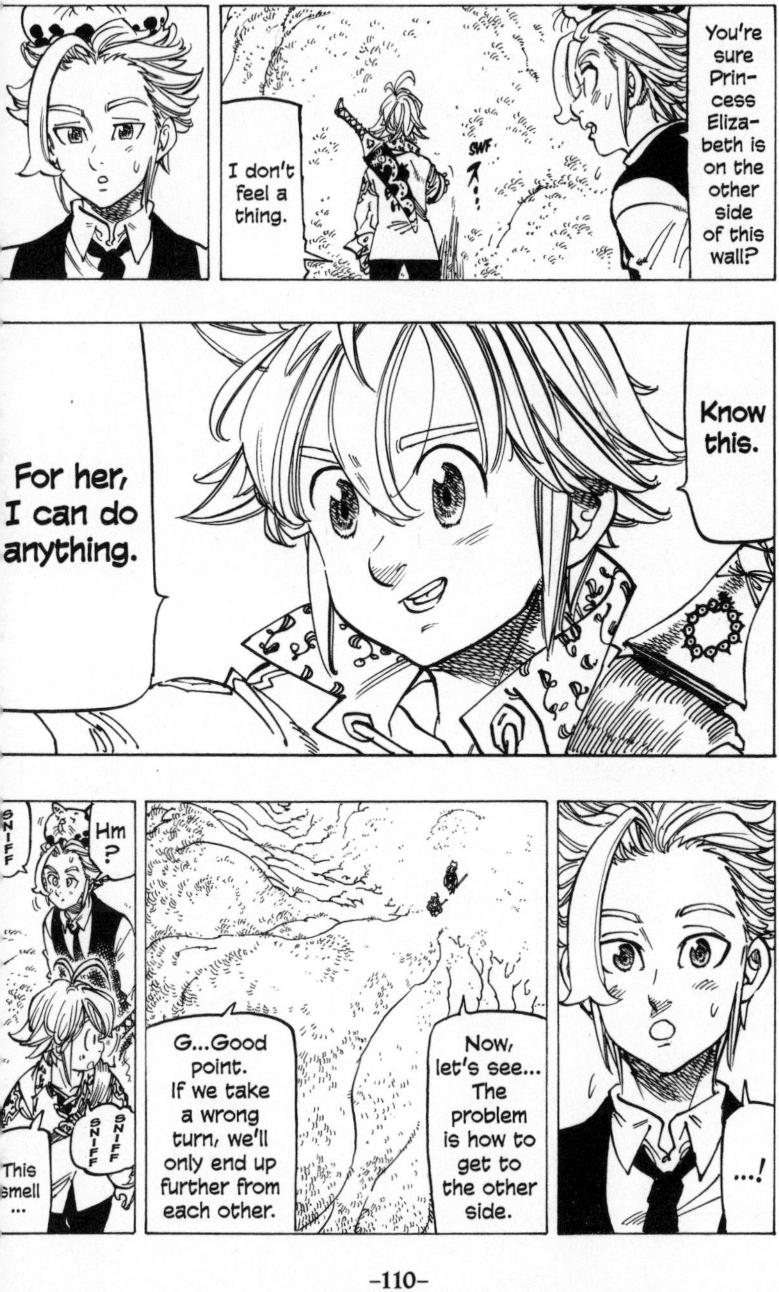
You're sure Princess Elizabeth is on the other side of this wall?
SWF
I don't feel a thing.
Know this.
For her, I can do anything.
...!
Now, let's see... The problem is how to get to the other side.
G...Good point. If we take a wrong turn, we'll only end up further from each other.
Hm?
SNIFF
SNIFF SNIFF
This smell ...

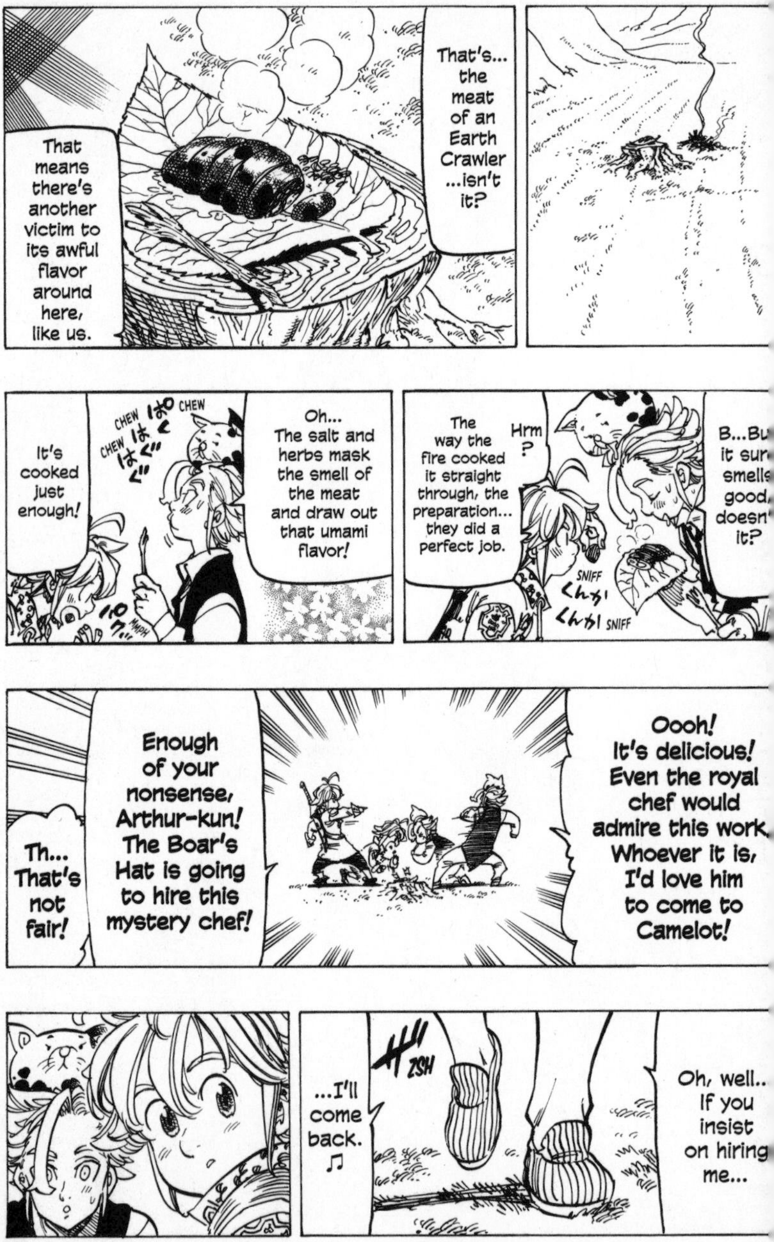
That's... the meat of an Earth Crawler ...isn't it?
That means there's another victim to its awful flavor around here, like us.
B...Bu it sur smells good, doesn' it?
SNIFF くんか くんか SNIFF
Hrm?
The way the fire cooked it straight through, the preparation... they did a perfect job.
Oh... The salt and herbs mask the smell of the meat and draw out that umami flavor!
CHEW ぱく CHEW はぐ CHEW はぐ
It's cooked just enough!
パク MMPH
Oooh! It's delicious! Even the royal chef would admire this work. Whoever it is, I'd love him to come to Camelot!
Enough of your nonsense, Arthur-kun! The Boar's Hat is going to hire this mystery chef!
Th... That's not fair!
Oh, well... If you insist on hiring me...
ZSH
...I'll come back. ♫

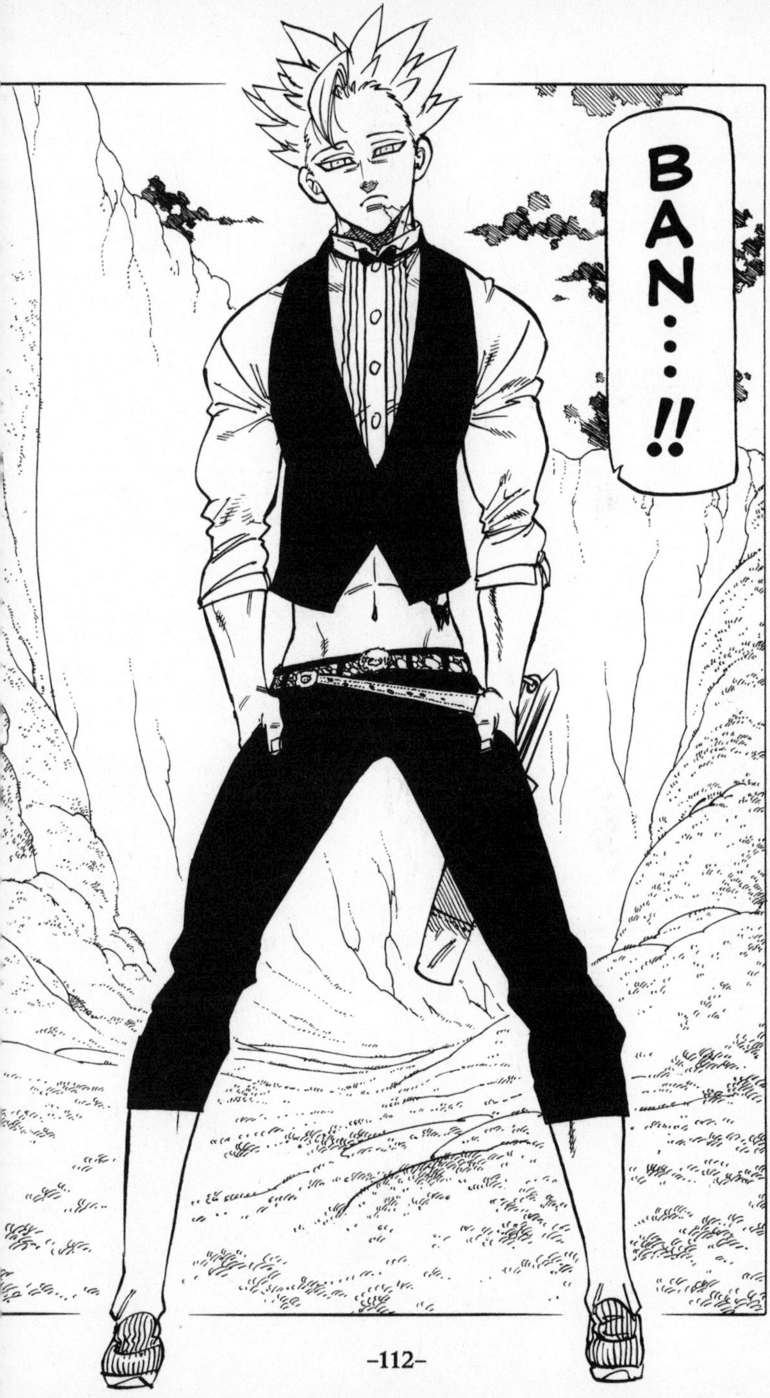
BAN...!!

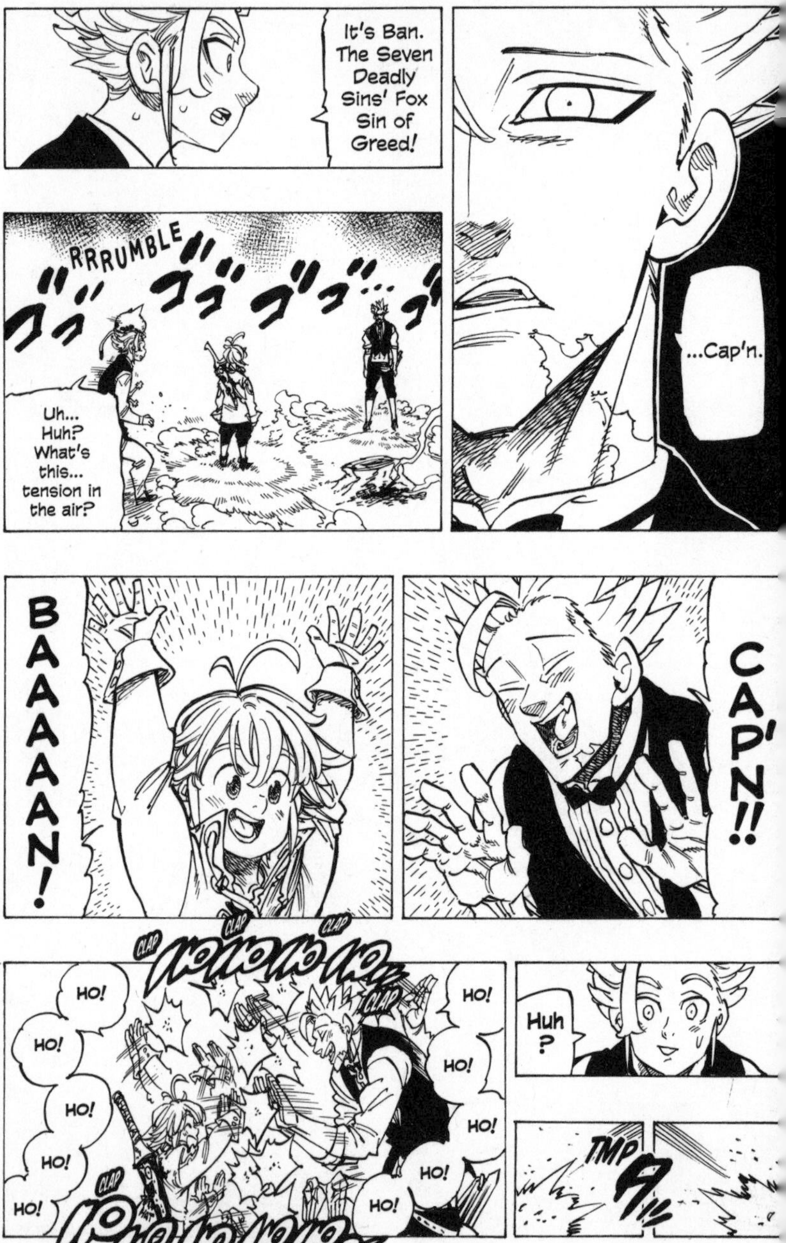
It's Ban. The Seven Deadly Sins' Fox Sin of Greed!
RRRUMBLE
Uh... Huh? What's this... tension in the air?
...Cap'n.
BAAAAAN!
CAP'N!!
CLAP
HO!
HO!
HO!
HO!
HO!
HO!
HO!
HO!
HO!
HO!
CLAP
Huh?
TMP

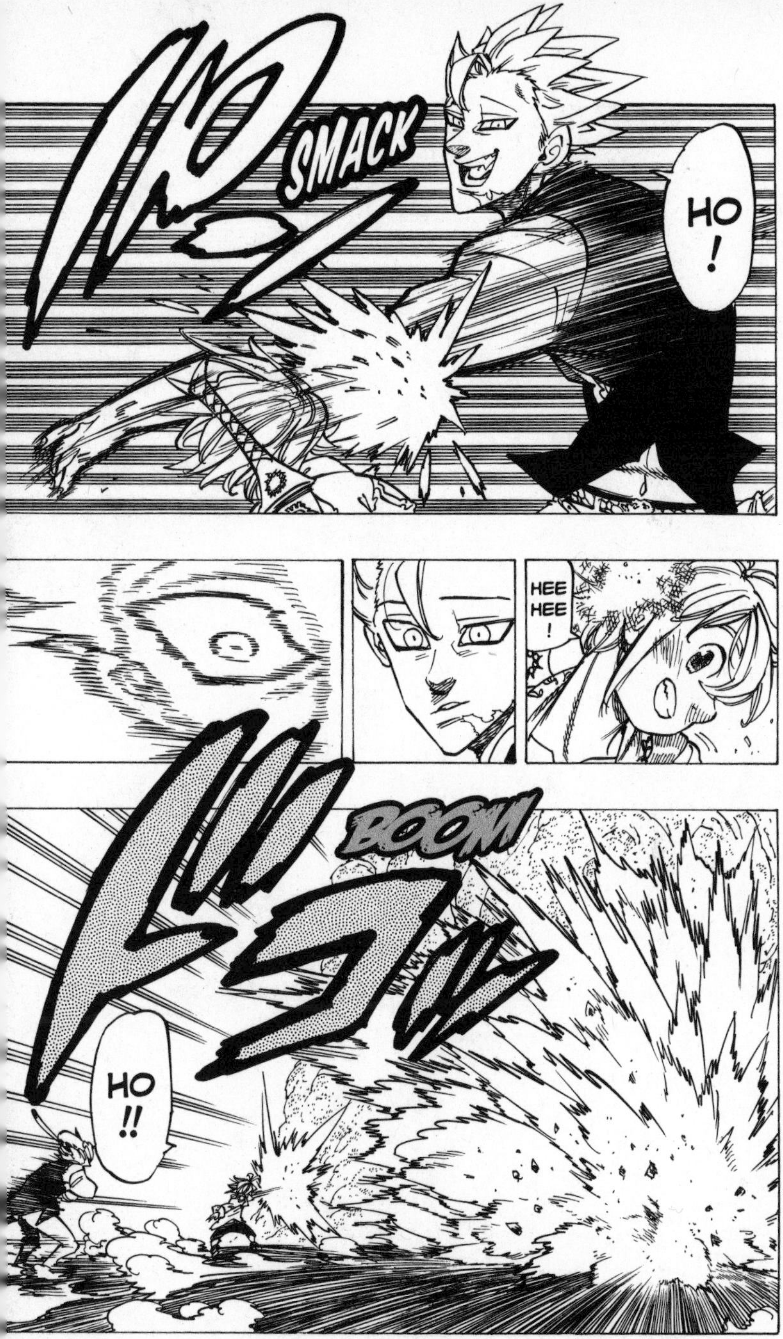
SMACK
HO!
HEE HEE!
BOOM
HO!!

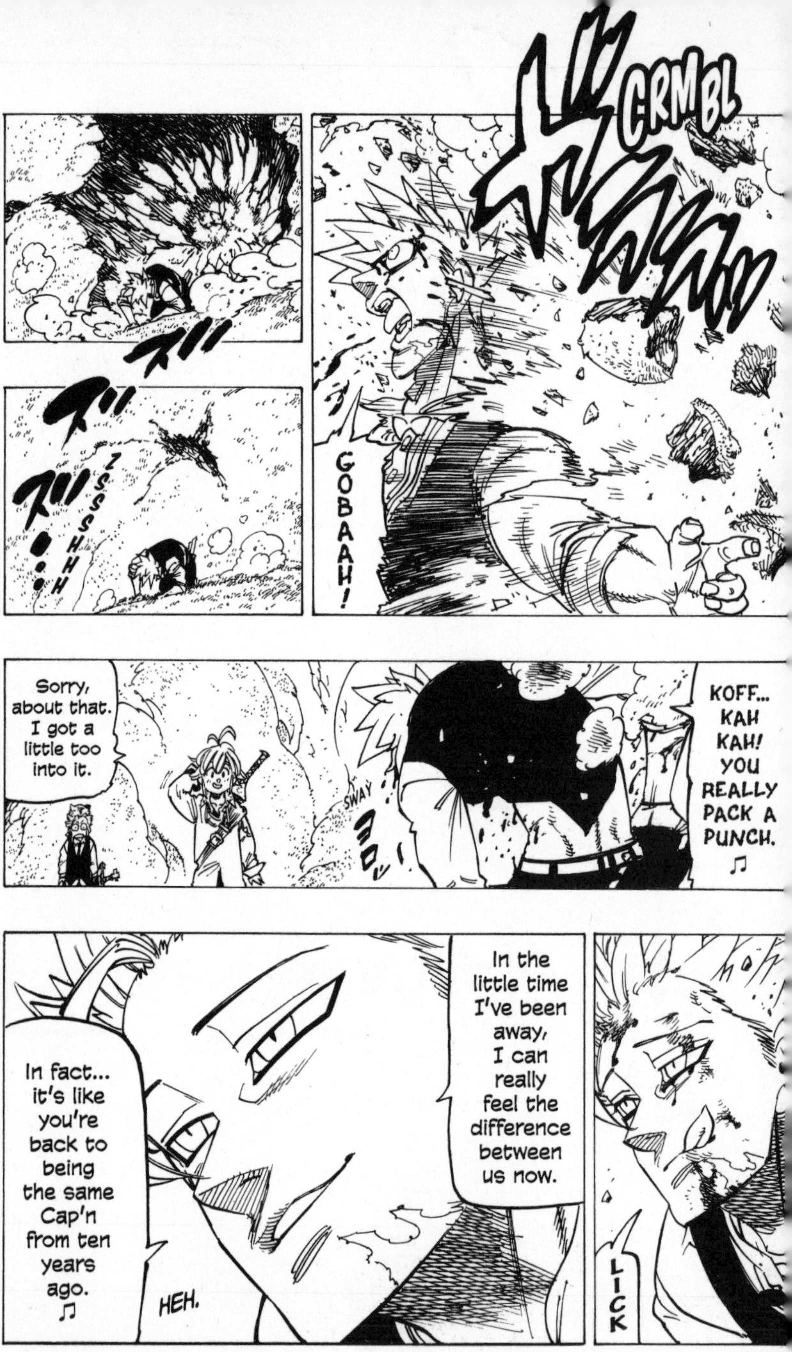
CRMBL
GOBAAAH!
ZSSSHHH
KOFF... KAH KAH! YOU REALLY PACK A PUNCH. ♫
SWAY
Sorry, about that. I got a little too into it.
LICK
In the little time I've been away, I can really feel the difference between us now.
In fact... it's like you're back to being the same Cap'n from ten years ago. ♫
HEH.

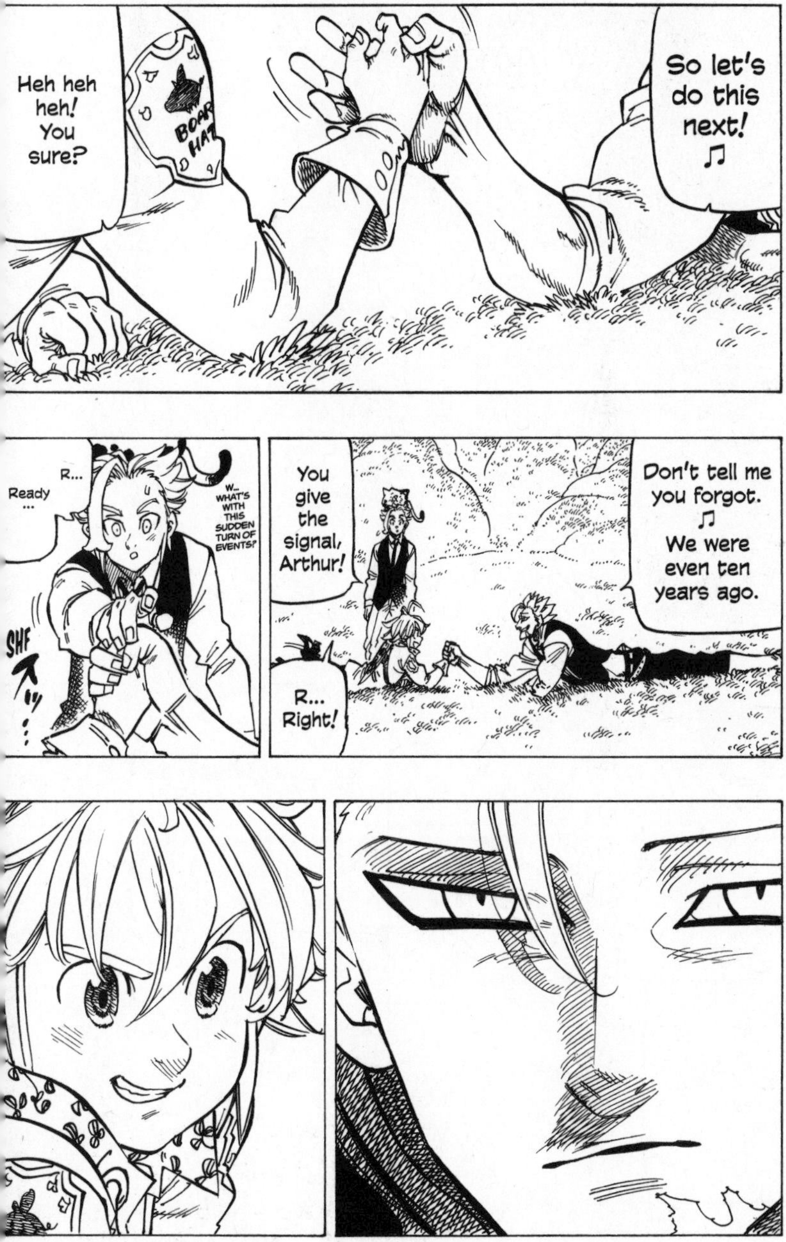
So let's do this next! ♫
Heh heh heh! You sure?
Don't tell me you forgot. ♫ We were even ten years ago.
You give the signal, Arthur!
R... Right!
W... WHAT'S WITH THIS SUDDEN TURN OF EVENTS?
R...
Ready ...
SHF

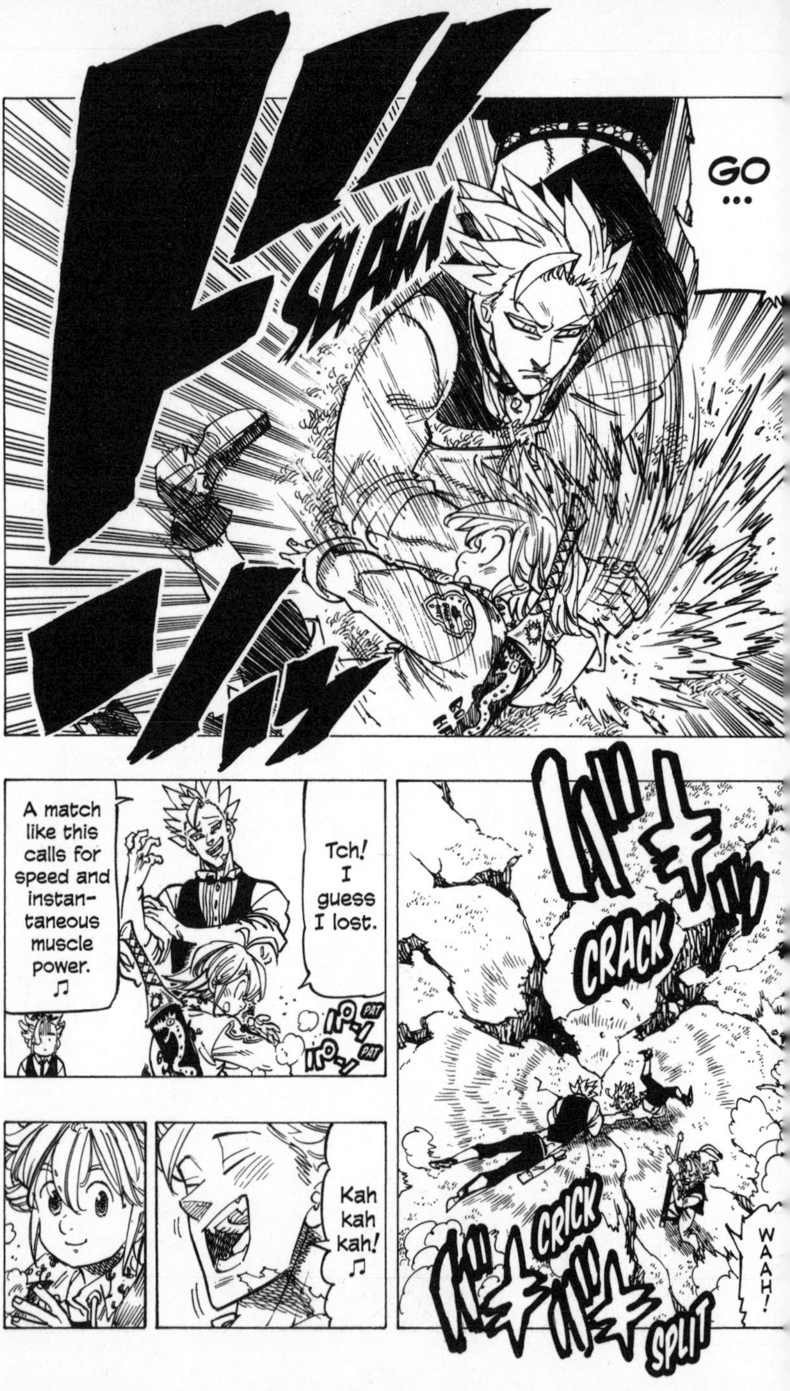
GO...
SLAM
CRACK
CRICK
SPLIT
WAAH!
Tch! I guess I lost.
A match like this calls for speed and instan-taneous muscle power. ♫
PAT
PAT
Kah kah kah! ♫

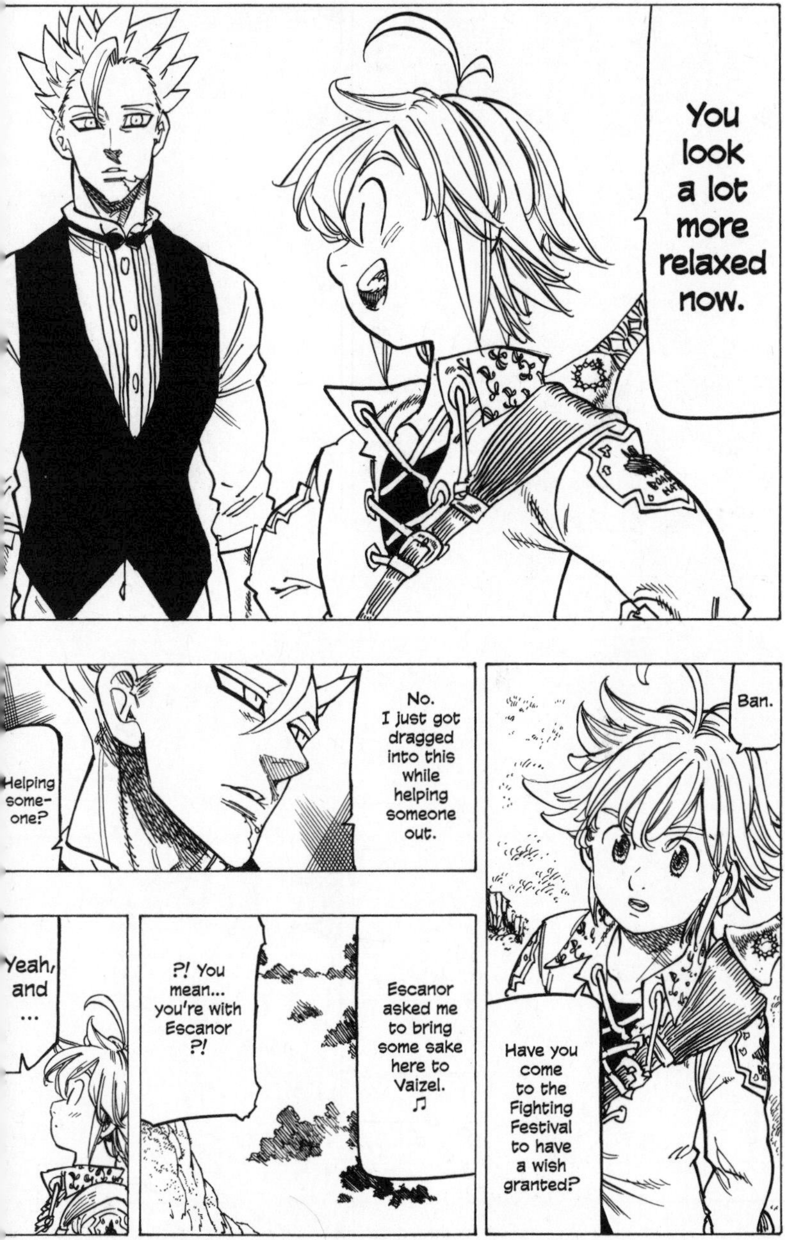
You look a lot more relaxed now.
Ban.
Have you come to the Fighting Festival to have a wish granted?
No. I just got dragged into this while helping someone out.
Helping some-one?
Escanor asked me to bring some sake here to Vaizel. ♫
?! You mean... you're with Escanor ?!
Yeah, and ...

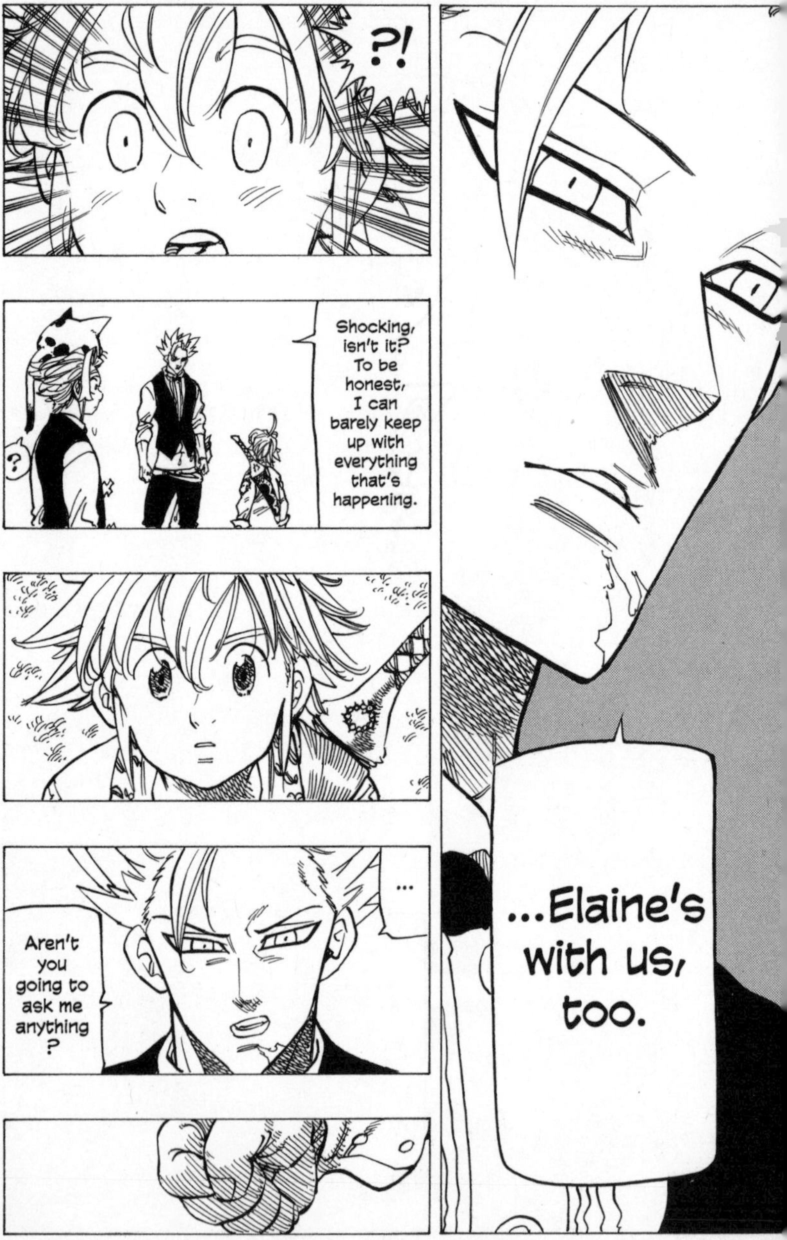
...Elaine's with us, too.
?!
Shocking, isn't it? To be honest, I can barely keep up with everything that's happening.
?
...
Aren't you going to ask me anything?

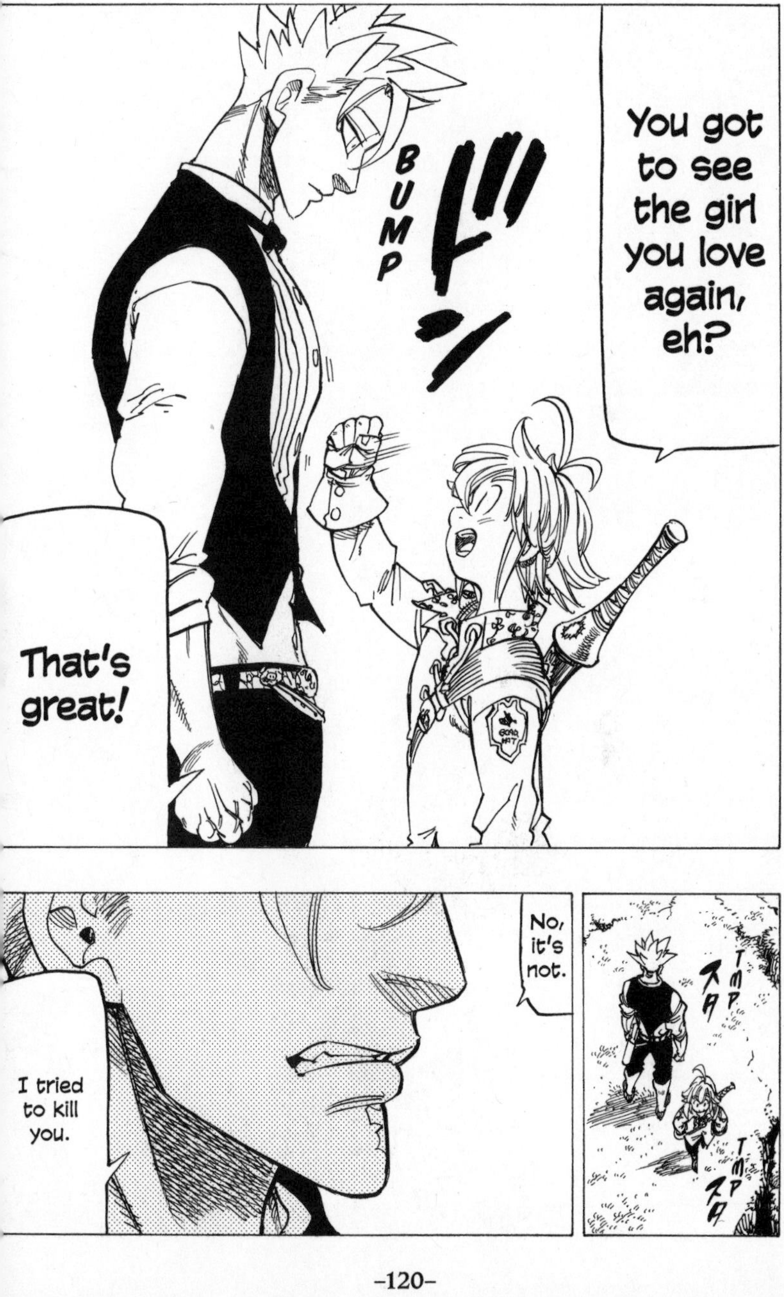
You got to see the girl you love again, eh?
BUMP
That's great!
TMP
TMP
No, it's not.
I tried to kill you.

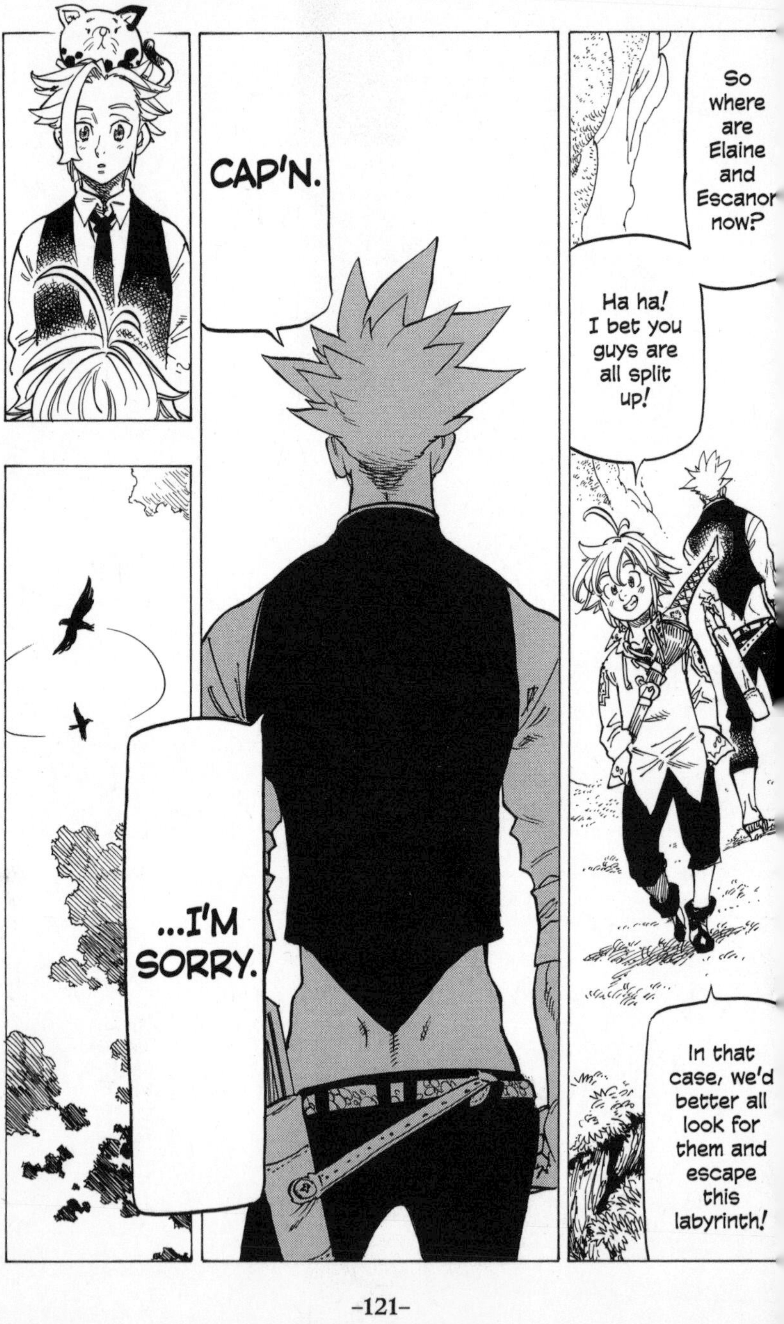
So where are Elaine and Escanor now?
Ha ha! I bet you guys are all split up!
In that case, we'd better all look for them and escape this labyrinth!
CAP'N.
...I'M SORRY.

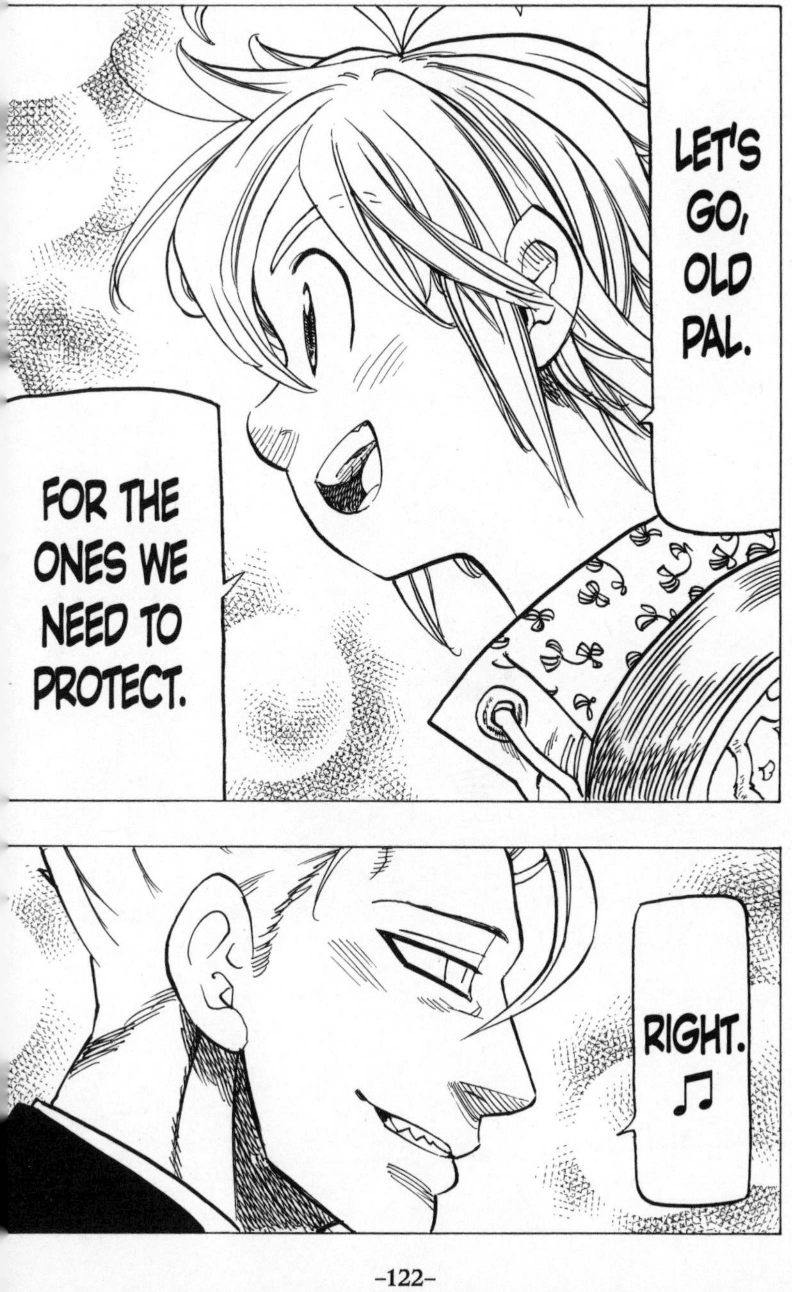
LET'S GO, OLD PAL.
FOR THE ONES WE NEED TO PROTECT.
RIGHT. ♫

Chapter 160 - Go!! Break Through

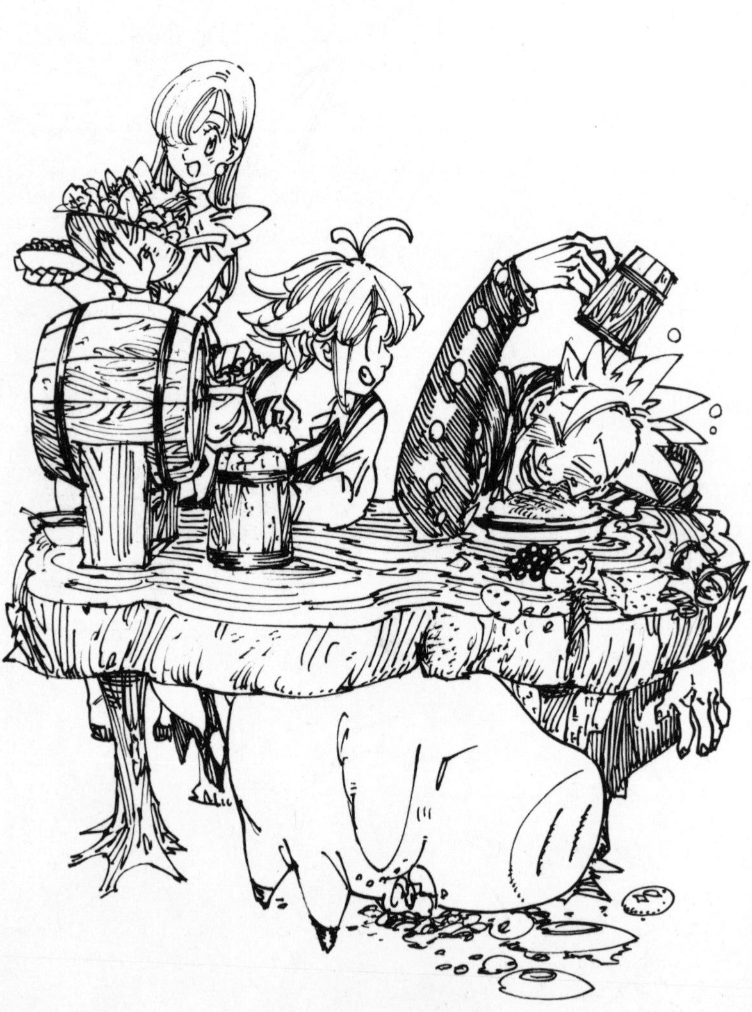

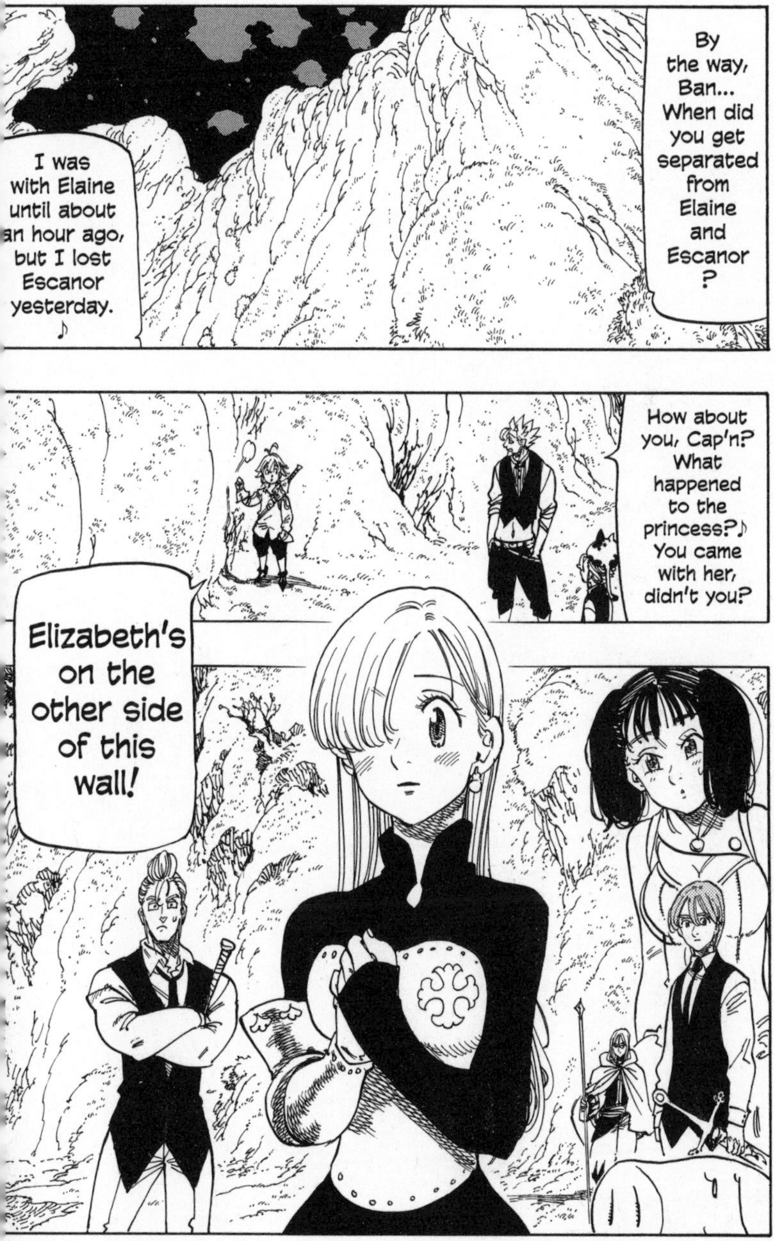
By the way, Ban... When did you get separated from Elaine and Escanor?
I was with Elaine until about an hour ago, but I lost Escanor yesterday. ♪
How about you, Cap'n? What happened to the princess?♪ You came with her, didn't you?
Elizabeth's on the other side of this wall!

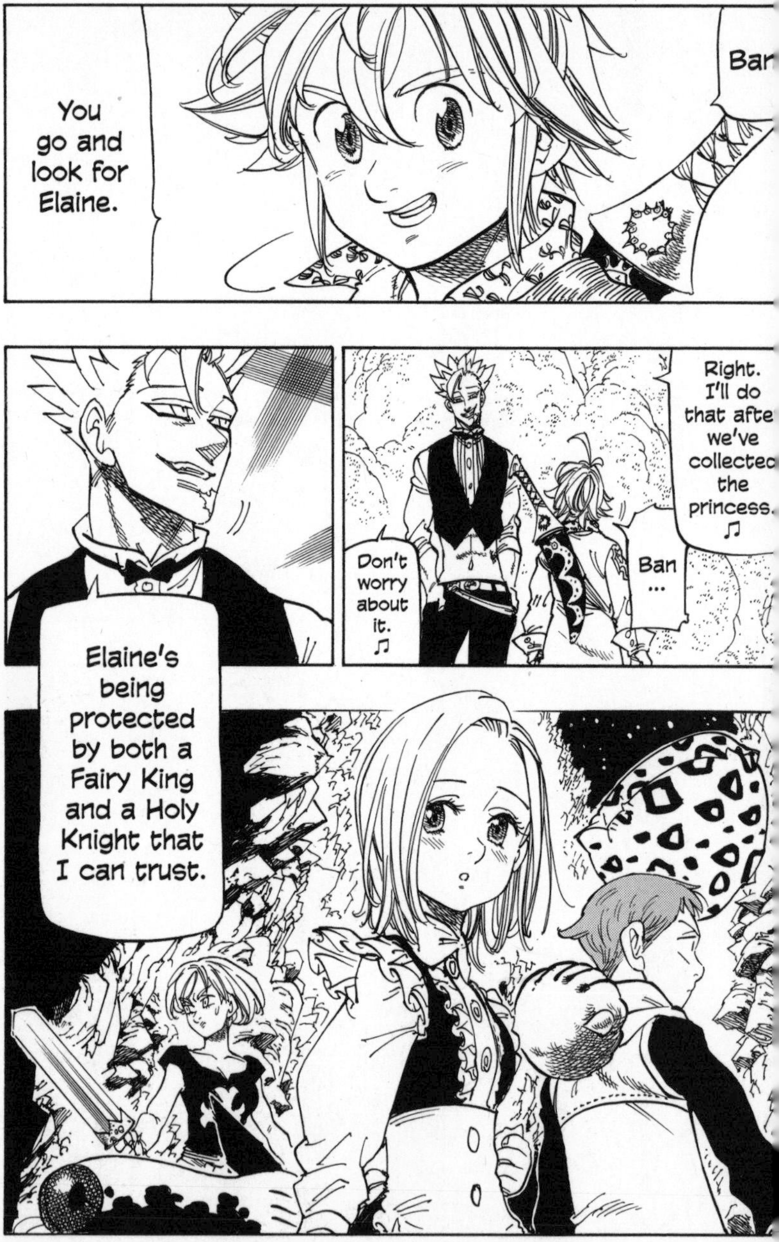
Ban
You go and look for Elaine.
Right. I'll do that afte we've collected the princess. ♫
Ban ...
Don't worry about it. ♫
Elaine's being protected by both a Fairy King and a Holy Knight that I can trust.

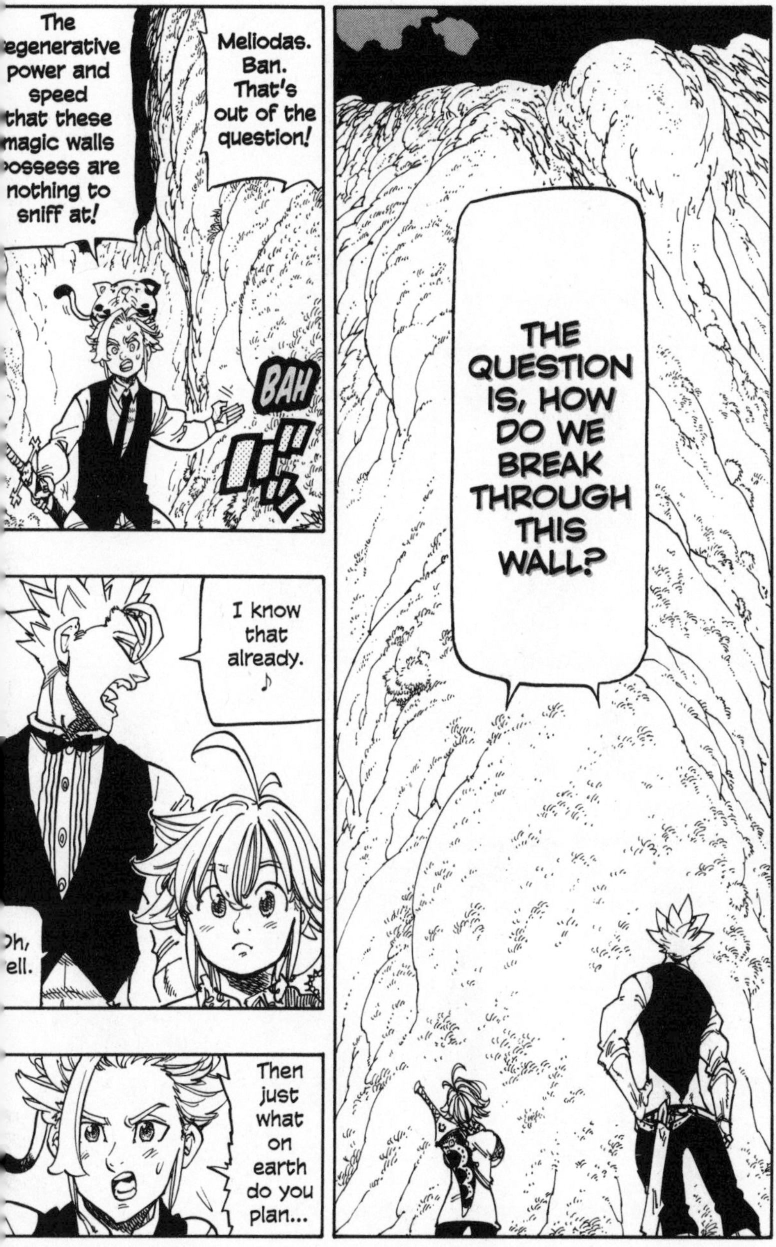
THE QUESTION IS, HOW DO WE BREAK THROUGH THIS WALL?
Meliodas. Ban. That's out of the question!
The regenerative power and speed that these magic walls possess are nothing to sniff at!
BAH
I know that already. ♪
Oh, well.
Then just what on earth do you plan...

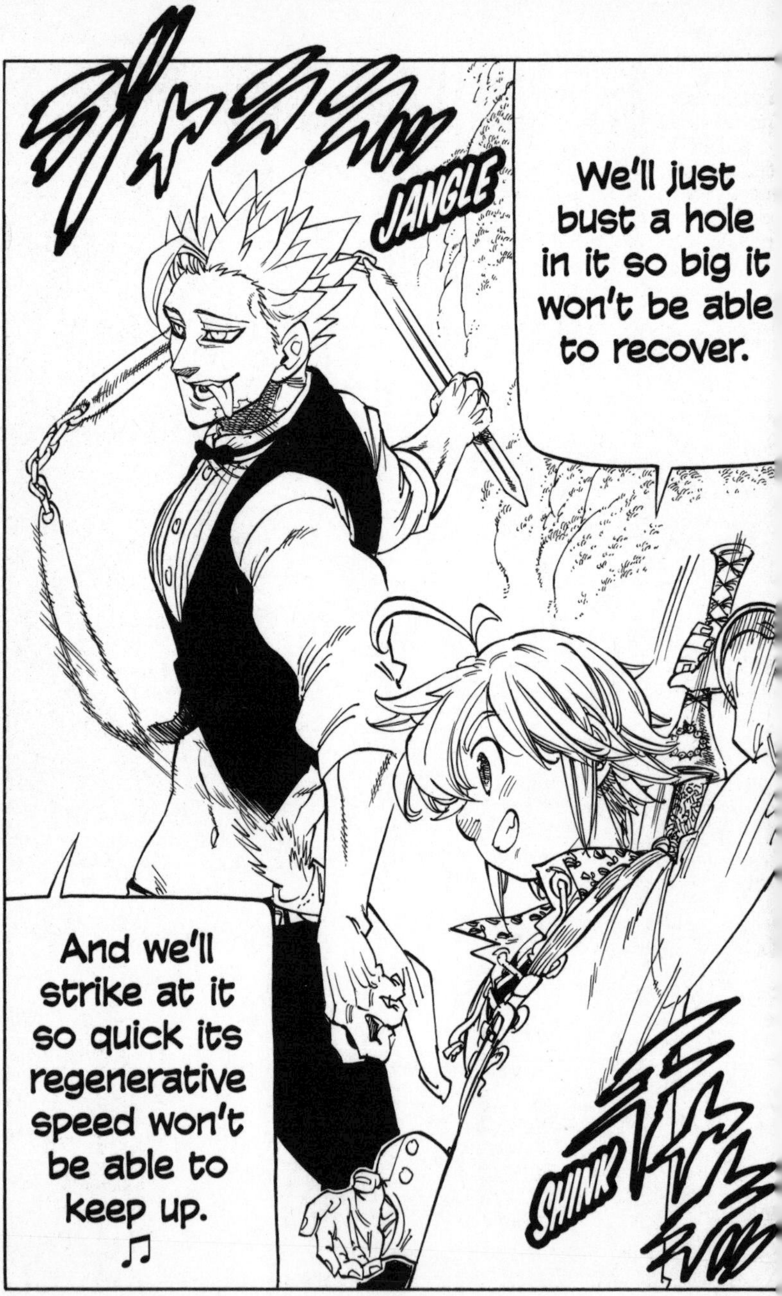
We'll just bust a hole in it so big it won't be able to recover.
JANGLE
And we'll strike at it so quick its regenerative speed won't be able to keep up. ♫
SHINK

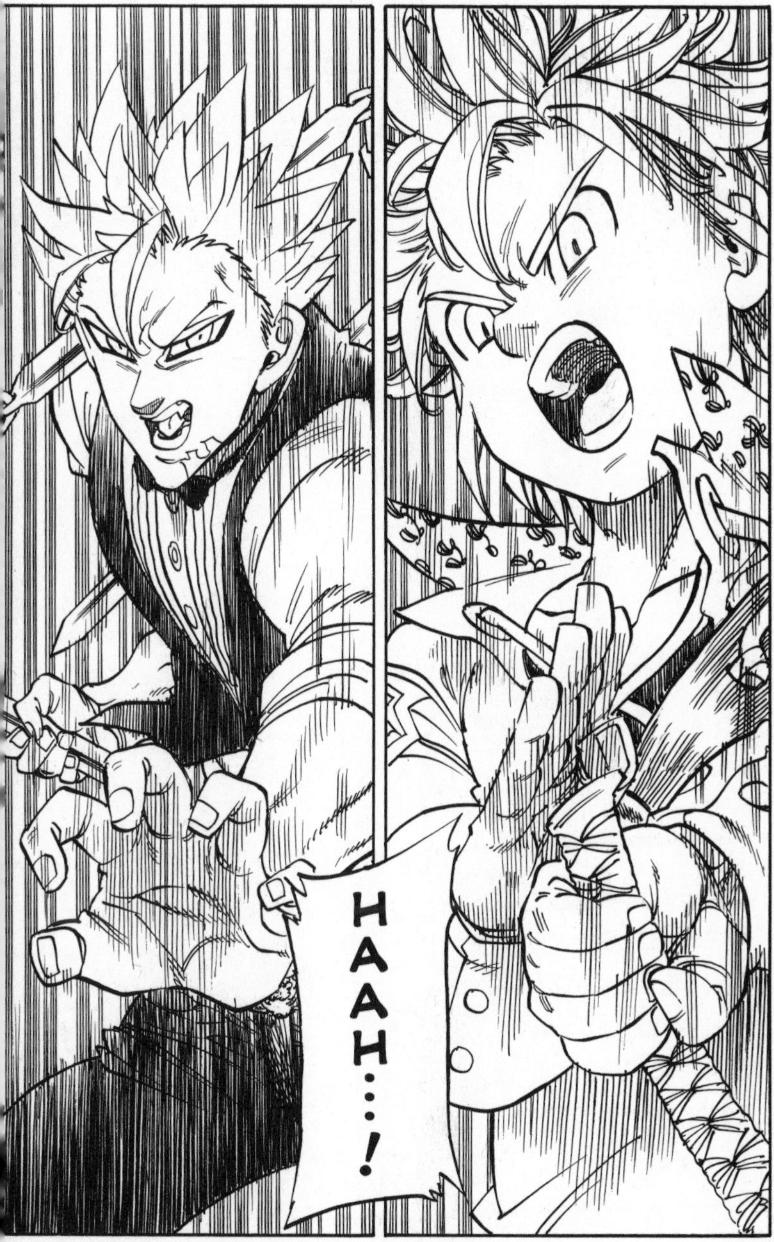
HAAH...!

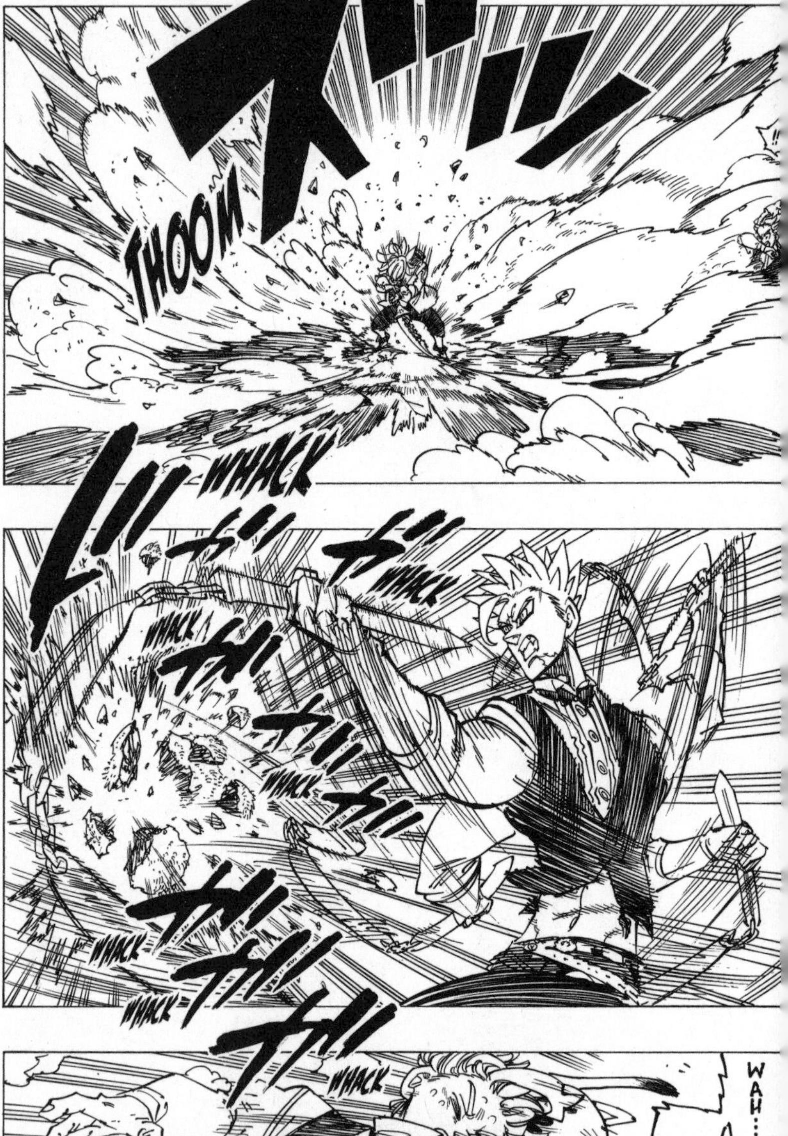
!!
THOOM
WHACK
WHACK
WHACK
WHACK
WHACK
WHACK
WHACK
WAH...
W-WHOA...!

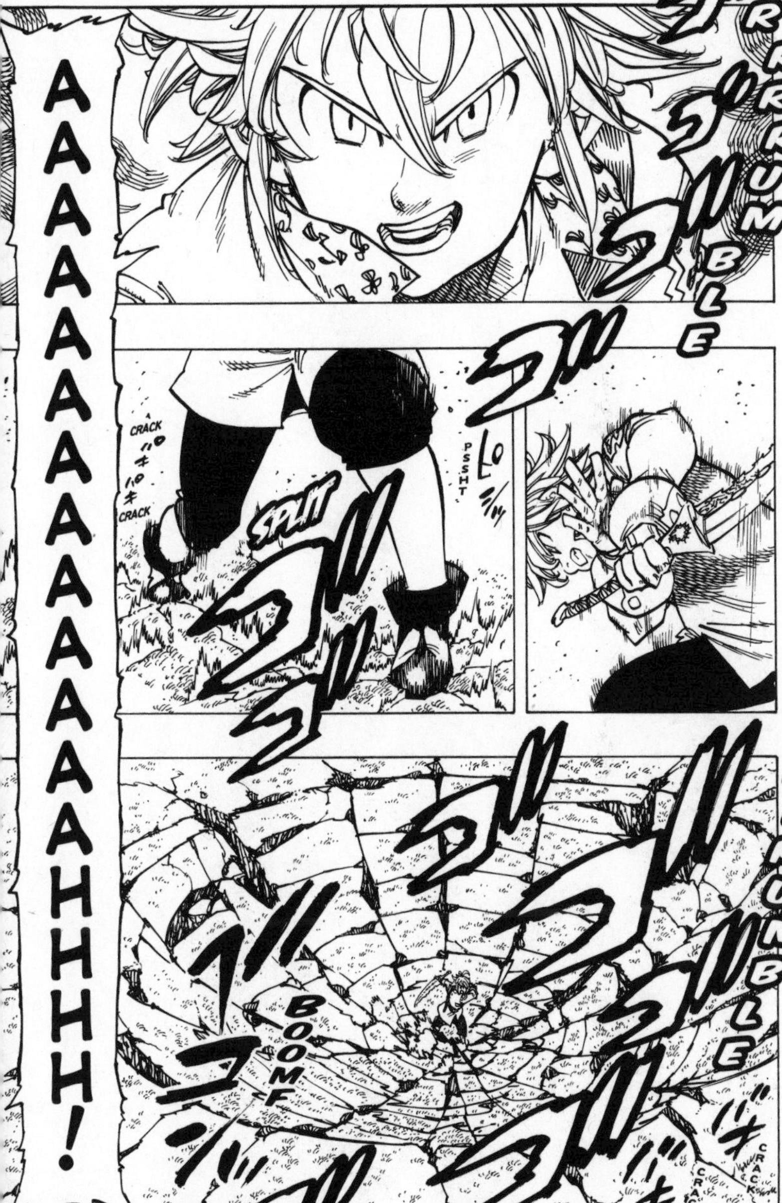
RRRRRUMBLE
PSSHT
SPLIT
CRACK
CRACK
RRRRUMBLE
CRACK
CRACK
BOOMF
AAAAAAAAAAAAAAAHHHH!

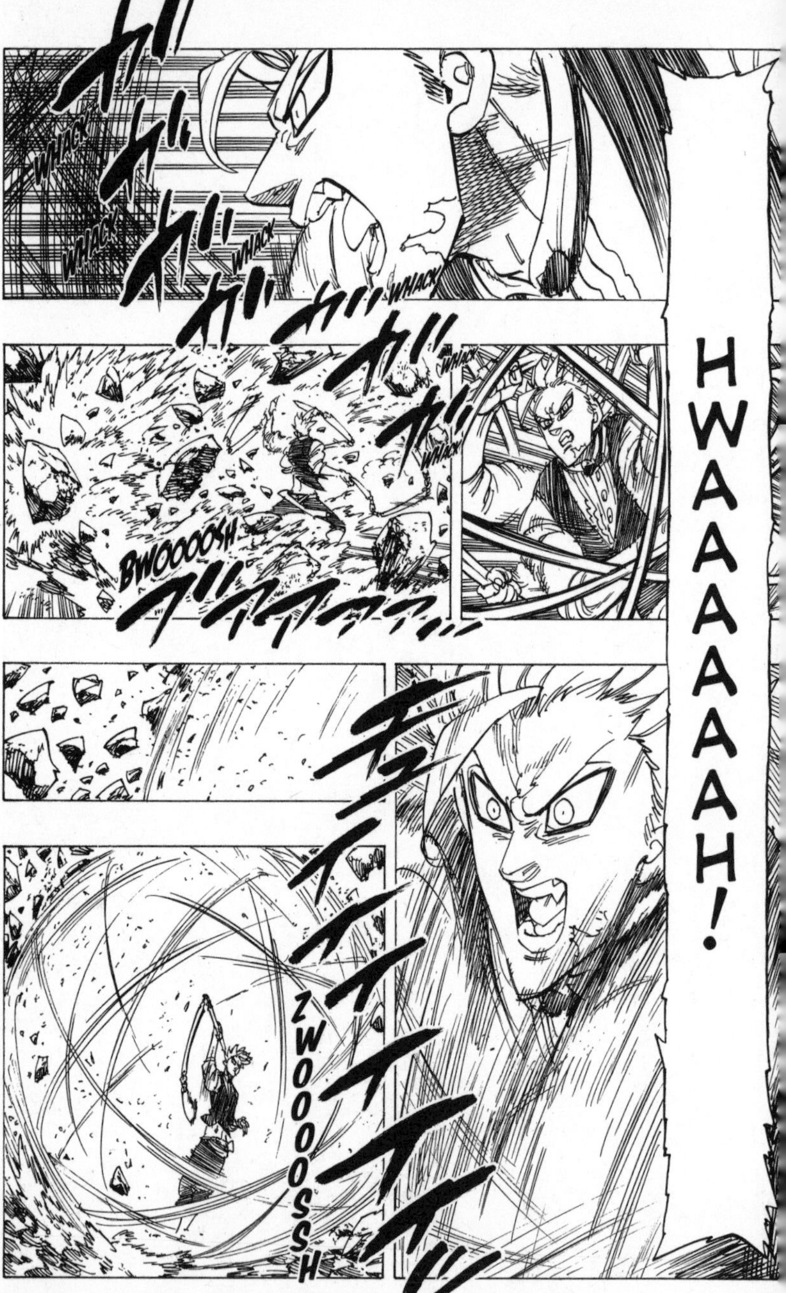
WHACK
WHACK
WHACK
WHACK
WHACK
WHACK
BWOOOOSH
ZWOOOOOOSSH
HWAAAAAAAH!

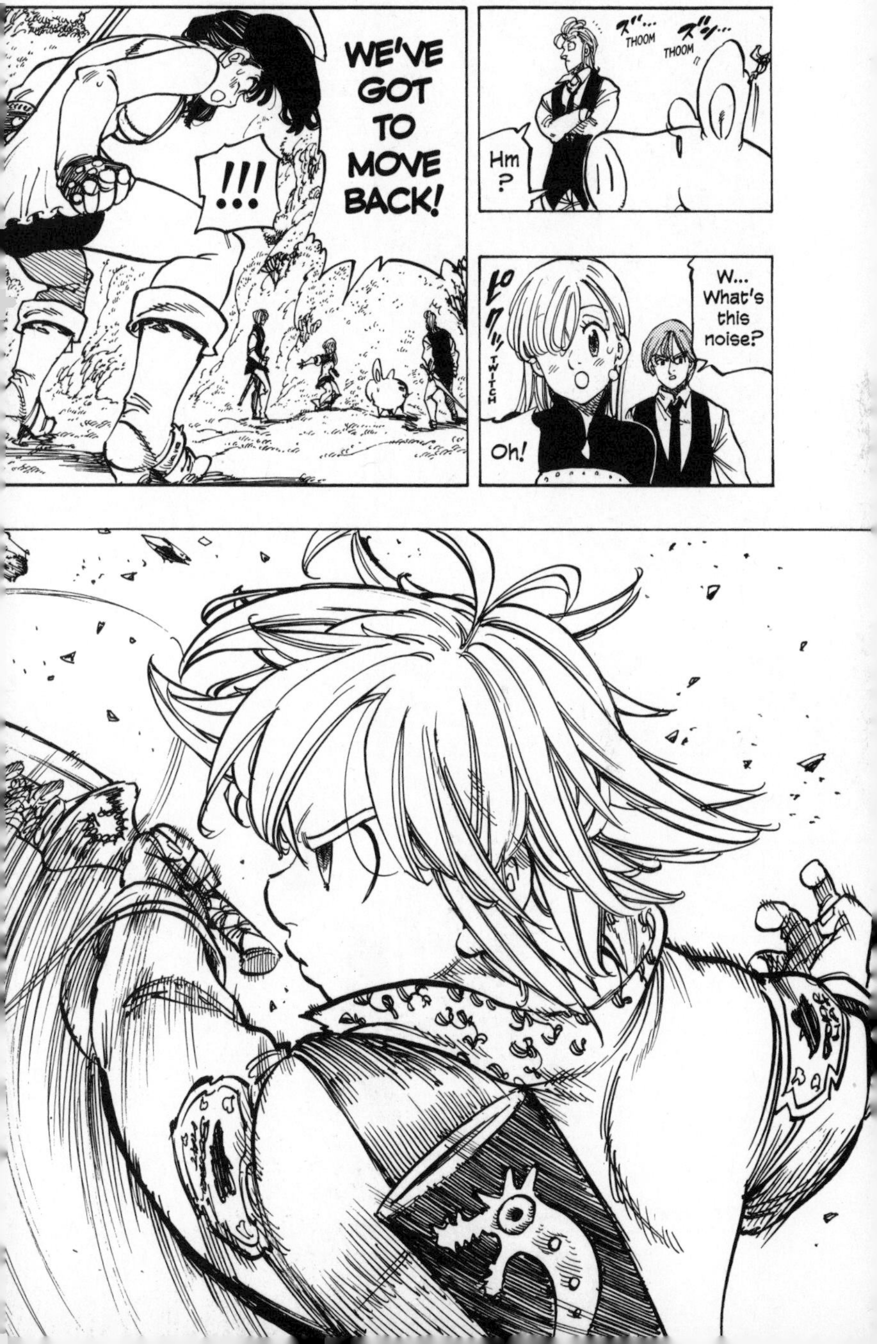
THOOM
THOOM
Hm?
W... What's this noise?
TWITCH
Oh!
WE'VE GOT TO MOVE BACK!
!!!

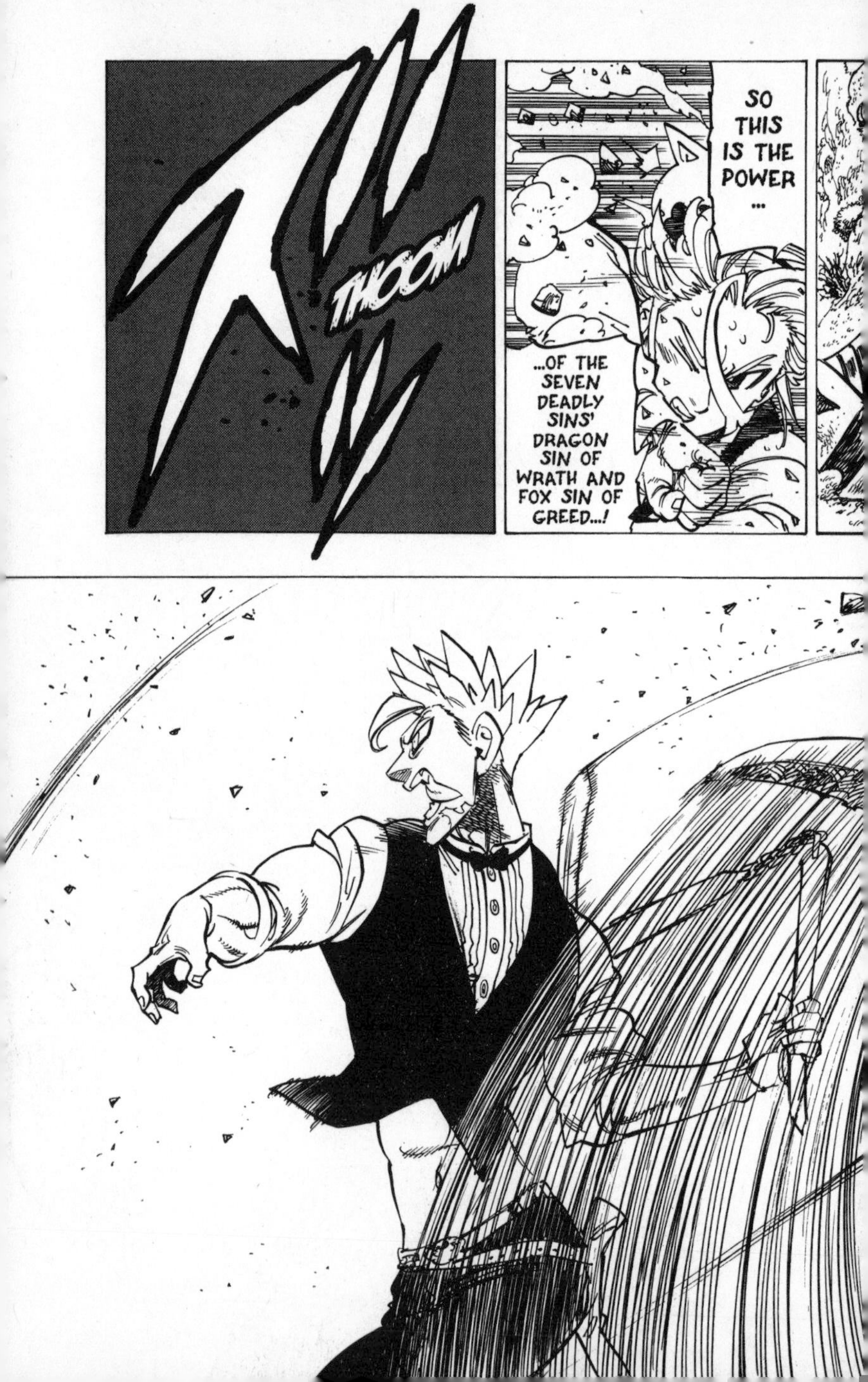
SO THIS IS THE POWER ...
...OF THE SEVEN DEADLY SINS' DRAGON SIN OF WRATH AND FOX SIN OF GREED...!
THOOM

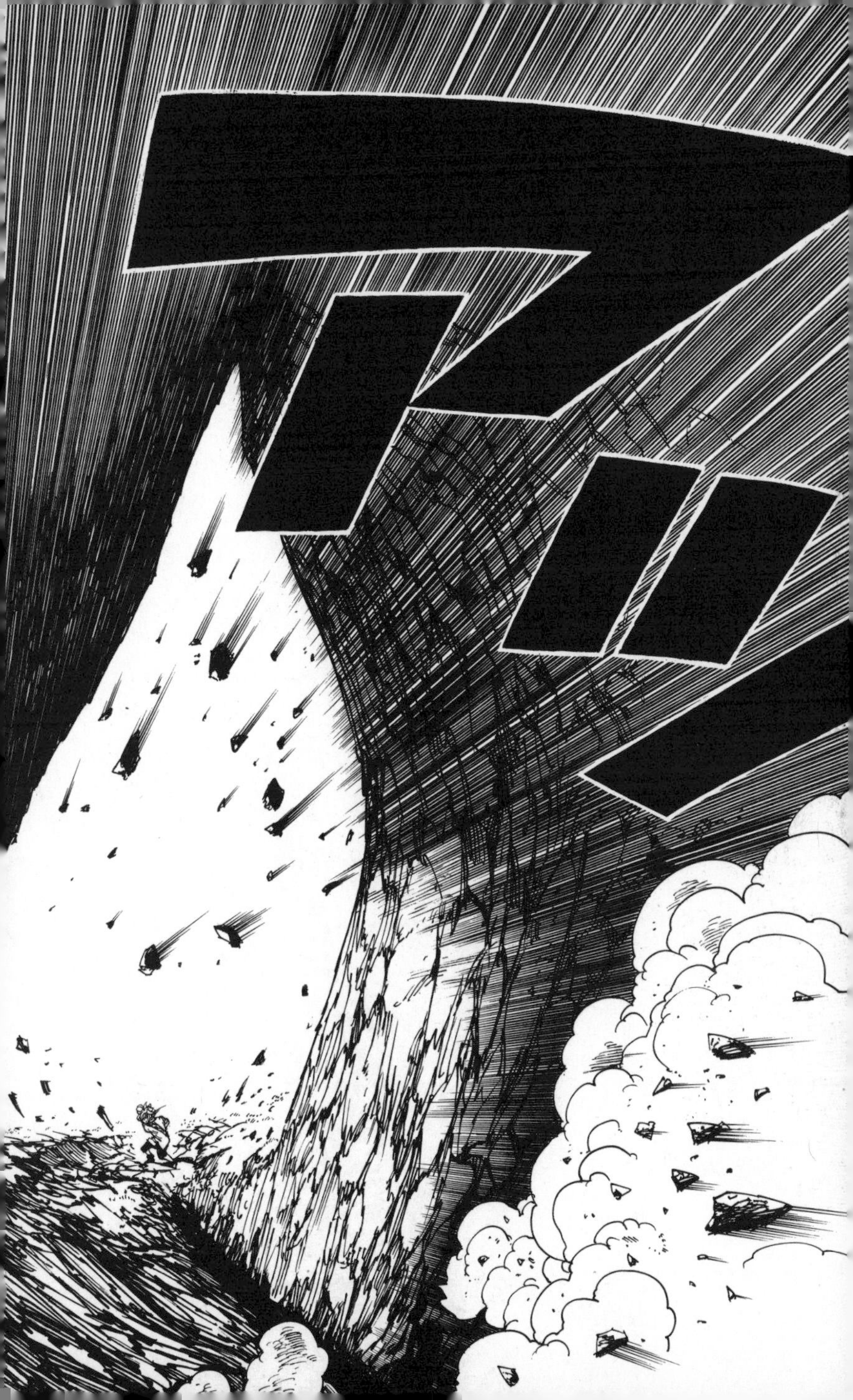

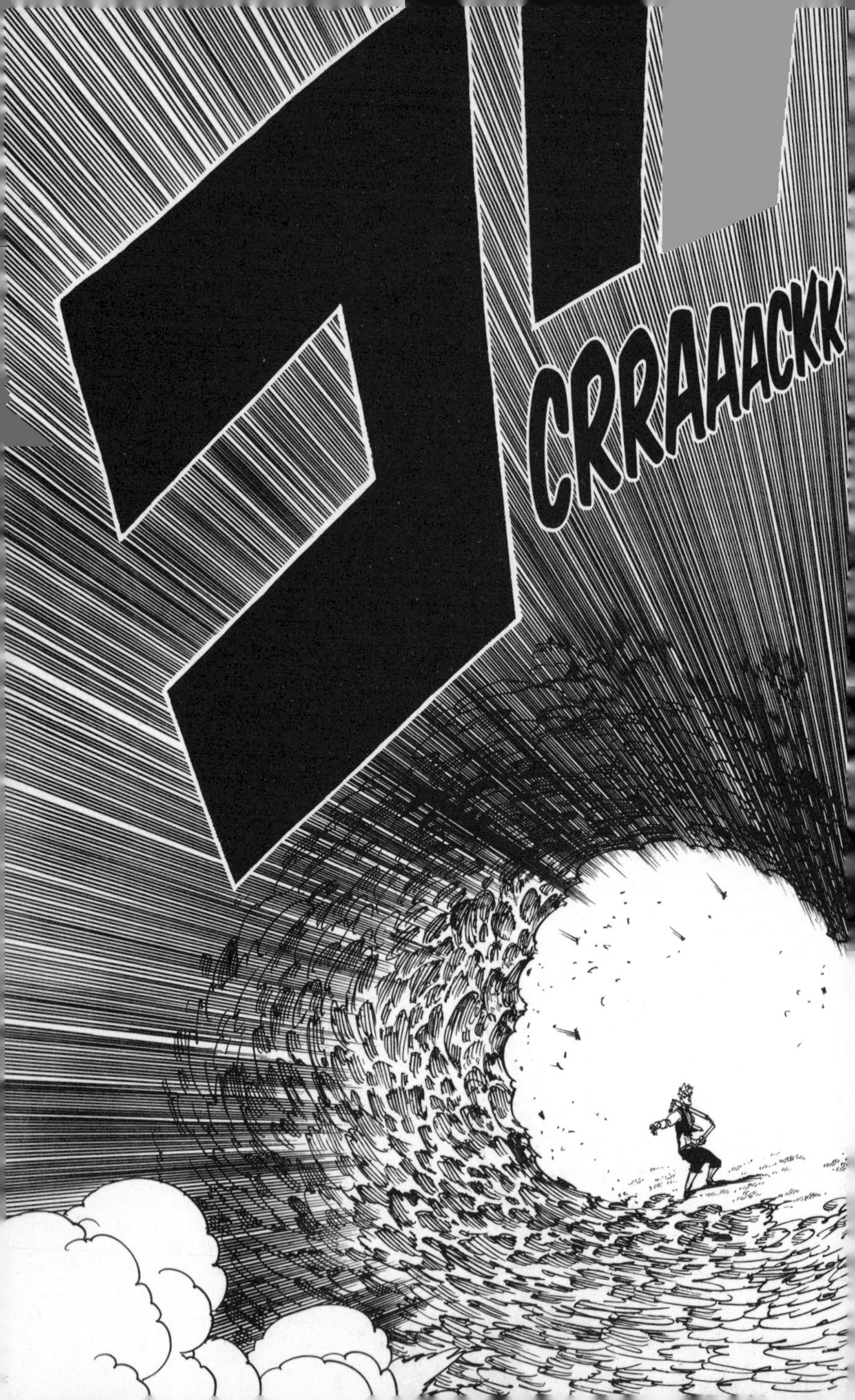
CRRAAACKK

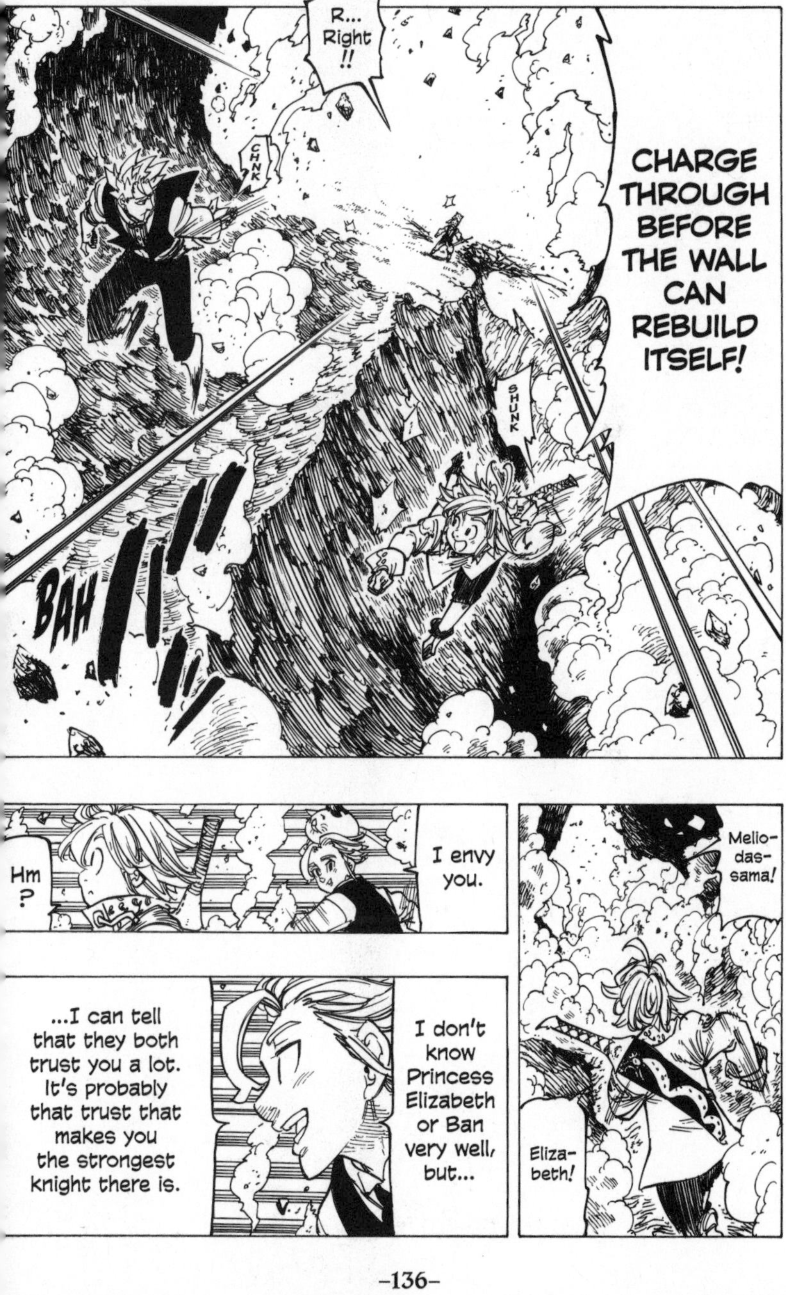
CHARGE THROUGH BEFORE THE WALL CAN REBUILD ITSELF!
R... Right!!
CHNK
SHUNK
BAH
Melio-das-sama!
Eliza-beth!
I envy you.
Hm?
I don't know Princess Elizabeth or Ban very well, but...
...I can tell that they both trust you a lot. It's probably that trust that makes you the strongest knight there is.

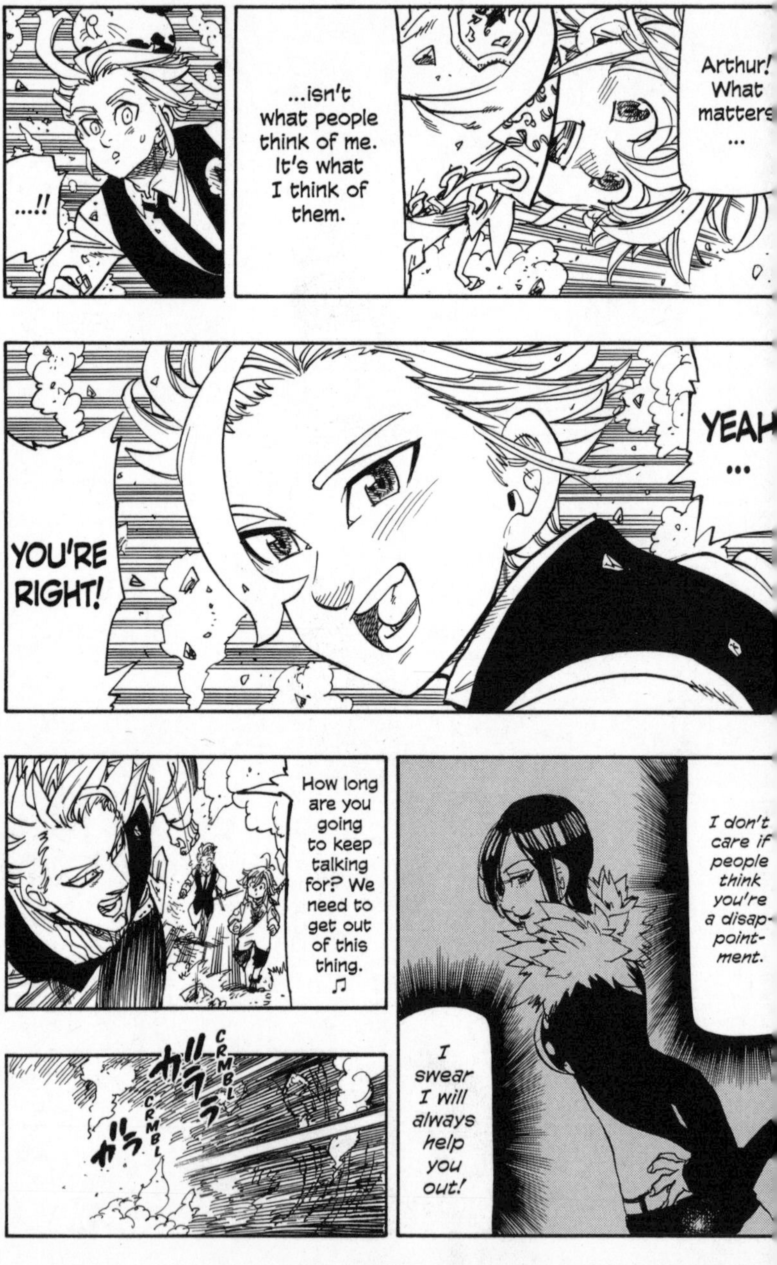
Arthur! What matters ...
...isn't what people think of me. It's what I think of them.
...!!
YEAH ...
YOU'RE RIGHT!
I don't care if people think you're a disappointment.
I swear I will always help you out!
How long are you going to keep talking for? We need to get out of this thing. ♫
CRMBL
CRMBL

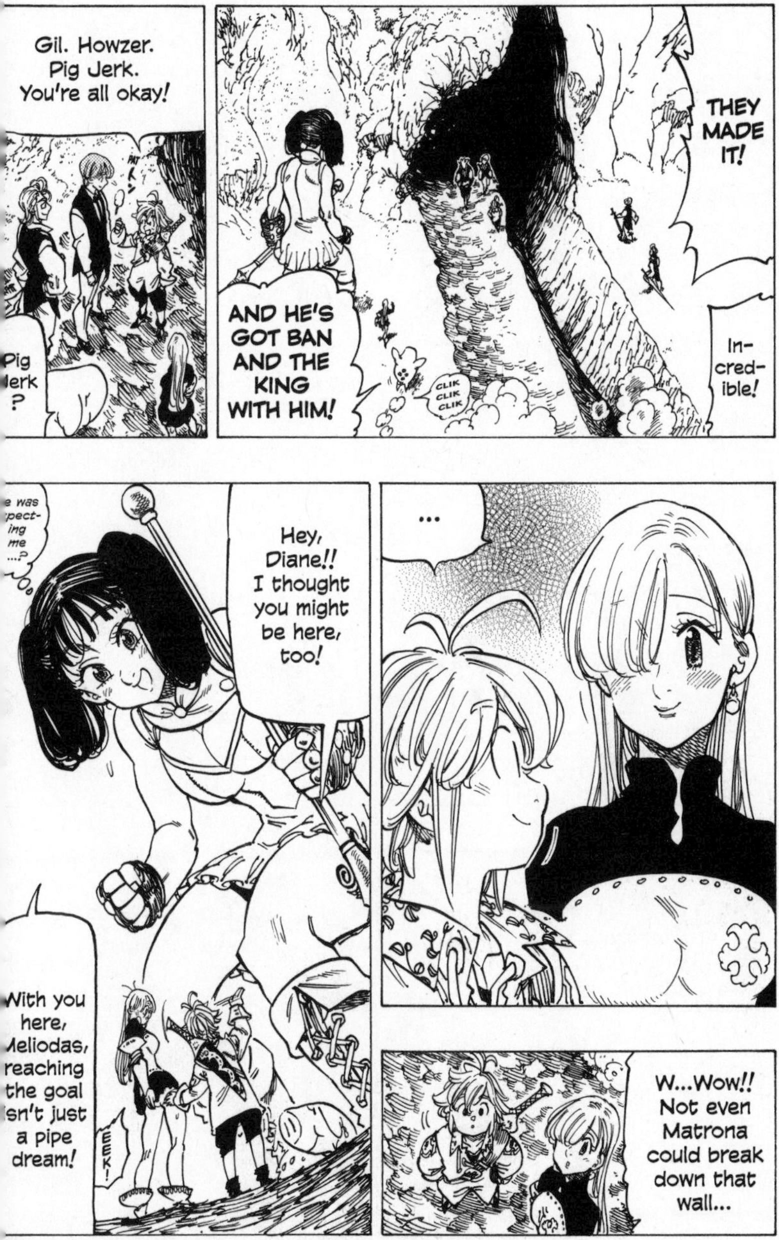
THEY MADE IT!
Incredible!
AND HE'S GOT BAN AND THE KING WITH HIM!
CLIK CLIK CLIK
Gil. Howzer. Pig Jerk. You're all okay!
Pig Jerk?
...
W...Wow!! Not even Matrona could break down that wall...
Hey, Diane!! I thought you might be here, too!
e was pect-ing me ...?
With you here, Meliodas, reaching the goal isn't just a pipe dream!
EEK!

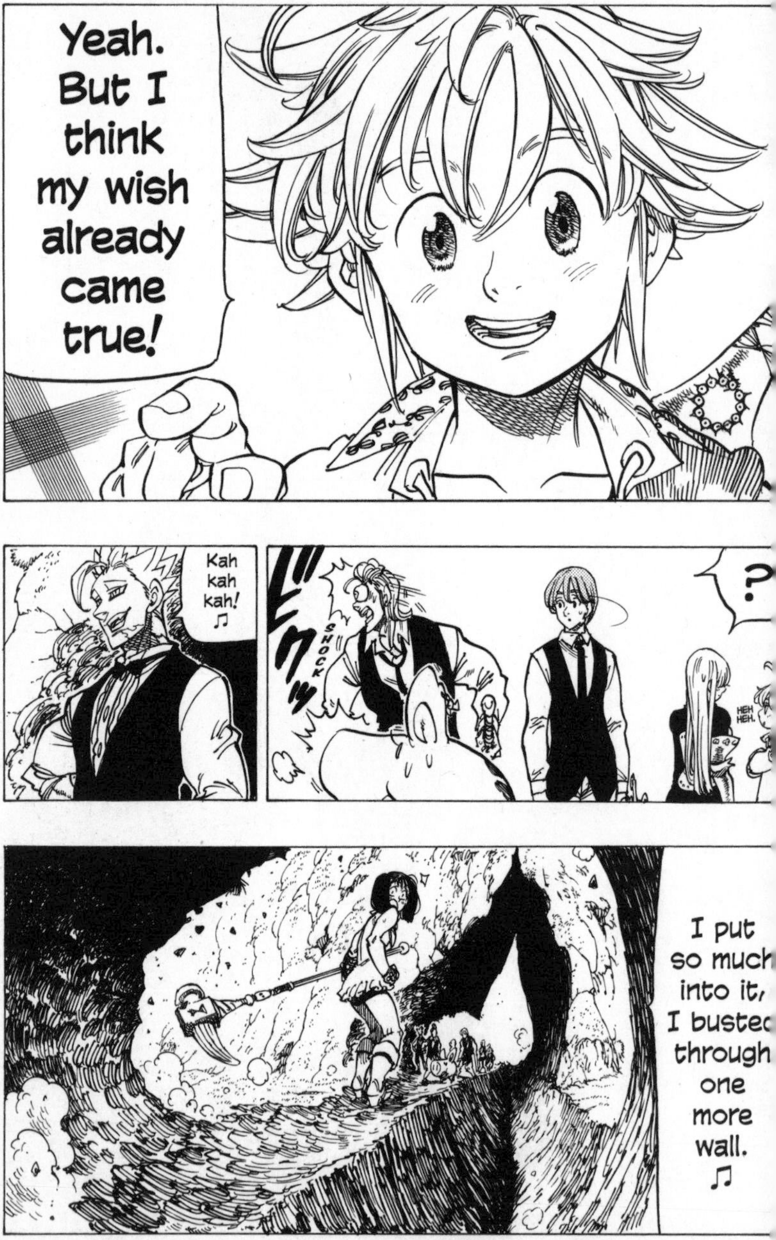
Yeah. But I think my wish already came true!
?
SHOCK
HEH HEH.
Kah kah kah! ♫
I put so much into it, I busted through one more wall. ♫

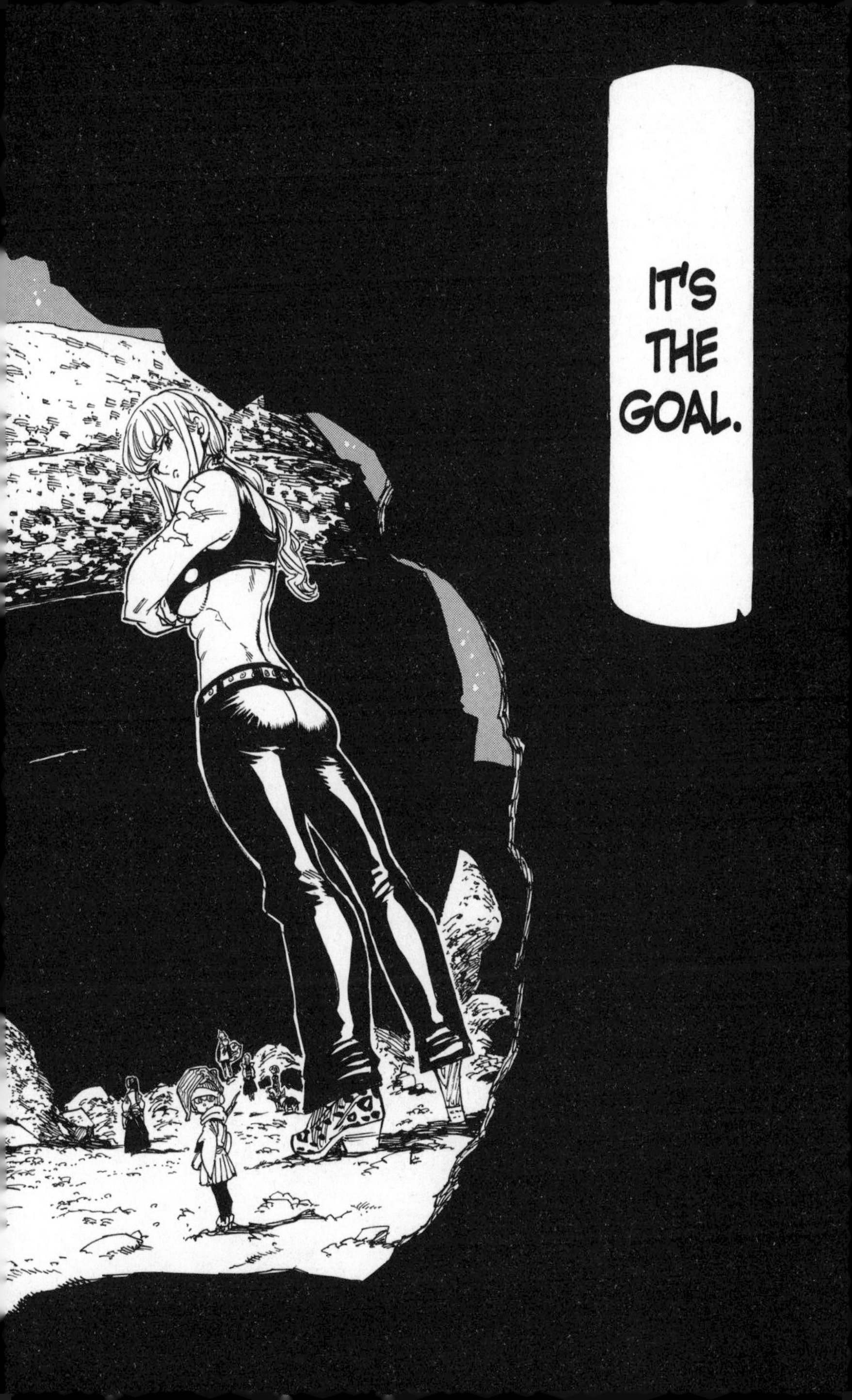
IT'S THE GOAL.

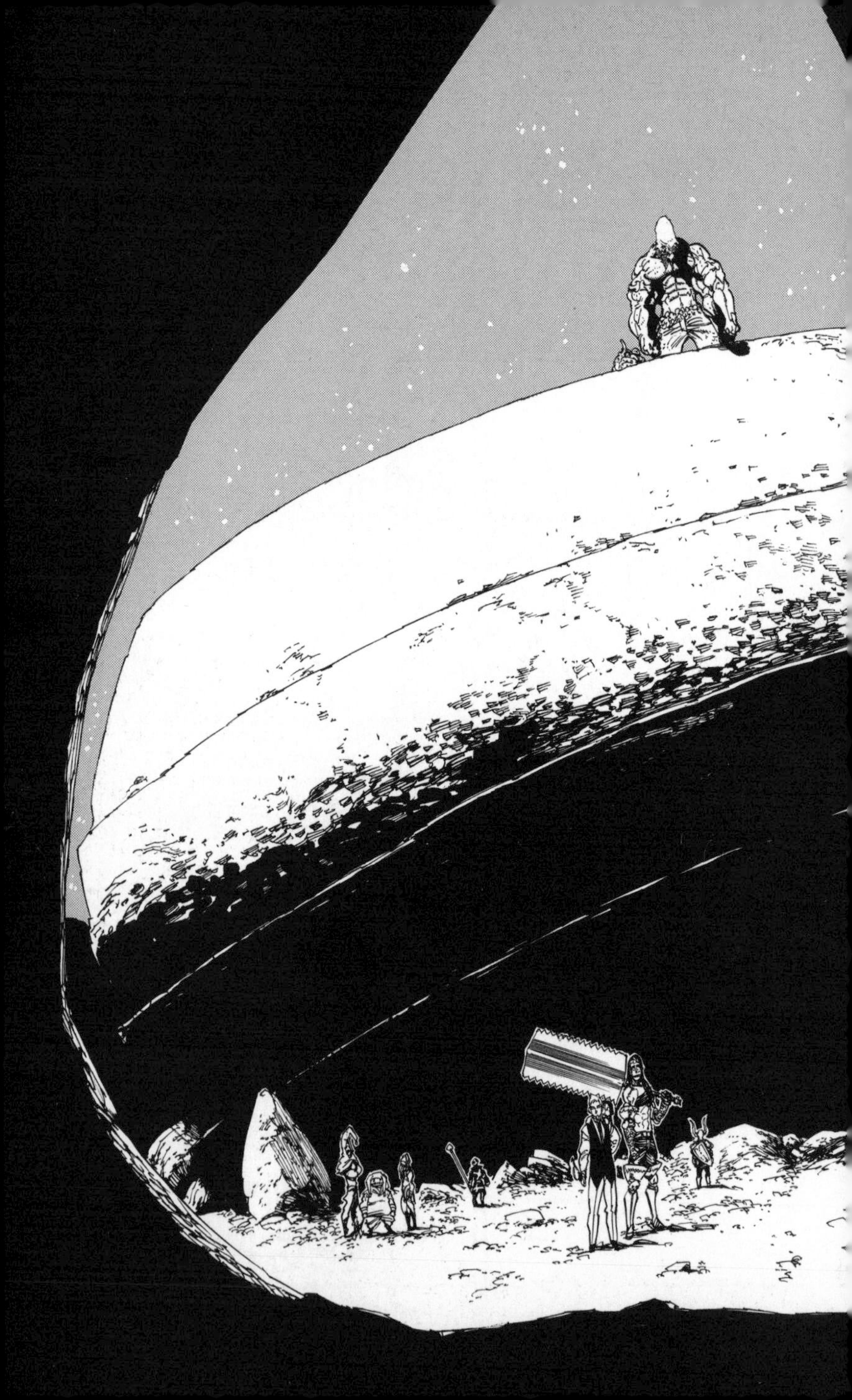

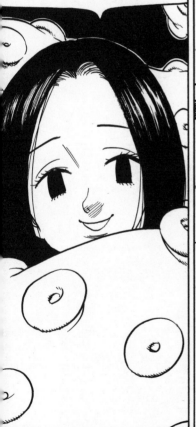

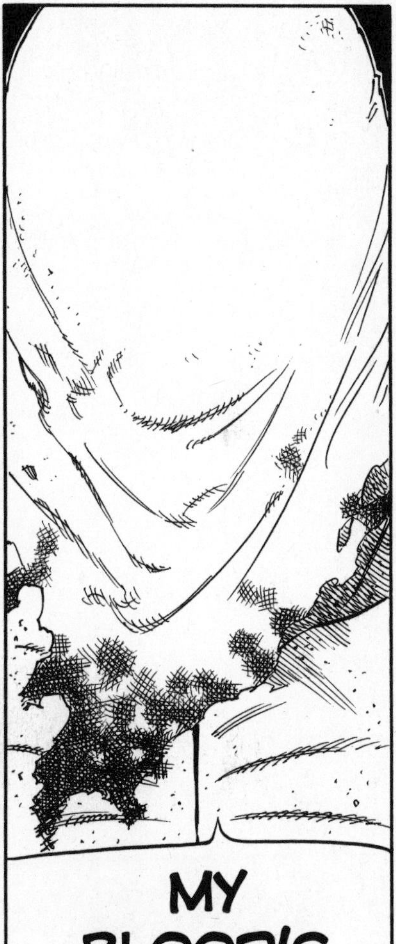
MY BLOOD'S BOILING. LET THE FESTIVAL BEGIN.
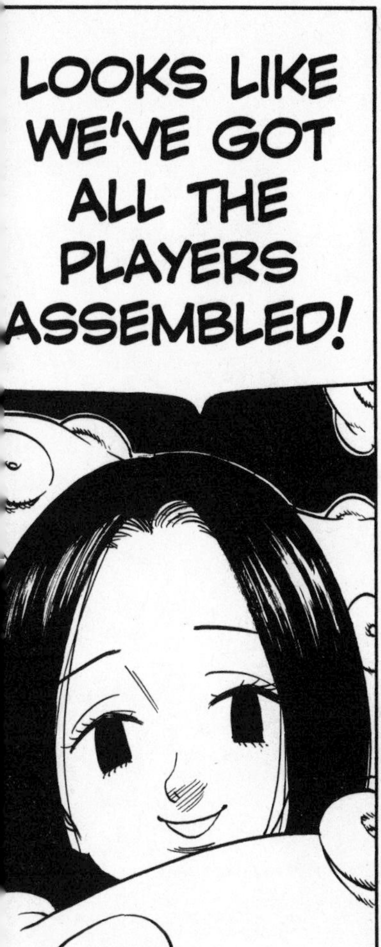
LOOKS LIKE WE'VE GOT ALL THE PLAYERS ASSEMBLED!

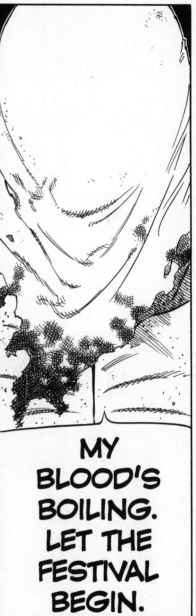

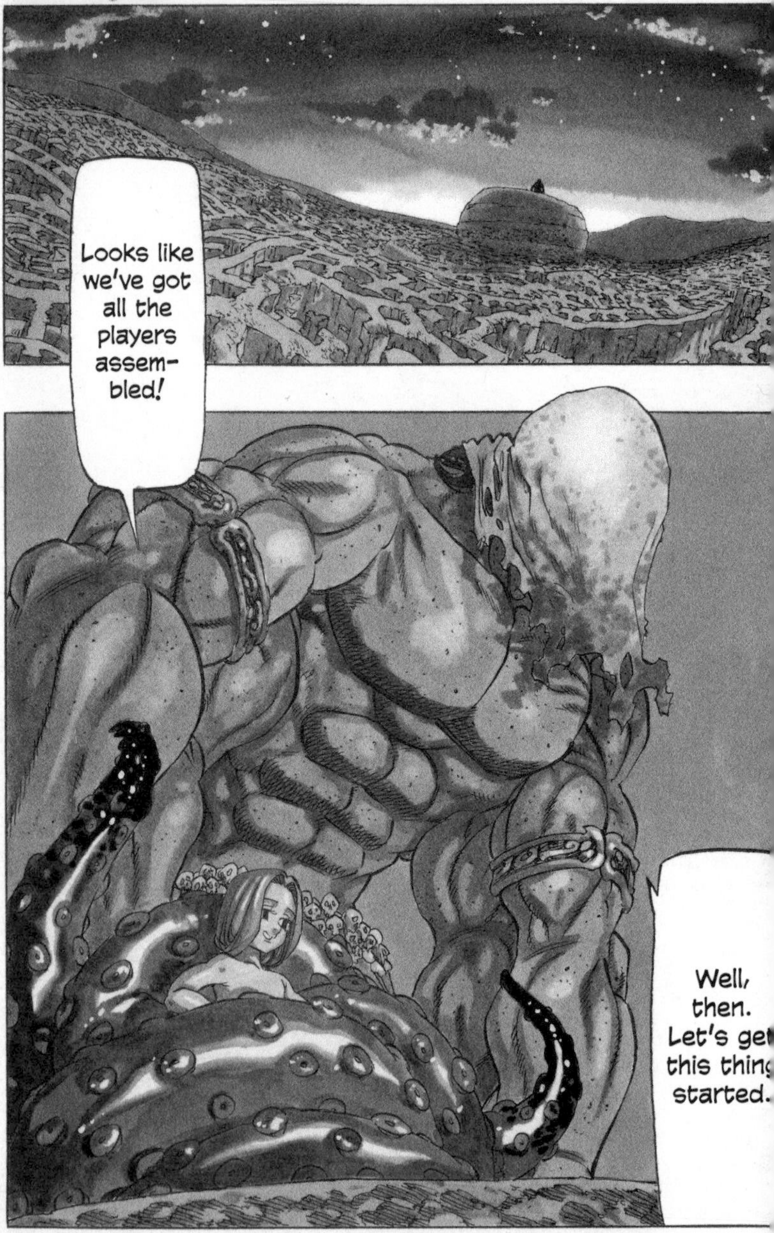
Looks like we've got all the players assembled!
Well, then. Let's get this thing started.

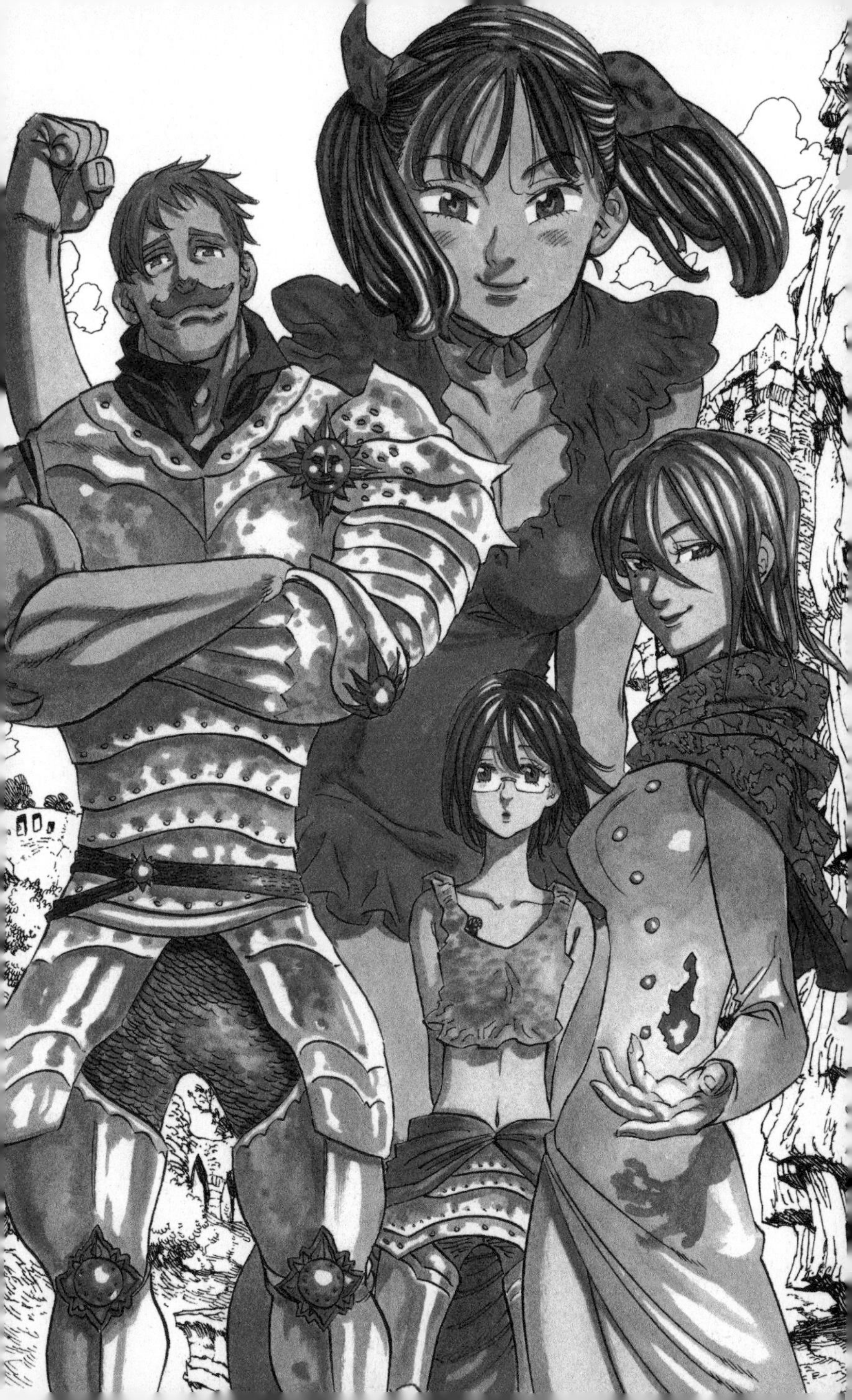

Chapter 161 - Legendary Figures

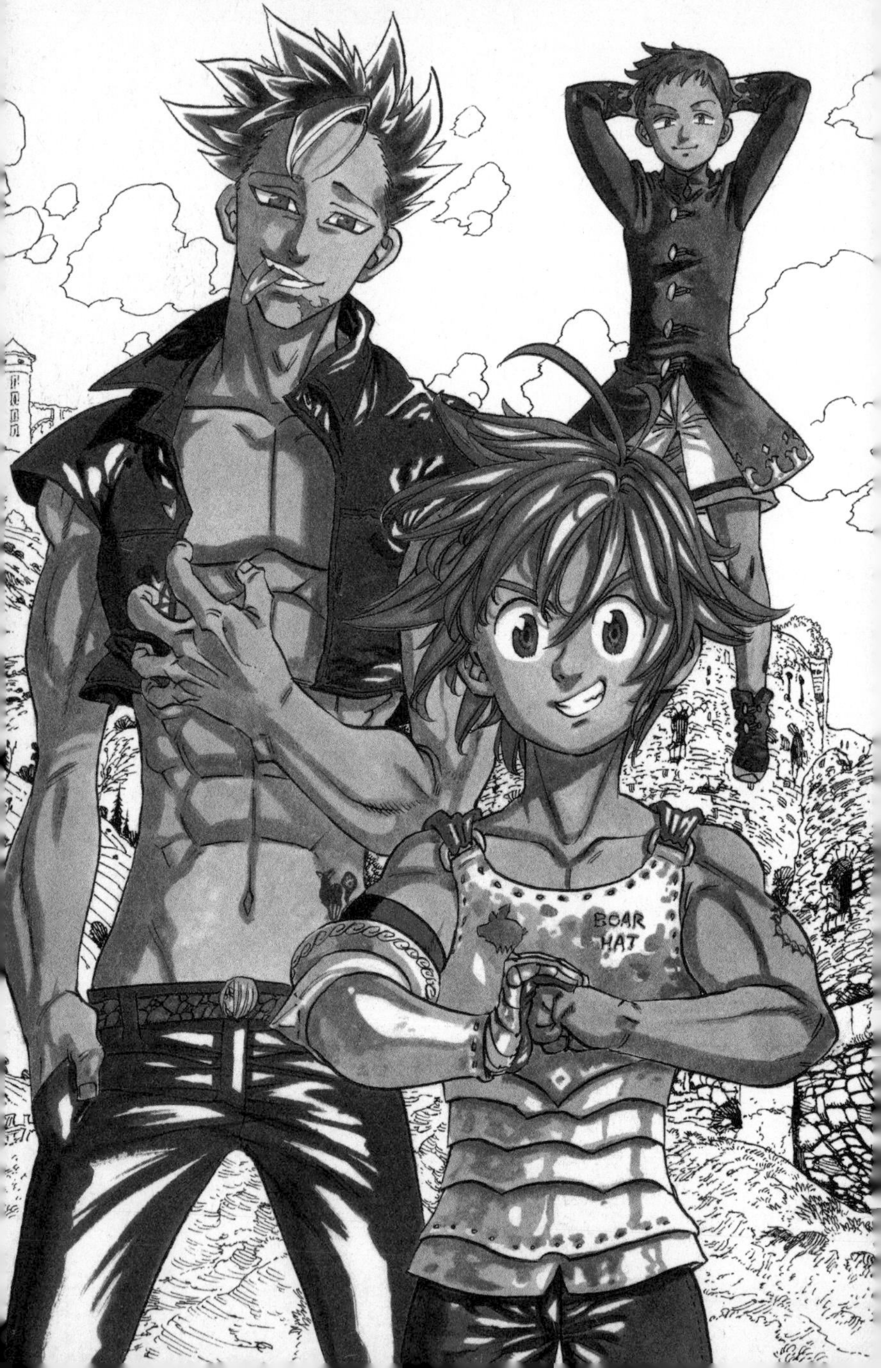
BOAR HAT

Candidate participants for the illusive Vaizel Fighting Festival. One of them is Selion, the son of Ban's benefactor Zhivago. The other is Diane's former best friend Dolores. I actually had originally planned on both of them being alive, but since that'd be just too convenient, and there was also the question of whether they'd be able to keep up with the current developments, they ended up not showing up in the end.

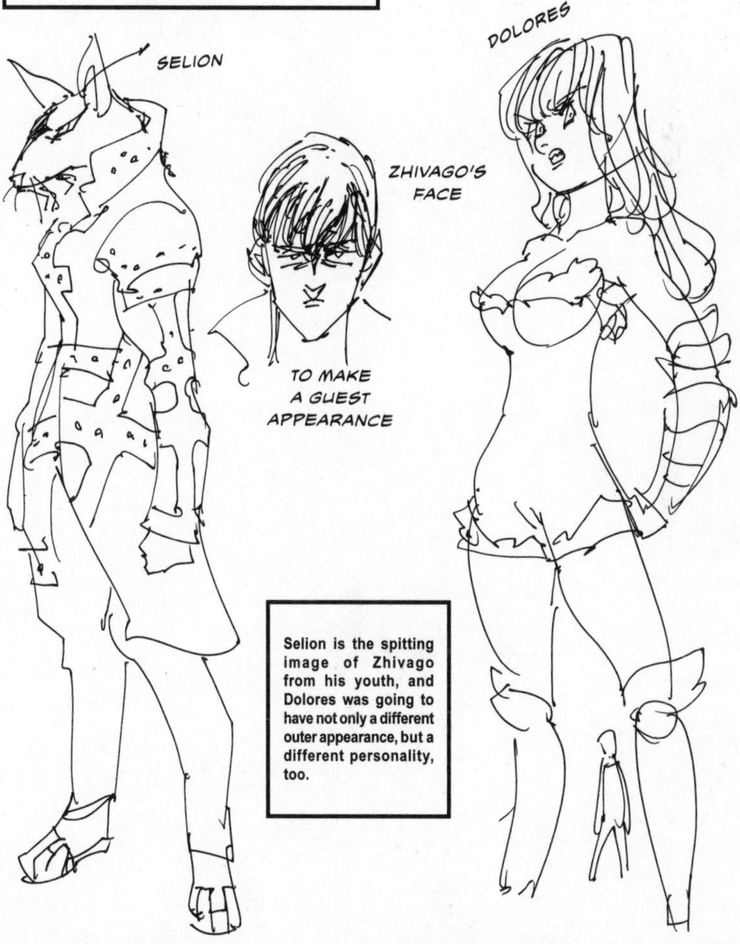
SELION
ZHIVAGO'S FACE
TO MAKE A GUEST APPEARANCE
DOLORES

Selion is the spitting image of Zhivago from his youth, and Dolores was going to have not only a different outer appearance, but a different personality, too.

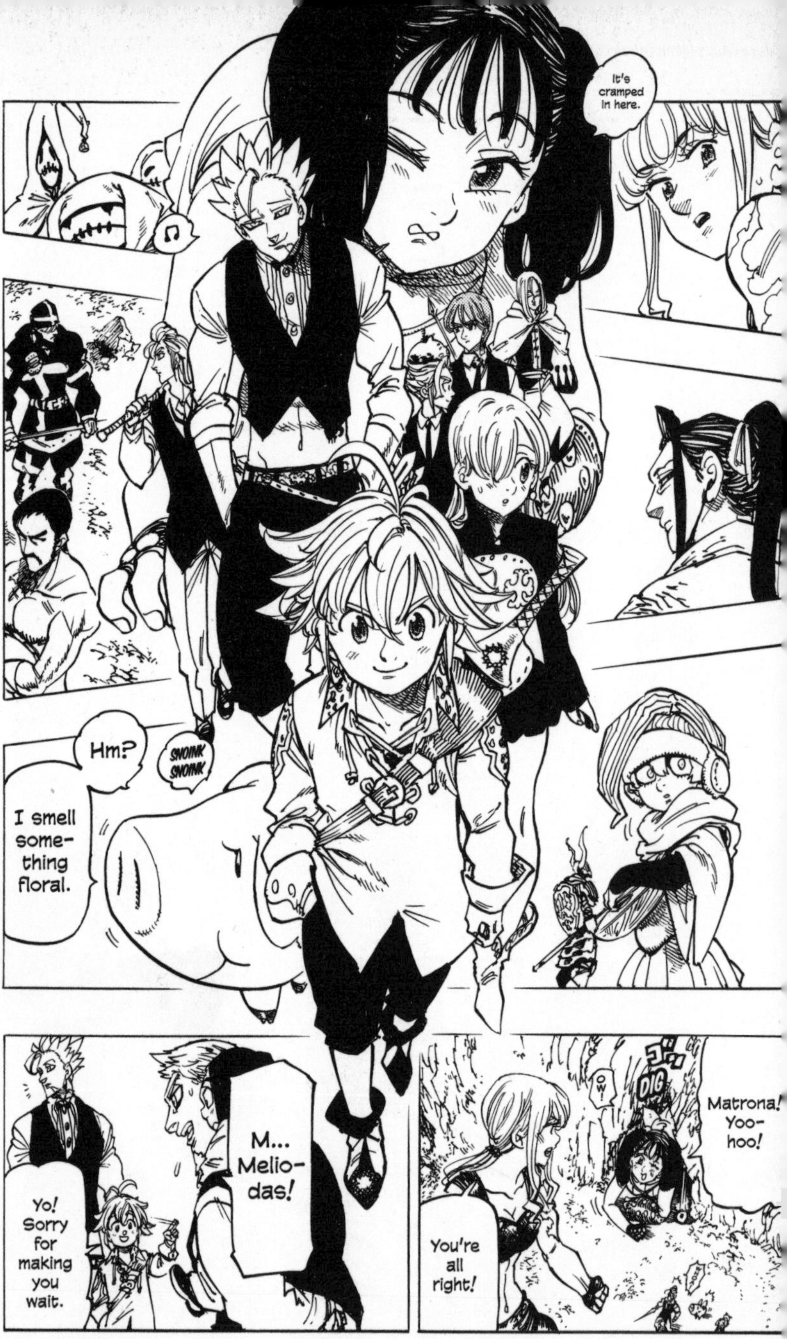
It's cramped in here.
♫
SNOINK SNOINK
Hm?
I smell something floral.
Matrona! Yoo-hoo!
DIG
OW!
You're all right!
M... Melio-das!
Yo! Sorry for making you wait.

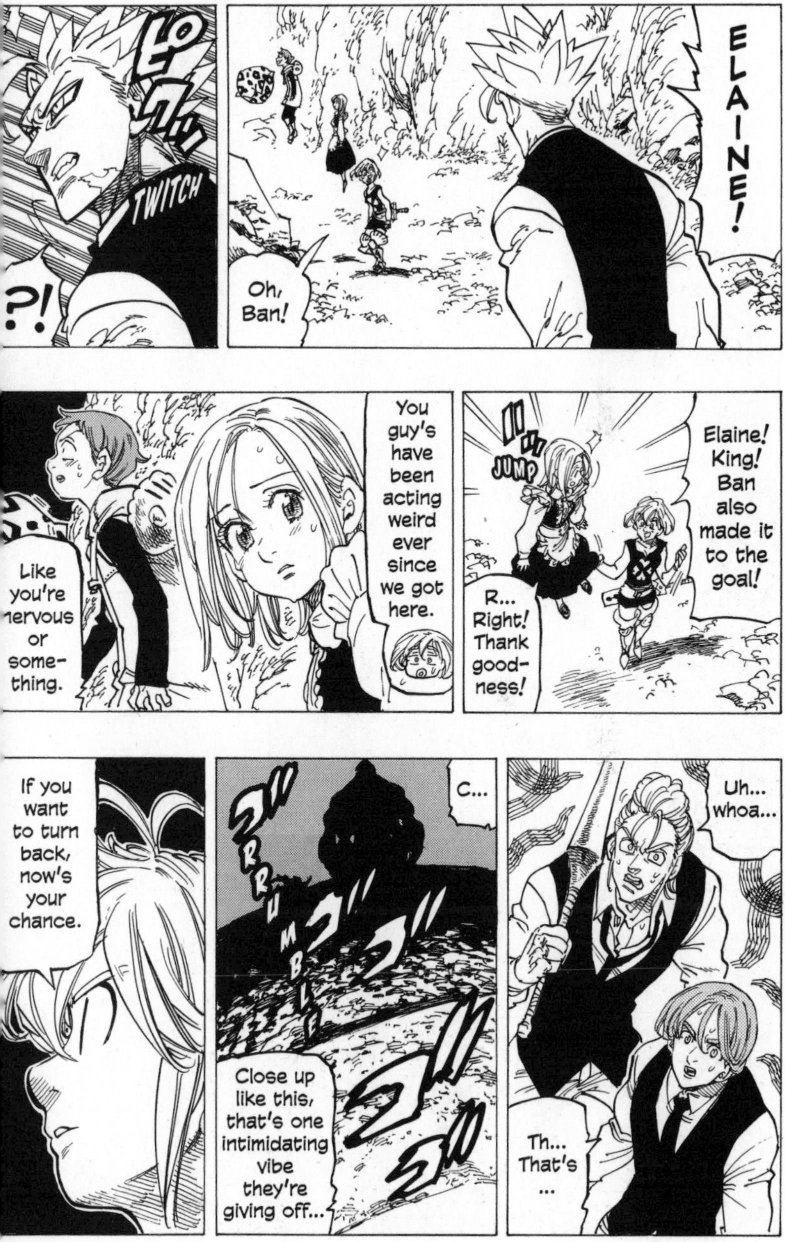
ELAINE!
Oh, Ban!
TWITCH
?!
Elaine! King! Ban also made it to the goal!
JUMP
R... Right! Thank goodness!
You guy's have been acting weird ever since we got here.
Like you're
ervous or something.
Uh... whoa...
Th... That's ...
C...
RRUMBLE
Close up like this, that's one intimidating vibe they're giving off...
If you want to turn back, now's your chance.

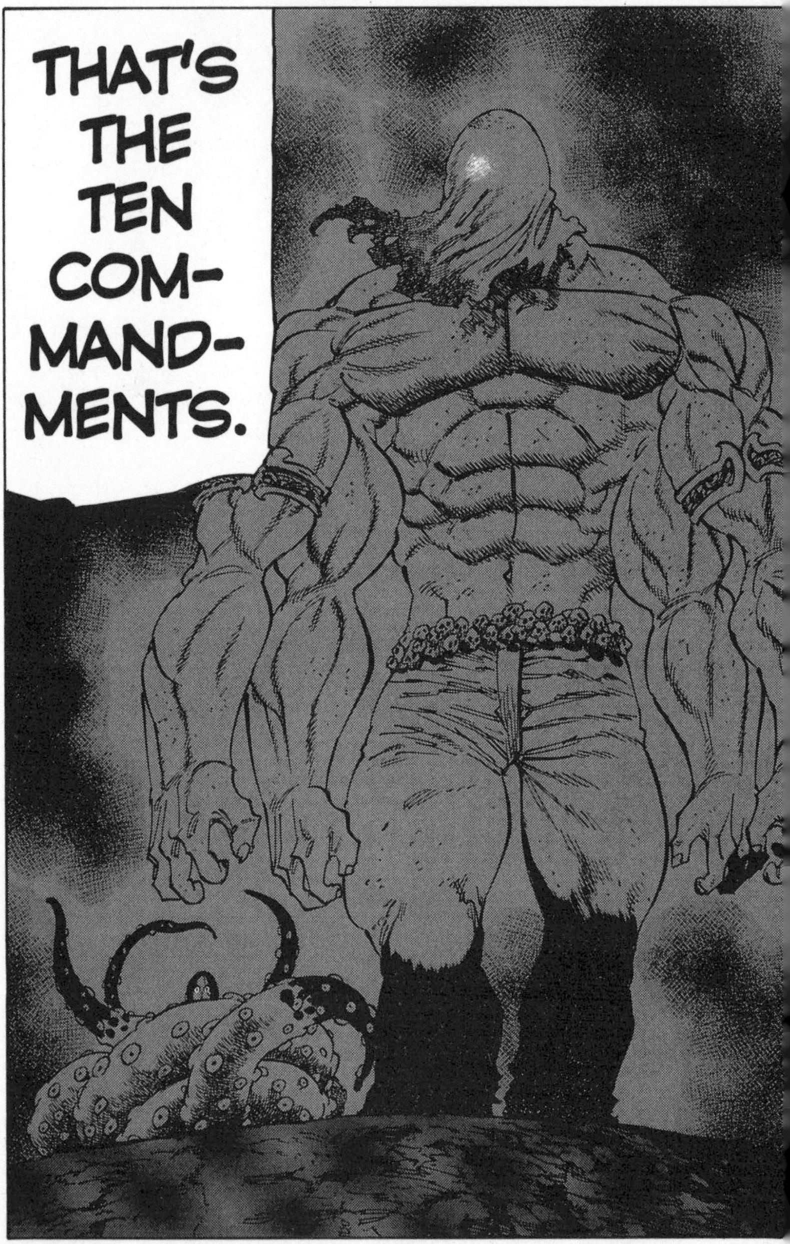
THAT'S THE TEN COM-MAND-MENTS.

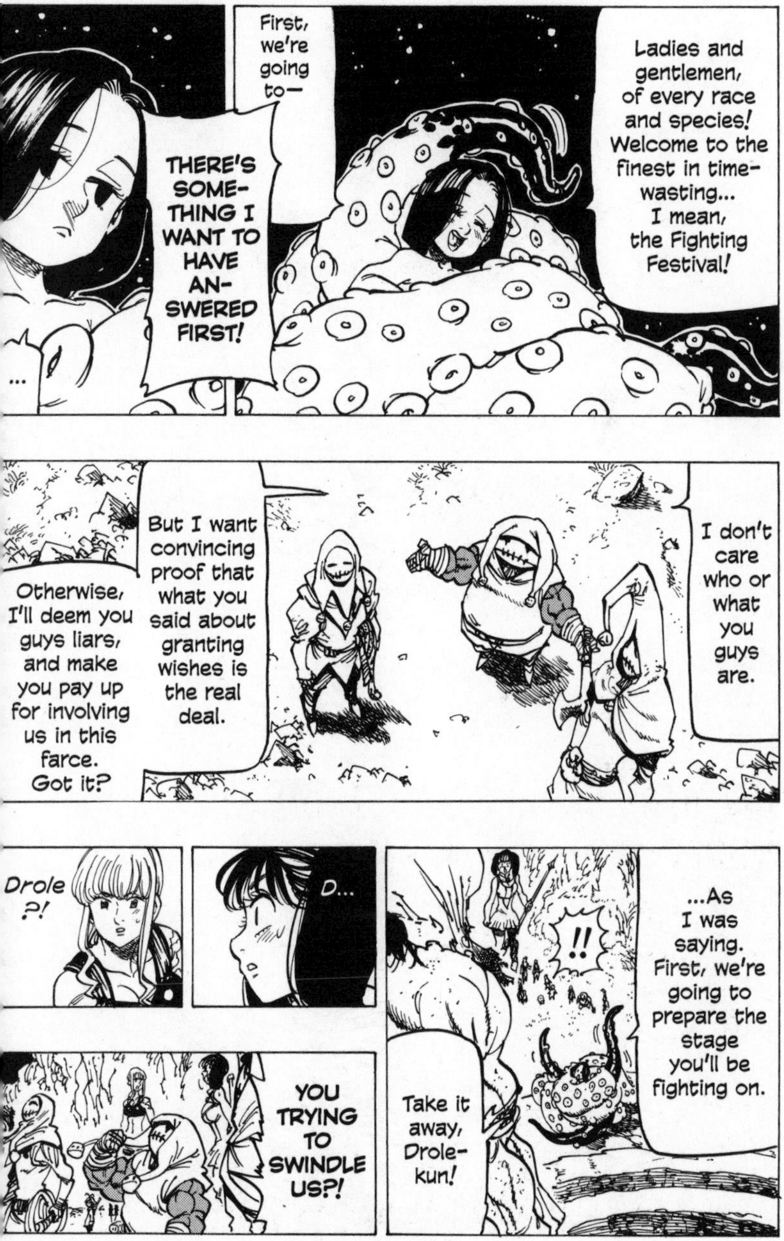
Ladies and gentlemen, of every race and species! Welcome to the finest in time-wasting... I mean, the Fighting Festival!
First, we're going to—
THERE'S SOMETHING I WANT TO HAVE ANSWERED FIRST!
...
I don't care who or what you guys are.
But I want convincing proof that what you said about granting wishes is the real deal.
Otherwise, I'll deem you guys liars, and make you pay up for involving us in this farce. Got it?
...As I was saying. First, we're going to prepare the stage you'll be fighting on.
!!
Take it away, Drole-kun!
D...
Drole?!
YOU TRYING TO SWINDLE US?!

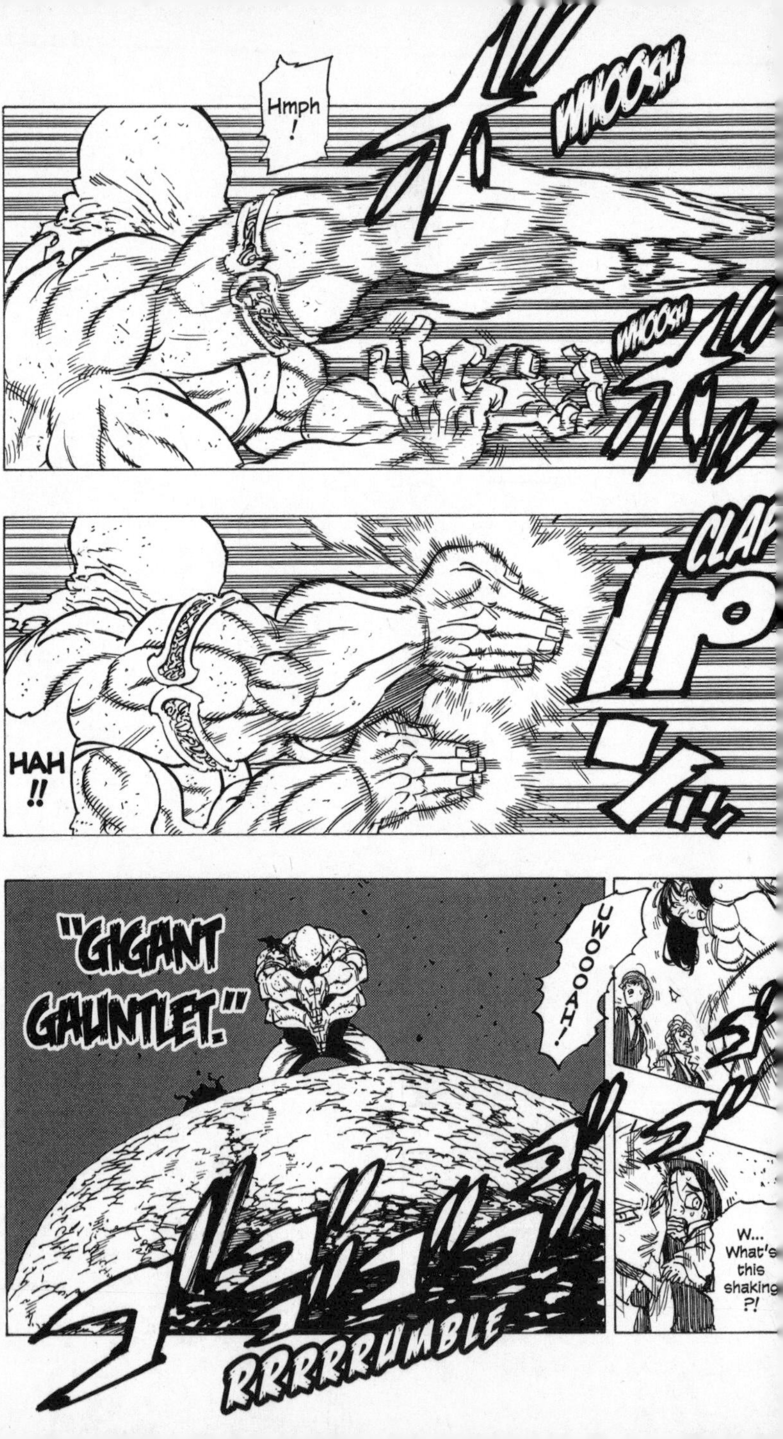
WHOOSH
Hmph!
WHOOSH
CLAP
HAH!!
"GIGANT GAUNTLET."
UWOOOOAH!
W... What's this shaking?!
RRRRRUMBLE

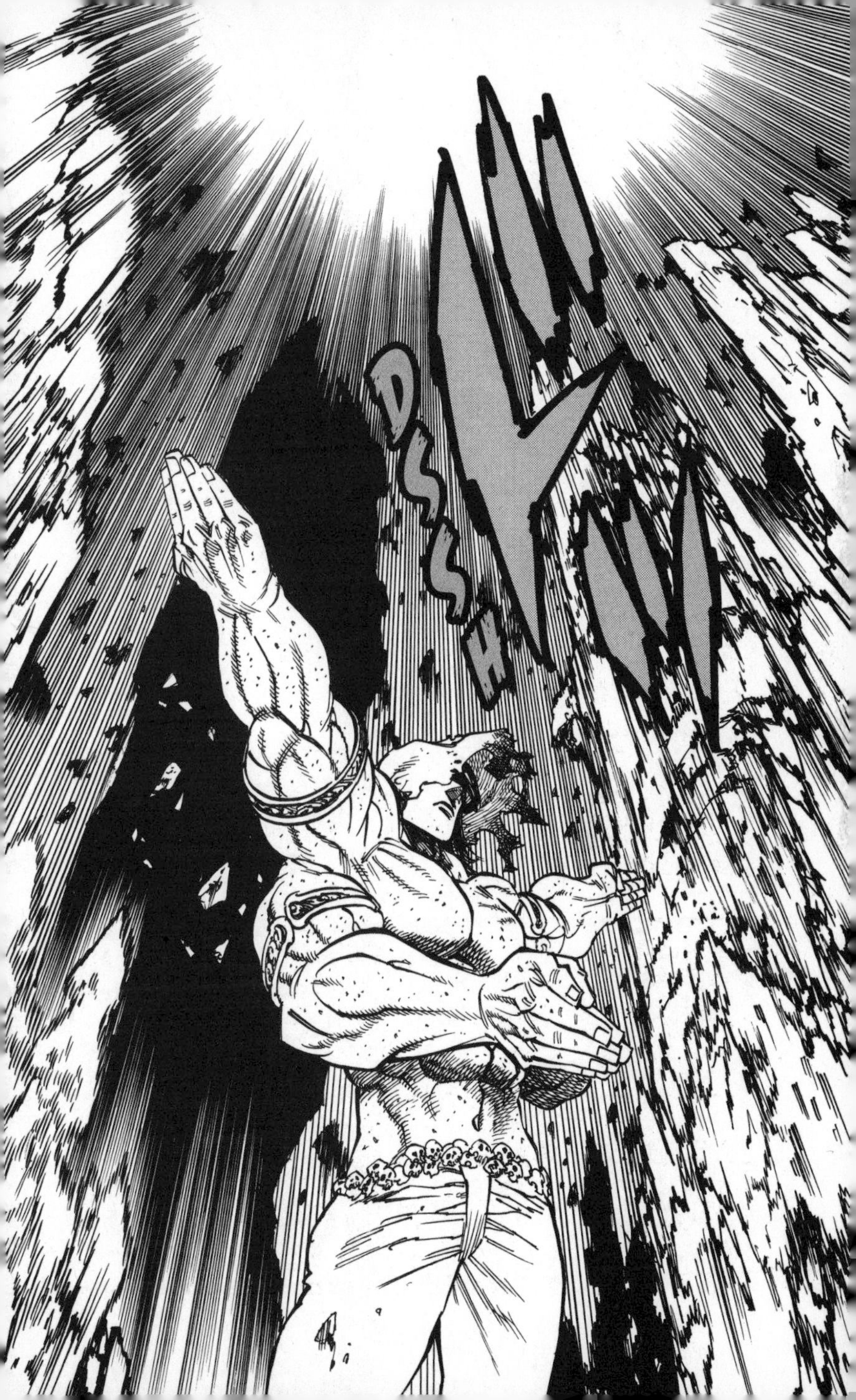
DASH
VWM

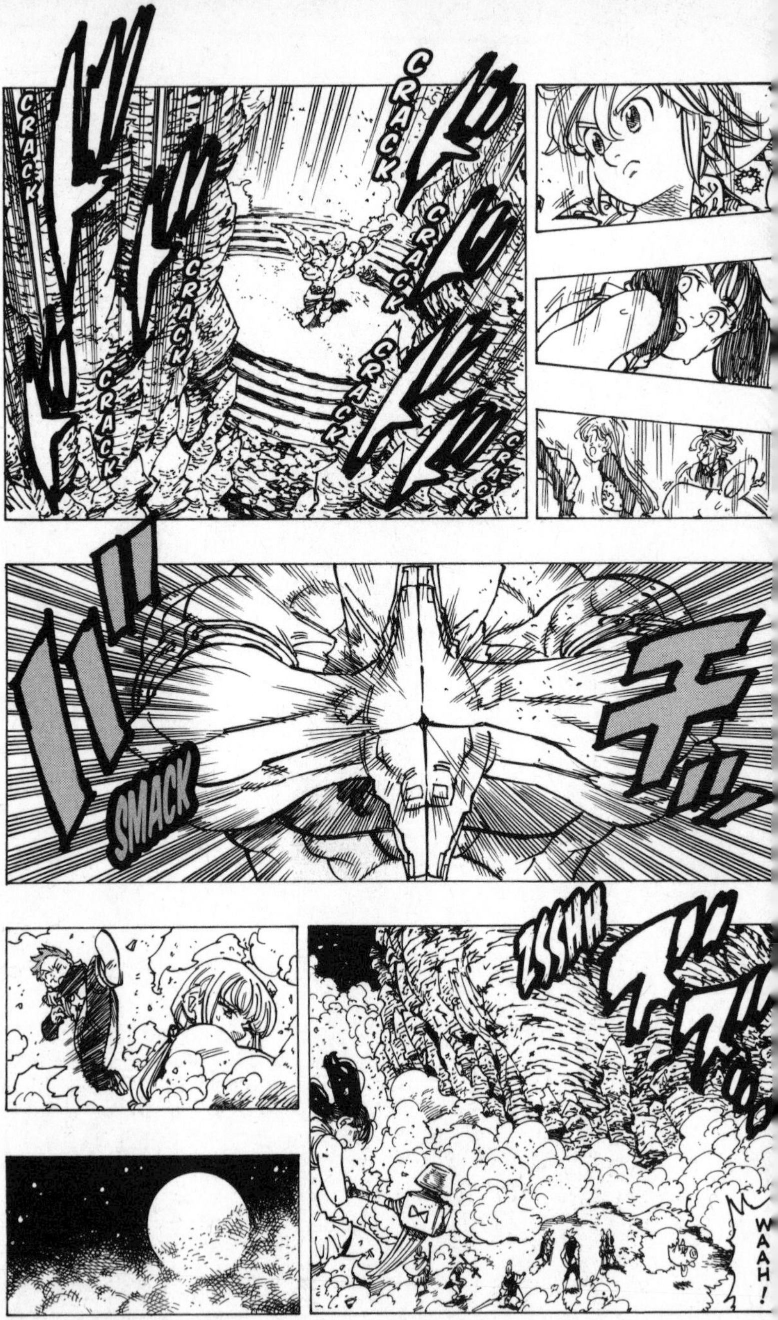
CRACK
CRACK
CRACK
CRACK
CRACK
CRACK
CRACK
SMACK
ZSSHH
WAAH!

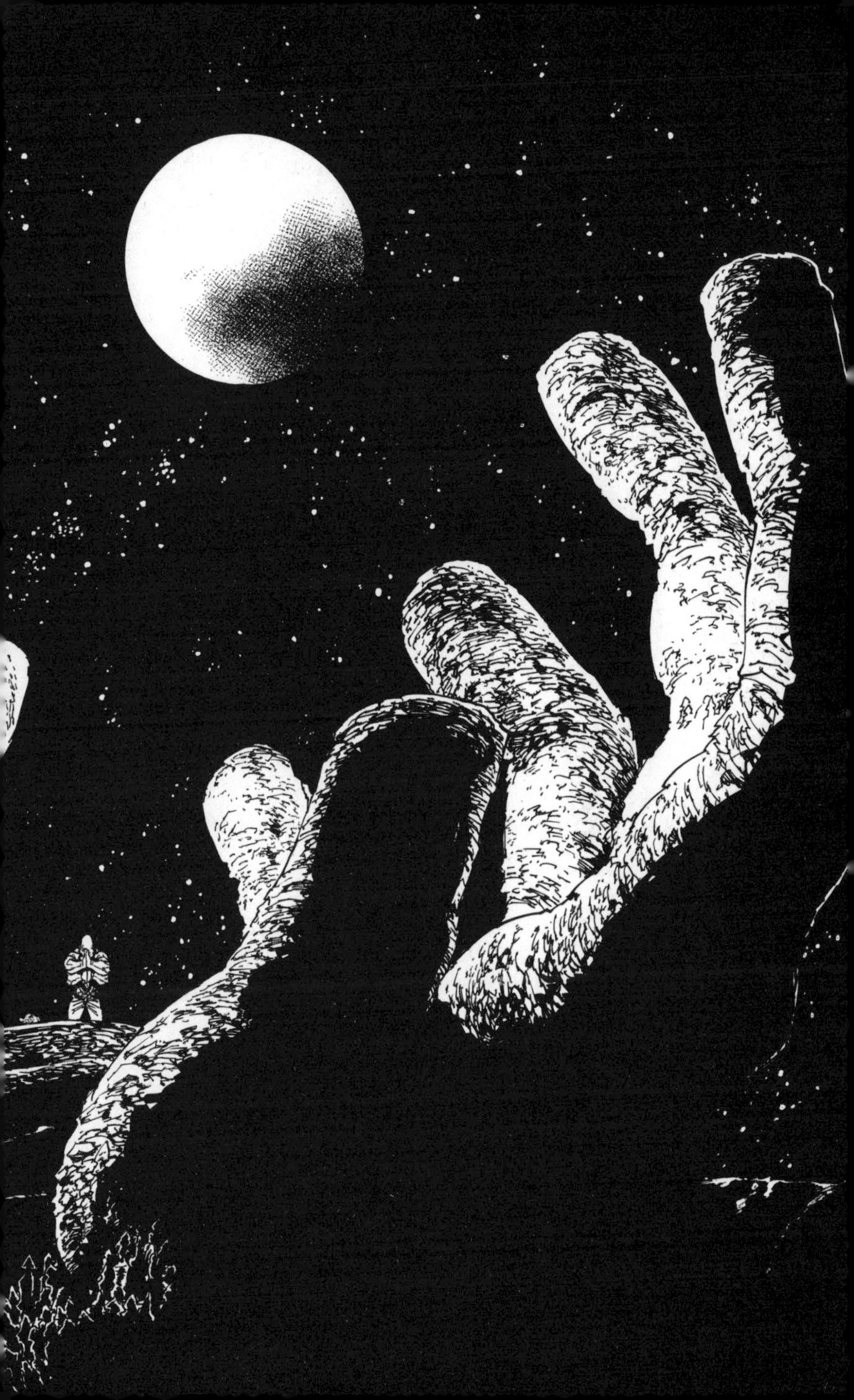

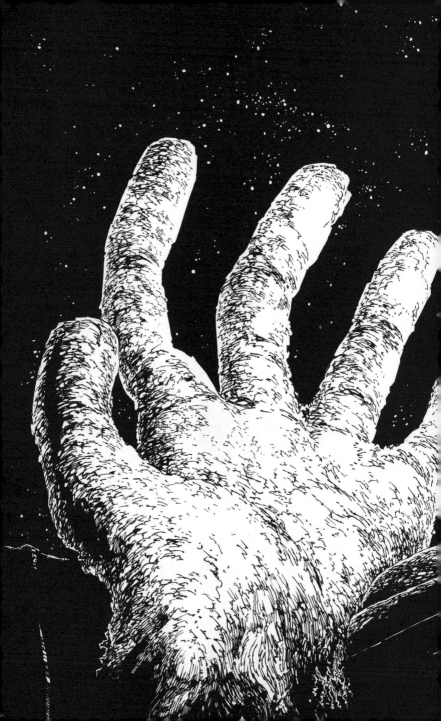

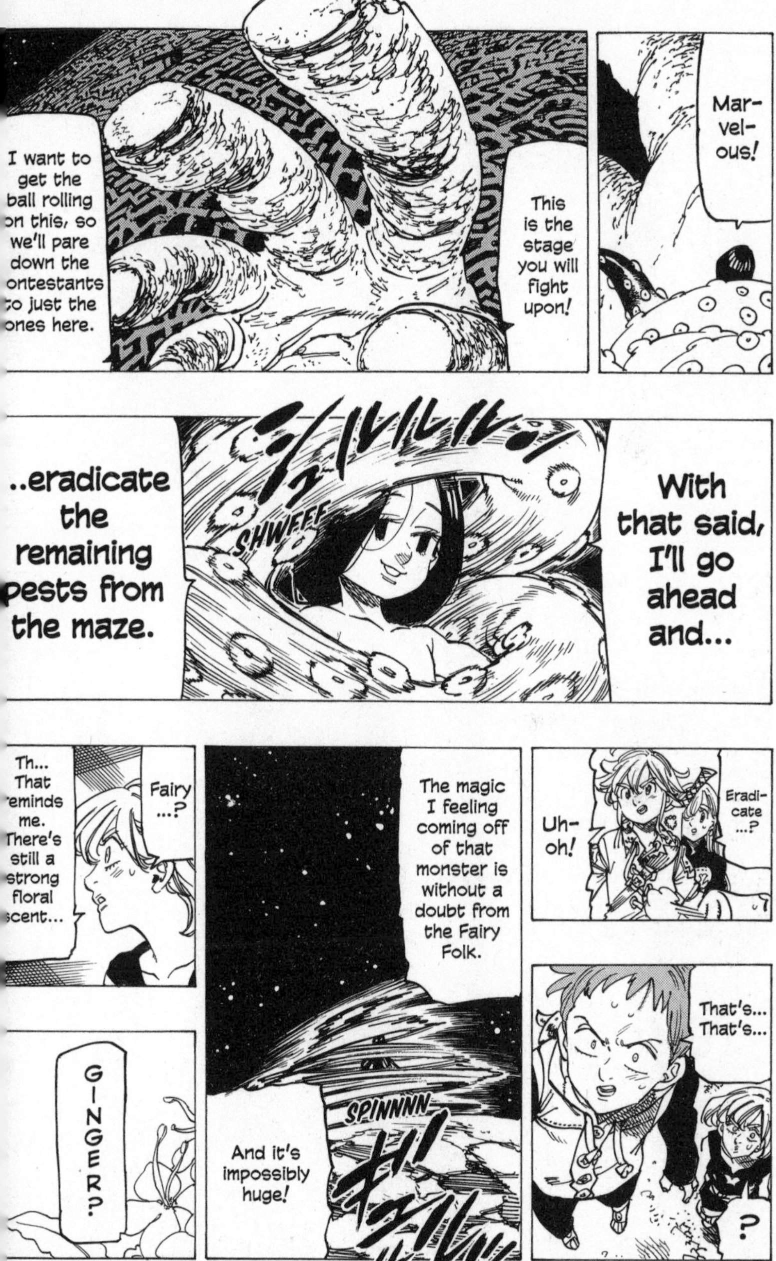
Marvelous!
This is the stage you will fight upon!
I want to get the ball rolling on this, so we'll pare down the contestants to just the ones here.
With that said, I'll go ahead and...
SHWEEE
..eradicate the remaining pests from the maze.
Eradicate ...?
Uh-oh!
That's... That's...
?
The magic I feeling coming off of that monster is without a doubt from the Fairy Folk.
SPINNNN
And it's impossibly huge!
Fairy ...?
Th... That reminds me. There's still a strong floral scent...
GINGER?

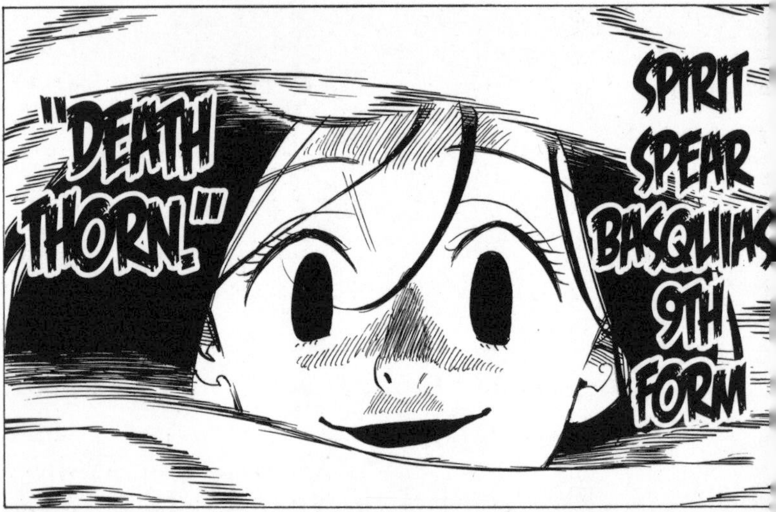
SPIRIT SPEAR BASQUIAS 9TH FORM
"DEATH THORN."

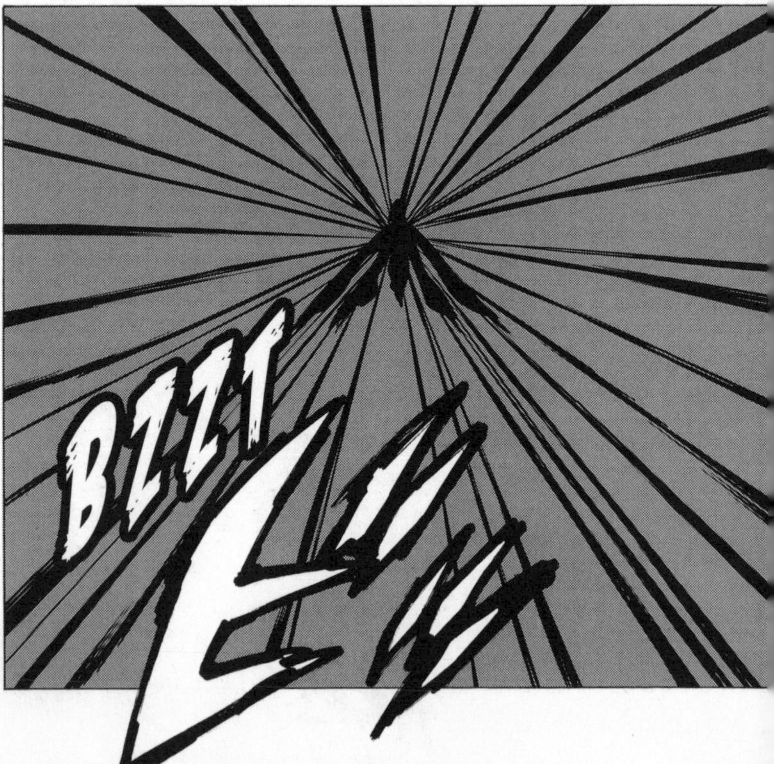
BZZT

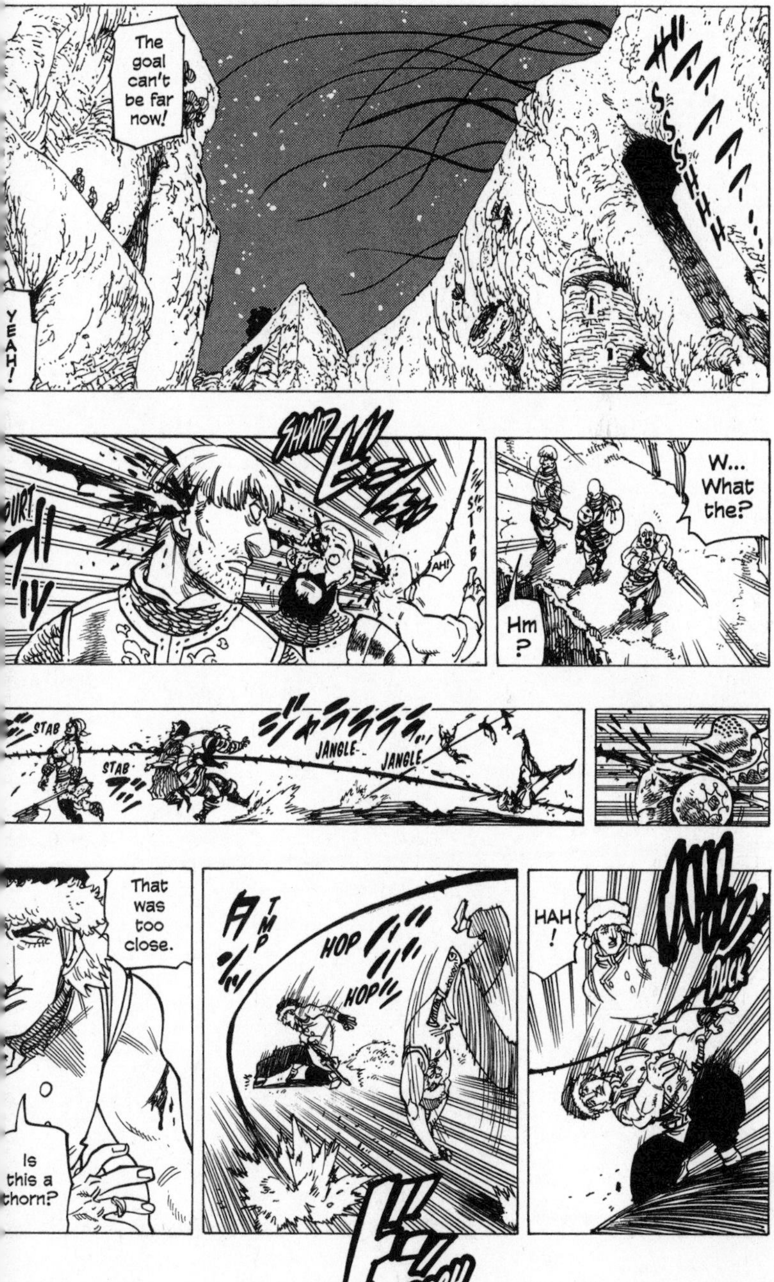
SSSHHH
The goal can't be far now!
YEAH!
W... What the?
Hm?
STAB
AH!
JANGLE
JANGLE
STAB
STAB
DUCK
HAH!
TMP
HOP
HOP
DSSH
That was too close.
Is this a thorn?

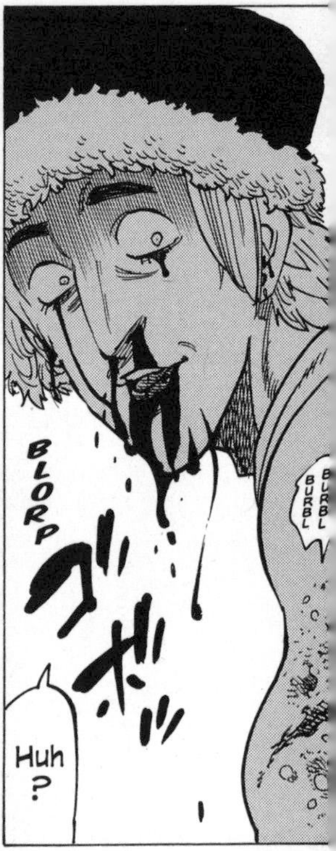
BURBL BURBL
BLORP
ゴボッ
Huh?
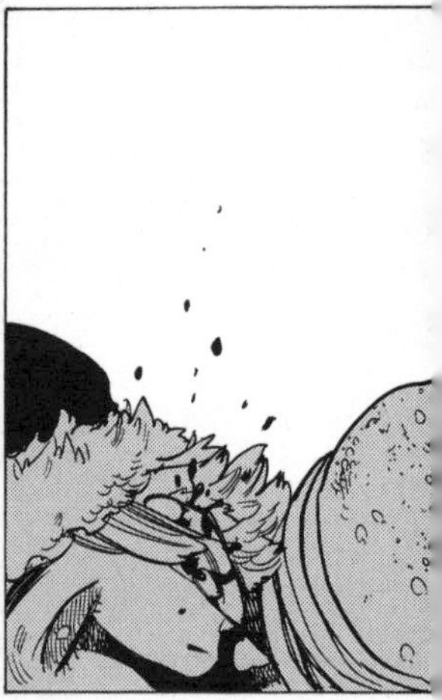
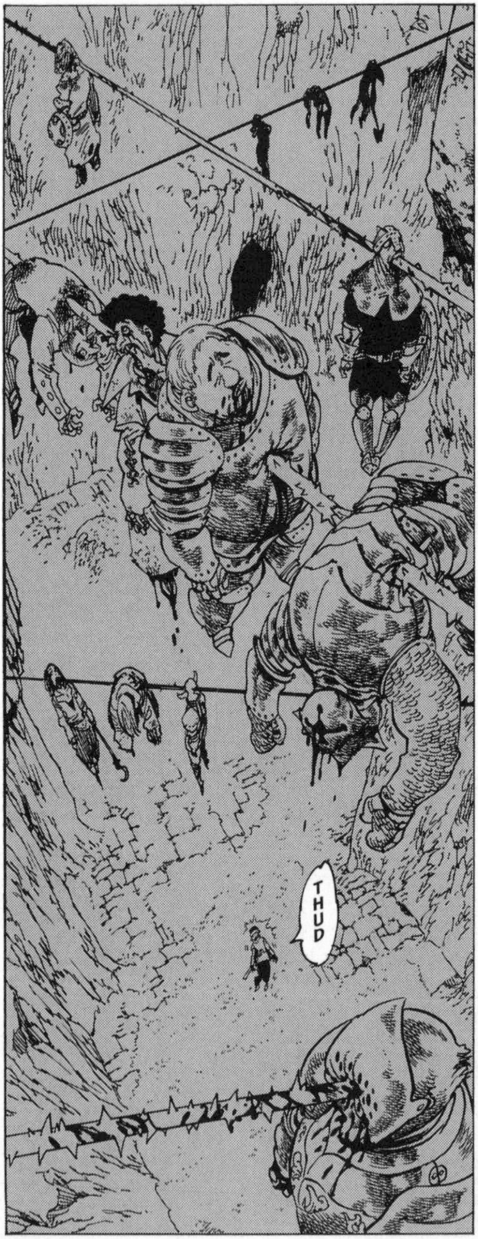
THUD

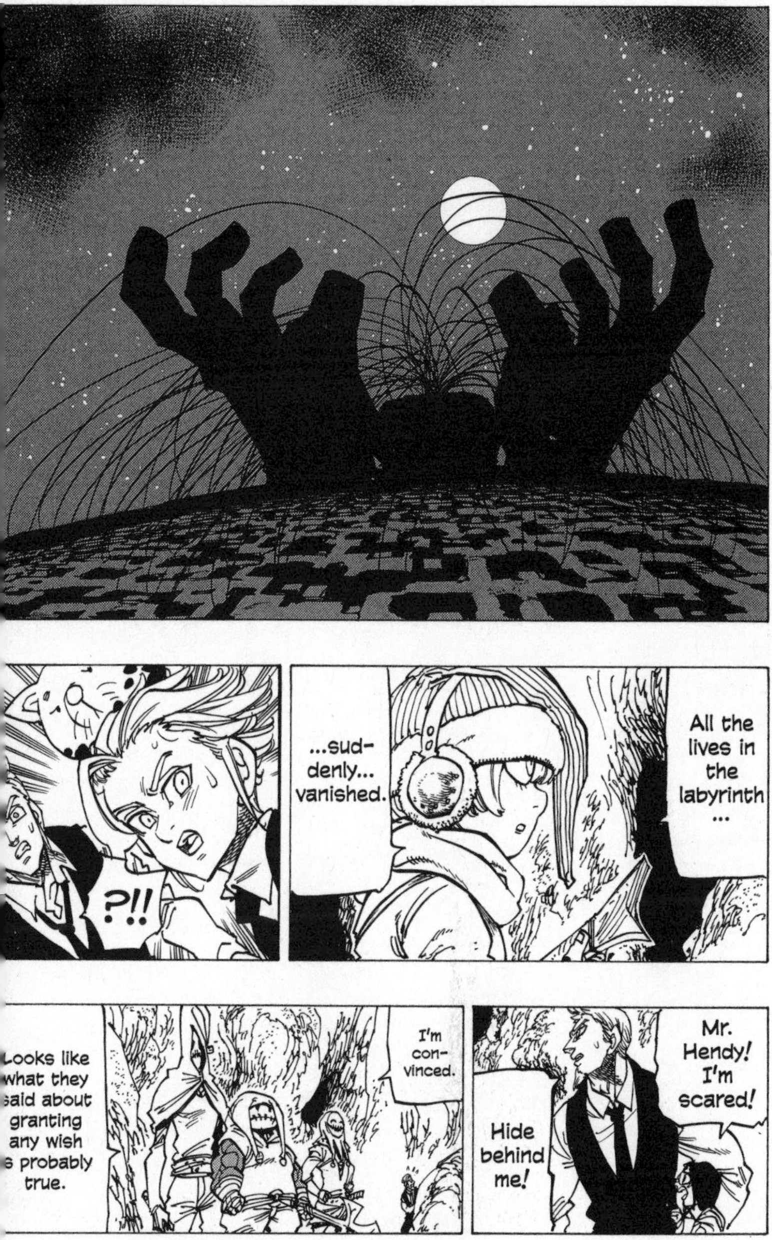
All the lives in the labyrinth ...
...sud-denly... vanished.
?!!
Mr. Hendy! I'm scared!
Hide behind me!
I'm con-vinced.
Looks like what they said about granting any wish is probably true.

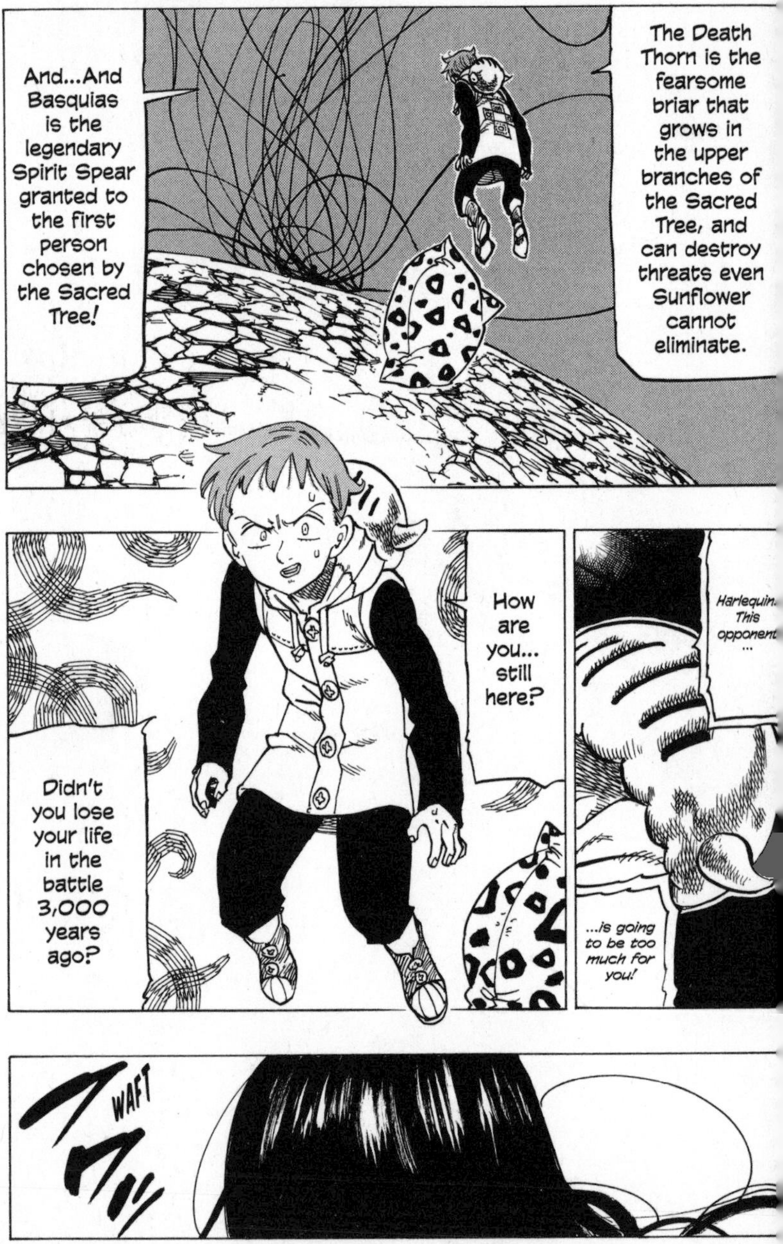
The Death Thorn is the fearsome briar that grows in the upper branches of the Sacred Tree, and can destroy threats even Sunflower cannot eliminate.
And...And Basquias is the legendary Spirit Spear granted to the first person chosen by the Sacred Tree!
Harlequin. This opponent...
...is going to be too much for you!
How are you... still here?
Didn't you lose your life in the battle 3,000 years ago?
WAFT

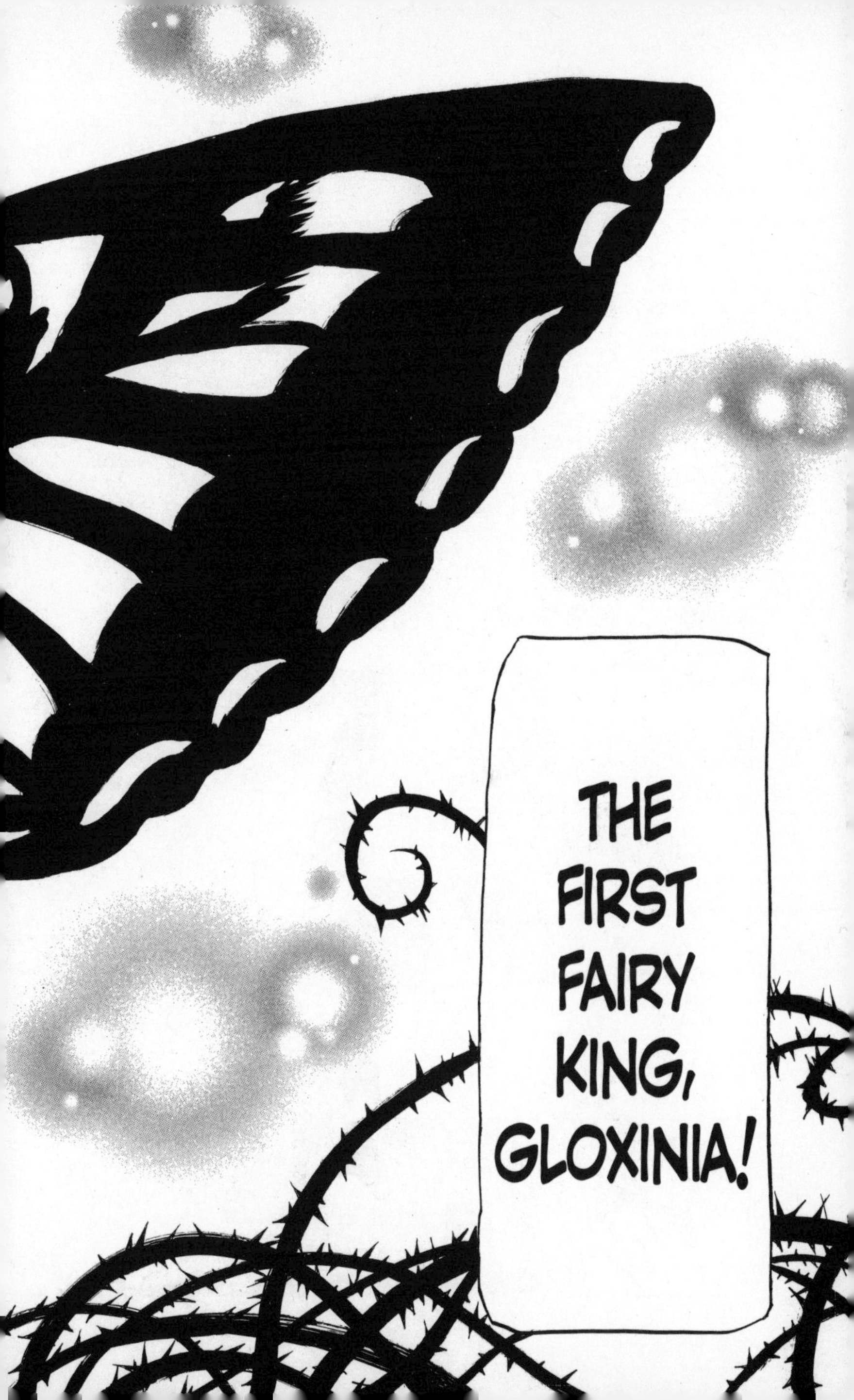
THE FIRST FAIRY KING, GLOXINIA!

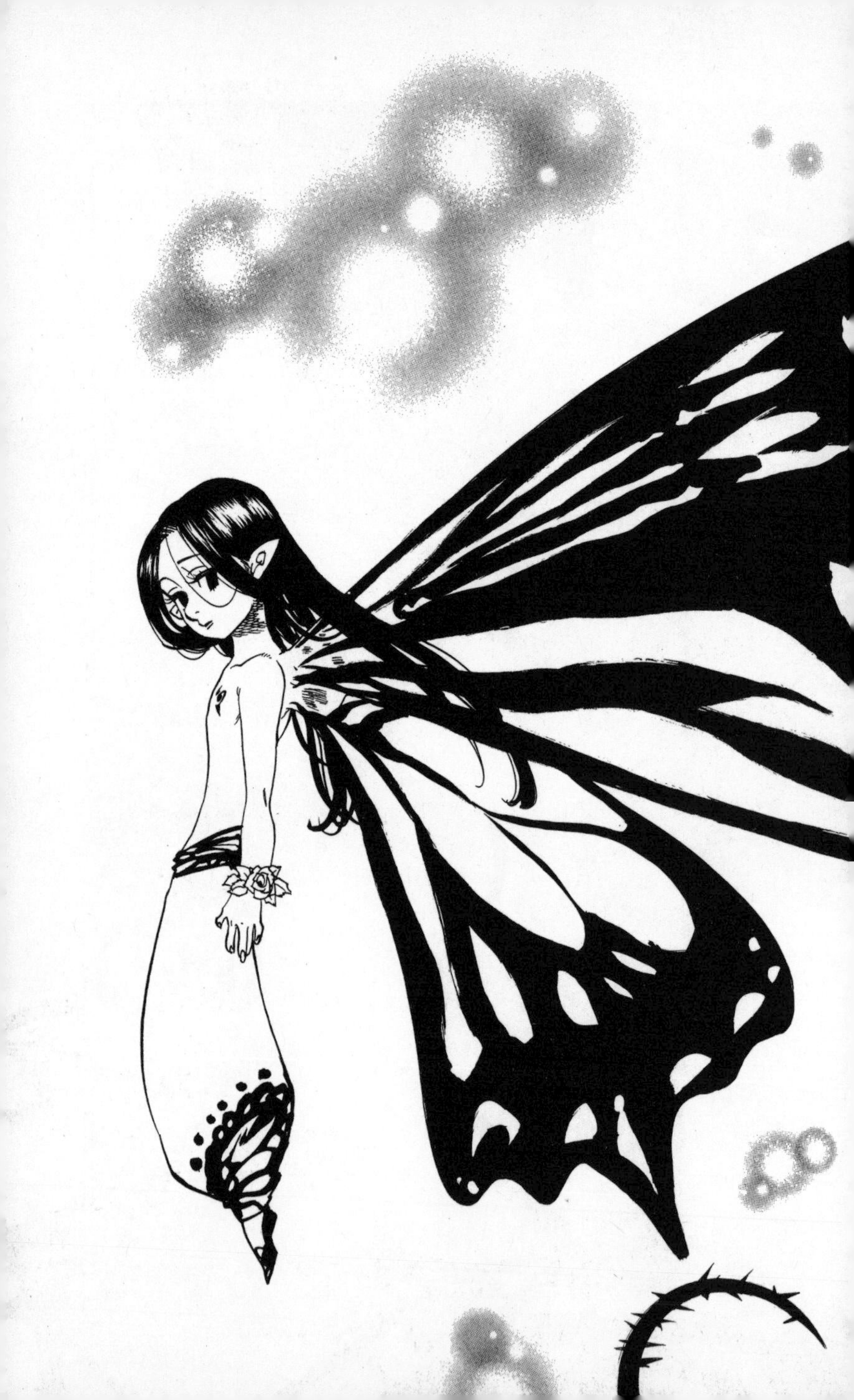

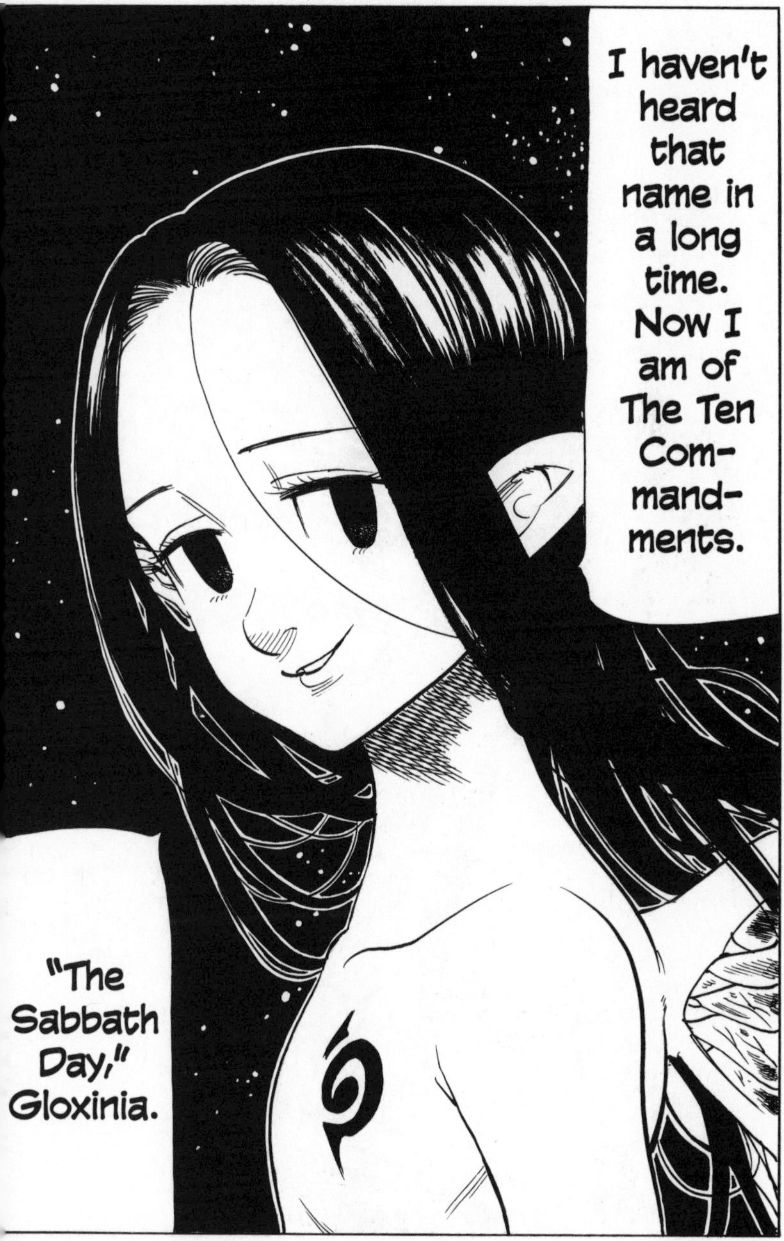
I haven't heard that name in a long time. Now I am of The Ten Commandments.
"The Sabbath Day," Gloxinia.

Chapter 162 - Who Will Share Their Fate?!

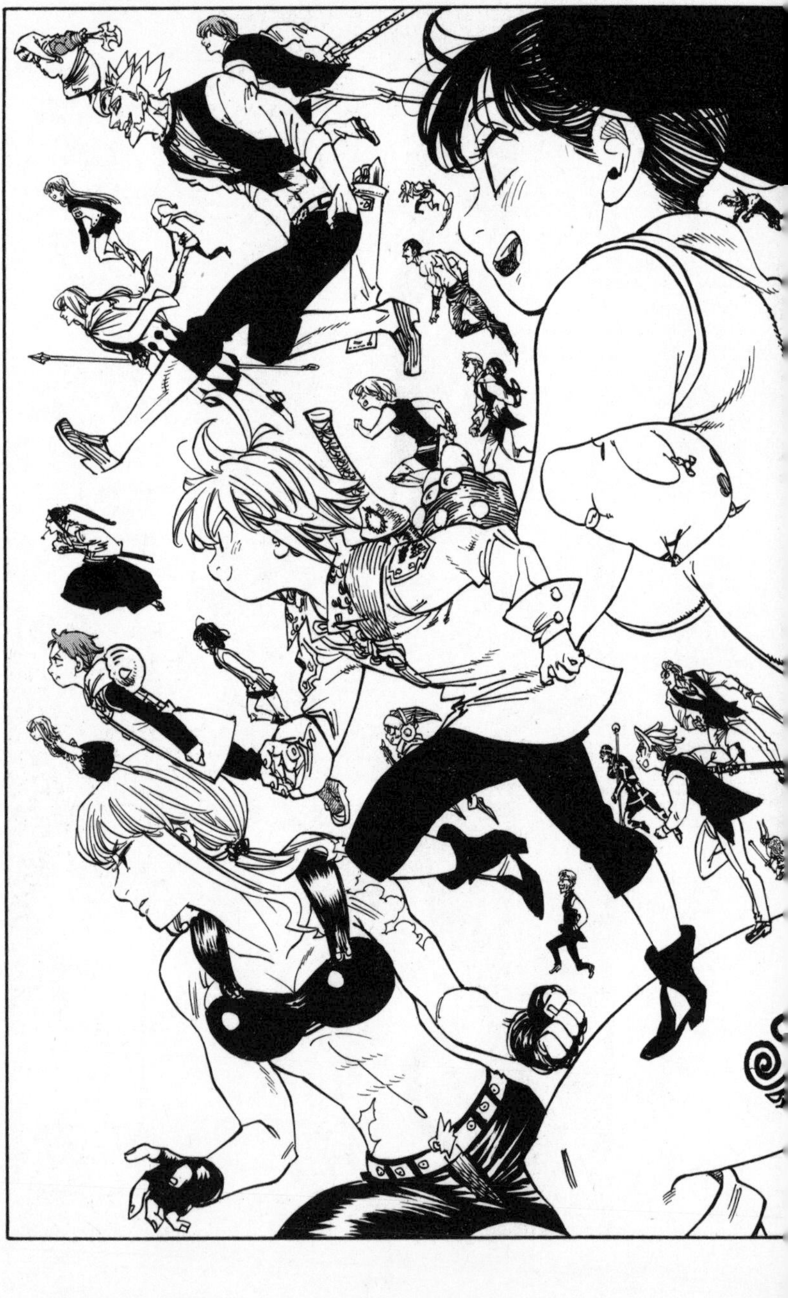

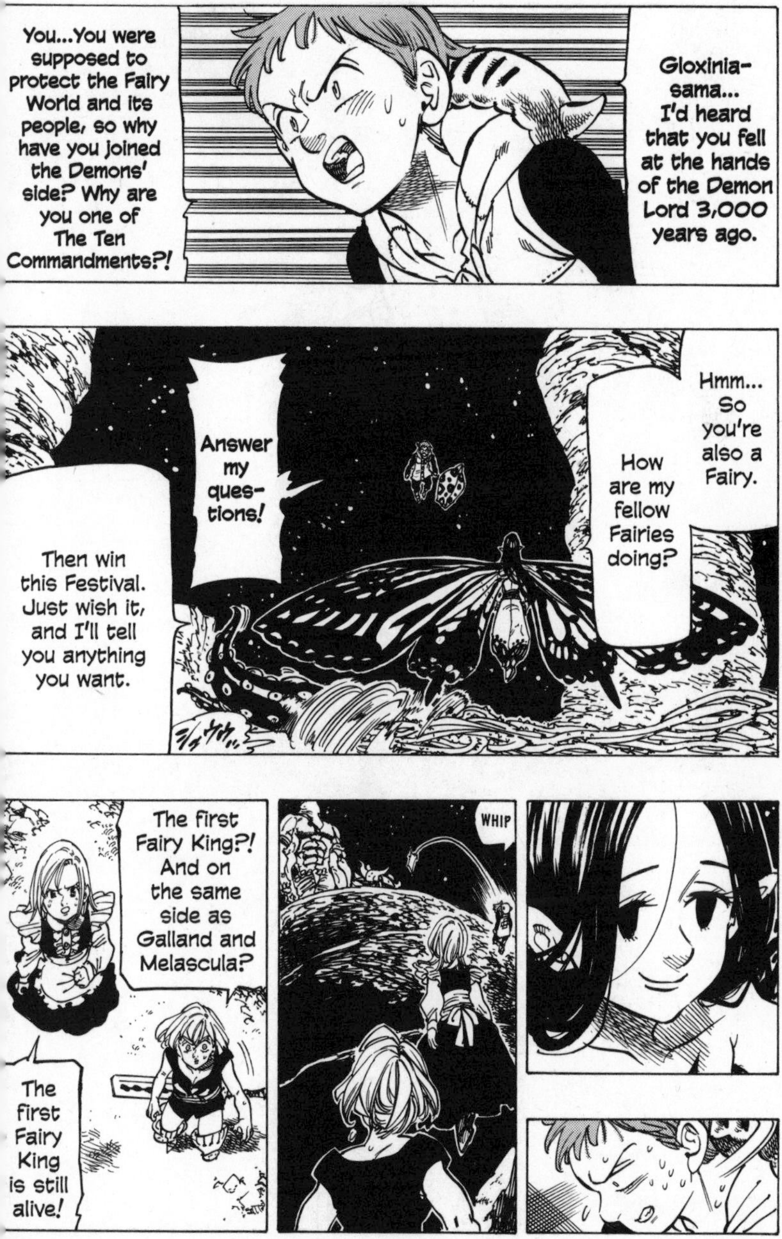
Gloxinia-sama... I'd heard that you fell at the hands of the Demon Lord 3,000 years ago.
You...You were supposed to protect the Fairy World and its people, so why have you joined the Demons' side? Why are you one of The Ten Commandments?!
Hmm... So you're also a Fairy.
How are my fellow Fairies doing?
Answer my questions!
Then win this Festival. Just wish it, and I'll tell you anything you want.
WHIP
The first Fairy King?! And on the same side as Galland and Melascula?
The first Fairy King is still alive!

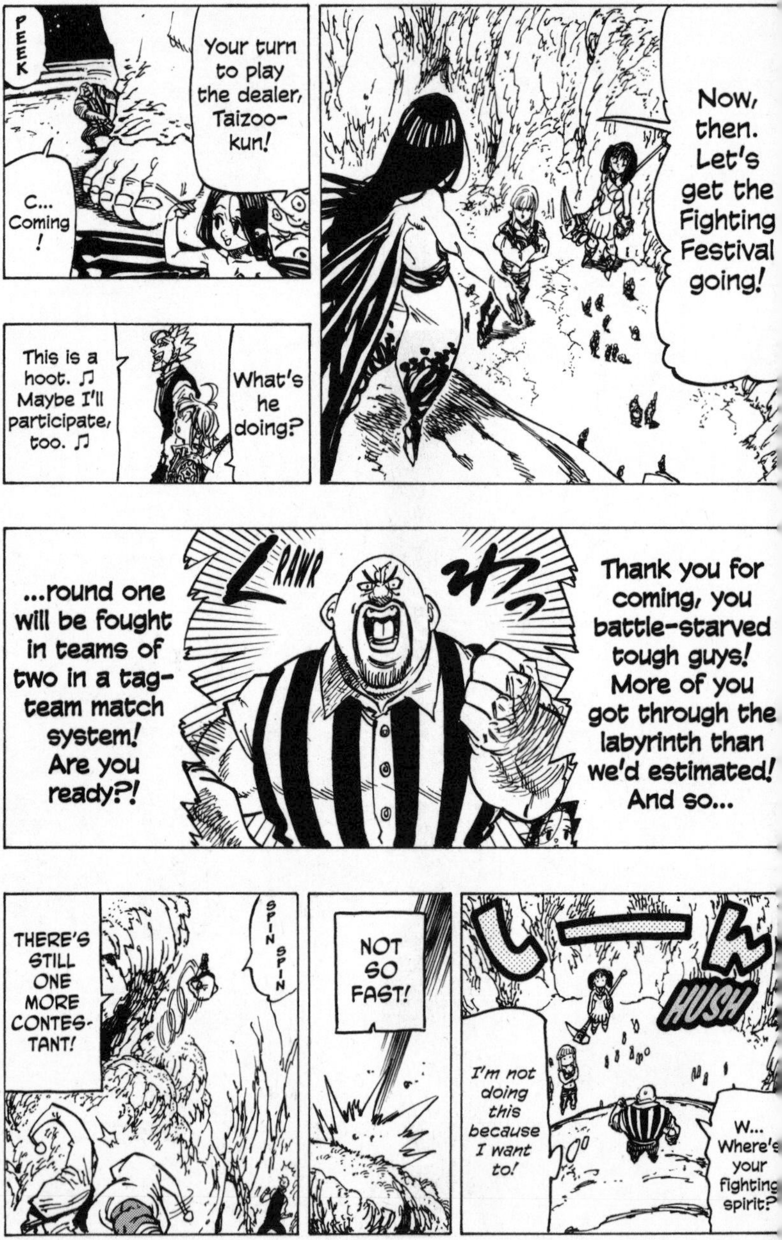
Now, then. Let's get the Fighting Festival going!
PEEK
Your turn to play the dealer, Taizoo-kun!
C... Coming!
What's he doing?
This is a hoot. ♫ Maybe I'll participate, too. ♫
Thank you for coming, you battle-starved tough guys! More of you got through the labyrinth than we'd estimated! And so...
RAWR
...round one will be fought in teams of two in a tag-team match system! Are you ready?!
HUSH
W... Where's your fighting spirit?
I'm not doing this because I want to!
NOT SO FAST!
SPIN SPIN
THERE'S STILL ONE MORE CONTES-TANT!

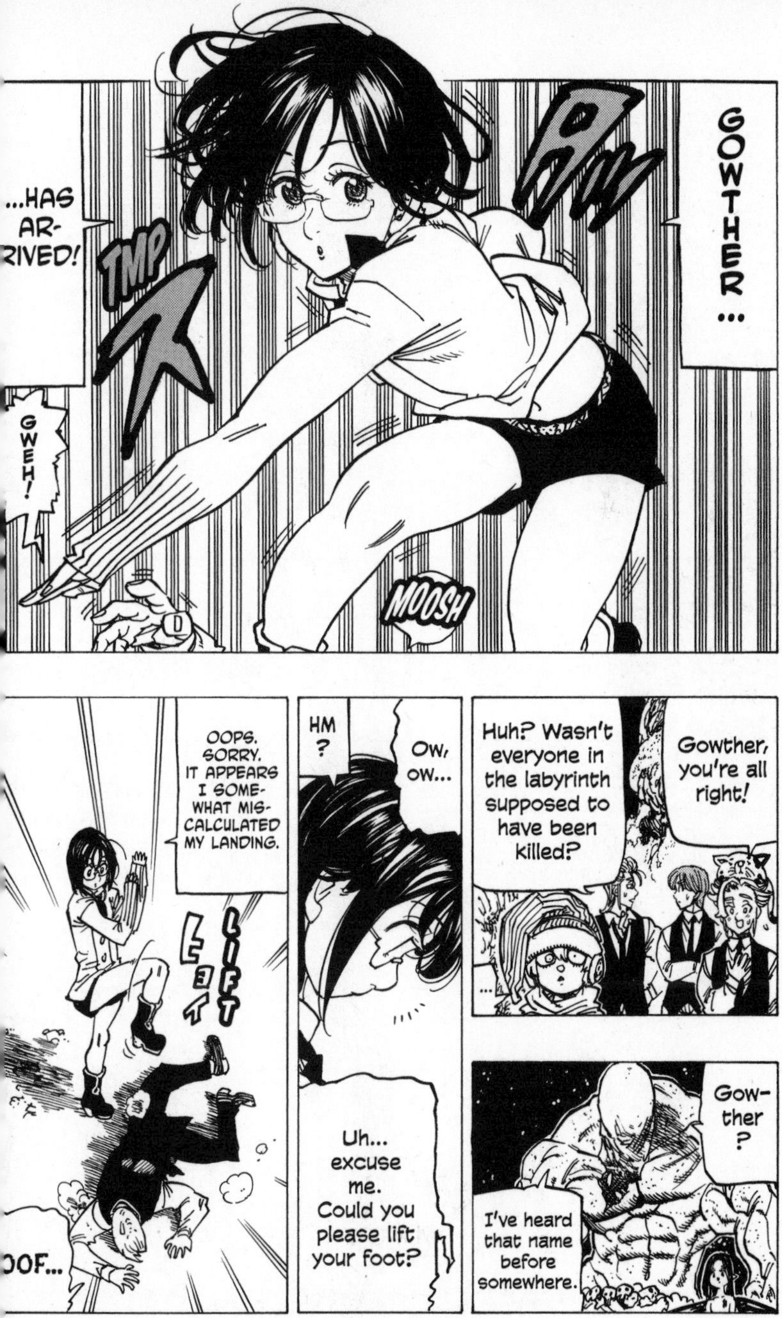
GOWTHER...
BAM
...HAS AR-RIVED!
TMP
GWEH!
MOOSH
Gowther, you're all right!
Huh? Wasn't everyone in the labyrinth supposed to have been killed?
...
Gow-ther?
I've heard that name before somewhere.
HM?
Ow, ow...
Uh... excuse me. Could you please lift your foot?
OOPS. SORRY. IT APPEARS I SOME-WHAT MIS-CALCULATED MY LANDING.
LIFT
LIFT
OOF...

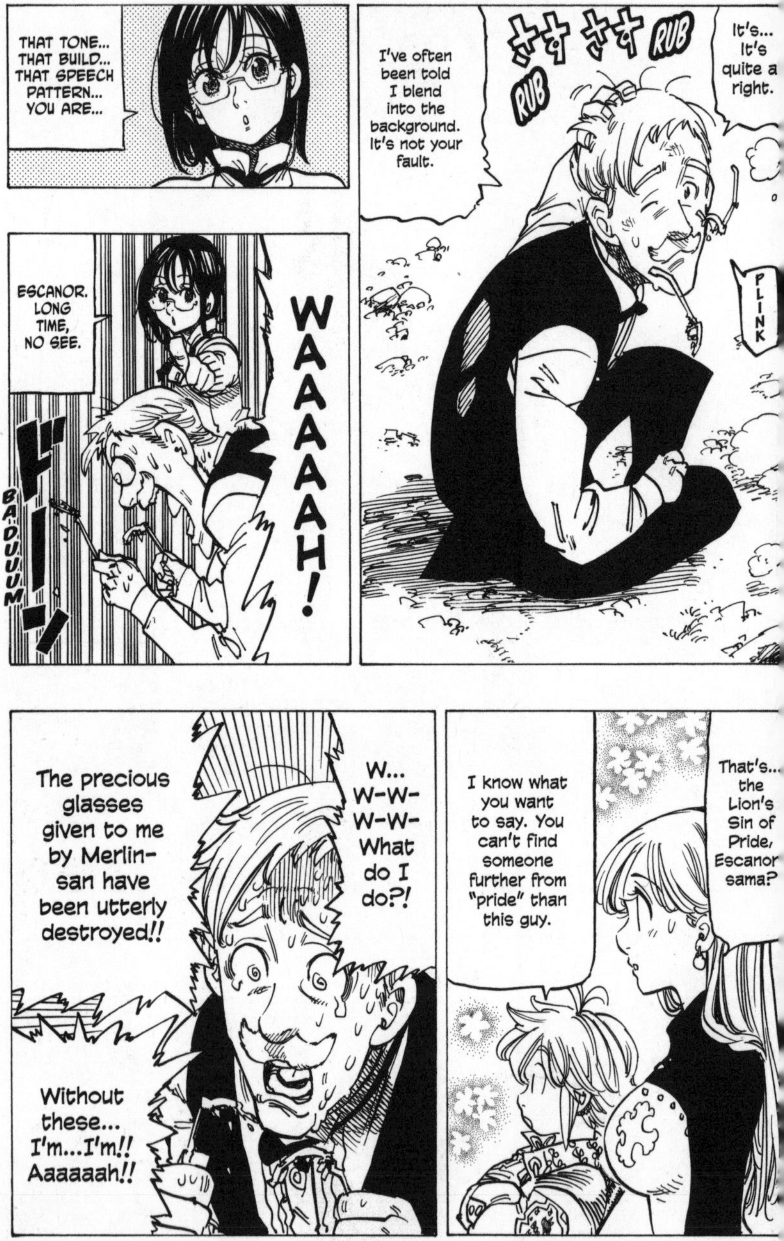
It's... It's quite a right.
RUB
RUB
I've often been told I blend into the background. It's not your fault.
PLINK
THAT TONE... THAT BUILD... THAT SPEECH PATTERN... YOU ARE...
ESCANOR. LONG TIME, NO SEE.
WAAAAAAH!
BA-DUUUUM
That's... the Lion's Sin of Pride, Escanor sama?
I know what you want to say. You can't find someone further from "pride" than this guy.
W... W-W-W-W-What do I do?!
The precious glasses given to me by Merlin-san have been utterly destroyed!!
Without these... I'm...I'm!! Aaaaaah!!

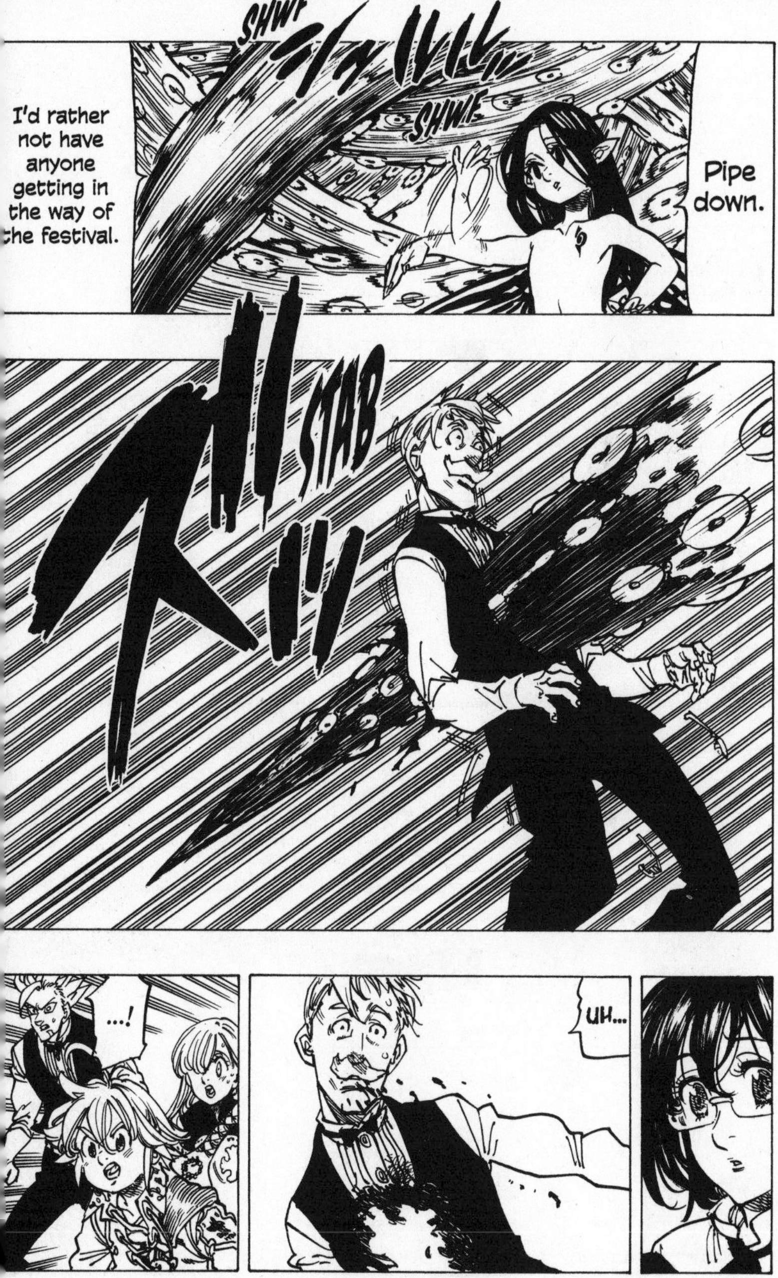
SHWF
SHWF
Pipe down.
I'd rather not have anyone getting in the way of the festival.
STAB
UH...
...!

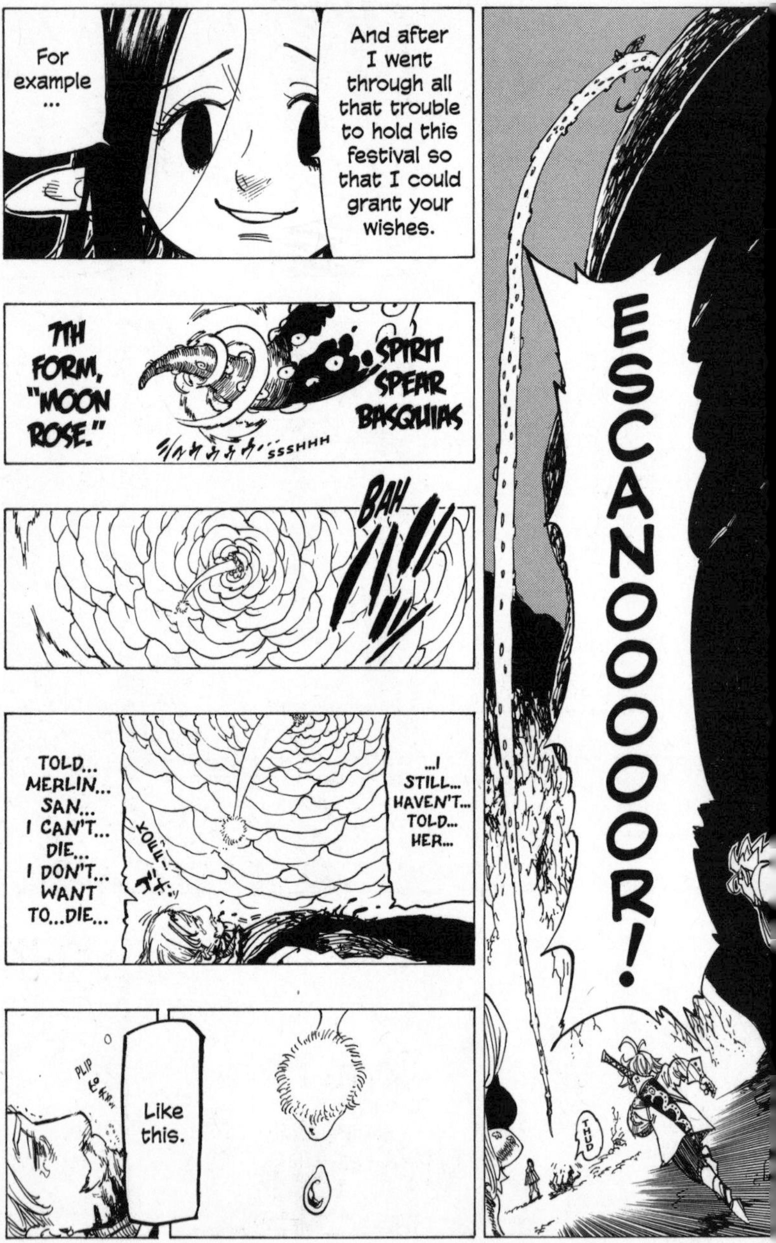
ESCANOOOOOOR!
THUD
And after I went through all that trouble to hold this festival so that I could grant your wishes.
For example ...
SPIRIT SPEAR BASQUIAS
7TH FORM, "MOON ROSE."
SSSHHH
BAH
...I STILL... HAVEN'T... TOLD... HER...
TOLD... MERLIN... SAN... I CAN'T... DIE... I DON'T... WANT TO...DIE...
KOFF
Like this.
PLIP

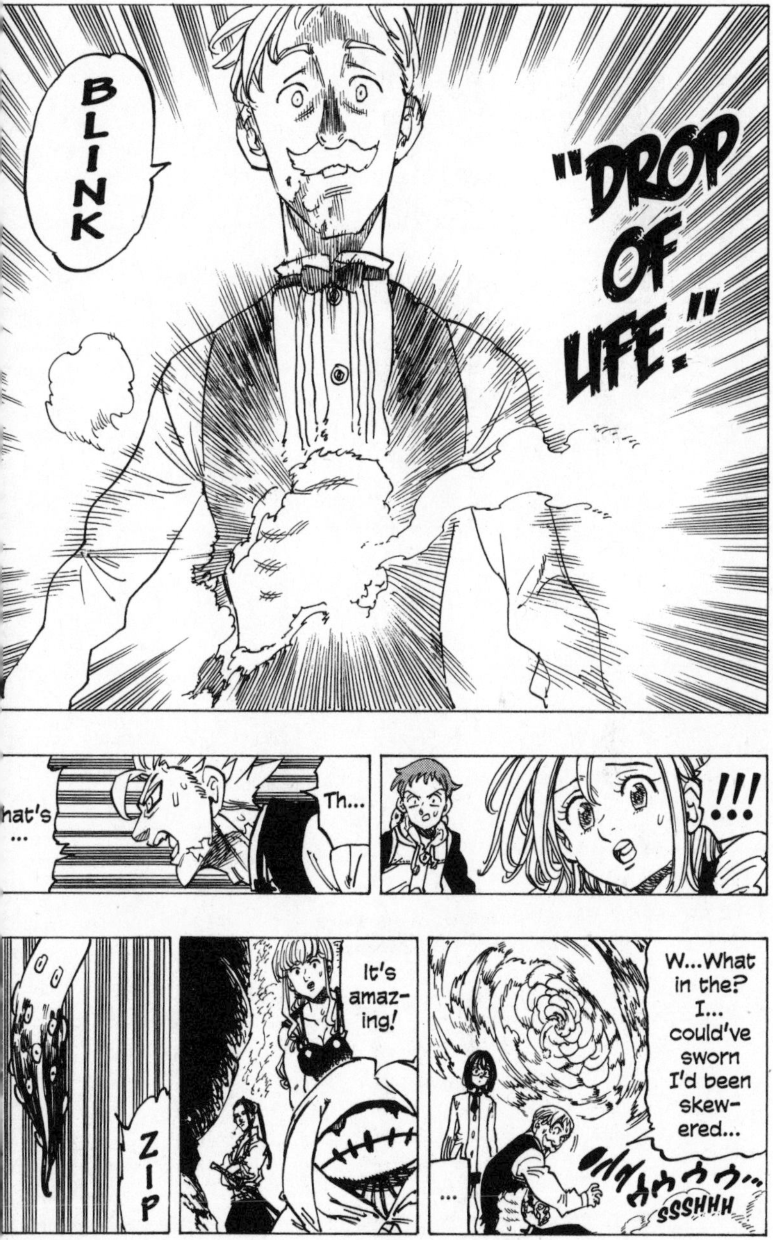
"DROP OF LIFE."
BLINK
!!!
Th...
hat's ...
W...What in the? I... could've sworn I'd been skewered...
SSSHHH
...
It's amazing!
ZIP

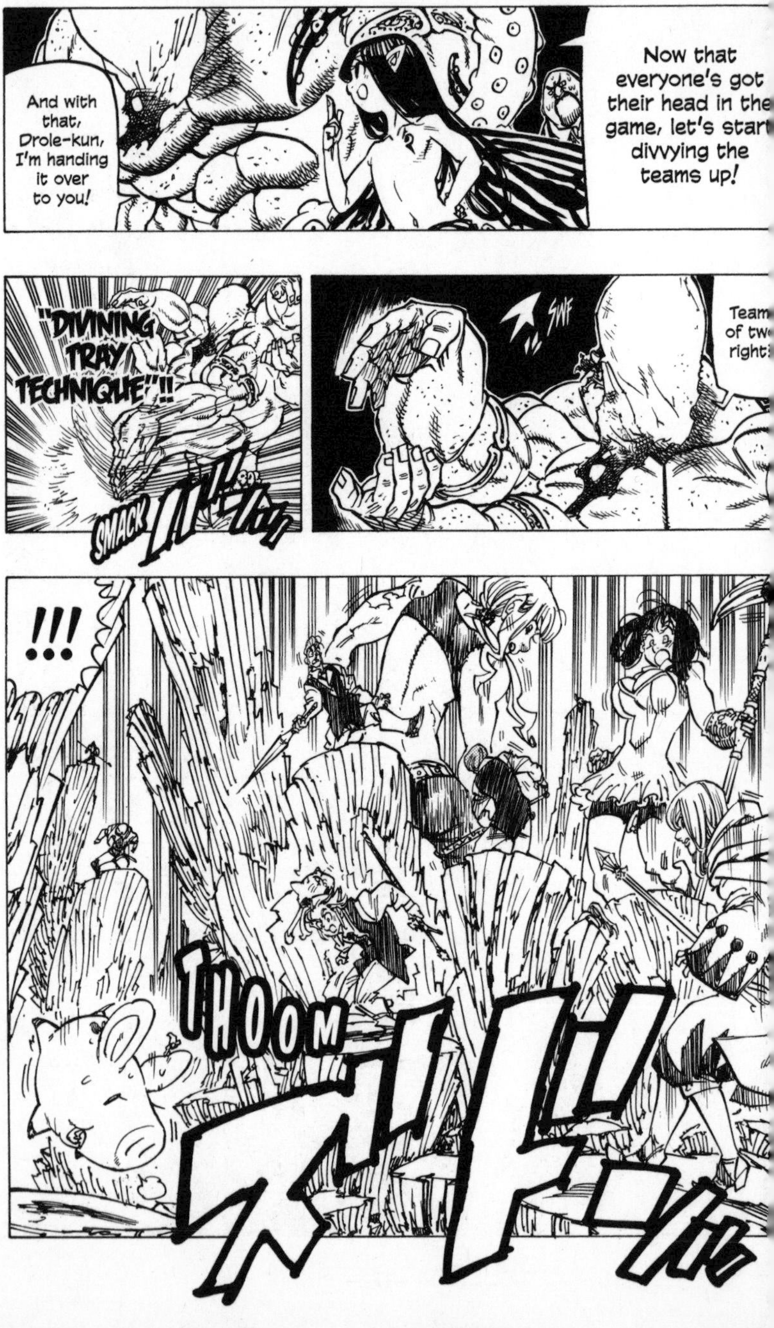
Now that everyone's got their head in the game, let's start divvying the teams up!
And with that, Drole-kun, I'm handing it over to you!
Team of tw right!
SWF
"DIVINING TRAY TECHNIQUE"!!
SMACK
!!!
THOOM

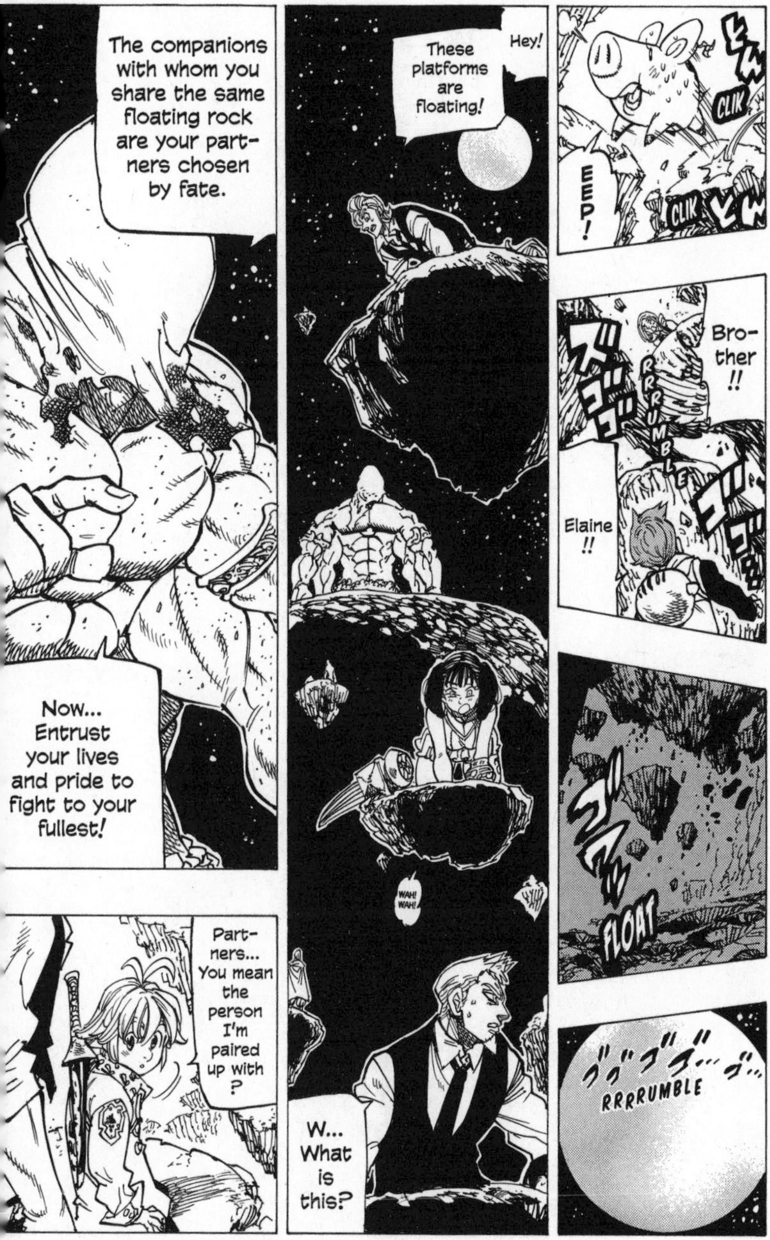
CLIK
EEP!
CLIK
Brother!!
RRRUMBLE
Elaine!!
FLOAT
RRRRUMBLE
Hey!
These platforms are floating!
WAH! WAH!
W... What is this?
The companions with whom you share the same floating rock are your partners chosen by fate.
Now... Entrust your lives and pride to fight to your fullest!
Partners... You mean the person I'm paired up with?

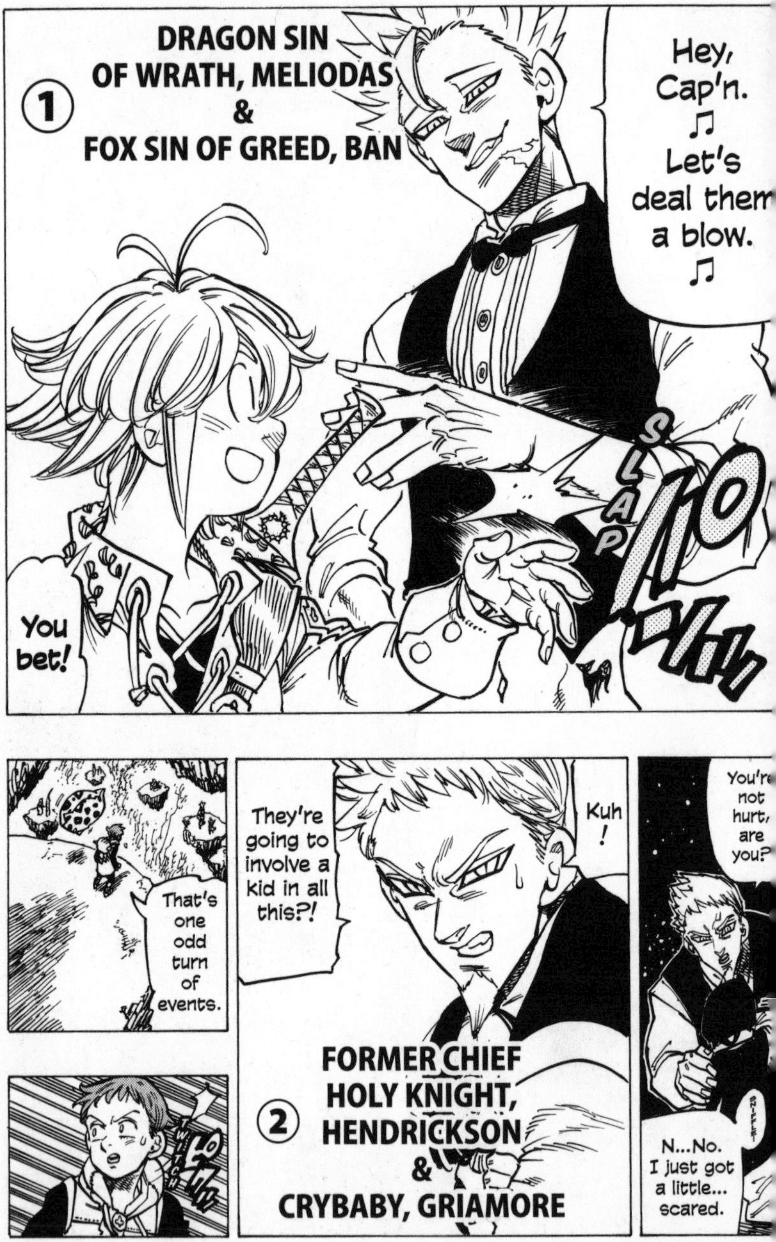
Hey, Cap'n. ♫ Let's deal them a blow. ♫
① DRAGON SIN OF WRATH, MELIODAS & FOX SIN OF GREED, BAN
SLAP
You bet!
You're not hurt, are you?
SNIFFLE
N...No. I just got a little... scared.
Kuh!
They're going to involve a kid in all this?!
② FORMER CHIEF HOLY KNIGHT, HENDRICKSON & CRYBABY, GRIAMORE
That's one odd turn of events.
TWITCH

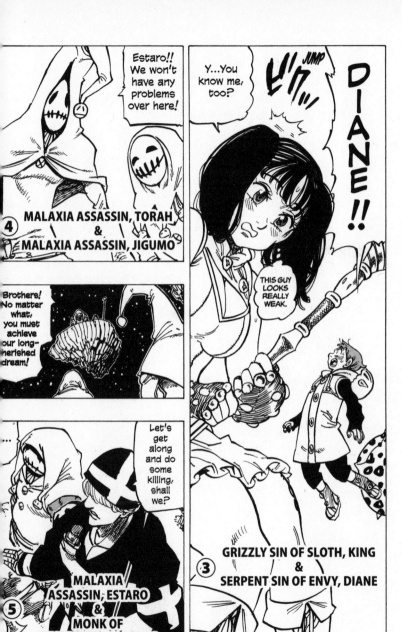

JUMP
Y...You know me, too?
DIANE!!
THIS GUY LOOKS REALLY WEAK.
3
GRIZZLY SIN OF SLOTH, KING & SERPENT SIN OF ENVY, DIANE
Estaro!! We won't have any problems over here!
4
MALAXIA ASSASSIN, TORAH & MALAXIA ASSASSIN, JIGUMO
Brothers! No matter what, you must achieve our long-herished dream!
...
Let's get along and do some killing, shall we?
5
MALAXIA ASSASSIN, ESTARO & MONK OF DESTRUCTION, ARBUS

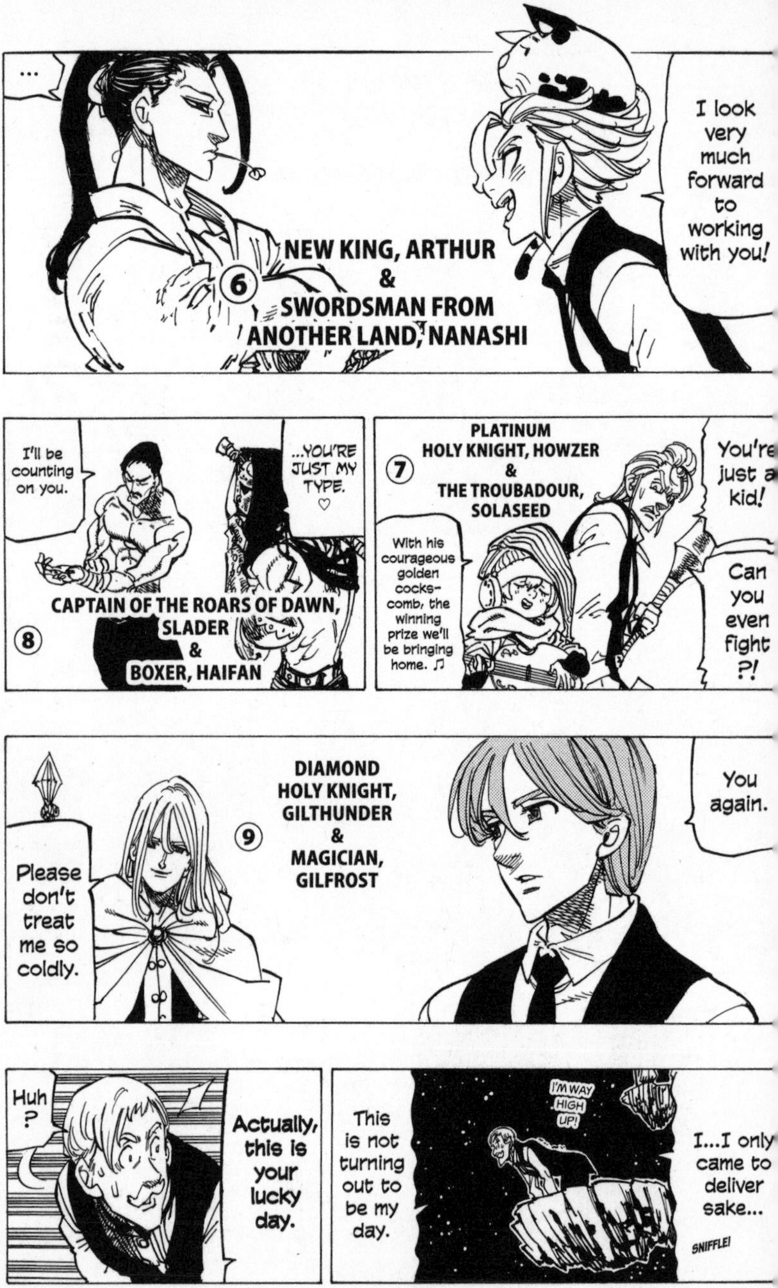
I look very much forward to working with you!
6 NEW KING, ARTHUR & SWORDSMAN FROM ANOTHER LAND, NANASHI
...
You're just a kid!
Can you even fight?!
7 PLATINUM HOLY KNIGHT, HOWZER & THE TROUBADOUR, SOLASEED
With his courageous golden cocks-comb, the winning prize we'll be bringing home. ♫
...YOU'RE JUST MY TYPE. ♡
I'll be counting on you.
8 CAPTAIN OF THE ROARS OF DAWN, SLADER & BOXER, HAIFAN
You again.
9 DIAMOND HOLY KNIGHT, GILTHUNDER & MAGICIAN, GILFROST
Please don't treat me so coldly.
I...I only came to deliver sake...
SNIFFLE!
I'M WAY HIGH UP!
This is not turning out to be my day.
Actually, this is your lucky day.
Huh?

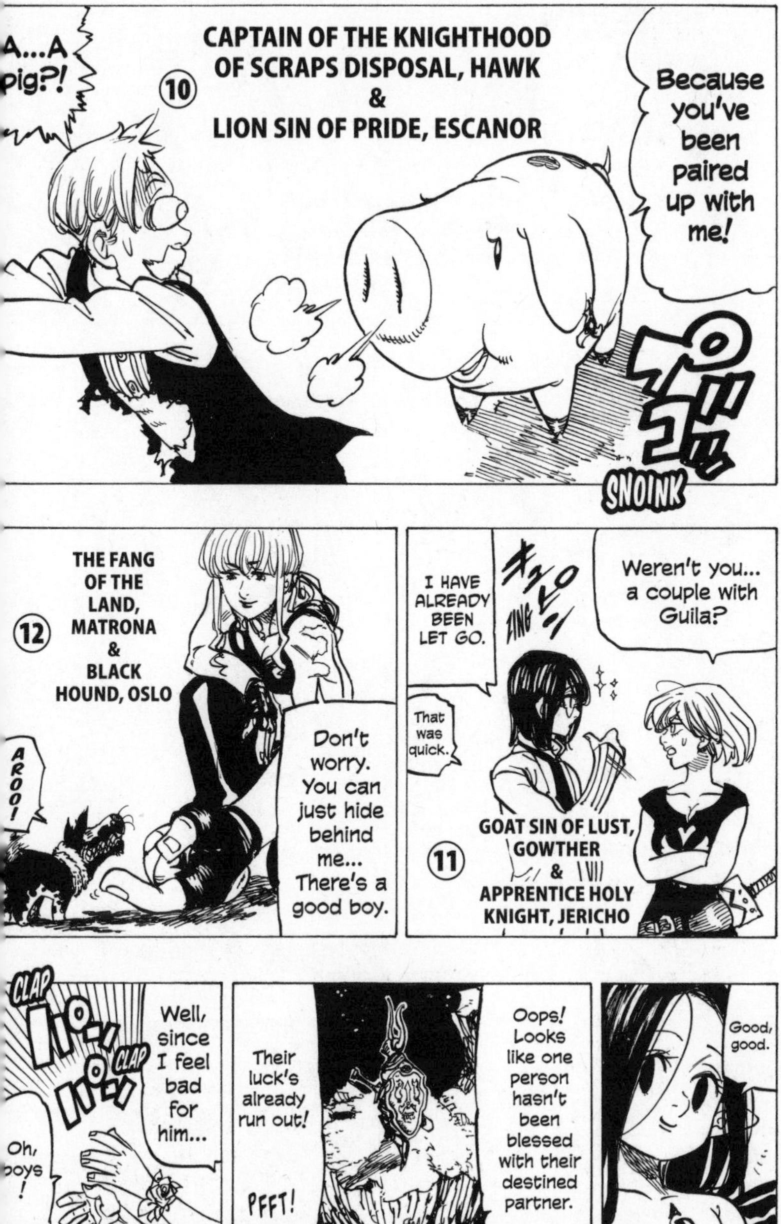
Because you've been paired up with me!
10 CAPTAIN OF THE KNIGHTHOOD OF SCRAPS DISPOSAL, HAWK & LION SIN OF PRIDE, ESCANOR
A...A pig?!
SNOINK
Weren't you... a couple with Guila?
I HAVE ALREADY BEEN LET GO.
ZING
That was quick.
11 GOAT SIN OF LUST, GOWTHER & APPRENTICE HOLY KNIGHT, JERICHO
12 THE FANG OF THE LAND, MATRONA & BLACK HOUND, OSLO
Don't worry. You can just hide behind me... There's a good boy.
AROO!
Good, good.
Oops! Looks like one person hasn't been blessed with their destined partner.
Their luck's already run out!
PFFT!
Well, since I feel bad for him...
CLAP
CLAP
Oh, boys!

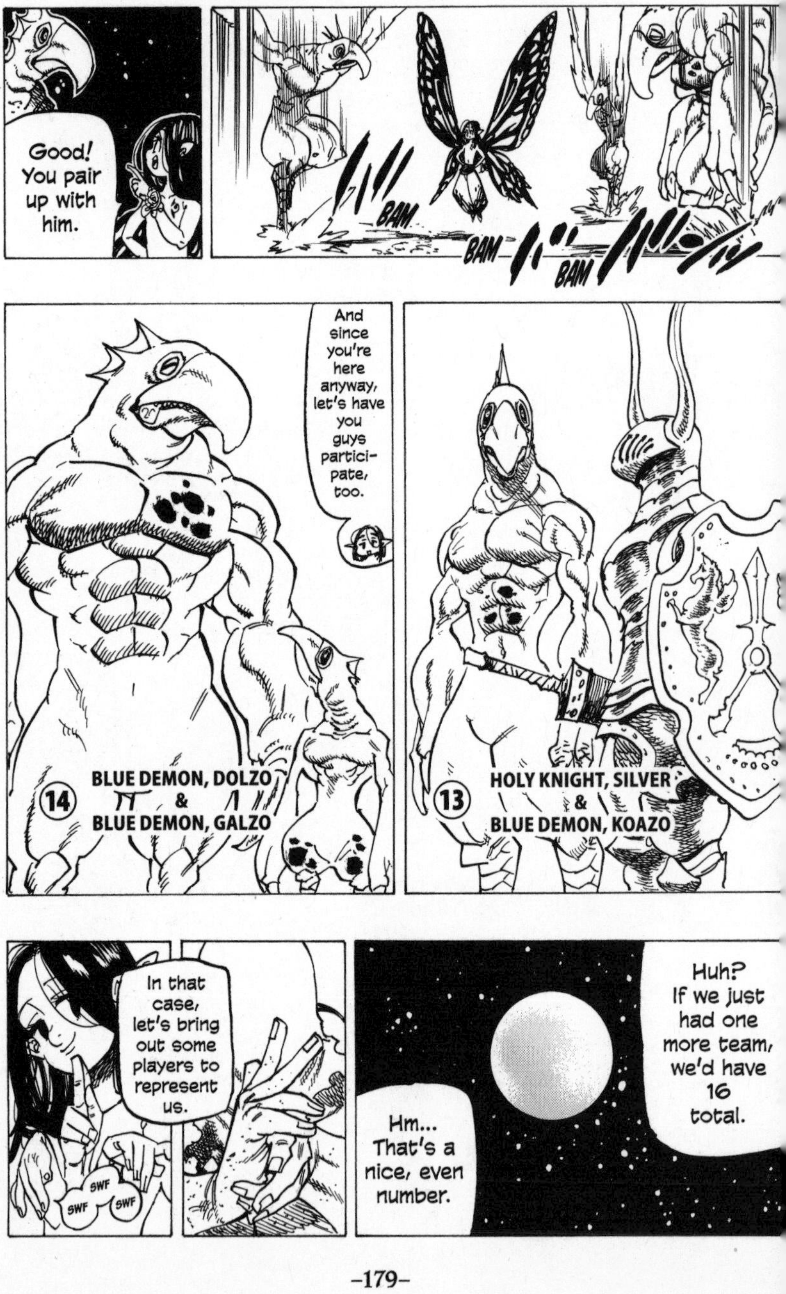
BAM
BAM
BAM
Good! You pair up with him.
13
HOLY KNIGHT, SILVER & BLUE DEMON, KOAZO
And since you're here anyway, let's have you guys partici-pate, too.
14
BLUE DEMON, DOLZO & BLUE DEMON, GALZO
Huh? If we just had one more team, we'd have 16 total.
Hm... That's a nice, even number.
In that case, let's bring out some players to represent us.
SWF
SWF
SWF

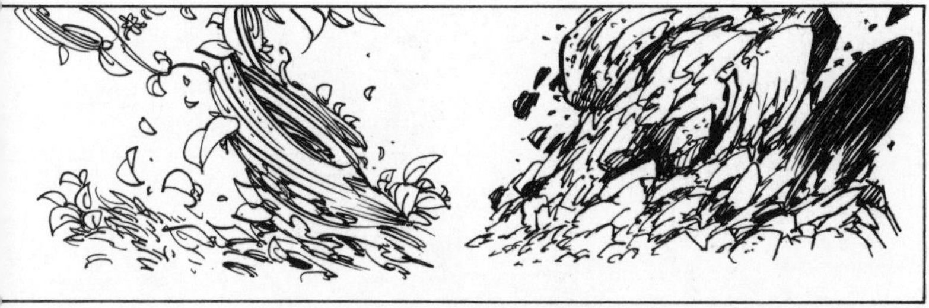

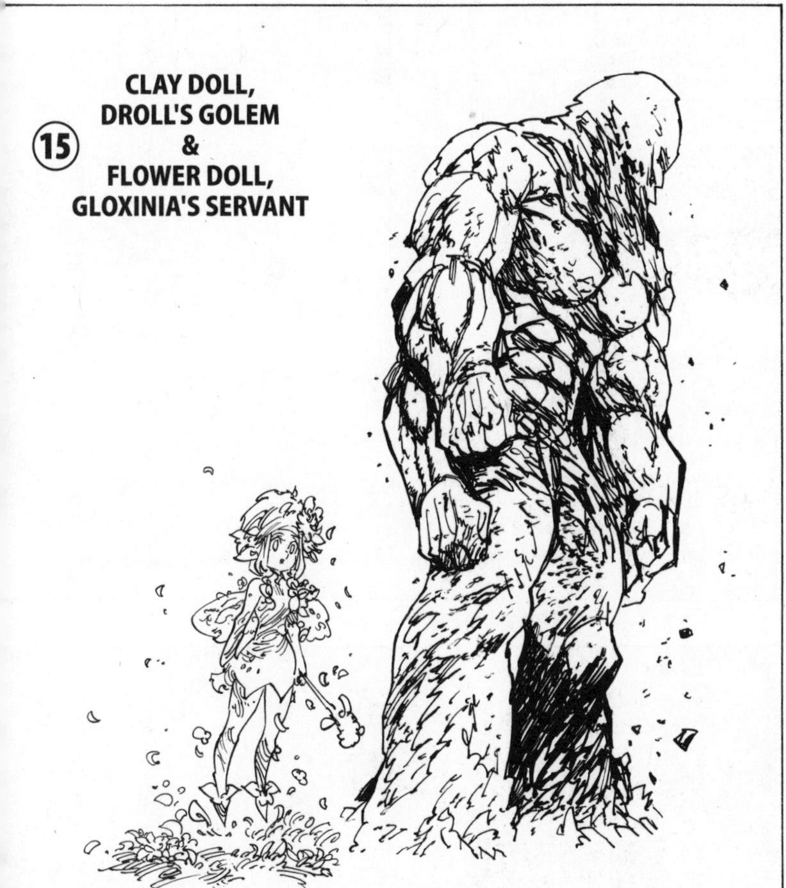
15
CLAY DOLL,
DROLL'S GOLEM
&
FLOWER DOLL,
GLOXINIA'S SERVANT

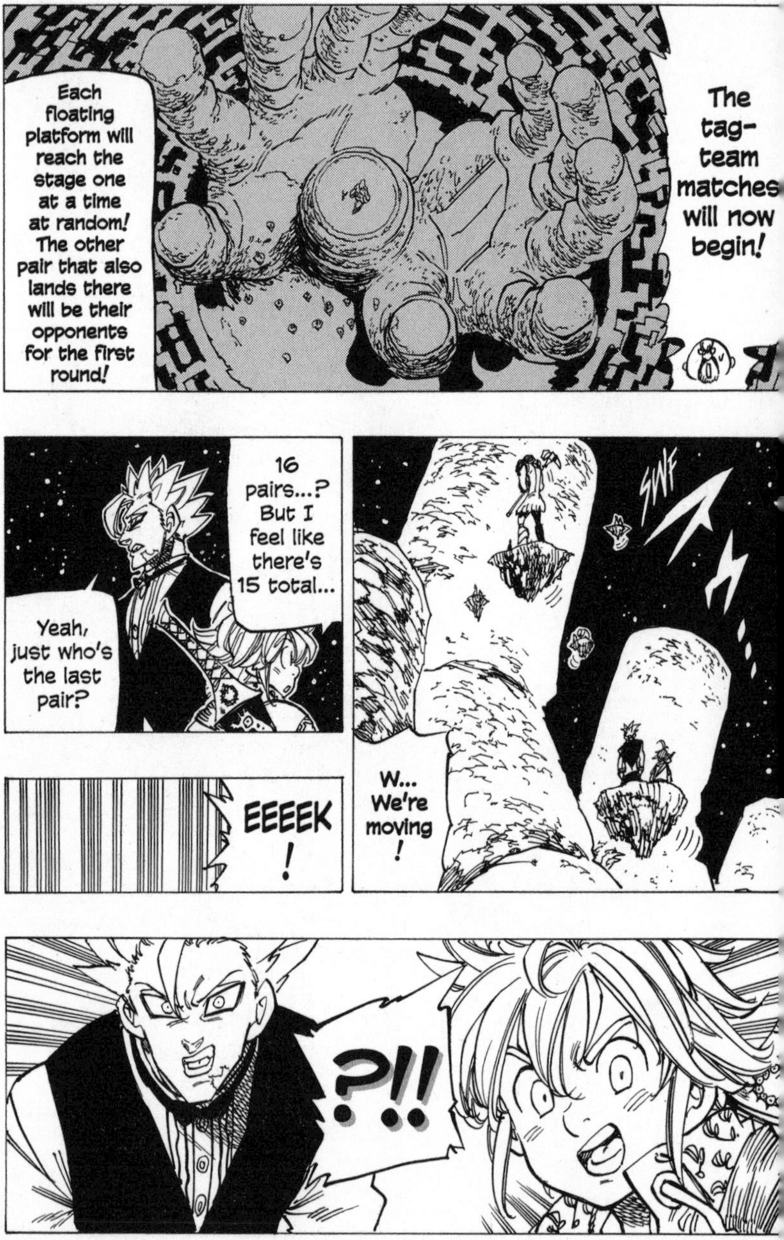
The tag-team matches will now begin!
Each floating platform will reach the stage one at a time at random! The other pair that also lands there will be their opponents for the first round!
W... We're moving!
16 pairs...? But I feel like there's 15 total...
Yeah, just who's the last pair?
EEEEK!
?!!

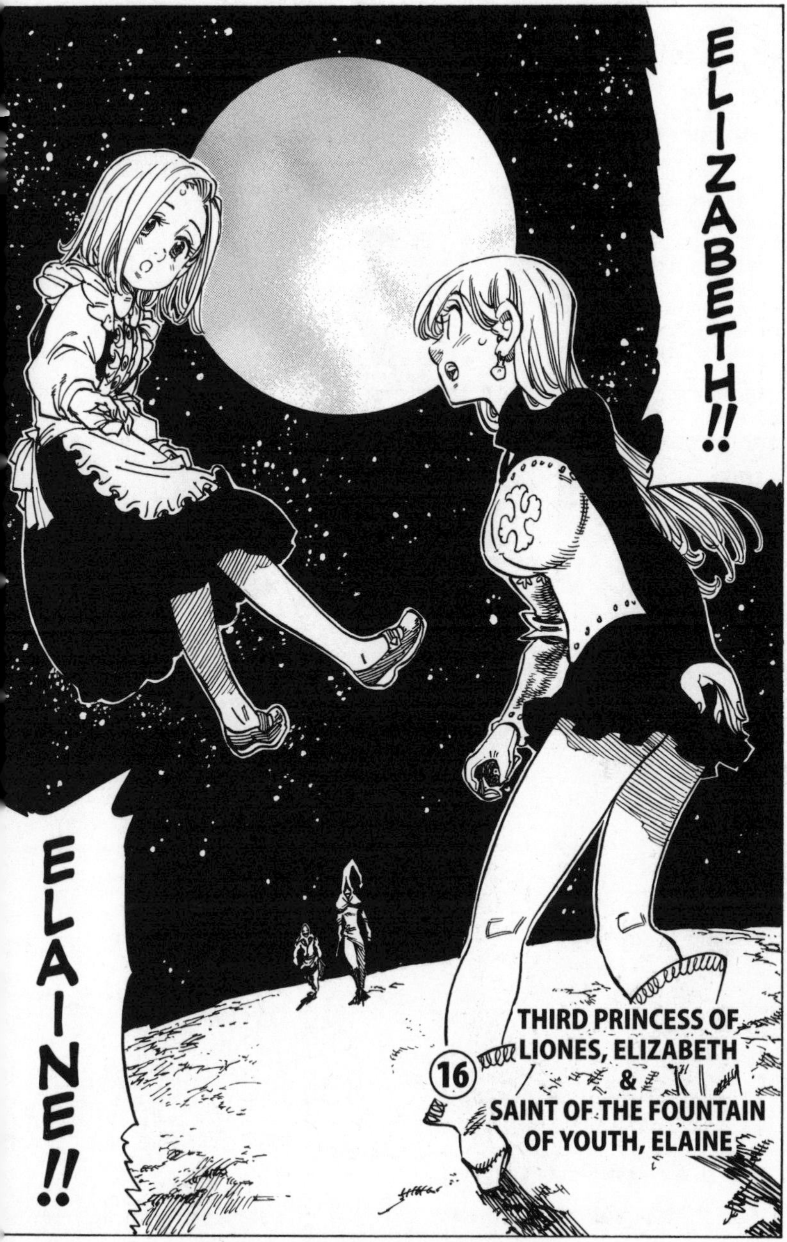
ELIZABETH!!
ELAINE!!
16
THIRD PRINCESS OF LIONES, ELIZABETH & SAINT OF THE FOUNTAIN OF YOUTH, ELAINE

To Be Continued in Volume 21...

"THE SEVEN DEADLY SINS" ILLUSTRATION CORNER

"THE DRAWING KNIGHTHOOD" SPACE

This time we're featuring participants from abroad!

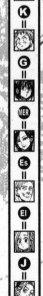

SPECIAL PRIZE

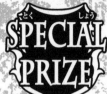

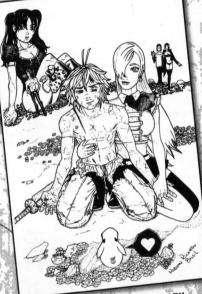

HUDSON RICARDO-SAN / BRAZIL

E "Thinking back on it even now, you were a hero back then, too, Hawk!"

H "Aw, shucks. I only did what any friend would! Snoink!"

BAN
SEVEN DEADLY SINS
ARTWORK of ACHMAD FAUZI
SCRETCHME.DEVIANTART.COM

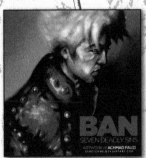

ACHMAD FAUZI-SAN / INDONESIA

Es "I swear, if I ran into Ban on the roadside in the dead of night, I'd faint."

H "Yeah? Well, I'd poop myself."

E "Hawk-chan..."

七つの大罪

MAGUERRAMOVA-SAN / FRANCE

MER "Hmm...it seems that everyone's gender has been switched for some reason."

K "Heh heh! Escanor's wanted poster is downright terrifying!"

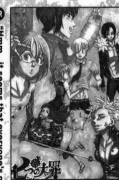

MUTIA RIZANATI-SAN / INDONESIA

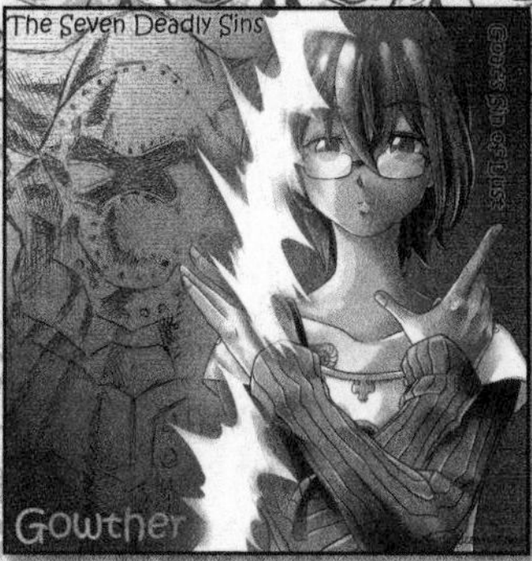
The Seven Deadly Sins
Gowther

"Whoever wants to be fed to my double bow, Harlitt, step forward... Swoon!"

"How much does he mean what he says?"

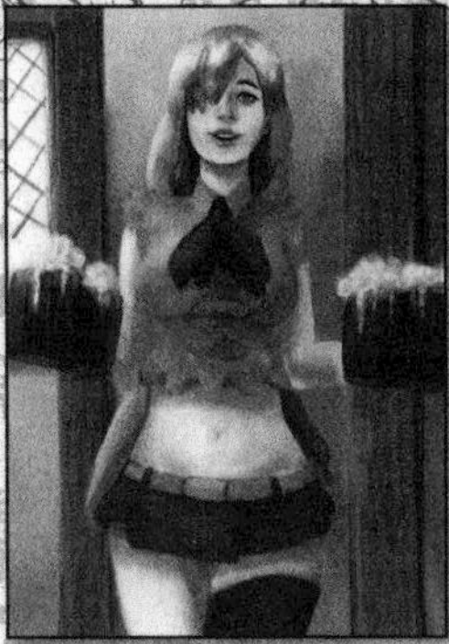

C0GGIE-SAN / USA

H "Boar's Hat is the only establishment in the whole wide world that would hire a princess to be a waitress."

M "That's one of our selling points!"

H "The barkeep's the greatest friend you could ask for. Right, Elizabeth-chan?!"

E "To me, Meliodas-sama is...uh... well... (blush)"

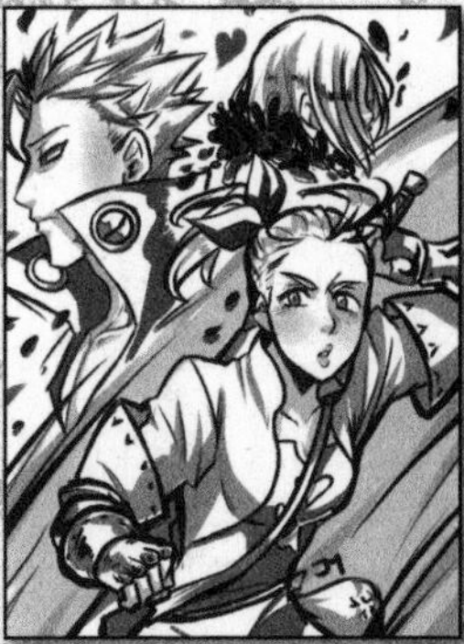

JULYMARTE-SAN / ITALY

MER "Are these three in what they call a 'love triangle'?"

E "Hmmm... I get the feeling it's not as simple as that."

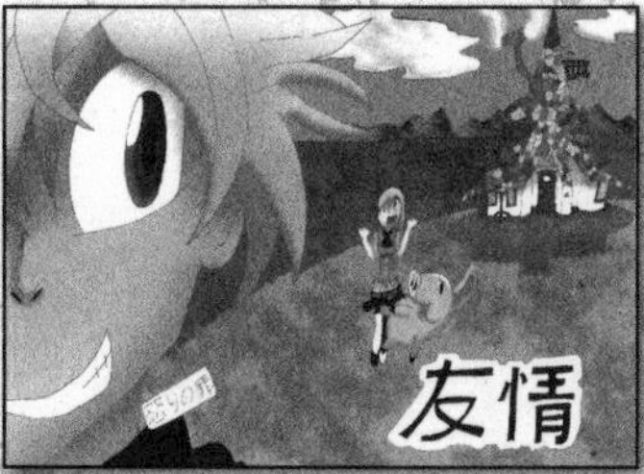
友情

NATSU9000-SAN / SCOTLAND

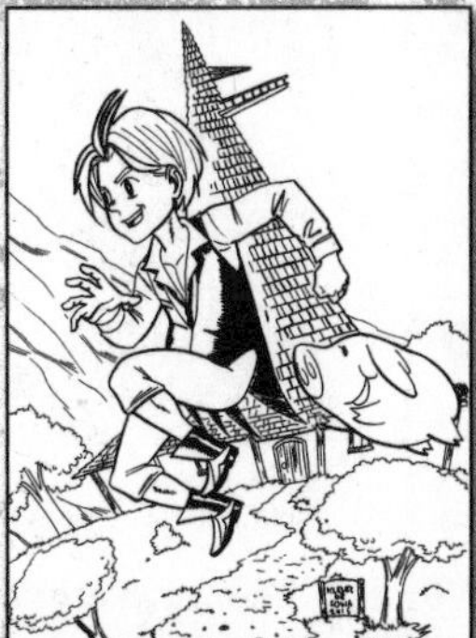

KLEBER DE SOUSA-SAN / BRAZIL

H "If it's a walk you're going on, I'm tagging along!"

M "I've got to go guard Elizabeth while she's taking her bath!"

H "Then I have to stop you!"

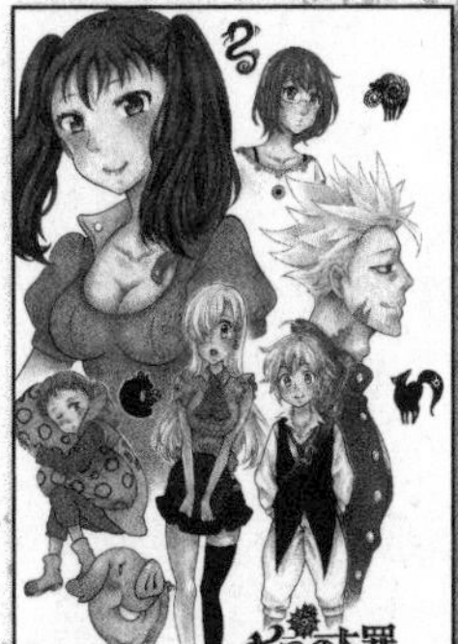
七つの大罪

JUISHAN LIANG-SAN / TAIWAN

E "I believe that it's because I met everyone that I'm stronger than ever."

M "You're way stronger than you used to be."

E "Meliodas-sama...!"

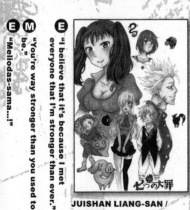

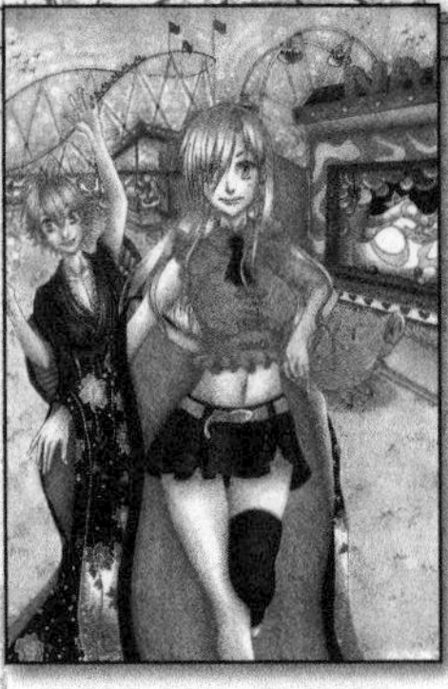

DICOP-SAN / FRANCE

M “Nothing says a festival like a kimono! And kimonos look best when they're being stripped off!”

E “Ha wa wa wah! Ah...Um...!”

H “Guys, this is an amusement park we're in!”

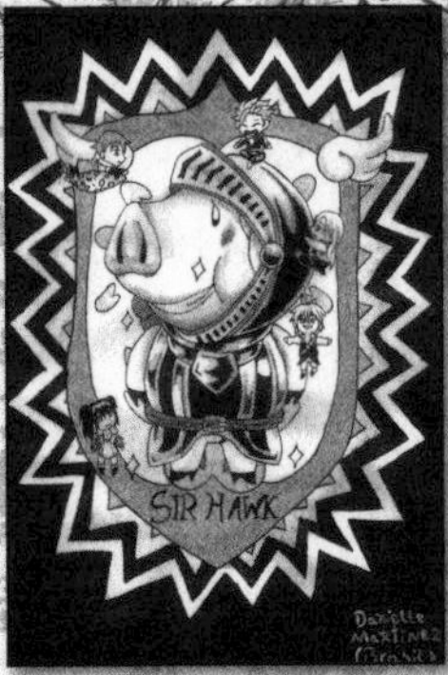
SIR HAWK

DANIELLE MARTINEZ-SAN / BRAZIL

H “Look! This is the new costume for the Knighthood of Scraps Disposal! Oof...! B-But it's a little tight around the waist...”

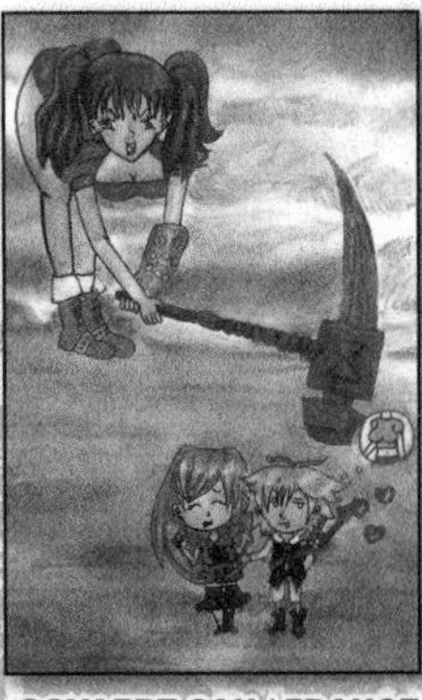

GOVAERT-SAN / FRANCE

D “Captain, you pervert!”

B “Diane's striking with everything she's got!♫”

M “That would kill me.”

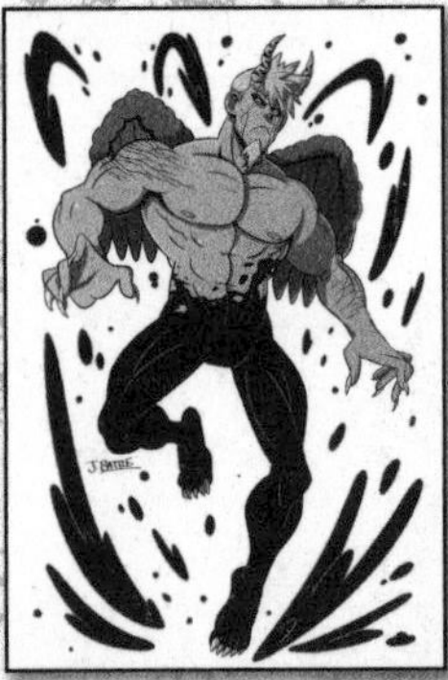

BARONBATTLE-SAN / USA

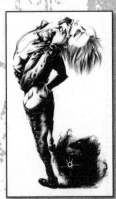

K “I'll have you know, I still haven't forgiven him for what he did.”

H “I'm not really mad about it anymore.”

K “Mr. Pig, you are crazy.”

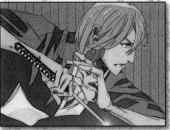

M “The way Gil's so serious that he can't even take a joke reminds me an awful lot of Hendrickson.”

D “Ah ha ha! You're right!”

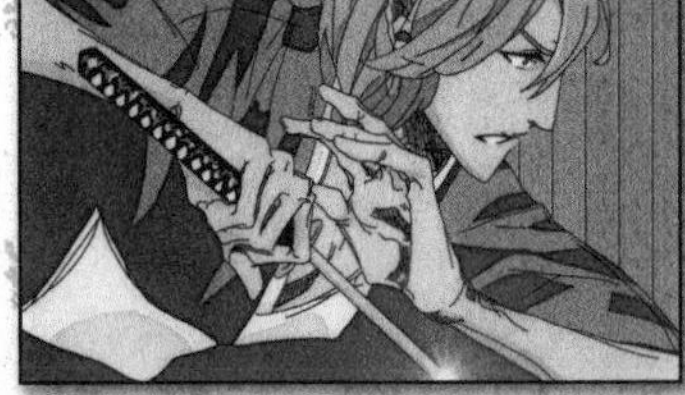

MARINA TORRIJOS VELASCO-SAN / SPAIN

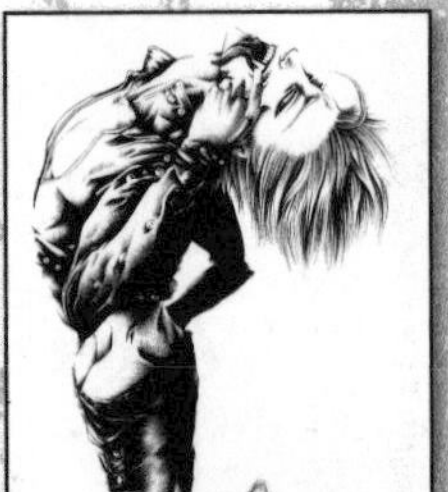

GRETA DONELLA-SAN / ITALY

B “What're you staring at? I'll bite you to death.♫”

B “Snoooink! But then we'll be bound for life!”

M "More than ten years ago, Dreyfus was always calling Hendrickson 'Hendy! Hendy!' and bothering him with his teasing."

H "Pfffft!

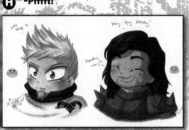

ISABELL DIETRICH-SAN / GERMANY

E "In Escanor's presence, even Ban behaves himself."

B "Kah kah! ♫ That's because he's terrifying!"

K "...(Do you really feel that way?)"

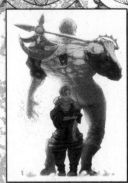

DESORIENTER-SAN / USA

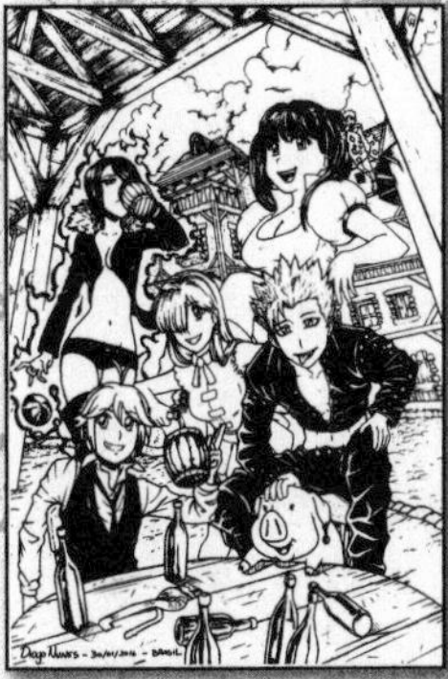

E "Wow, the Hawk-chan in this picture is super adorable...!"

M "You think it might be an impostor?"

H "I'm the real one! Snoink!!"

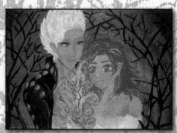

DIOGO NUNES-SAN / BRAZIL

El "Ban, thank you for protecting the Fairy King's Forest."

B "What else was I going to do? After all, you asked me to."♫

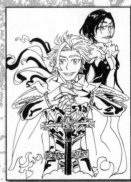

ILIREA-SAN / USA

B "That guy's head is totally blank."

G "I am sorry to say but I am actually simulating thinking about something deeply."

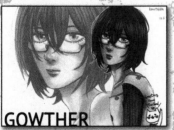

GOWTHER

KANTHIDA PACHANATIP-SAN / THAILAND

Es "M-Merlin-san, what is the nature of your relationship...with that young man?!"

MER "Well...I suppose, you could say he's my master."

Es "Aaaaah!"

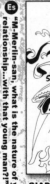

GIADA CROCI-SAN / ITALY

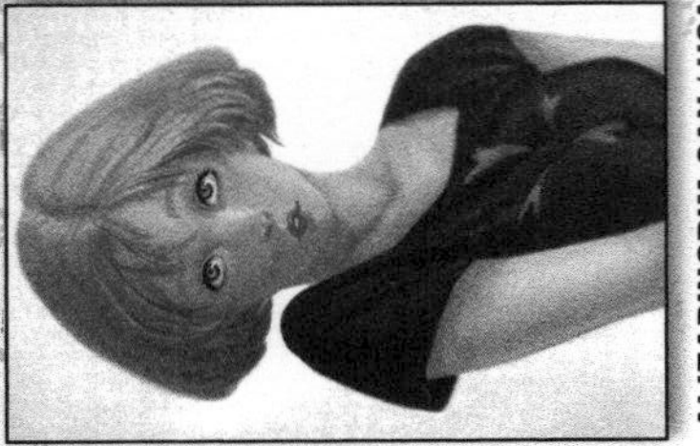

ALIZARINCRIM-SAN / USA

EI "Jericho, you're amazing!"

J "W-What makes you say that?"

EI "Because Ban and I love you, and we don't even like Humans!"

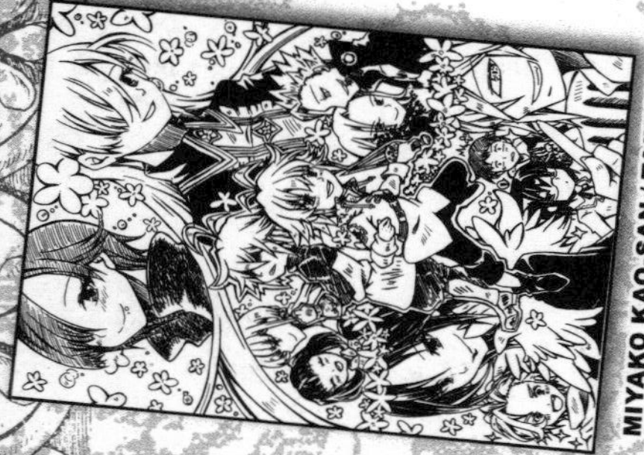

MIYAKO KAO-SAN / TAIWAN

"I like it, I like it! Everyone looks so young. Wait...hm? How come I'm nowhere in the picture?!"

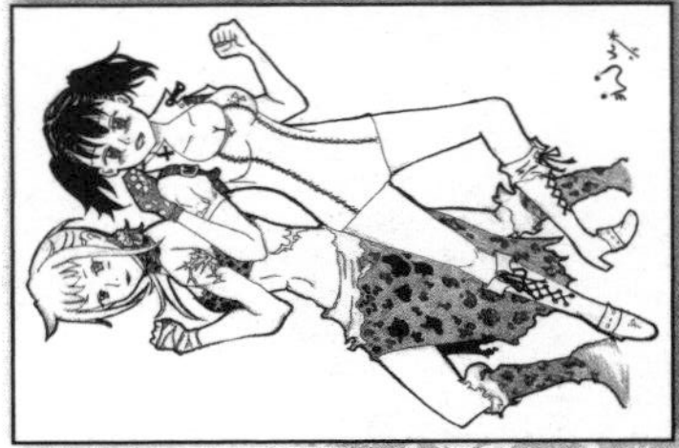

WU-SAN / TAIWAN

D "We've got to win the Fighting Festival for Zol and Della's sakes, Matrona!"

K "I'll be cheering you on too, Diane!"

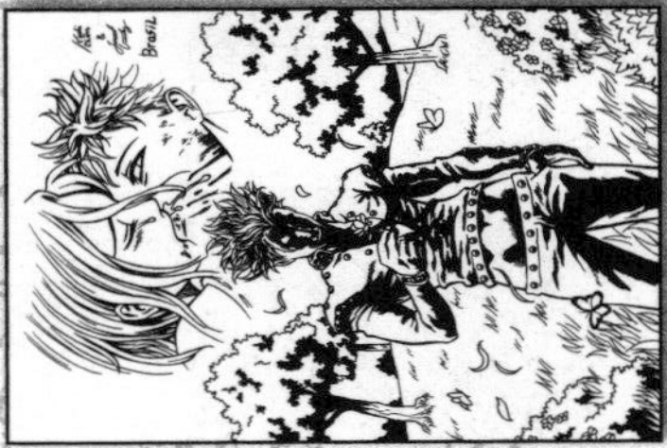

ISRAEL GUEDES-SAN / BRAZIL

Es "At first glance, Ban-san may look scary, but he's more earnest than anybody else... He puts his whole heart into things."

K "I...I guess that's one way to put it."

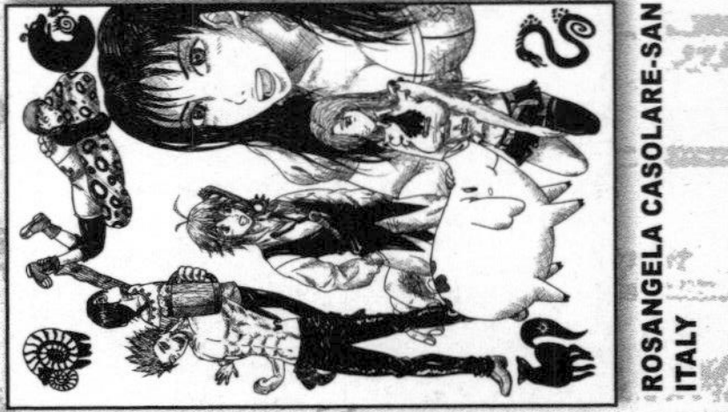

ROSANGELA CASOLARE-SAN / ITALY

K "Knock it off, Gowther! Don't grab my leg while I"m flying, okay?"

G "Then let me ride on your cushion, too."

K "No way!"

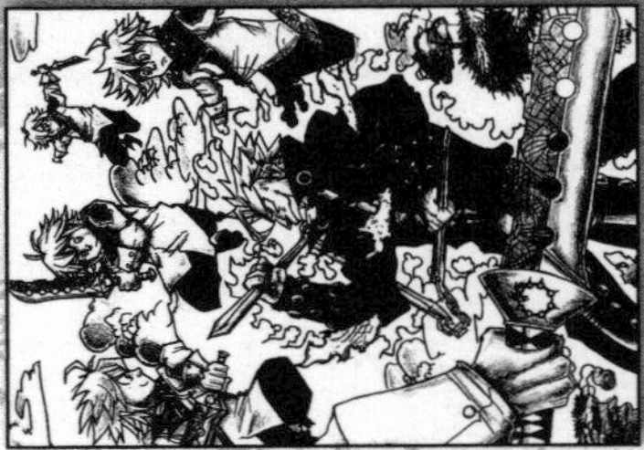

CORAZON-SAN / USA

B "Hah hah... ♫ Nice one, Cap'n! Now, bring on even more!" ♫

M "Hee hee hee! Promise you won't regret it?"

K "Those two are at it again."

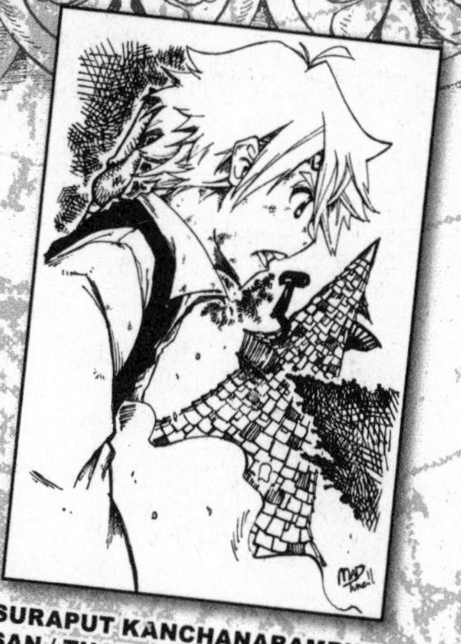

SURAPUT KANCHANABAMRUNG-SAN / THAILAND

"I love the serious faces Meliodas-sama sometimes show. Oh, and of course his usual expressions, too."

"You're such a girl."

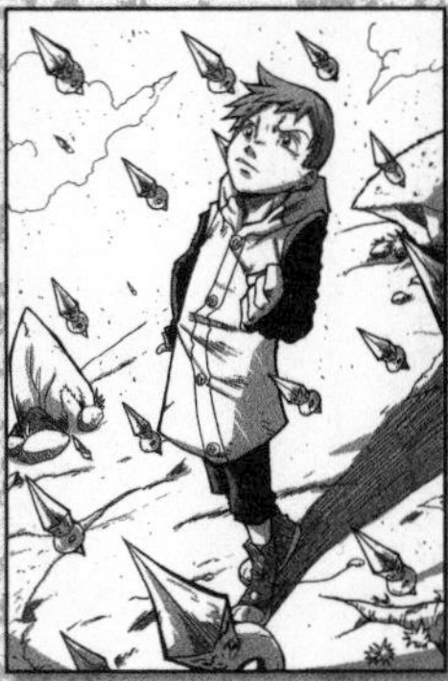

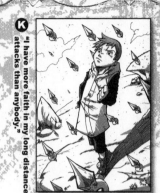

STASZAK-SAN / FRANCE

K "I have more faith in my long distance attacks than anybody."

Es "Not so fast, King-kun! Have you forgotten about Merlin-san?"

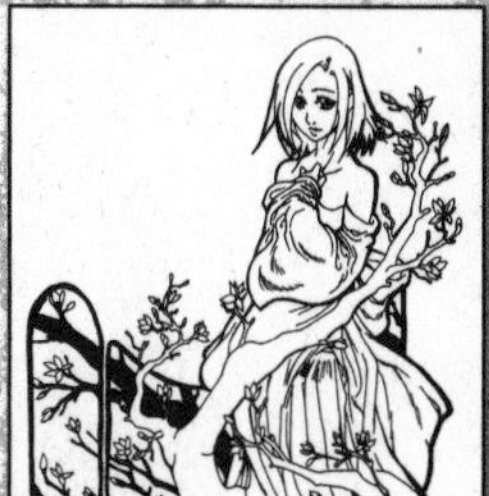

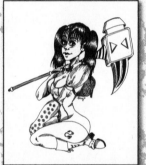

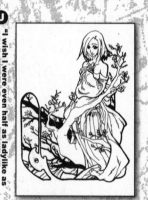

ANA MACIAS KHAENGKHAN-SAN / SPAIN

J "I wish I were even half as ladylike as Elaine."

B "For starters, you can stop sitting cross-legged."♪

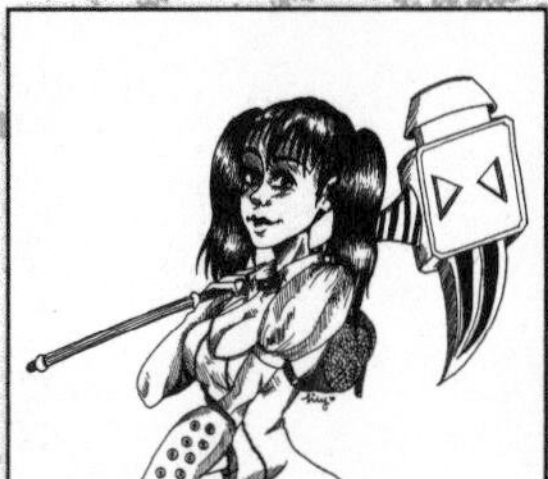

PATROCIELLO ILARIA-SAN / ITALY

K "I always did believe cute girls look best with hammers."

M "Say that again?"

B "Oh, really?"

H "I don't get Fairies' tastes. Same goes for his little sister, Elaine."

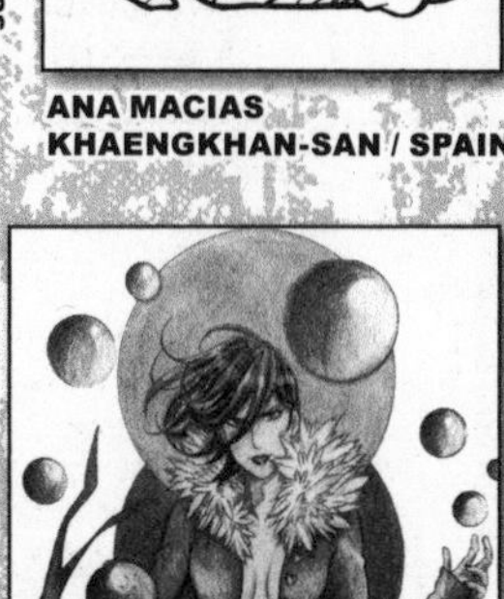

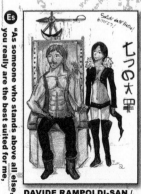

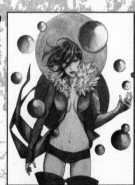

CORAL DIAZ CANO-SAN / SPAIN

Es "I think Merlin-san is the strongest of anybody in The Seven Deadly Sins."

B "That's coming from you?"

K "I agree."

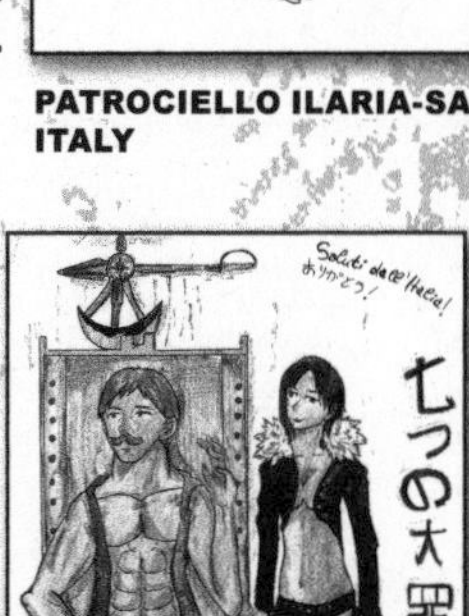
七つの大罪

DAVIDE RAMPOLDI-SAN / ITALY

Es "As someone who stands above all else, you really are the best suited for me, Merlin. Don't you agree?"

MER "Heh... I'm honored you by your compliment."

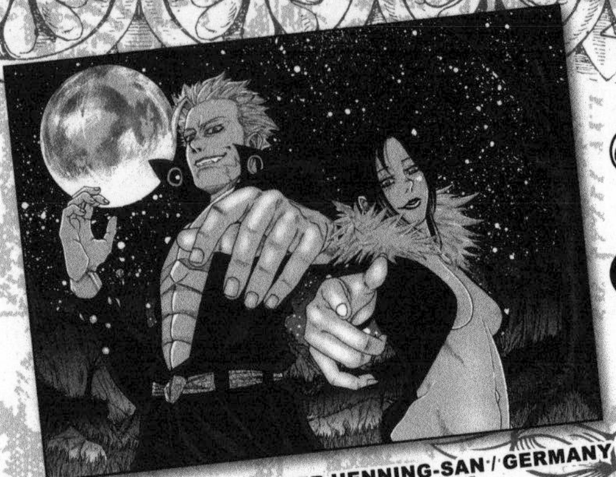

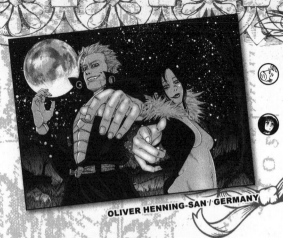

"Eeeek! A vampire and a witch! Oh, wait... It's just Ban and Merli

"When you put the two of them together, they really do have a creepy vibe about them."

OLIVER HENNING-SAN / GERMANY

All "Yeaaah!"

M "It feels like all the players have assembled! All right, everyone! Let's give it our all!"

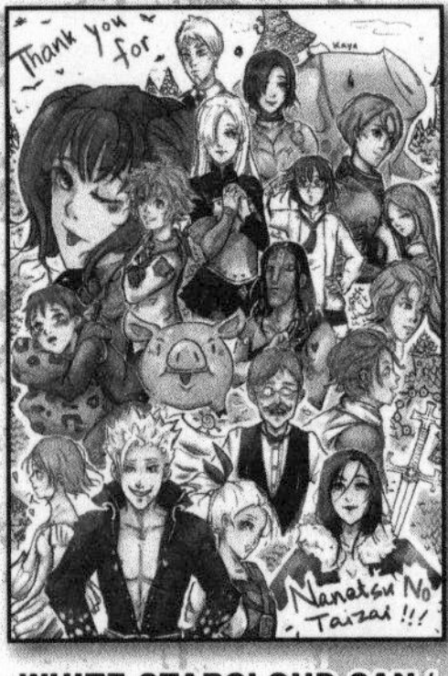
Thank you for
Nanatsu No Taizai !!!

WHITE-STARCLOUD-SAN / BELGIUM

H "This guy's got it bad."

K "Huh? What is it I like so much about Diane? I guess how she's so big and peppy... Actually, I like everything about her!"

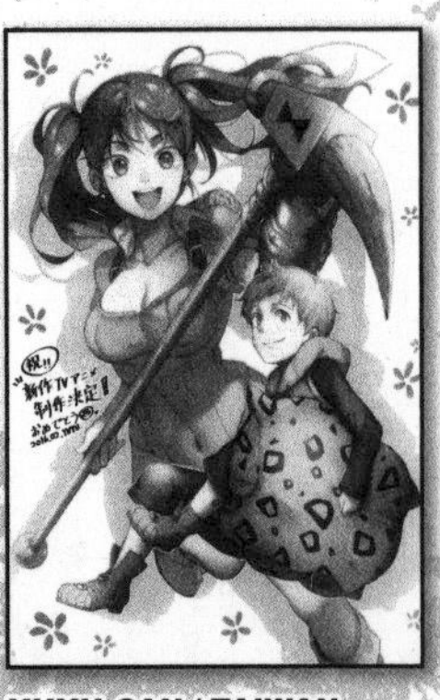

YUYU-SAN / TAIWAN

Now Accepting Applicants for the Drawing Knighthood!

- Draw your picture on a postcard, or paper no larger than a postcard, and send it in!
- Don't forget to write your name and location on the back of your picture!
- You can include comments or not. And colored illustrations will still only be displayed in B&W!
- The Drawing Knights whose pictures are particularly noteworthy and run in the print edition will be gifted with a signed specially made pencil board!
- And the best overall will be granted the special prize of a signed shikishi!!

Send to:
The Seven Deadly Sins Drawing Knighthood
c/o Kodansha Comics
451 Park Ave. South, 7th floor,
New York, NY 10016

- Submitted letters and postcards will be given to the artist. Please be aware that your name, address, and other personal information included will be given as well.

A new
series
from the
creator
of *Soul
Eater*, the
megahit
manga and
anime seen
on Toonami!

"Fun and lively...
a great start!"
 -Adventures in
   Poor Taste

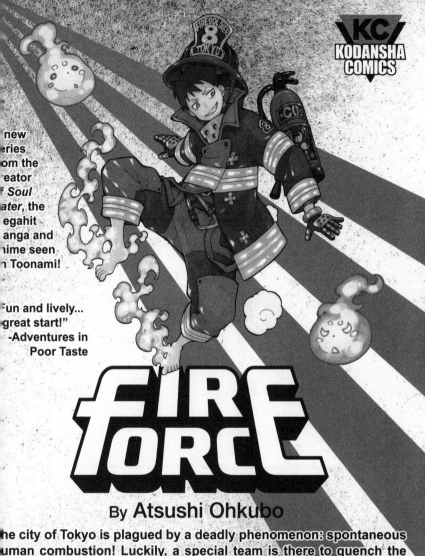

FIRE FORCE

By Atsushi Ohkubo

The city of Tokyo is plagued by a deadly phenomenon: spontaneous human combustion! Luckily, a special team is there to quench the inferno: The Fire Force! The fire soldiers at Special Fire Cathedral 8 are about to get a unique addition. Enter Shinra, a boy who possesses the power to run at the speed of a rocket, leaving behind the famous "devil's footprints" (and destroying his shoes in the process). Can Shinra and his colleagues discover the source of this strange epidemic before the city burns to ashes?

KC KODANSHA COMICS

New action series from Takei Hiroyuki, creator of the classic shonen franchise Shaman King!

In medieval Japan, a bell hanging on the collar is a sign that a c has a master. Norachiyo's bell hangs from his katana sheath, but he nonetheless a stray — a ronin. This one-eyed cat samurai travels across dishonest world, cutting through pretense and deception with his blad

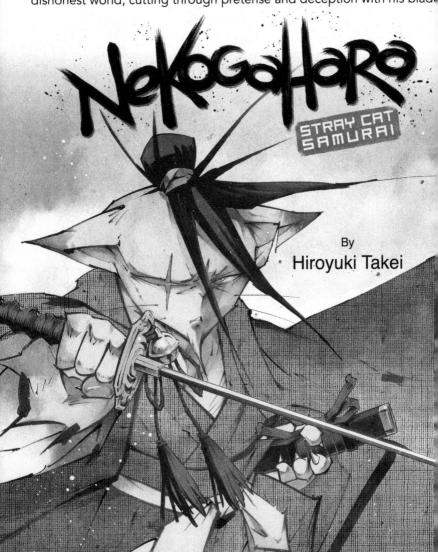

Nekogahara

STRAY CAT SAMURAI

By
Hiroyuki Takei

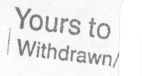

The Seven Deadly Sins volume 20 is a work of fiction. Names, characters, places, and incidents are the products of the author's imagination or are used fictitiously. Any resemblance to actual events, locales, or persons, living or dead, is entirely coincidental.

A Kodansha Comics Trade Paperback Original.

Published in the United States by Kodansha Comics, an imprint of Kodansha USA Publishing, LLC, New York.

Publication rights for this English edition arranged through Kodansha Ltd., Tokyo.

First published in Japan in 2016 by Kodansha Ltd., Tokyo.

ISBN 978-1-63236-350-3

Printed in the United States of America.

www.kodanshacomics.com

9 8 7 6 5 4 3 2 1

Translation: Christine Dashiell
Lettering: James Dashiell
Editing: Lauren Scanlan
Kodansha Comics edition cover design: Phil Balsman